Programmed Environments
Curriculum

Programmed Environments Curriculum

JAMES W. TAWNEY

University of Kentucky
Programmed Learning
Environments Project

with

DEBORAH STEVENS KNAPP

CAROL DOEHNER O'REILLY

SANDRA SLOAN PRATT

CHARLES E. MERRILL PUBLISHING COMPANY
A Bell & Howell Company
Columbus   Toronto   London   Sydney

PUBLISHED BY
Charles E. Merrill Publishing Company
A Bell & Howell Company
Columbus, Ohio 43216

This book was set in Times Roman, Typewriter, Helvetica, and Souvenir Demi.
The Production Editor was Cynthia Norfleet Donaldson.
The cover was prepared by Ron Starbuck.

International Standard Book Number:
0–675–08265–X

Library of Congress Catalog Card Number:
79–84488

2 3 4 5 6 7 8—83 82 81 80

Printed in the United States of America

Preface

These curricula for the severely developmentally delayed and an inservice training/supervision program are products of the Programmed Environments Project, funded by the Bureau of Education for the Handicapped in 1972. It arises out of the whole rights to education for the handicapped movement, which culminated in the landmark suit, PARC v. Commonwealth of Pennsylvania (1971).

The objectives of the project, generally, were to develop curriculum and teacher training materials and models to teach the severely handicapped and to explore instructional technology developments—demands created by the Pennsylvania decree and others that followed it. It has taken nearly seven years to complete this phase of the project.

While the path we took did not meet the immediate need in 1973, we began field validation in right to education classes in 1975. This continued until 1978, when the validation effort was completed. During this period, we accomplished several objectives simultaneously: We trained teachers, provided direct instruction to some 300 children, developed a data-based training/supervision system, obtained data to document the extent to which severely handicapped children can learn under our validation conditions, and, perhaps most important, acquired data on the academic performance of severely developmentally retarded children in public schools.

The decision in PARC v. Pennsylvania and the implementation of PL 94–142 (1975) ushered in a new era for the severely developmentally retarded, assuring them of equal access to educational opportunities. We now understand that young children with severe and multiple handicapping conditions will never again be placed in large institutions, remote from community life. We assume that these persons will benefit from education; that is, when instructed, they will acquire a broader repertoire of increasingly complex tasks. We acknowledge that, as yet, there is no substantial data base to support the assumption of educability. But the information we obtained contributes, in small part, to the emerging data base.

This curriculum was developed in the classroom. It was written by a professional staff. All are former teachers. And it was validated, as noted, in right to education classes, as they have come to be called. The teacher training procedures and data systems developed in validation appear in this edition. This was done for two reasons: So that users might replicate training and data verification on their own, and to give teachers a system to record their efforts and the academic performance of their students. While PL 94–142 is not an ''accountability'' law, unless the teacher has clear objectives, documentation that alternative strategies have been employed, and records of the child's performance, teachers of the severely developmentally retarded are in a tenuous position when negotiating an individual education plan with a dissatisfied parent. Thus, whether or not there is a national experimental replication of the project, as has been suggested, the materials and procedures exist for obtaining data—systematically or individually.

The Programmed Environments Curriculum is representative of our increasingly precise instructional technology. It emerges in a new era of teacher education, one that emphasizes technical competence, particularly in the application of demonstrated principles of learning. This curriculum evolved from a functional analysis of concept acquisition and daily living skills. It offers highly structured programs, taught with defined, specific procedures.

Our debt to those who participated with us is large (see *Acknowledgments*). There are others whose contributions are less direct, but, nevertheless, influential. These include B. F. Skinner, who started it all, and Sidney Bijou, whose functional analysis of retarded development provided the perspective from which we viewed the students for whom this curriculum was developed. Directly and indirectly, Warren Steinman, Keith Scott, Lawrence Stolurow, and Samuel Kirk contributed to the professional repertoire of the senior author, and his gratitude is expressed.

Regretfully, Lee Wright Hipsher, who collaborated with the senior author on an earlier curriculum, lived on the other side of the mountain when this curriculum was developed. Still, her earlier contributions are evident and not forgotten.

J.W.T.

Acknowledgments

Long-term projects like the Programmed Environments Curriculum are the cumulative result of positive efforts from a large number of persons in many agencies. Assistance comes in many forms—moral support, direct effort, and the like. For each and every type, we are most grateful.

This project began as a cooperative effort between the Bluegrass Association for Mental Retardation and the University of Kentucky. That cooperative relationship continues, a tribute to the sagacity of Carleton Scully, the BGA executive director, and the sensitivity of Ellen Perry, preschool coordinator, and Marjorie Allen and Dorothy Ward, project coordinators.

The development of field sites was greatly facilitated by individuals at each site. A. B. Harmon in the Louisville (and now the Jefferson County) Schools has supported our research and training efforts since 1969, when precursors to this project began. Albin Lee, who supported the 1976–78 validation effort, and Fred Goeshel, principal of Churchill Park School, deserve special thanks. And Betsy Holton managed many of the administrative details at our Louisville site and should be commended, also.

In Albuquerque, Gary Adamson and the Van Ettens, Glen and Carlene, assisted us in the public schools. They, along with Claire Hummel, director of special education in the Albuquerque schools, coordinated our field validation at the University of New Mexico.

In the Boston area, Katie Best and Liz Fleming provided initial contacts. Cynthia Gillis, Massachusetts State Department of Education, made additional contacts, arranged meetings, and facilitated our intra-state contracting.

Our Virginia contacts were James Micklem and Sara Irby, Virginia State Department of Education. In Philadelphia, we learned much from Dick Glean and Ed McHugh.

During the last year of the project, our field validation coordinator was Terry Lee. Alone on the road, travelling from site to site, she collected the inter-observer reliability data. More importantly, she addressed the unique challenges at each locale and eased the flow of communication to and from the sites.

Many project staffers, whose primary responsibility was in another area of the Programmed Environments Project, contributed to the development of the curriculum and training program. Sandra Deaton and Stan Aeschleman served as directors of administration and research, respectively, during my sabbatical. Karen Blum devised the teacher/child observation system and also participated in on- and off-site training. Her persistence in administering each activity insured the quality of the data base. Patti Cole developed the computer storage system; Joni Baldwin and Monica Campbell aptly entered the data into it.

Only those who have lived through it can imagine the amount of typing required through the first version of this curriculum to the last: Joy Huston, Yvonne Howitz, and

Sheppy Kerr can, for they have lived through it. Special mention is due Ms. Kerr who, in secretarial, then administrative, and then product development roles, kept her good humor and improved ours.

We recognize Alice Williams, Kathy Bartholomew, and Pam Smith, who contributed to the writing of the motor development programs and the data base underlying them.

The dual role of field trainer (data collector and teacher training supervisor) was challenging, and successful implementation was dependent upon the direct efforts of these persons. Their exemplary performance at each site deserves special mention: Alice Williams, Louisville; Susan Hayes, then Jerry Ammer, Boston College; and Jim Leon, then Terry Brito, University of New Mexico, Albuquerque (Terry deserves special mention for her professional approach to field training, and, on a personal level, for enlivening the 1978 summer field training; her daughter, Tori, our unofficial project mascot, also deserves special mention for humanizing us throughout the same time period).

Roger Mazur and Marianne Kopaczynski shared field trainer responsibilities in the Boston Public Schools; Maggie Stein developed the contact for field validation at the SEEM Collaborative in Winchester, Mass., and assisted in obtaining data there; and Betty Burmeister of Virginia arrived in Lexington well after training had begun and systematically exceeded each criterion check in record time.

We are also grateful for the equivalent amount of effort expended to keep things running smoothly at the geographically dispersed sites:

Albuquerque Public Schools

Pearl Thompson, principal, Buena Vista Elementary School

Bill Castill, principal, McCullom Elementary School

Carlene Van Etten and Lyn Pike, special education coordinators, McCullom Elementary

Teachers: (1976–1977)

Kathleen Dwor	Bonnee Burnett	Leon Bartels
Stephen Moody	Patricia Kelley	Patricia Gonzales
Gail Woods	Keri Hattox	Sharon Kern
Wesa Ramsey	Diana Herrera	Kyra Robbins
Belva Whitfield		

(1977–1978)

Kathleen Dwor	Patricia Gonzales	Alice Maechtlen
Diana Herrera	Sue Ann Voris	Michael Rouden
Keri Hattox Small	James Raborn	Barbara Hooten
Rebecca Martin		

Boston Public Schools

Roger D. Mazur, principal, Carter Developmental Day Care Center

Michael Sallen, principal, Agassiz School

Cornelius Cronin, principal, Condon School

Thomas Clegg, principal, Blackstone School

Teachers: (1977–1978)

Spencer Gould	Elizabeth Kilgoar	Ruth Marks	Marylou Webber
Dale Greenwood	Cleopatra Knight	Judy Rothbard	
James Harrington	Linda Markel	Kathleen Sullivan	

SEEM Collaborative
Winchester, Massachusetts

Richard Gorham, principal, Buzzell and Swain Schools

Edward Callahan, principal, Veterans Memorial Elementary School

Leonard D'Orlando, principal, Reading Memorial High School

Charles Papandreau, principal, Barrows School

Robert Lyons, executive director, SEEM Collaborative

Charles Faneuff, assistant director, SEEM Collaborative

Teachers: (1977–1978)

Diana Cavallo	Lorraine Zacchinni	Sheila Tessier
Deborah Chamberlin	Maureen Quinn	Elizabeth Irwin
Vilma Merrill	Leonard Chin	Norma Carlson
Lauren Mills	Marilyn Skantz	Jana Leichtman
Susan Kelly		

Bluegrass Association for Mental Retardation Preschool
Lexington, Kentucky

Ellen Perry, director

Teachers: (1975–1976)

Marty Chastain	Pam Hayden Boone	Judy Hoagland
Bonnie Brinly Younger	Gail Edwards Isaacs	Jenny Shire

(1976–1977)

Marty Chastain	Vaughnetta R. Collins	Terri Monroe
Bonnie Brinly Younger	Judy Hoagland	Polly McAlister
Pam Hayden Boone		

(1977–1978)

Marty Chastain	Polly McAlister	Melanie Garner
Ruth Bucholtz	Sue Foley	Don Brooks
Judy Hoagland	Vaughnetta R. Collins	

Philadelphia Public Schools

Ed McHugh, principal, Hill School

Teachers: (1975–1976)

Deborah Hicks	Michael Birmbaum	Mary Rzepski
Michael Kobkawski	Barbara Kristal	Judy Soffer
Elizabeth Stoff	Lynore Ehmer	

Jefferson County (Kentucky) Public Schools

Fred Goeschel, principal, Churchill Park School

Patricia Andrews, principal, Jeffersontown Special Education Center

Teachers: (1977–1978)

Patricia Gale	Mary Ellen Orr	Debbie Sheridan
Nancy Goodman	Angela Rueff	Pamela Smith
Debra Hauter	Ann Sautel	Alexis Varney
Elizabeth Herman Hull	Brenda Sheehan	Wei Hsi Walsh

(1976–1977)

Kathy Bartholomew	Jacquelyn Dunion	Pamela Smith
Nancy Beal	Patty Gifford	Barbie Turner
Jane Binford	Nancy Goodman	Wei Hsi Walsh
Laurel Davis	Angela Rueff	

Boston College

Dr. N. J. Hemphill, principal, Roberts Center

Teachers: (1977–1978)

Patricia Caro
Margaret Press

(1976–1977)

Patricia Caro   Pamela Parsons   Joseph Wolczak
Margaret Press   Brigitta Rosenthal

Virginia Department of Education

William Wysong, principal, McKinley School, Arlington

William Havens, principal, Ashlawn School, Arlington

Raymond Tolson, principal, George Mason Center, Arlington

Ralph Voight, principal, Nellie Custis, Arlington

Betty Rubright, principal, Northern Virginia Training Center, Fairfax

Betty B. Burmeister, trainer

Sara G. Irby, assistant supervisor, Title VI-D, Division of Special Education

Teachers: (1977–1978)

Jeanne S. Austin   Elizabeth A. Braun   Leslie Duff   Connie L. Scott
Karen E. Bayer   Janis Lee DePoy   Lyn Herman   John Sucher
Valerie Blane   Ann Dougherty   Pamela Mallon

Dedication

Within any long-term, complex effort, there are participants whose commitment deserves recognition. The development of the Programmed Environments Curriculum was no exception. We dedicate this curriculum to the teachers who wrote it, for their commitment to the tasks, their students, and to their profession. We also dedicate this curriculum to the students whose task performance documented it.

Equally, this work is dedicated to William E. Johnston, Jr., deceased, who served as the project officer during the major part of the funding period. Bill played by the rules of the game, yet facilitated the project in good times and in bad. He would have been very proud, we think, of the finished product.

Contents

Preface, v

INTRODUCTION, 0

    Program List, 11

INSTRUCTIONAL PROGRAMS, 12

    The Curriculum, 1

    Receptive Language Skills, 13

    Expressive Language Skills, 45

    Cognitive Skills, 79

    Fine Motor Skills, 149

    Gross Motor Skills, 173

    Eating Skills, 231

    Dressing Skills, 261

    Grooming Skills, 383

ACCOMPANYING MATERIALS, 420

    Class Observation Record, 421

    Data Sheet for 4/5 and Rate Data Programs, 447

    Data Sheet for Skill Analysis and Chain Programs, 449

CHARTS, 450

Actions, 451

Basic Motor Actions, 453

Body Parts, 455

Common Objects, 457

Cued Commands, 459

Foods, 461

Phonemes, 463

Stimulus, 467

DIRECTIONS FOR USING THE CURRICULUM, 471

Module 1:   Program Selection, 472

Module 2:   The Programs, 477

Module 3:   General Instructional Procedures, 482

Module 4:   Types of Programs, 491

SUPPLEMENTARY INFORMATION, 528

Module 5:   Reinforcement and Instructional Control, 529

Module 6:   Developing Instructional Programs, 535

Module 7:   Individual Educational Programs (IEP), 548

BIBLIOGRAPHY, 554

GLOSSARY, 557

Programmed Environments
Curriculum

Introduction

Program List, 11

The Curriculum

The Programmed Environments Curriculum is more than a curriculum; it is an integrated learning system. This conceptualization is important for two reasons: The components of the curriculum may be used by the classroom teacher to generate more programs; and the total system may be used for inservice teacher training, teacher supervision, and for direct instruction with children.

The complete program consists of the curriculum and instructional modules, a video training tape and module posttests, and forms for data collection. It is possible for a school system to use the modules, training tape, and posttests for inservice training. During field validation, many teachers received 3 hours of graduate credit for taking the course, "Direct Instruction with the Severely Developmentally Retarded." Then using the direct instruction format, system supervisors observed class instruction and used the program structure for remediation to technically assist teachers and aides.

There is an underlying organization in this curriculum and its components: The profile, class observation forms, instructional programs, supplementary charts, and data sheets. On one level, these materials provide a structure for the assessment, instruction, documentation, and instructional modification process. On a second level, the curriculum consists of a set of completed instructional programs, which specify everything needed to carry out instruction; a defined set of instructional procedures, including a decision-making system or parameters for program revision; and a set of task-analyzed programs, less precisely specified.

These programs (or system structures) were devised to help classroom teachers generate new curriculum sequences, or modify ours, as needed. We provide a model for curriculum development, parameters for program revision, and task analyses that may be transformed into complete programs. Thus, teachers can use the model to develop new curricula where ours does not meet a child's need.

No curriculum can be just picked up and used and still adequately meet the needs of children whose abilities and handicaps are as diverse as the severely developmentally delayed. Few curricula, if any, can be used without serious study and analysis. Thus, this curriculum, or integrated learning system, is both a starting point and a model for curriculum development. The classroom teacher who initiates the programs with a child who lacks skills presented in the programs can also specify needs not covered and use the same format and procedures to develop equivalent programs. Time and management factors permitting, teachers should be able to structure a comprehensive program in each content area for each child, if each child approximates those in the validation target population.

Programming Model

This curriculum has been described as highly programmed. It represents, as noted in the preface, "a functional analysis of concept acquisition and daily living skills." The structure is based on an *errorless learning* model. It is primarily an experimental laboratory procedure for comparing the behavior of human and infra-human species under different stimulus presentation conditions (Bijou, 1968; Moore & Goldiamond, 1964; Sidman & Stoddard, 1966; Sidman & Stoddard, 1967; & Terrace, 1967) and has been translated into an instructional procedure by Tawney and Hipsher (1970), Tawney (1972), and others. Tawney (1977b) analyzes and describes the equivalences between laboratory and instructional procedures.

TABLE 1
Percent—Correct Responding Data
All Sites—Academic Year 1977–78

Program Name	Ave %—Correct	Population (N)	Range
RESPONDING TO SOCIAL STIMULATION	80	1	80—80
MAKING CHOICES	100	2	100—100
USING GESTURES TO INDICATE WANTS	88.25	4	78—97
SITTING DURING ACTIVITY	95	1	95—95
INITIATING PLAY ON CUE	86	1	86—86
ATTENDING TO VOICE	78.33	6	65—90
FOLLOWING SIMPLE CUED COMMANDS	91.89	48	73—107
ATTENDING TO OWN NAME	79.66	6	73—84
USING OBJECTS ON CUE	93.12	8	74—100
IDENTIFYING BODY PARTS	96	5	86—100
IDENTIFYING EASILY HANDLED OBJECTS	89.75	8	79—100
IDENTIFYING LARGE OBJECTS	94.50	4	88—100
IDENTIFYING PEOPLE	97.50	2	95—100
IMITATING WORDS	93	3	88—100
PRODUCING SOUNDS ON REQUEST	94.75	4	82—100
ATTENDING TO OBJECTS	90	1	90—90
FINDING HIDDEN OBJECTS	84.80	10	76—96
FINDING SOURCE OF SOUND	93.33	6	82—100
MATCHING—LEVEL A	88	15	78—100
SORTING	80	7	71—91
IMITATING ACTIONS	96	1	96—96
PUTTING OBJECTS IN SEQUENCE	88.76	17	74—100
LINING UP OBJECTS	91	9	79—100
PAIRING EQUAL SETS	92.31	16	75—100
SELECTING EQUIVALENT AMOUNTS	91.18	16	80—100
MAKING SETS EQUAL	93.20	5	88—100
MATCHING EQUAL SETS—1	97.66	9	93—100
MATCHING EQUAL SETS—2	93.75	8	84—100
MATCHING EQUAL SETS—3	96	3	93—100
COUNTING RATIONALLY—1	94.66	3	94—96
COUNTING RATIONALLY—2	94	1	94—94
NAMING HOW MANY—3	94	1	94—94
SELECTING NAMED AMOUNTS—1	97	2	94—100
SELECTING NAMED AMOUNTS—2	94	2	94—94
SELECTING NAMED AMOUNTS—4	90	1	90—90

Mean of Means   91.35

Total Uses   236

This programming model was selected because, in experimental settings under certain conditions, learners demonstrated nearly error-free learning. These studies suggest that one should expect learning to occur, no matter how disabled the learner, if the conditions of instruction are clearly specified and carefully arranged. This assumption, integrated with the belief that the abilities of the severely developmentally delayed have been underestimated, led us to incorporate the concept of errorless learning into this curriculum. Collectively, this approach represents a positive view of human potential and sets aside, until shown otherwise, any notion that the upper limit of human potential for the severely handicapped, or the rest of us for that matter, can reasonably be estimated.

When this project began, the senior author for one believed that it would be possible to develop instructional programs that would teach a child from the first steps of instruction through the posttest at 90 percent correct responding. Then with the development of a decision-making model, students should perform nearly without error. We have approximated that, as shown in Table 1, which lists the percent correct responding on the instructional programs that incorporate a 4 out of 5 correct responding program step criterion. This table reflects data from the 1977–78 validation year. A field validation report, in preparation and available from the senior author through the ERIC system, describes the full scale data collection effort.

Concept of Retarded Development

Mental retardation and developmental retardation, despite the similarities of the terms, are not the same thing. The distinction between them is concisely spelled out in Bijou's (1966) functional analysis of retarded development. He described the retarded individual as "one who has a limited repertory of behaviors shaped by events that constitute his history" [p. 2]. We steadfastly adhere to Bijou's definition, and have incorporated it into the majority of our publications and proposals. This is because it (a) directs our attention to observable stimulus-response relationships, (b) encourages us to focus on child-environment interactions, (c) specifies the ways that inadequate environments may retard development, and (d) suggests ways that we can modify environments.

(Tawney, 1977a, p. 231)

Again, this concept emphasizes a positive view of human development and suggests that the potentially deleterious effects of a poor environment can be overcome by early intervention, within a highly programmed model. This conceptualization is an integral part of this curriculum.

Daily Instruction Model

Teachers can use this curriculum in a one-to-one, or small group, intensive direction session, lasting perhaps 10 to 15 minutes, depending upon the ability of the learner. The instructional programs provide a comprehensive educational program in each "content" area for the teacher who uses the material for direct instruction, and a model for other curriculum development.

REFERENCES

Bijou, S. W. A functional analysis of retarded development. In N. Ellis (Ed.), *International review of research in mental retardation* (Vol. 1). New York: Academic Press, 1966.

Bijou, S. W. Studies in the experimental development of left-right concepts in retarded children using fading techniques. In N. Ellis (Ed.), *International review of research in mental retardation* (Vol. 3). New York: Academic Press, 1968.

Moore, R., & Goldiamond, I. Errorless establishment of a visual discrimination using fading procedures. *Journal of the Experimental Analysis of Behavior,* 1964, *7,* 269–272.

Sidman, M., & Stoddard, L. Programming perception and learning for retarded children. In N. Ellis (Ed.), *International review of research in mental retardation* (Vol. 2). New York: Academic Press, 1966.

Sidman, M., & Stoddard, L. The effectiveness of fading in programming a simultaneous form discrimination for retarded children. *Journal of the Experimental Analysis of Behavior,* 1967, *10,* 3–15.

Tawney, J. & Hipsher, L. *Systematic Language Instruction* (Project No. 7–1205). Washington, D.C.: U.S. Office of Education, 1970.

Tawney, J. New considerations for the severely and profoundly handicapped. In R. Kneedler and S. Tarver (Eds.), *Changing Perspectives in Special Education.* Columbus: Charles Merrill, 1977. (a)

Tawney, J. *Practice What You Preach* (Project No. 119163A). Washington, D.C.: U.S. Office of Education, 1977. (b)

Terrace, H. Stimulus control. In W. Honig (Ed.), *Operant behavior: Areas of research and application.* New York: Appleton-Century-Crofts, 1967.

This curriculum has been designed for and field-tested with children generally considered to manifest moderate, severe, or profound developmental retardation and attendant multiple handicapping conditions. The curriculum could potentially be used with any individual who is acquiring skills that are typically learned by normal children from birth through 3 years of age.

Typical entry behaviors found in our population include:

- Little or no vocal behavior;
- limited motor gestural behavior;
- inability to follow simple commands;
- limited self-help skills;
- inconsistent or no bowel or bladder control;
- limited social interaction with other children and adults;
- no reciprocal social reinforcement of others;
- a high rate of stereotyped behavior and/or socially disruptive behavior;
- a low rate of behaviors that might generally be called *constructive play behavior;* and
- no obtained score on a standardized test of intelligence (due to being considered untestable or to responding inconsistently when tested).

VALIDATION PROCEDURES

This curriculum was developed by a general validation procedure that involved developing and revising a program until one child demonstrated a high level of correct responding, using the program with other children and teachers, and then revising for validation with more children and teachers in other cities.

During 3 years of validation, our programs have been used by and revised for over 300 children in five different parts of the country. At all points, validation teachers recorded response-by-response data on child performance during all steps of the programs used. In addition, periodic data samples were taken on teachers as they used the programs to insure that the conditions specified were, in fact, used. Thus, we attempted to verify that our specified program procedures directly affected child performance in a positive way.

By accumulating data on both teacher and child performance during use of the programs, we can say that our programs are "effective," or that they work under the set of conditions outlined in this product.

COMPONENTS OF THE CURRICULUM

The curriculum consists of 79 programs, covering language, cognitive, motor, and self-help skills, as well as all information and record forms necessary for using the programs. Specific curricular components include:

1. Screening materials:
   a. *Profile:* A chart showing all programs available, organized by area and sequenced in approximate order of acquisition (page 7).
   b. *Class Observation Record:* A form suggesting observational strategies for initial screening of skills (pages 421-46).
2. Instructional programs, each containing:
   a. *Program Overview:* A narrative which includes:
      - A *rationale* for the functioning of the skill;

- a description of *entry behaviors* typically required for successful acquisition of the skill, with suggested *adaptations* for sensory or motor impairments;
- the behavioral *objective* for the program; and
- *suggestions* for generalization to other conditions and continuation to other skills after completion of the program.

b. *Program:* Description of the instructional procedures for teaching the skill, including:

- Specified *strategies* and performance *criteria* for the pretest, all teaching steps or phases, and the posttests;
- reference to a *chart* (if applicable) for suggested options on materials, cues, concepts, or responses; and
- *information on modifying* the program for students who fail to meet criteria during the teaching steps.

3. **Accompanying materials** for using the programs:

a. *Data Sheets:* Standard forms for recording response-by-response performance on the program from pretest through posttests (See extra sheets on pages 447 and 449).

b. *Charts:* Lists of suggested options on materials, cues, concepts, or responses for specified programs.

The curriculum is accompanied by a training program for teachers. This program describes how to use the curriculum and includes suggestions for general instructional procedures.

CURRICULUM OVERVIEW

Introduction

Because skills do not develop in isolation, we feel it is important for persons using this curriculum to understand the order in which skills taught by our instructional programs are typically acquired. In the following description, titles of all programs have been included in parentheses for easy reference.

Two points should be made regarding the following description. First, for organizational purposes, the description has been split into two sections—Response Building (motor and self-help skills), and Stimulus Shaping (social, language, and cognitive skills). However, this categorization is quite arbitrary and cannot adequately describe the complex process of learning. Therefore, to get a more complete picture across curricular areas, refer to the Profile on page 7 while reading this description.

Second, although typical patterns of skills acquisition as described here often occur, it is obvious that all children do not learn skills in these patterns, particularly children exhibiting specific sensory and motor handicapping conditions. This description is only a general overview with greater detail presented in each program on the skill, entry behaviors, and adaptations for sensory and motor impairments. Note that the order of programs in the Profile is not necessarily the order in which they should be taught.

Response Building

Skills in the motor and self-help areas can be roughly categorized as *response building,* since the child learns to produce the motor components of the desired response for either basic gross and fine motor actions or their specific applications in eating, dressing, and grooming skills. Based on the existence of these responses in the child's behavioral repertoire, he can use them as he learns to recognize and respond appropriately to increasingly more complex cues in the environment. (This

PROFILE

	SOCIAL/LANGUAGE		COGNITIVE	MOTOR		SELF-HELP		
	Receptive	Expressive	Cognitive	Fine Motor	Gross Motor	Eating	Dressing	Grooming
			Selecting a Specified Quantity / Counting Rationally / Matching Equal Sets				Zipping Jacket / Snapping / Unbuttoning / Hooking / Unbuckling	Brushing Hair / Brushing Teeth
			Selecting Equivalent Amounts			Eating with a Fork		Washing Face / Washing Hands
			Pairing Equal Sets				Zipping Pants / Unzipping Pants / Untying / Unhooking / Putting On T-Shirt / Taking Off T-Shirt	
	Identifying People		Sorting / Lining Up Objects / Putting Objects in Sequence				Putting On Shirt / Putting On Pants / Taking Off Shirt / Taking Off Pants / Putting Socks On	Wiping Nose
	Identifying Body Parts / Identifying Objects	Naming Objects / Naming Actions	Identifying Simple Pictures / Matching			Eating with a Spoon	Putting Shoes On / Putting Mittens On / Unzipping Jacket / Putting Hat On	Drying Face / Using a Napkin / Drying Hands
	Responding to Signal Words / Attending to Own Name	Shaping Words / Producing Sounds on Request	Imitating Actions / Finding Source of Sound	Placing In/On	Walking	Drinking from a Cup	Unsnapping / Pulling Off	
	Following Cued Commands	Indicating Preferences / Responding Vocally to Model	Finding Hidden Objects / Repeating Teacher Model / Responding to Teacher Model	Manipulating Objects	Standing Up / Crawling on Hands and Knees / Standing / Sitting Up / Crawling on Stomach	Eating Finger Foods / Chewing		
	Attending to Voice / Responding to Social Interaction	Making Sounds	Attending to Objects / Focusing Attention	Grasping / Reaching for Objects	Sitting / Controlling Head Movements			

7

differential responding to specific stimuli is described in Stimulus Shaping.) Note that this curriculum does not include toileting skills, which are covered more extensively in Foxx and Azrin (1975). See the Bibliography (p. 556) for details.

At birth, the child's responses consist of reflex actions elicited by specific stimuli and random voluntary actions, such as arm flailing or leg kicking. The child gradually learns *control over these voluntary gross motor actions, typically from the head downward.* His neck muscles strengthen, enabling him to turn his *head,* hold it up when given shoulder support, and finally to lift it and keep it erect (Controlling Head Movements). As his neck muscles strengthen, he gains *upper trunk control* so that he needs less and less support to maintain a sitting position (Sitting). During this time, his arms and legs increase in maneuverability and strength so that he can propel himself forward on his stomach with his head up (Crawling on Stomach). The *arm, leg, and trunk control and maneuverability* combine to enable him to reposition himself on the floor (Sitting Up). As his leg strength and trunk control increases, he begins to support weight on his legs and balance in a standing position (Standing). At the same time, his *balance, strength and coordination* increase so that he can crawl forward on his hands and knees, move into a standing position, and take the first few steps—first with assistance, and then alone (Crawling on Hands and Knees, Standing Up, Walking).

At the same time these gross motor responses are increasing, the child is learning dexterity or arm and hand control. The child learns to voluntarily grasp and hold light objects (Grasping) and to bat at, then directly reach for, objects close to him (Reaching for Objects). As his mouth control increases for chewing common foods (Chewing), he applies his *reaching and grasping skills* for simple self-feeding (Eating Finger Foods). Gradually he increases his rate of *simple hand, wrist, and arm actions,* while interacting with toys and other objects (Manipulating Objects). He also learns to direct these simple actions to fit objects together (Placing In/On). One application of this increasing control is the skill of grasping and bringing a cup to his mouth to drink (Drinking from a Cup). Other applications are simple *grasp-and-pull behavior chains* that increasingly require better eye-hand coordination for the grasp (Pulling Off, Unsnapping, Putting Hat On, Unzipping Jacket, Putting Mittens On). In addition, the child learns to coordinate simple *grasp-and-rub tasks* (Drying Hands, Using a Napkin, Drying Face, Wiping Nose).

As the child's trunk control and balance improves, these skills combine with his increasing arm and hand control to form behavioral chains, requiring him to reposition his arms, legs, or head to complete the task (Putting Shoes and Putting Socks On; Washing Hands, Face). With increasing *trunk control and maneuverability,* he learns more difficult and complex behavioral chains (Putting On and Taking Off Pants, Shirt, T-Shirt). As his grasping skills and *eye-hand coordination skills* improve, he learns to use utensils to feed himself (Eating with a Spoon, Fork), to open and close increasingly more difficult fastenings (Unhooking, Untying, Unzipping and Zipping Pants, Unbuckling, Hooking, Unbuttoning, Snapping, Zipping Jacket), and to perform brushing tasks (Brushing Teeth, Hair).

With these basic strength, balance, and coordination skills and their applications to simple self-help skills, the child can go on to learn skills requiring greater ability and dexterity, as well as more complex behavioral chains for appropriate self-care skills. See the Bibliography for other available curricula covering these more difficult skills.

Stimulus Shaping

Skills in the language, social, and cognitive areas can be roughly categorized as *stimulus shaping,* since the child learns to differentially respond to specific stimuli. In other words, he learns to recognize and respond appropriately to increasingly more complex cues in the environment. (The response the child uses is, of course, based on his motor skills as described in Response Building.)

At birth, the child's voluntary responses are essentially random. When such *random actions* as making eye contact, touching, or vocalizing result in a consequence that is considered "reinforcing" to the child, the *rate of those behaviors increases,* leading to more frequent eye contact, touching, or vocalizing (Responding to Social Interaction, Focusing Attention, Making Sounds). As the frequency of such behaviors increases, the child randomly exhibits *more sustained attention* to specific stimuli at an increasing rate (Attending to Voice, Attending to Objects).

From random responding, the child slowly *increases the rate of his responding to adult actions directed toward him.* When the adult imitates the child's random actions or sounds, the child responds to this in some way (Responding Vocally to Model, Responding to Teacher Model). In other words, the child responds to a request for a response, although he may respond indiscriminately to some simple cues, such as to words with accompanying gestures or to models of the child's random actions (Following Cued Commands, Repeating Teacher Model).

At the same time, the child begins to *use certain responses to indicate his preferences* to the adult. He gestures, with or without accompanying sound, to indicate preferred objects or activities (Indicating Preferences) and uses sound consistently to request an offered object (Producing Sounds on Request). In addition, he *seeks out preferred objects* which have been placed out of sight while he watches or which are out of sight but are producing sound (Finding Hidden Objects, Finding Source of Sound).

Gradually, the child's responding to cues becomes more differentiated. He learns to recognize and *respond appropriately to words that signal upcoming events,* gestures, or cues (Attending to Own Name, Responding to Signal Words). He also learns to *imitate* actions performed by an adult (Imitating Actions), as well as to produce a consistent approximation of modeled words (Shaping Words). With these skills, the child has the basis for vocal and motor imitation, as well as language.

From this, the child learns to *respond appropriately to cues that are considered "symbolic," words or pictures* that represent concrete objects or actions. He learns to indicate or identify common elements of his environment when the adult names them (Identifying Objects, Body Parts, People). He also learns to name those common elements on his own (Naming Objects, Actions). In addition, he begins to associate simple pictures with their referent (Identifying Simple Pictures). With these basic receptive and expressive language skills, he is ready to expand his vocabulary and syntax to communicate with others. Note that our language programming ends at this point since these are the skills necessary to enter most other existing language curricula. See the Bibliography for follow-up curricula.

At the same time that the child is learning to respond to symbolic cues, he is also *learning to "abstract" or to respond to specific characteristics of objects, or groups of objects.* He learns to match identical objects and pictures, as well as to separate a group of objects into categories based on their main identifying characteristics (Matching, Sorting). He also learns to *organize objects,* first placing them sequentially in a designated space (Putting Objects in Sequence), then placing them in a row with no position cues (Lining Up Objects).

From this, the child *uses one-to-one correspondence* to compare groups of objects without necessarily using words to describe or define his actions. First he learns to put two equal sets of objects in correspondence by pairing the objects in the two sets (Pairing Equal Sets). Then he learns to make two unequal sets equal by pairing the corresponding objects and adding or subtracting extras (Selecting Equivalent Amounts). With these skills he scans different sets to find the ones with an equal or corresponding number of items (Matching Equal Sets). To this point, the child can perform a variety of functional tasks requiring him to get a specified amount by using correspondence, not necessarily by counting; for example, he can set the table by matching the place mats to the number of chairs.

When the child can identify and name a variety of objects, he then learns the *names of the numbers* based on his one-to-one correspondence skills. He first says the number names as he places each object, insuring that he pairs the name with the corresponding object (Counting Rationally). Then he uses this counting skill to determine the number of objects requested (Selecting a Specified Amount). Now he can use number names to perform functional tasks; for example, he can set the table when told that four places are needed.

With these basic skills in imitation, object identification and naming, abstraction of essential characteristics of objects, organization of groups of objects, and one-to-one correspondence and counting, the child can go on to learn a variety of tasks that might be considered "academic" in that they are presented in normal kindergarten or primary classes. See the Bibliography for further curricula.

RECEPTIVE SKILLS

1 Responding to Social Interaction
2 Attending to Voice
3 Following Cued Commands
4 Attending to Own Name
5 Responding to Signal Words
6 Identifying Objects
7 Identifying Body Parts
8 Identifying People

Receptive Skills

EXPRESSIVE SKILLS

1 Making Sounds
2 Responding Vocally to Model
3 Indicating Preferences
4 Producing Sounds on Request
5 Shaping Words
6 Naming Actions
7 Naming Objects

Expressive Skills

COGNITIVE SKILLS

1 Focusing Attention
2 Attending to Objects
3 Responding to Teacher Model
4 Repeating Teacher Model
5 Finding Hidden Objects
6 Finding Source of Sound
7 Imitating Actions
8 Matching
9 Identifying Simple Pictures
10 Putting Objects in Sequence
11 Lining Up Objects
12 Sorting
13 Pairing Equal Sets
14 Selecting Equivalent Amounts
15 Matching Equal Sets
16 Counting Rationally
17 Selecting a Specified Quantity

Cognitive Skills

FINE MOTOR SKILLS

1 Reaching
2 Grasping Objects
3 Manipulating Objects
4 Placing In/On

Fine Motor Skills

GROSS MOTOR SKILLS

1 Controlling Head Movements
2 Sitting
3 Crawling on Stomach
4 Sitting Up
5 Standing
6 Crawling on Hands and Knees
7 Standing Up
8 Walking

Gross Motor Skills

EATING SKILLS

1 Chewing
2 Eating Finger Foods
3 Drinking from a Cup
4 Eating with a Spoon
5 Eating with a Fork

Eating Skills

DRESSING SKILLS

1 Pulling Off
2 Unsnapping
3 Putting Hat On
4 Unzipping Jacket
5 Putting Mittens On
6 Putting Shoes On
7 Putting Socks On
8 Taking Off Pants
9 Taking Off Shirt
10 Putting On Pants (Coat, Jacket)
11 Putting On Shirt (Coat, Jacket)
12 Taking Off T-Shirt
13 Putting On T-Shirt
14 Unhooking
15 Untying
16 Unzipping Pants (Skirt)
17 Zipping Pants (Skirt)
18 Unbuckling
19 Hooking
20 Unbuttoning
21 Snapping
22 Zipping Jacket

Dressing Skills

GROOMING SKILLS

1 Drying Hands
2 Using a Napkin
3 Drying Face
4 Wiping Nose
5 Washing Hands
6 Washing Face
7 Brushing Teeth
8 Brushing Hair

Grooming Skills

Instructional Programs

Receptive Language Skills, 13

Expressive Language Skills, 45

Cognitive Skills, 79

Fine Motor Skills, 149

Gross Motor Skills, 173

Eating Skills, 231

Dressing Skills, 261

Grooming Skills, 383

Responding to Social Interaction

Rate Data

Skill:

In this program the child increases the frequency with which he responds to another person. This response may be gurgling, cooing, smiling, and turning toward or making any voluntary action that indicates awareness of and a positive response to the other person. This basic responsiveness is important for developing positive relations with others and for developing skills in any type of situation involving another person.

Entry Behaviors:

S makes a few voluntary movements which would be appropriate to increase. These movements may be very simple actions such as head turning, smiling, or vocalizing. (You do not want to increase negative behaviors such as screaming or pulling away.) Although S may respond to certain kinds of stimuli (loud noises, bright light, movement), he remains passive or tries to withdraw when another person interacts with him. Accept any positions or movements that S has taken in the past when demonstrating attention to things in his environment (e.g., Focusing Attention). Note that the definition is flexible and requires no adaptation. With a motorically involved child, it is very important to identify and increase responses that indicate his awareness.

Objective:

S makes a positive response during social interactions. S must initiate his response correctly at least 30 times during at least five different interactions, anytime during a 10-minute session.

positive response = any voluntary movement or sound that is a sign of pleasure: Gurgling, cooing, smiling, laughing, making sounds, clapping, grasping (not reflexive), turning toward you, moving a body part (arm, leg, finger). Negative behaviors such as crying, hitting, screaming, or pulling away are incorrect.

social interaction = playing with S, talking to or physically stimulating him, and the like. See the Stimulus Chart, page 467.

Cycle:

None specified. However, you may repeat the program with specific interactions to increase S's responsiveness to particular kinds of interactions, or to other different interactions. Or, you may repeat to increase the variety of S's responses, requiring him to make a certain number of different responses.

Follow-Up:

Continue to interact with S and reinforce his responding. Present many different
types of interactions. Shape the response into a more refined action if necessary. Reinforce specific kinds of responses as introduced in Making Sounds
(vocalizations) and Focusing Attention (eye contact). Use S's responsiveness
to you to encourage his motor development, such as in Reaching or Controlling
Head Movements. Frequently perform the social interactions S prefers, guiding
him to make a specific response to the interaction (e.g., play patty-cake, and
he may learn to clap his hands).

Program for Receptive Skill 1

Materials:

Select a variety of materials as desired.

Chart:

Stimulus Chart (for social interactions), page 467.

GENERAL STRATEGY

Interaction:

Begin to interact with S, performing a game or some action with him, as well as talking to him. Note that with some children, your touch and movement of them may be particularly effective. However, with other children, your touch may elicit negative responses. Choose interactions depending on the individual child. Continue to interact for approximately 30 seconds.

Latency:

S can initiate his response anytime during the interaction.

Correction:

Anytime S is not responding, assist him to clap or make some appropriate response. If he makes a response unassisted after guidance, count this as correct since S has responded to this interaction. Note that all unassisted positive responses are correct regardless of when they occur. If S withdraws or resists guidance at any time, go on to another type of interaction.

Natural Consequence:

Continue the interaction as long as he continues to respond. Note that all of S's unassisted responses are counted.

Other Trials:

Repeat the strategy. Vary the types of interactions for a 10-minute session.

Modification:

S has not met step criterion after four sessions.

	CONDITIONS	BEHAVIOR	CRITERIA
		S makes a positive response...	during a 10-minute session
PRE	Interact with S for 10 minutes, varying events and materials.	unassisted	30 times during 5 different types of interactions
S/1	Interact with S for 10 minutes, varying events and materials. Correct if needed.	"	5 times, any type of interaction
S/2	"	"	10 times, during 2 different types of interactions
S/3	"	"	15 times, 3 different types
S/4	"	"	20 times, 4 different types
S/5	"	"	25 times, 5 different types
S/6	"	"	30 times, 5 different types
POST 1	Same as PRE	unassisted	30 times, 5 different types for each test
POST 2	New Types of Interactions		
POST 3	New Setting		

MODIFICATIONS

If S withdraws from you or resists at first, do not try to work with him for 10 minutes. Break down the length of the session, and then gradually increase the time. For example, start with a 1-minute session. When S no longer withdraws or resists during the 1-minute interval, increase it to 2 minutes, and so forth. For such a child, select very slow, calming interactions that do not startle or frighten him. Use assistance as little as possible.

Attending to Voice

Rate Data

Skill:

This program teaches a child to increase the frequency of eye contact with a speaker. Communication is built on this sustained attention to the vocalizations of others.

Entry Behaviors:

1. S frequently <u>responds positively to adults</u> during social interactions and has certain games and events that he prefers (e.g., Responding to Social Interaction). However, S does not maintain eye contact when someone is talking to him as part of those stimulus events.

2. S frequently <u>turns toward noise and movement</u> but does not maintain eye contact over 1-2 seconds. S frequently makes eye contact with another person but only for 1-2 seconds (e.g., all cycles of Focusing Attention).

3. S <u>hears your voice</u> when you are close to him. Sometimes S turns toward a loud or unusual voice, but not often. If S has an hearing impairment, adapt the program by always tapping S's shoulder or moving his body and head around toward you before beginning the stimulus event.

4. S <u>sees well enough to make eye contact</u> with the person who is talking. Or, adapt by redefining the response (e.g., "S keeps his head turned toward you as you are speaking").

5. S <u>turns his head</u> to face you when you are immediately in front of him or to his left or right (e.g., Controlling Head Movements). Or, adapt by always positioning yourself within S's line of sight, and do not change positions.

Objective:

S maintains eye contact with the speaker for at least 5 seconds. S must initiate his response correctly 25 times during a 10-minute session.

Cycle:

None specified.

Follow-Up:

Continue to reinforce S's attending throughout the day. Give individual trials on a regular basis, taking data to insure that S's performance is or becomes consistent in a variety of natural situations. Require S's attention whenever speaking directly to him, in particular when giving a command. This follow-up is extremely important.

Increase the time S attends to speech. In addition, reinforce his attending when you are conversing with another person. Introduce the sequence--S listens, then responds (motor response--Following Cued Commands, or vocal response--Responding Vocally to Model or Producing Sounds on Request). Combine with gross motor skills, having S creep or crawl toward the speaker.

Program for Receptive Skill 2

Materials:

Select a variety of materials as desired.

Chart:

Stimulus Chart (for events), page 467.

GENERAL STRATEGY

Arrangement:

In a quiet area, sit in front of S within his range of vision.

Stimulus Event:

Encourage S to look at you by vocalizing continuously--talk, sing, whisper, say
nursery rhymes, change your voice tone or intensity, and so forth. During the
event, give an appropriate command ("LISTEN." "LOOK AT ME."). To get initial
eye contact, you may also make vocal sounds (e.g., whistle or click your tongue),
move your face closer to S to attract his attention, or hold a small noise-making
toy (e.g., squeeze toy, clicker) close to your face and manipulate it. (The toy
should be small enough to hide in your hand so that you can remove it from sight
by closing your hand without drawing attention away from your face.) Begin a
different stimulus event if S has not made eye contact within 30 seconds.

Once S makes initial eye contact, continue to provide a stimulus, but only
through vocalizing.

Latency:

S must sustain his attention as soon as he has made initial eye contact.

Correction:

None. Go on to a new stimulus event.

Other Trials:

Repeat the strategy. Vary the stimulus event and your position in relation to
S (in front of, to S's left or right) but keep within S's range of vision.

Modification:

S has not met step criterion after four sessions.

CONDITIONS	BEHAVIOR	CRITERIA
	S maintains eye contact for 5 seconds...	during a 10-minute session
PRE Present a stimulus event. As soon as S looks, vocalize only.	unassisted	25 times
S/1 "	"	5 times
S/2 "	"	10 times
S/3 "	"	15 times
S/4 "	"	20 times
S/5 "	"	25 times
POST 1 Same as PRE	unassisted	25 times for each test
POST 2 New Setting		
POST 3 New Teacher		

MODIFICATIONS

If S does not look for 5 seconds, increase sustained eye contact gradually. At first go through the steps, increasing the rate at which S gives attention for 3-second intervals. Then repeat for 4-second intervals. Finally run the program as written (5-second intervals).

Following Cued Commands

4/5 Data

Cycle

Skill:

This program teaches the child to respond to simple commands by using all naturally available cues to comprehend what is expected of him. (The available cues include the words in the command, the tone of voice used, accompanying gestures, and the situational context.) This skill is taught by adding and then fading extra cues that further clarify the desired response (i.e., physical prompts, exaggerated models). Once the child comprehends such cued commands, he can use words alone to obtain the same information (receptive language per se).

Entry Behaviors:

1. S responds to other people (e.g., Responding to Social Interaction, Focusing Attention--Eye Contact, and possibly, Responding to Teacher Model). This responding insures that the child attends to the command and will make some response.

2. S sustains his attention on a particular target for brief periods (e.g., Attending to Objects, Attending to Voice). The more S attends to his environment, the more readily he will focus on the command.

3. S performs the action without physical assistance. Select commands only for actions S can already perform. Or, adapt by accepting an approximation of the response.

4. S hears the command. Or, adapt by giving the sign for the command as you say it. Also, give specified gestural cues. Note that for "cued commands," S does not have to rely on words alone; therefore, an hearing impaired child can perform correctly without adaptations just by using the visual cues (e.g., gestures) instead of, or in addition to, the command. However, since this program introduces commands, it is also appropriate to introduce specific signs at this point if the child will be using them later.

5. S sees the cues that accompany the command (i.e., gestures, the presence of particular objects, the situation). Or, adapt by adding extra auditory or tactile cues.

Objective:

Given a cued command, S performs the requested action without assistance. S must initiate his response within 5 seconds of the command and respond correctly to one command 4 out of 5 trials.

cued command = a verbal command given with accompanying gestures and context cues. See the Cued Commands Chart, page 459.

Cycle:

Record each different command that S can perform. Each cycle teaches one command. Repeat the program as needed to teach a variety of commands.

Follow-Up:

Continue to have S perform each command in a variety of situations. Increase the number of people for whom S performs. Always use cued commands to convey your meaning, relying on physical guidance as little as possible. Continue to expand the number of commands S can comprehend by using all available cues. As S performs different cued commands with more proficiency, begin to use words alone, gradually fading your gestures (e.g., Responding to Signal Words).

To develop S's communication skills, encourage him to use gestures and cued commands to convey his meaning to you (e.g., Indicating Preferences). If S is developing speech, encourage him to imitate the key word in the command (e.g., Shaping Words).

Teach S more and more difficult tasks by using cued commands and directions (e.g., self-help skills). This increases S's use of cues to learn new skills and provides experiences needed for acquiring generalized imitation (e.g., Imitating Actions). As S performs appropriately in many situations, wait to give a command so that he learns to initiate the task using just situational cues, a large step toward independence.

Program for Receptive Skill 3

Materials:

Select materials appropriate to the command.

Chart:

Cued Commands Chart (for suggested commands), page 459.

GENERAL STRATEGY

Arrangement:

Wait for the opportunity, or set up a situation where the command is appropriate.

Attention:

Draw S's attention to you.

Command:

Give the command paired with a gesture that normally accompanies that command ("SIT DOWN"; then pat the seat of the chair). Note: Use the same phrase and gesture throughout the program.

Cues:

model = use of any repeated or exaggerated gestures along with a demonstration of the desired response to convey your interest.

full guidance = repeat the command, and physically assist S to perform the entire response.

partial guidance = repeat the command, and physically assist S to start or do any part of the response, but do not assist the entire response.

Latency:

S must initiate his response within 5 seconds of the command or delayed cue. When guidance cues are given, S is to respond immediately.

Correction:

Use general correction procedures.

Natural Consequence:

Present a situation that naturally follows the response (e.g., after S sits down, music time begins).

Other Trials:

Repeat the strategy. Vary the situation in which the command is given.

Modification:

S has not met step criterion after four errors.

CONDITIONS	BEHAVIOR	CRITERIA
	S performs the requested action...	
PRE Arrange the situation, and get S's attention. Give the command. Present the natural consequence.	unassisted	4 correct out of 5 trials
S/1 Arrange the situation, and get S's attention. Give the command, and immediately model. If S does not begin to respond correctly, provide full guidance. Correct if needed. Present the natural consequence.	given a model and, if necessary, delayed full guidance	4 correct out of the last 5 trials for each step
S/2 Same as S/1, but provide only partial guidance.	given a model and, if necessary, delayed partial guidance	
S/3 Arrange the situation, and get S's attention. Give the command, and immediately model. Correct if needed. Present the natural consequence.	given a model	
S/4 Arrange the situation, and get S's attention. Give the command. If S does not begin to respond correctly, present the model. Correct if needed. Present the natural consequence.	given a delayed model, if necessary	
S/5 Arrange the situation, and get S's attention. Give the command. Correct if needed. Present the natural consequence.	unassisted	
POST 1 Same as PRE	unassisted	4 correct out of 5 trials for each test
POST 2 New Phrase (same command)		
POST 3 New Setting		

MODIFICATIONS

If S does not attend to the gestures, use a primary reinforcer. Hold an edible at S's eye level, and move it slowly to the desired focal point. Fade the use of the edible gradually.

Practice the response. Give appropriate gestures, label what he is doing, and assist him as needed to perform the response (e.g., say "Sit," pat the chair, and guide S to sit down). Repeat this several times before each trial. Gradually fade how much practice S gets before each trial (e.g., give five chances to practice, then one trial; give four chances to practice, then one trial; and so on).

Attending to Own Name

4/5 Data

Skill:

This program teaches a child to respond to a specific attention signal by turning his face toward the person who calls his name. (Note that the program
teaches the child to look up after his name is spoken; it does not teach him to
identify himself by name.) This skill is built by fading all attention-getting
cues other than the child's name. Besides improving his on-task performance,
this behavior is an early step in language where the child learns to respond to
one specific word--his own name.

Entry Behaviors:

1. S attends briefly to a speaker (e.g., Focusing Attention, Attending to
   Voice). Although S may understand little of what is said, he is aware
   of speech.

2. S responds to some simple commands given with gestures, although he may
   only respond to ones that signal reinforcing activities (e.g., Following
   Cued Commands). This response provides the natural reinforcement for his
   reaction (e.g., you call his name to get his attention to tell him to come
   or to do something).

3. S hears his name called. If S has an hearing impairment, reconsider the
   rationale for this program since you will probably need to use something
   other than speech to draw S's attention to you. Or, adapt by positioning
   yourself within S's range of vision and use signing in addition to speech.

Objective:

S turns his face toward the person who calls his name. S must initiate his
response within 5 seconds of the command and respond correctly 4 out of 5
trials.

Cycle:

None specified.

Follow-Up:

Continue to provide S with opportunities to attend when you call his name, as
well as when other people call him. Always provide him with a reason to attend
to his name (e.g., to come to lunch, to help with chores). Vary the situations
in which you call for S when he is at a distance (e.g., when you are in another
room, or you are both outside). Reinforce S's response to other spoken words
not given with any gestures or cues (e.g., Responding to Signal Words). To
develop his expressive language, have him imitate all or part of his name after
you say it (e.g., Shaping Words).

Program for Receptive Skill 4

Materials:

Use objects and activities S prefers (for the natural consequence).

Chart:

None

GENERAL STRATEGY

Arrangement:

Conduct the program in a room that is relatively quiet so that S will easily hear his name called. Position yourself at the distance specified for the step (e.g., 5 feet from S, 10 feet, or anywhere in the same room). Vary your direction relative to S (e.g., behind, beside, in front of S).

Command:

Say S's name in a firm voice ("TODD").

Cues:

auditory or visual cue = draw S's attention to you in some way, either with an auditory cue (e.g., clap your hands) or a visual cue (e.g., hold up a toy that you will let S play with later). You may vary which cue you use (e.g., clap your hands on one trial, shake a toy on the next).

physical guidance = go to S, and assist him to turn his face toward you.

Latency:

S must initiate his response within 5 seconds of the command or delayed cue. When guidance cues are presented, S is to respond immediately.

Correction:

Use general correction procedures.

Natural Consequence:

Direct S to another activity (e.g., present a cued command, and assist him if necessary to perform the action: Sit down for snacktime; Take this, giving S a toy; Come here to begin a group activity).

Other Trials:

Repeat the strategy. Vary your position relative to S for each trial (behind, beside, in front of S). Give trials at appropriate times during the day rather than consecutively (e.g., at lunchtime, at worktime, when S needs to attend to his name) and then perform an activity as a natural consequence.

Modification:

S has not met step criterion after four errors.

CONDITIONS	BEHAVIOR	CRITERIA
	S turns his face toward the speaker...	
PRE Position yourself any-where in the room. Give the command. Present the natural consequence.	unassisted	4 correct out of 5 trials
S/1 Position yourself with-in 5 feet of S. Give the command, followed imme-diately by an auditory or visual cue. If S does not begin to re-spond correctly, provide physical guidance. Correct if needed. Present the natural consequence.	given an auditory or visual cue and, if necessary, delayed physi-cal guidance	4 correct out of the last 5 trials for each step
S/2 Position yourself within 10 feet of S. Give the command, followed imme-diately by an auditory or visual cue. Correct if needed. Give the natural consequence.	given an auditory or visual cue	
S/3 Position yourself any-where in the room. Give the command. If S does not begin to respond correctly, repeat the command, followed imme-diately by an auditory or visual cue. Correct if needed. Present the natural consequence.	given a delayed auditory or visual cue if neces-sary	
S/4 Position yourself any-where in the room. Give the command. Correct if needed. Present the natural consequence.	unassisted	
POST 1 Same as PRE	unassisted	4 correct out of 5 trials for each test
POST 2 New Setting		
POST 3 New Teacher		

MODIFICATIONS

Sit directly in front of S so that he faces you. When he consistently responds in this position, move to his side, then farther away. Finally position your-self behind him so that he must turn to make eye contact.

Sit directly in front of S, and hold a reinforcer (e.g., candy, small toy) in front of your face as you call his name. After S responds with this cue, call his name but do not hold up the reinforcer. Instead, give it to him after he looks. Finally stop using the reinforcer. Note: Always provide the natural consequence in addition to the reinforcer.

Responding to Signal Words

4/5 Data

Cycle

Skill:

In this program the child learns to associate a specific word or phrase with the activity that it signals. For example, when an adult says "car," the child may begin to pull the adult toward the door in anticipation of a ride. Often the first words learned are those that signal or precede reinforcing events. This skill is taught by introducing, then fading cues (other than the signal word) that indicate that the event is to occur. After learning that specific words signal specific events, the child later expands his vocabulary to recognize a variety of words.

Entry Behaviors:

1. S responds to some cued commands for routine tasks (e.g., Following Cued Commands). Although S may not be able to comprehend the specific words of a command, he is usually able to perform the desired action by using your model, gestures, or other cues to understand what is expected of him. In addition, he may respond to his own name when it is called out as an attention signal (e.g., Attending to Own Name).

2. S hears the signal word, which is spoken with intonation cues such as loudness, pitch, or rhythm. Or, adapt by teaching S to respond to a visual signal, such as signing. Note that the intent of the program is to introduce symbols, not simple gestures or other situational cues.

3. S sees the teacher. Or, adapt by giving extra tactile cues to replace the visual cues (which are faded in the program).

4. S makes an unassisted response that indicates he predicts the upcoming event. (You may help S participate in the event after he has made an initial response.)

Objective:

After hearing a signal word, S makes an appropriate anticipatory response when he hears a word or command that signals the start of an activity or event. S must initiate his response within 5 seconds of the signal word and respond correctly 4 out of 5 trials.

signal word = a word or short phrase that is associated with a reinforcing event (e.g., car signals that you will go for a ride; lunchtime signals that you get out your lunchbox; swimming signals that you will go to the pool; up signals that you will pick the child up). Select words that you regularly use in conjunction with events that are reinforcing to the child.

<u>anticipatory response</u> = any action (gesture, movement, sound) that S typically makes during the reinforcing event. S must initiate his response within 5 seconds of the signal word and respond correctly 4 out of 5 trials.

Cycle:

Record each different command that S can perform. Each command is a cycle. Each cycle teaches one signal word. Repeat to teach S to respond to other signal words.

Follow-Up:

Continue to use the signal words at appropriate times. Vary the situation so that S learns to respond to the word whenever it is used. Establish other routines with S so that he learns to predict more events by their signal words. As you introduce a new word, repeat it at appropriate times. For example, say <u>roll</u> enthusiastically each time before and as you roll the ball to S. The repetition of the same word with the same object or action will give S experiences needed for Identifying Objects, Body Parts, and People, as well as Naming Actions. Reinforce S's attempts to imitate as you repeat the key word (e.g., Shaping Words).

Program for Receptive Skill 5

Materials:

Select materials appropriate to the signal word to be taught.

Chart:

None.

GENERAL STRATEGY

Arrangement:

Set up a situation appropriate to the signal word.

Command:

Give the signal word with appropriate intonation cues ("LUNCHTIME").

Cues:

model = present a demonstration of the reinforcing event or present exaggerated gestures or motions indicating the event.

partial guidance = assist S to start or perform some part of the response he typically makes during the reinforcing event (e.g., start S in the direction of his lunchbox).

Latency:

S must initiate his response within 5 seconds of the command or delayed cue.

Correction:

Use general correction procedures.

Natural Consequence:

Immediately begin the reinforcing event. You may assist S if needed during the event.

Other Trials:

Repeat the strategy as often as appropriate. If it is appropriate to give several trials in the same session, separate the trials by interspersing other activities between them.

Modification:

S has not met step criterion after four errors.

CONDITIONS	BEHAVIOR	CRITERIA
	S makes an anticipatory response...	
PRE Arrange the situation. Give the command. Present the natural consequence.	unassisted	4 correct out of 5 trials
S/1 Arrange the situation. Give the command and immediately model. If S does not begin to respond correctly, provide partial guidance. Correct if needed. Present the natural consequence.	given a model and, if necessary, delayed partial guidance	4 correct out of the last 5 trials for each step
S/2 Arrange the situation. Give the command. If S does not begin to respond correctly, present the model and provide partial guidance. Correct if needed. Present the natural consequence.	given a delayed model and partial guidance if necessary	
S/3 Arrange the situation. Give the command. If S does not begin to respond correctly, present the model. Correct if needed. Present the natural consequence.	given a delayed model if necessary	
S/4 Arrange the situation. Give the command. Correct if needed. Present the natural consequence.	unassisted	
POST 1 Same as PRE	unassisted	4 correct out of 5 trials for each test
POST 2 New Setting		
POST 3 New Teacher		

MODIFICATIONS

Add a step at the beginning where you provide partial guidance immediately after the command.

Practice the response. Select a signal word for an event that may be repeated several times in a row (e.g., Up for picking up S and swinging him). Before a trial, practice the event. Say Up, pick up S, and swing him. Repeat this several times. Then give the signal word alone and whatever cues are described for the step. Gradually fade the number of practices before each trial (e.g., five chances to practice, one trial; three chances to practice, one trial) until S responds without practice.

Identifying Objects

4/5 Data

Cycle

Skill:

In this program the child learns to recognize the names of objects he uses often in his environment. He learns to select an object from a group through a process which includes introducing then fading auditory and visual cues that enhance the discriminability of the object. The child who learns the skill will follow verbal commands without additional cues.

Entry Behaviors:

1. S <u>uses a variety of common objects</u> with minimal assistance (e.g., self-help skills). If S cannot use objects because of physical limitations, he should be able to indicate in some way that he is aware of the uses of the objects (e.g., opens his mouth when he sees a spoon or cup).

2. S <u>responds to a variety of cued commands</u> for routine tasks (e.g., Following Cued Commands). Although S may or may not be able to comprehend the specific words of a command, he is usually able to perform the desired action by using your model, gestures, or other cues to understand what is expected of him. Typically, S associates a specific word with a specific reinforcing event and anticipates the event whenever that word is spoken (e.g., Responding to Signal Words).

3. S <u>visually discriminates between different objects</u>. Usually S demonstrates this skill by spontaneously using different objects correctly (he shows he can tell a sock from a mitten by attempting to put each one on correctly, without direction). S may also demonstrate visual discrimination by matching objects that are similar in appearance (e.g., Matching-Objects). If S is visually impaired, he should be able to discriminate objects by touch. Adapt the program by having him feel the objects, perform an activity with them if necessary, then select the indicated object.

4. S <u>hears the command</u>, or can lip-read. If S is hearing impaired, you may adapt the program, using signing instead of or in addition to vocal language.

5. S <u>makes some motor response</u> to indicate his choice (points to a specified object, looks at it, picks it up). Select a response appropriate to S's capabilities.

Objective:

When presented with a choice of three <u>objects</u>, S selects the specified object. S must initiate his response within 5 seconds of the command and respond correctly 4 out of 5 trials for each of two different objects that are specified at random.

object = an item that can be easily handled and for which there is a duplicate available. (This program is not appropriate to teach objects that are large or do not have a duplicate that can be used. See Cycle and Follow-Up for suggestions for teaching large objects.)

Cycle:

Record each object S can identify. Each cycle teaches two objects. Repeat as needed to teach other small, easily handled objects. Once S recognizes the names of a variety of familiar objects and can associate those objects with their pictures (e.g., Identifying Simple Pictures), repeat the program to teach large objects (especially those not readily available), using pictures instead of the real objects.

Follow-Up:

Have S respond to a variety of commands that include each new word he learns. Help S generalize these new concepts by teaching him to recognize a variety of objects of the same class (e.g., cup--short red one with a handle; large green cup). Teach S to recognize the pictures of objects he has learned (e.g., Identifying Simple Pictures). Teach S to imitate the names of the objects he has learned (e.g., Shaping Words) and to name the object on his own (e.g., Naming Objects). Have S help with household or school tasks by sorting the objects he has learned (e.g., Sorting). Informally introduce the names of other objects that S sees or uses daily, such as bed, sink, or tree. Encourage S to say the names of these objects.

Program for Receptive Skill 6

Materials:

Select two objects (called targets) to be taught. Obtain a duplicate for each (called samples). In addition, have at least three other objects available to use as distractors.

Chart:

Common Objects Chart, page 457.

GENERAL STRATEGY

Cue:

present sample = select a visual characteristic of the target and its sample (the roundness of a ball, the bristles of a brush). Point out this attribute and describe it ("Look how round the ball is," as you circle the ball with your finger). Then hold up the sample or give it to S, and say its name emphatically... "Ball." If S is vocal, have him try to say the word.

Arrangement:

Display three choices, both targets and one distractor.

Command:

Give an appropriate command for S to indicate one of the targets ("GIVE ME THE CUP" or "POINT TO THE SPOON").

Latency:

S must initiate his response within 5 seconds of the command or delayed cue.

Correction:

Use general correction procedures.

Natural Consequence:

Allow S to interact with the object. Guide S to use the object appropriately (brush his hair with the hairbrush, pretend to drink from the cup).

Other Trials:

Repeat the strategy. Vary trials between the two targets to be identified. Note that S must always meet criterion on both targets. Also, vary the distractor and the arrangement of choices.

Modification:

S has not met step criterion after four errors.

CONDITIONS	BEHAVIOR	CRITERIA
	S selects the specified target...	for each target
PRE Display the choices, and give the command. Present the natural consequence.	unassisted	4 correct out of 5 trials (each target)
S/1 Present the sample. Display the choices, and give the command. Correct if needed. Present the natural consequence.	with sample present	4 correct out of the last 5 trials for each step (each target)
S/2 Present the sample; then remove it. Display the choices, and give the command. Correct if needed. Present the natural consequence.	with sample present, then removed	
S/3 Display the choices, and give the command. If S does not begin to respond correctly, present the sample, and then remove it, repeating the command. Correct if needed. Present the natural consequence.	with delayed sample, which is removed	
S/4 Display the choices, and give the command. Correct if needed. Present the natural consequence.	unassisted	
POST 1 Same as PRE	unassisted	4 correct out of 5 trials for each test (each target)
POST 2 New Command		
POST 3 New Objects (Same type of object, such as a different cup and spoon)		

MODIFICATIONS

When you present the sample, demonstrate the appropriate use of the object at the same time. Allow S to perform the appropriate action with the object. Then give the command. After S's response, present the natural consequence as described.

Identifying Body Parts

4/5 Data

Cycle

Skill:

This program teaches the child to recognize the names of the parts of his body.
By presenting, then fading, physical guidance and visual cues, the child is taught
to point to body parts when requested to do so. With this skill, the child can
follow verbal commands requiring the use of parts of his body (e.g., "Close your
eyes," "Blow your nose," "Clean your ears," "Put your arms in the sleeves").

Entry Behaviors:

1. S recognizes the names of several common objects (e.g., Identifying Objects).
   Typically, the child learns some routine verbal commands (without gestural
   cues) and signal words (e.g., Responding to Signal Words) before he learns
   specific nouns. Often the first nouns learned are very familiar objects and
   toys. As his receptive vocabulary increases, however, he learns the words
   for specific body parts.

2. S demonstrates body awareness in several ways. For example, he is taught or
   can already perform self-help skills requiring the use of the body parts to
   be learned; he responds in some way when he sees his image reflected in a
   mirror (e.g., touches the mirror or his body, vocalizes, smiles); and S
   imitates some simple motor actions requiring the use of the body parts to be
   learned (e.g., Imitating Actions).

3. S responds to a variety of cued commands for routine tasks (e.g., Following
   Cued Commands). Although S may or may not be able to comprehend the specific
   words of a command, he is usually able to perform the desired action by using
   your model, gestures, or other cues to understand what is expected of him.

4. S sees your model. Or, adapt by having S touch the appropriate body part as
   you give the model (e.g., have S touch your foot as you name it, then wiggle
   it).

5. S hears the command or can lip-read. If S is hearing impaired, you may adapt
   the program using signing instead of or in addition to verbal language.

6. S makes some motor response to indicate the body part (points to, looks at).
   Select a response appropriate to S's capabilities.

Objective:

S indicates the specified body part. S must initiate his response within 5
seconds of the command and respond correctly 4 out of 5 trials for each of two
body parts specified at random.

Cycle:

Record each body part S can identify. Each cycle teaches two body parts. Repeat as needed to teach the names of other body parts. <u>Note</u>: This program is functional when S has a need to recognize the names of the parts of his body (e.g., S is working on self-help programs). Teach body parts whose names are used most frequently in those commands. See the Body Parts Chart (page 455) for suggested vocabulary.

Follow-Up:

Have S respond to a variety of commands requiring the use of different parts of his body (e.g., "Put your hands on the table" or "Close your eyes"). Play games that use specific body parts, such as Simon Says or Peek-A-Boo. Continue to teach self-help skills that require S to use the body parts he has learned to identify. Also, give more detailed descriptions for directions in dressing skills (e.g., "Put your arm or hand in here" or "Bend your knee and put your leg here"). Teach S the names of other body parts that are less frequently used in commands (e.g., elbow, neck, knee). Ask S to say the names of the body parts he has learned. Then have him name body parts from the picture of a person.

Program for Receptive Skill 7

Materials:

Have a wall mirror available (especially for S's body parts that he cannot see, such as his facial features).

Chart:

Body Parts Chart, page 455.

GENERAL STRATEGY

Warm-Up:

Sit with S in front of a mirror. Direct his attention to the mirror if necessary. Begin an activity in which you play with S, and ask him to repeat simple motor actions that you demonstrate (e.g., cover your eyes). Do this at the beginning of every session.

Cue:

model = touch one of your body parts and name it; then perform an appropriate response with it (e.g., Wiggle your fingers).

Command:

Give an appropriate command for S to indicate one of his body parts ("TOUCH YOUR NOSE"). Emphasize the name of the body part.

Cues:

full guidance = assist S to indicate the specified part of his own body (have S touch, point to).

partial guidance = physically assist S to start or perform any part of the response, but do not assist the entire response.

Latency:

S must initiate his response within 5 seconds of the command or delayed cue. When guidance cues are given, S is to respond immediately.

Correction:

Use general correction procedures.

Natural Consequence:

Have S do something with the specified body part (cover his eyes, wiggle his fingers, put his foot into his shoe). Name the part during this activity.

Other Trials:

Repeat the strategy. Vary trials between the two body parts. Note that S must always meet criterion on both body parts.

Modification:

S has not met step criterion after four errors.

	CONDITIONS	BEHAVIOR S indicates the speci- fied body part...	CRITERIA for each body part
PRE	Give the command. Present the natural consequence.	unassisted	4 correct out of 5 trials (each part)
S/1	Present the model, then give the command. If S does not begin to respond correctly, pro- vide full guidance. Correct if needed. Pre- sent the natural conse- quence.	with a model and, if necessary, delayed full guidance	4 correct out of the last 5 trials for each step (each part)
S/2	Present the model, then give the command. If S does not begin to re- spond correctly, provide partial guidance. Correct if needed. Present the natural consequence.	with a model and, if necessary, delayed partial guidance	
S/3	Present the model, then give the command. Correct if needed. Present the natural consequence.	with a model	
S/4	Give the command. If S does not respond correct- ly, present the model, and repeat the command. Correct if needed. Pre- sent the natural conse- quence	with a delayed model if necessary	
S/5	Give the command. Cor- rect if needed. Present the natural consequence.	unassisted	
POST 1	Same as PRE	unassisted	4 correct out of 5 trials for each test (each part)
POST 2	New Command (e.g., "Show me your ___.")		
POST 3	New Setting		

MODIFICATIONS

Use one child who already recognizes the names of several body parts as a peer
model. Ask him to indicate the body part you name, then ask S to do so. Use
the peer model for each trial, then every other trial. Gradually fade the use of
the peer model until S can respond correctly without this cue.

At first do not vary the trials between the two body parts. Instead, give
five trials for one body part, then five trials for the other. Gradually reduce the consecutive number of trials for each body part until you are alternating trials between the two. Finally give trials in random order for each
body part.

Give the warm-up before every trial, and draw attention to the body parts to be
taught by performing some action with them. Require S to imitate your actions.
Gradually fade the use of the warm-up until it is given only at the beginning
of each session as in the original strategy. (If trials are presented with a
warm-up for each, intersperse them throughout the day.)

Identifying People

4/5 Data

Cycle

Skill:

This program teaches a child to recognize the names of his classmates. By introducing, then fading, physical guidance and visual cues, the child will point to a classmate who is named by the teacher. With this skill, the child can follow verbal commands that require him to recognize the names of other students in his class.

Entry Behaviors:

1. S <u>recognizes the names of members of his family and of some common objects</u> (e.g., Identifying Objects). Typically, the names of close family members and pets are learned much earlier than the names of classmates. Often the child who is reinforced enough by peers to learn their names already has at least a small vocabulary consisting of some nouns, verbs, and auxiliary words.

2. S <u>has interacted positively</u> with the two children whose names he will learn. Do not teach this program until S discriminates different classmates by showing preferences (e.g., smiles when one classmate sits next to him).

3. S <u>responds to a variety of cued commands</u> for routine tasks (e.g., Following Cued Commands). Although S may or may not be able to comprehend the specific words of a command, he is usually able to perform the desired action by using your model, gestures, or other cues to understand what is expected of him.

4. S <u>recognizes his own name</u> and typically demonstrates this skill by turning toward a person who calls his name (e.g., Attending to Own Name).

5. S <u>hears</u> or lip-reads. If S is hearing impaired, adapt by using signing instead of or in addition to spoken names.

6. S <u>sees</u> so that he will be able to associate a classmate's name with his appearance. If S is visually impaired, reconsider teaching this program. Or, adapt by having S recognize the classmate either from the feel of his hair and facial features (e.g., touches each peer before one is named) or from his voice (e.g., S listens to each peer before one is named). <u>Note:</u> It may take longer to teach the program using these tactile and auditory cues.

7. S <u>makes some motor response</u> to indicate the specified child (e.g., points to, looks at, walks over to, gives something to the child named). Select a response appropriate to S's capabilities.

Objective:

S points to, or otherwise identifies, a classmate at teacher request. S must initiate his response within 5 seconds of the command and respond correctly 4 out of 5 trials for each of two peers specified at random.

Cycle:

Record each person who S can identify. Each cycle teaches the names of two people. Repeat as needed to teach the names of other people, two at a time.

Follow-Up:

Give S a variety of commands to interact with the person named ("GO SIT BY MARY" or "GIVE THE BOOK TO TOMMY"). Teach S the names of other people he sees everyday. Have his parents work on this skill at home, for neighbors, frequent visitors, and the like. Ask S to identify photographs of people, also. Teach S to recognize his printed name; then label his possessions in the room. Assign each child his own desk, coat, book, or locker to further generalize identity and ownership.

Program for Receptive Skill 8

Materials:

Have available only those needed for the activity (e.g., books, toys).

Chart:

None.

GENERAL STRATEGY

Activities:

You, S, and two other students are in a group facing each other. Begin an activity in which everyone can participate (ball rolling), or provide something for everyone to do. Call the children by name during this activity ("It's Susan's turn"..."Eric, show me what you have"). Continue the activity throughout the session.

Command:

Give an appropriate command for S to indicate one of the classmates ("GIVE THE BALL TO JOHN" or "POINT TO SUE"). Emphasize the name.

Cues:

<u>physical guidance</u> = assist S to indicate the person you specify (e.g., have S touch, point to, perform a specified activity with).

<u>pointing cue</u> = point to the child you specify.

Latency:

S must initiate his response within 5 seconds of the command or delayed cue. When guidance cues are given, S is to respond immediately.

Correction:

Use general correction procedures.

Natural Consequence:

Have S interact in some way with the specified classmate (e.g., trade toys, roll the ball to each other, shake hands). Call them both by name during this activity.

Other Trials:

Repeat the strategy. Vary the command between the names of the two classmates. You may also vary the activity if desired. <u>Note</u>: You may give each classmate the chance to indicate the specified child. However, record only S's responses. Note that S must always meet criterion on both names.

Modification:

S has not met step criterion after four errors.

	CONDITIONS	BEHAVIOR	CRITERIA
		S indicates the spec-ified classmate...	for each name
PRE	Begin an activity. Give the command. Present the natural consequence	unassisted	4 correct out of 5 trials (each name)
S/1	Begin an activity. Give the command with the <u>pointing cue</u>. If S does not begin to respond correctly, provide <u>physical guid-ance</u>. Correct if needed. Present the natural consequence.	with a pointing cue and, if necessary, delayed physical guidance	4 correct out of the last 5 trials for each step (each name)
S/2	Begin an activity. Give the command with the <u>pointing cue</u>. Correct if needed. Present the natural consequence.	with a pointing cue	
S/3	Begin an activity. Give the command. If S does not begin to respond correctly, present the <u>pointing cue</u>, and repeat the command. Correct if needed. Present the natural consequence.	with a delayed pointing cue if necessary	
S/4	Begin an activity. Give the command. Correct if needed. Present the natural consequence.	unassisted	
POST 1	Same as PRE	unassisted	4 correct out of 5 trials for each test (each name)
POST 2	New Command (e.g., "WHERE'S SUE?")		
POST 3	New Setting (everyone still facing each other)		

MODIFICATIONS

Select as a peer model one child who already knows the names of several class-mates. Ask him to indicate the specified classmate; then ask S to do so. Use the peer model for each trial, then every other trial, and so forth, until S can respond correctly without him.

Use an extra cue in which you name the classmate ("This is Sue." Point to Sue) or emphasize something about the classmate ("Janet has curly hair." Touch Janet's hair). Add this cue to any step, but make sure it is eventually removed.

Making Sounds

Rata Data

Skill:

This program increases the frequency with which the child produces any vocal
sounds. Although the child produces these sounds indiscriminately (without
meaning), this experimentation is a first step toward speech. From these
randomly emitted sounds, he will learn to produce specific words to communicate.

Entry Behaviors:

1. S <u>responds in some way to the environment</u> (e.g., Responding to Social Interaction, Focusing Attention, and/or any voluntary motor response). Although
   S responds, usually his responses include few vocal sounds. Use any stimulus
   events that concentrate on S's sensory abilities and to which S responds. See
   the Stimulus Chart, pages 467-70. If S is hearing impaired, he may randomly
   produce sounds, but this activity usually ceases when he does not hear his own
   sound. Because of this, it is important that you provide stimuli and systematically reinforce all vocal attempts.

2. S spontaneously <u>cries as a reflex</u> when hungry, wet, and/or in pain. Usually
   S produces random vocal sounds; but this is a rare event. If S has never
   produced any vocal sounds, consult a speech therapist to determine the func-
   tionality of S's speech articulators.

3. S has <u>functional speech articulators</u>. If there is any question, consult a
   speech therapist or language development specialist. If necessary, adapt by
   requiring fewer different vocal sounds or by lowering the criterion. See the
   Phonemes Chart, pages 463-65.

Objective:

S produces <u>vocal sounds</u> when presented with eliciting stimuli. S emits at least
40 sounds, including at least five different ones, anytime during a 10-minute
interval.

<u>vocal sound</u> = a syllable; a vowel, consonant, or combination that can be clearly
distinguished. For example, each of the following is one vocal sound: <u>ah</u>, <u>mm</u>,
<u>bah</u>, <u>guh</u>, <u>uhr</u>, <u>duh</u>, <u>ee</u>. See the Phonemes Chart. Whining, crying, or other
inappropriate sounds should not be counted.

Cycle:

None specified. You may repeat the program to increase babbling (i.e., repeating
one sound several times--<u>ba-ba-ba-ba</u>). Rather than count each syllable separately,
count each episode as "one" sound.

Follow-Up:

Continue to present stimuli to increase the number of different sounds S spontaneously produces. Use a variety of stimulus events, and reinforce sounds
made in different situations and when other people are present. Whenever S
emits a sound, imitate the sound and reinforce when S repeats that sound or
makes another--a strategy used in Responding Vocally to Model--to build S's
responding to models for later shaping specific speech sounds. In addition,
begin to require S to emit a sound before you give him something he wants--a
strategy used in Producing Sounds on Request--to build the use of sound to
communicate preferences. While S's speech skills are developing, work on other
communication skills. Reinforce when S communicates his wants gesturally or
with sound (e.g., Indicating Preferences). Talk to S frequently and to others
in his presence, and reinforce when S looks at the speaker (e.g., Attending to
Voice). Give S commands by using words with gestures and other context cues (e.g.,
Following Cued Commands), and assist him to respond only if needed.

Program for Expressive Skill 1

Materials:

Collect a variety of stimulus objects.

Chart:

Stimulus Chart (for suggested events) page 467; Phonemes Chart, page 463 (for suggested events for specific sounds).

GENERAL STRATEGY

Eliciting Stimuli:

In a play situation, present an object or perform an activity (about 15 seconds each) to elicit sounds. During the event, <u>make noises and talk to</u> S. Pause to allow him to vocalize. (Insure that stimuli are not presented too rapidly.) Continue presenting different objects and events for 10 minutes. Anytime S emits a sound, imitate that sound.

Latency:

S must initiate his response anytime during the 10 minutes.

Correction:

None. If S does not emit any sound after about 15 seconds, change to a new eliciting event.

Other Trials:

Repeat the strategy. Vary eliciting events to encourage S to make a variety of sounds. Present as many different objects and events as possible during the 10-minute session.

Modification:

S has not met criterion for a step after four sessions.

	CONDITIONS	BEHAVIOR	CRITERIA
		S emits vocal sounds...	during a 10-minute session
PRE	Present eliciting events for 10 minutes.	unassisted	40 sounds, including 5 different
S/1	"	"	any 5 sounds
S/2	"	"	10 sounds, at least 2 different
S/3	"	"	15 sounds, at least 3 different
S/4	"	"	20 sounds, at least 4 different
S/5	"	"	30 sounds, at least 5 different
S/6	"	"	40 sounds, at least 5 different
POST 1	Same as PRE	unassisted	40 sounds, including 5 different sounds, for each test
POST 2	New Setting		
POST 3	New Teacher		

MODIFICATIONS

If S is emitting sounds that do not contain phonemes (e.g., gurgling, giggling), change the definition of a response to accept these sounds. Go through the steps to increase the rate of these sounds. This strategy will increase the probability that S will also spontaneously produce a vocal sound with phonemes (vowels, consonants, or combinations). After S has produced at least three vocal sounds with phonemes during each session for a week, begin again at S/1 and count only responses meeting the definition found in the Objective.

Responding
Vocally to Model

Rate Data

Skill:

In this program the child increases the frequency with which he produces any sound after a verbal model. This skill is developed in an interactive situation where a stimulus for producing vocal sounds is presented, as in Making Sounds. Once the child emits a sound, provide a verbal model. The child is expected to respond to the model. He may make **any** sound to meet criterion. This inter- action builds the responding needed for later speech work to shape the child's responses into specific sounds.

Entry Behaviors:

1. S frequently emits vocal sounds, especially during interactions (e.g., Making Sounds). Although S emits sounds, he does not attempt to respond to other people's sounds. Rather, his sounds are produced without any attempt to interact vocally. S may occasionally use sound to indicate his preferences (e.g., Indicating Preferences), but he does not usually attempt to imitate a sound or word you give as a model.

2. S's attention can be directed toward the person interacting with him while a verbal model is given (e.g., Focusing Attention: Eye Contact and/or Attending to Voice). However, S does not attempt to "talk back" or interact vocally with the person, although he may make other nonvocal responses (e.g., a smile, gestures).

3. S hears the verbal model. Or, adapt by adding extra cues with the verbal model, such as placing S's hand on your lips or throat to feel the sound being produced. Consult with a speech therapist for other alternatives.

4. S has intact and functional speech articulators. Or, adapt by lowering criterion to require fewer different sounds.

Objective:

When presented with a model that is repetitious of a sound elicited from S, S produces a vocal response. S must initiate his response within 5 seconds of the model at least 30 times during a 10-minute session.

vocal response = any vocal sound (vowel, consonant, or vowel-consonant combina- tion), not necessarily an imitation, produced after the model. (See Phonemes Chart, page 463.)

Cycle:

None specified.

Follow-Up:

Continue to encourage S to interact with you. Have others imitate S's sounds, and encourage S to respond to them. As S responds more frequently, initiate the sequence yourself (i.e., do not wait for S to emit the first sounds). Model (make) a sound, and reinforce if S responds. Continue to model, and reinforce each closer approximation of the sound. This strategy is designed to develop specific speech sounds, as in Shaping Words. In addition, require S to emit sounds or make gestures to obtain something he desires (e.g., Indicating Preferences). Note that the use of sound to communicate wants is more fully developed in Producing Sounds on Request, which may be taught concurrently with this program.

Talk to S and others frequently. Reinforce S when he looks at the speaker (e.g., Attending to Voice). Request S to do things for you, and accompany your requests with gestures and other context cues. Provide S with minimal assistance (e.g., Following Cued Commands).

Imitate S's motor actions. Reinforce him when he imitates your motor response (e.g., Responding to and Repeating Teacher Model). To respond to other's sounds and actions is a step toward the development of verbal and/or motor imitation.

Program for Expressive Skill 2

Materials:

Collect a variety of stimulus objects.

Chart:

Stimulus Chart (for suggested events), page 467; Phonemes Chart (for events for specific sounds), page 463.

GENERAL STRATEGY

Eliciting Stimuli:

In a play situation, present an object or perform an activity (about 15 seconds) to elicit a sound from S. As soon as S emits a sound...

Verbal Model:

Draw S's attention to your face or mouth in some way, such as by placing your face in his line of sight. Then enthusiastically imitate the sound S just produced.

Latency:

S must initiate his response within 5 seconds of the model.

Correction:

None. Go on to another eliciting stimulus.

Other Trials:

Repeat the strategy. Vary eliciting stimuli to encourage S to initiate sounds for you to model. Present as many models as possible during the 10-minute session. Note that only one response per model is counted.

Modification:

S has not met step criterion after four sessions.

CONDITIONS	BEHAVIOR	CRITERIA
	S produces a vocal response to the model...	during a 10-minute session
PRE Present eliciting stimuli until S emits a vocal sound. As soon as S completes the production, present the verbal model.	unassisted	30 responses, 5 different sounds
S/1 "	"	any 5 responses
S/2 "	"	10 responses, 2 different sounds
S/3 "	"	15 responses, 3 different sounds
S/4 "	"	20 responses, 4 different sounds
S/5 "	"	30 responses, 5 different sounds
POST 1 Same as PRE	unassisted	30 responses, 5 different sounds, for each test
POST 2 New Setting		
POST 3 New Teacher		

MODIFICATIONS

If S does not produce a consistent response to the model, add a step. Repeat your command with additional cues. Fade (decrease the number of times you present) these cues until you reach the conditions of the original strategy (one model for a response).

Indicating
Preferences

Rate Data

Skill:

In this program the child increases the frequency with which he communicates his preferences to others through gestures or motions. The child's motions may include pointing to a desired object that is out of reach, or tugging or pulling at another person to bring him to the desired object. Any motion or set of motions that communicates S's intent to the teacher is acceptable. These gestures are an early form of communication and are often paired with nonspecific vocal sounds. As the child's vocal skills develop, this gestural communication becomes subordinate to speech.

Entry Behaviors:

1. S <u>responds positively</u> to the environment and <u>shows preferences</u> for certain objects and activities (e.g., Responding to Social Interaction, Reaching, Focusing Attention, Manipulating Objects). These preferences provide S with a reason to communicate. In this program a preferred object or activity is withheld temporarily until S indicates that he wants that particular object or activity.

2. S <u>makes some responses</u> to indicate his preferences. Select any socially acceptable responses within his capabilities. Although S can make some responses, he is unable to communicate specifically what he wants because his actions are so undifferentiated (e.g., crying, waving arms in no particular direction, making sounds without any apparent referent). If S can already communicate with sound but without gestures, reconsider the rationale for this program and consider developing speech immediately (e.g., Producing Sounds on Request, Shaping Words).

3. S <u>sees the choices</u>. Or, adapt by using tactile and auditory cues to enable S to recognize the objects or activities available.

Objective:

S <u>gestures</u> to indicate his preference. S must initiate his response correctly at least 10 times to three or more different objects or activities during a 10-minute interval.

<u>gestures</u> = a specific item or the occurrence of a specific activity (e.g., reaches for, points to, takes you by the hand). Although vocalization is not required, always reinforce any vocal sound S produces in addition to the gesture. This strategy will facilitate performance on other speech programs.

53

Cycle:

None specified. However, you may repeat the program with specific objects or activities to expand S's use of different gestures, requiring him to make at least five different gestures.

Follow-Up:

Continue to reinforce S's gestures in appropriate situations (when objects are out of reach or when he wants you to do something for him). Reinforce more and more meaningful gestures so that his nonverbal communication techniques improve. For example, if S is indicating an object by swinging his arm toward it, you may shape the arm swing into a pointing response. Vary the objects and setting to encourage a variety of different gestures.

Reinforce when S pairs a vocal sound with the gesture. (This use of sound to communicate overlaps somewhat with Producing Sounds on Request.) When S uses sound, require him to make closer approximations of the word (e.g., Shaping Words). As S's use of sound develops, require S to vocalize and use the gestures only as needed to communicate his meaning. At this point, do not reinforce S's gestures without accompanying speech.

Program for Expressive Skill 3

Materials:

Collect materials appropriate to the stimulus events.

Chart:

Stimulus Chart (for activities and objects), page 467.

GENERAL STRATEGY

Arrangement:

Play situation with favorite objects available.

Stimulus Event:

Note: The purpose of the stimulus event is to interest S in an object or activity so that he will want to continue the interaction after he is interrupted. This preference provides the stimulus for S's communication. Change events if S has not emitted a response indicating his interest within 30 seconds.

For example, stimulate S to interact with the materials. After S shows an interest in the object, remove it. Place it within view but just out of his reach.

OR, if you use a record player or TV, turn it on and get S's attention. Then turn it off.

OR, if you are engaging S in an activity, begin the activity; then stop after S shows signs of enjoyment.

Command:

Give an appropriate command (e.g., "WHAT DO YOU WANT?").

Latency:

S must initiate his response within 5 seconds of the command.

Correction:

Repeat the command, and assist S if needed to make an appropriate response.

Natural Consequence:

Present S with the object and/or perform the desired activity.

Other Trials:

Repeat the strategy. Vary stimulus events for 10 minutes.

Modification:

S has not met step criterion after four sessions.

CONDITIONS	BEHAVIOR	CRITERIA
	S indicates a specific object or activity...	during a 10-minute session
PRE Present a stimulus event. When S indicates interest, interrupt it and give the command. Present the natural consequence.	unassisted	10 responses (at least 3 different objects or activities indicated)
S/1 Present a stimulus event. When S indicates interest, interrupt it and give the command. Correct if needed. Present the natural consequence.	"	3 responses (any object or activity indicated)
S/2 "	"	5 responses (at least 2 different objects or activities indicated)
S/3 "	"	8 responses (at least 2 different objects or activities indicated)
S/4 "	"	10 responses (at least 2 different objects or activities indicated)
S/5 "	"	10 responses (at least 3 different objects or activities indicated)
POST 1 Same as PRE	unassisted	10 responses (at least 3 different objects or activities indicated) for each test
POST 2 New Setting		
POST 3 New Events		

MODIFICATIONS

Reevaluate the activities and objects used to insure that S prefers them. Then try a new strategy. Do not present a stimulus event as described. Rather, place a highly reinforcing object out of reach, and draw S's attention to it. Give the command and, if needed, assist S to point. Gradually fade your assistance to point. When S can point, reintroduce the program strategy with the stimulus event.

Change the session time. Use the strategy (no stimulus event, highly reinforcing object out of reach), but present only one trial at regular times during the day (e.g., S must point to get a cookie at snacktime). Once S consistently responds in at least one situation, reintroduce the 10-minute session.

Producing Sounds on Request

4/5 Data

Skill:

In this program the child learns to emit some (any) vocal sound when asked to imitate ("Say ball"). This skill is taught by engaging in a large number of potentially reinforcing interactions with S, then fading the number and intensity of stimuli. The child is not required to imitate the model but can produce any sound. This responding is a necessary step to shape the response into a specific sound or word.

Entry Behaviors:

1. S responds in a variety of situations, although he does not usually make a vocal response when asked to imitate a word in a structured situation. This behavior is demonstrated by S's response to simple routine commands (e.g., Following Cued Commands). It may also be demonstrated in an interactive situation when a model is presented that is a repetition of his own previous sound (e.g., Responding to Teacher Model, Responding Vocally to Model).

2. S attempts to communicate his preferences in some way, such as by gesture or action or sound (e.g., Responding to Teacher Model, Responding Vocally to Model). spontaneously, he does not do so in response to a question or request.

3. S produces sounds (e.g., Making Sounds) but without attempting to imitate another person's speech. If S has any speech impairments, consult a speech therapist.

4. S hears the model. Or, adapt by adding visual or tactile cues. For example, place S's hand on your lips, mouth, or throat so he can feel the sound. You may wish to introduce sign language at this time by giving a sound and sign as the model and requiring S to make a sound and hand movement. Note that in this program, S does not have to imitate but can simply respond. Therefore, if you are introducing a sign, any attempt by S would be a response meeting criterion; then you may guide his hand if needed to complete the sign appropriately.

5. S sees the model. Or, adapt by adding tactile cues to have S feel the position of your mouth if necessary.

Objective:

When an object is presented and a command is given to imitate the object's name, S makes a vocal response. S must initiate his response within 5 seconds of the command and respond correctly 4 out of 5 trials.

Cycle:

None specified.

Follow-Up:

Continue to require S to imitate words (i.e., make some vocal response) to
obtain different objects or outcomes. Reinforce all of S's attempts to use
sound to communicate his preferences, a follow-up to Indicating Preferences,
as well as to this program. Have him imitate words spoken by a variety of
people so that he has many different speech experiences. As S learns to respond
consistently, require closer approximations of the sound before you reinforce
his response and give him the object (e.g., Shaping Words). Do not, however,
make this a very frustrating situation since this will hamper later speech work.
If you introduce signing in this program, require closer approximations of the
hand movements, and gradually fade your guidance. After S consistently responds
to a model to obtain different objects, have him imitate your sound without
having an object present as a stimulus. The more frequently S responds in a
structured situation (i.e., S attempts to imitate anytime you give a model),
the easier all later speech work will be (e.g., Shaping Words, Naming Objects/
Actions).

Program for Expressive Skill 4

Materials:

Choose five sounds you have heard S produce. For each sound, choose one object that begins with that sound (e.g., b--ball). Use toys, objects, or food to which S typically responds.

Chart:

None.

GENERAL STRATEGY

Cue:

practice the response = interact with S and the object until S emits some vocal sound.

Label:

Hold up the object, and draw S's attention to it, but keep it out of his reach. Name the object ("S, look...ball").

Command:

Give a command to imitate the name of the object ("SAY BALL). As specified, the word is said either in a normal voice or an exaggerated manner (e.g., loud, drawn out, staccato).

Cues:

object cue = manipulate the object, and draw S's interest. Allow him to play with the object.

repeated sound = articulate (repeat) one sound (phoneme) with exaggerated emphasis ("buh").

Latency:

S must initiate his response within 10 seconds of the command in S/1--S/3 and within 5 seconds of the command or delayed cue in S/4--S/6 and all tests.

Correction:

Use a brief time-out procedure. Hold the object out of sight, and look away from S for 3 to 5 seconds. Ignore any tantrum behaviors. Then go on to a new trial. If S does not respond and then consistently behaves inappropriately when he does not receive the object as a natural consequence for a response, discontinue the ongoing activity, and ignore S's inappropriate behavior.

Natural Consequence:

Give S the object after he emits some (any) sound.

Other Trials:

Repeat the strategy. Vary the object you present and the sound you emphasize. Be sure to space trials over time to maintain S's attention.

Modification:

S has not met step criterion after four errors.

CONDITIONS	BEHAVIOR S emits any sound...	CRITERIA
PRE Label the object, and give the command in a normal voice. Present the natural consequence.	unassisted, within 5 seconds	4 correct out of 5 trials
S/1 Practice the response. After S emits some sound, label the object, and give the command in an exaggerated manner. Immediately give the object cue and repeat the sound for up to 10 seconds. Correct if needed. Present the natural consequence.	after practicing and within 10 seconds of an exaggerated command with the object cue and repeated sounds	4 correct out of the last 5 trials for each step
S/2 Same as S/1, but omit the object cue. (S cannot manipulate the object until he makes a sound, although he receives verbal stimuli.)	after practicing and within 10 seconds of an exaggerated command with repeated sounds	
S/3 Label the object, and give the command in an exaggerated manner. Repeat the sound for up to 10 seconds. Correct if needed. Present the natural consequence.	within 10 seconds of an exaggerated command with repeated sounds	
S/4 Same as S/3, but repeat the sound for only 5 seconds (latency decreases).	within 5 seconds of an exaggerated command with repeated sounds	
S/5 Label the object, and give the command in an exaggerated manner. If S does not respond, repeat the sound once. Correct if needed. Give Present the natural consequence.	within 5 seconds of an exaggerated command with one delayed sound if necessary	
S/6 Label the object, and give the command in a normal voice. Correct if needed. Present the natural consequence.	unassisted, within 5 seconds	
POST 1 Same as PRE	unassisted, within 5 seconds	4 correct out of 5 trials for each test
POST 2 New Objects		
POST 3 New Teacher		

MODIFICATIONS

If S does not respond, add a step in which you give one trial each day only
during snacktime. Present a highly reinforcing snack to a peer, and have him
model a vocal sound. Then present the snack to S. Withhold the snack unless S
makes a vocal response within the defined latency period. Repeat this strategy
every snacktime until S responds vocally 4 out of 5 days. Then return to the
original step. (Insure that edibles are not used as reinforcers before snacktime.)

Shaping Words

Skill Analysis

Cycle

Skill:

This program develops the child's use of his speech articulators to repeat a word clearly enough to be understood. After the child can say the word, he can later learn to use it with meaning and without the model, thus initiating oral communication.

Entry Behaviors:

1. S <u>consistently makes some vocal response to a model</u> on command, although he does not accurately imitate the word (e.g., Producing Sounds on Request and Responding Vocally to Model). This responding is very important in speech work, and often a child who responds frequently can imitate simple actions (e.g., Imitating Actions), follow short simple commands given with cues (e.g., Following Cued Commands), and communicate his preferences in some way, preferably using sound (e.g., Indicating Preferences). Typically, S has frequently heard standard speech and attends to a speaker, although he may not understand the content of the conversation (e.g., Attending to Voice).

2. S <u>produces at least five different vocal sounds</u>, including one consonant. S may have produced these sounds while crying or whimpering, or during vocal play (e.g., Making Sounds). Select words to teach based on S's current vocal repertoire and the difficulty level of the required phonemes (see the Cycle, page 62, and the Phonemes Chart, pages 463-65). Note that this program develops the required phonemes but requires only a consistent approximation of the word. Further articulation work should be done after S has a working vocabulary.

3. S has the <u>articulators necessary to produce the required sounds</u>. Typically, S can chew and swallow properly. If S has any apparent significant organic impairment, consult a speech therapist for appropriate speech work.

4. S <u>hears the model</u>. Or, adapt by giving visual or tactile cues. Have S feel your mouth as you produce the word. You may use sign language. Present S with the model of the word and sign. Require him to repeat both. In this case, insure that S can already imitate the sign before this program.

5. S <u>sees the materials and model</u>. Or, adapt by adding tactile cues to help S identify the materials and model if necessary.

Objective:

S makes a <u>consistent approximation</u> of a word within 5 seconds of its model. S must initiate his response correctly 4 out of 5 trials.

<u>consistent approximation</u> = vocalization containing at least half the sounds in the word, including at least one vowel and one consonant (usually the initial consonant-vowel sound).

Cycle:

Record each word S imitates. Each cycle teaches one word at a time. Repeat to teach other words as needed. Typically, the first words learned are mono-syllabic or contain repeated sounds (MAMA), and begin with the easier consonants--<u>m</u>, <u>b</u>, <u>p</u>, <u>w</u>. For example: <u>baby</u>, <u>bib</u>, <u>big</u>, <u>bite</u>, <u>book</u>, <u>boy</u>, <u>bye-bye</u>, <u>cake</u>, <u>coat</u>, <u>cookie</u>, <u>cow</u>, <u>cup</u>, <u>ear</u>, <u>eat</u>, <u>eye</u>, <u>go</u>, <u>gum</u>, <u>hat</u>, <u>hot</u>, <u>keys</u>, <u>mama</u>, <u>milk</u>, <u>top</u>, <u>walk</u>, <u>water</u>.

Follow-Up:

Continue to have S say the word when you model it. When possible, encourage better articulation by gradually reinforcing a closer approximation. Teach S to use the word on his own by asking "What's this?" or "What am I doing?" (e.g., Naming Objects/Actions). Model the word only when necessary. Select other words to teach, particularly easy names of objects and actions that he enjoys. Combine the imitation of the word with recognition of its meaning (e.g., Identi-fying Objects/Body Parts/People). For example, present S with different commands: "Show me the ball" (S points). "Say <u>ball</u>" (S imitates). "What do you want?" or "What is this?" (S names). Note that S may learn to recognize (identifying = receptive language) and to say (naming = expressive language) the word con-currently or in either order.

Program for Expressive Skill 5

Materials:

Select one word to teach. Obtain appropriate objects to pair with the word.

Chart:

Phonemes Chart (for strategies specific to particular phonemes), page 463.

GENERAL STRATEGY

Arrangement:

Structure a relaxed situation, using objects as appropriate.

Attention:

Hold up the object or perform the action for the word to be taught.

Model:

Draw S's attention to your mouth, then give a model for the whole word or sound as specified for the part ("SAY_____").

Latency:

S must initiate his response within 5 seconds of the model.

Correction:

Use Suggestions for each part.

Natural Consequence:

Repeat the word, and allow S to interact with the object or perform the action.

Other Trials:

Repeat the strategy. Allow time between trials if needed. Have S engage in other short activities so that he continues to attend well during speech activities. Limit sessions to 10 minutes. 1 trial = 1 opportunity to perform perform 1 part.

Modification:

S has made no gains in average parts completed after two successive probes (2 weeks).

CONDITIONS	BEHAVIOR	CRITERIA
PRE Test *6 only. Get S's attention; then present a model for the whole word. Present the natural consequence.	*6. Target--S makes a consistent approximation of the word.	4 correct out of 5 trials

DAILY INSTRUCTION

Get S's attention; then present a model appropriate to the part. Assist if needed. Present the natural consequence.		Continue daily instruction/weekly probes until S performs *6 correctly 4 out of the last 5 trials
1. Demonstrate (position your mouth) how to produce the main vowel sound in the word. Present a model for the vowel sound ("SAY a").	1. S positions jaw, tongue, and lips to make the vowel sound.	at least 10 times
2. Present a model for the vowel sound ("SAY a").	2. S resonates and produces the vowel sound (resonates = vibrates the speech mechanisms, which produces a sound).	at least 10 times
3. Demonstrate how to position your mouth to produce one of the consonants from the word (usually the initial or final sound). Present a model for the consonant sound ("SAY m").	3. S positions his jaw, tongue, lip(s), and/or teeth to make the consonant sound.	at least 10 times
4. Present a model for the consonant sound ("SAY m").	4. S produces the consonant sound.	at least 10 times
5. Present a model for the consonant and vowel together as appropriate (either C-V "SAY m a" or V-C "SAY a m"). Note: If the word has more sounds than those covered to this point, repeat part(s) to teach other vowels, consonants, and/or combinations.	5. S produces the consonant-vowel combination.	at least 10 times
*6. Present a model for the whole word ("SAY MAMA"). Present the natural consequence.	*6 Target--S produces a consistent approximation of the word.	4 correct out of the last 5 trials
POST 1 Same as PRE	*6 Target--S produces a consistent approximation of the word.	4 correct out of 5 trials for each test
POST 2 New Setting		
POST 3 New Teacher		

Parts 1 and 3:

Sit behind S with both of you looking forward into a mirror. Demonstrate how to position your mouth. Guide S's jaws and lips into position (where possible). Gradually fade your guidance.

To improve jaw control, have S open and close his mouth slowly, stopping at different positions corresponding to different vowel sounds (e.g., ă--almost closed, ä--half open, ā--open). Model specific positions. Have S imitate as you model these different positions.

To improve tongue movements, have S: Stick his tongue straight out, then in; lick his lips, chew gum with his mouth closed; lick a candy stick held at a right angle to his mouth. Also, put peanut butter or marshmallow creme in parts of S's mouth where his tongue should touch for the sound (e.g., on top or bottom front lip, behind top or bottom front teeth, roof of mouth). Have S lick the food.

To improve lip movements, have S purse his lips, then stretch them wide apart (e.g., o͝o--pursed, ē--stretched). Model specific positions. Have S imitate you as you make funny faces.

Review Suggestions listed in Chewing (pages 235-36).

Pair the mouth position with one body position or action (e.g., Say oh! and throw up your arms in surprise). Whenever you give the model for the mouth position, perform the action. Gradually model only the mouth position.

Parts 2 and 4:

Present the sound frequently throughout the day. Model the sound itself, and use it in alliterative sentences and nonsense jingles (e.g., "Peter Piper picked").

Give auditory training on a sound by pairing that sound with a reinforcing event. Say ä, then ring a bell. Ring the bell every time you say ä, then have S ring it when you say it. When S can do this, intersperse ä with other sounds, insuring that S does not ring the bell for the other sound. Work on this until S recognizes the sound consistently.

Refer to the Phonemes Chart for specific phonemes. Provide a stimulus as suggested for the sound, and reinforce when he produces it. Gradually fade the amount of stimuli until you present just the model.

Pair the sound with one action, always the same (e.g., Say Oh! and raise your hands). Have S imitate both together. Then you make the sound, and he performs the action. Finally you do the action; he makes the sound (alone).

Repeat the model, and shape S's response by gradually requiring closer approximations. Guide if possible, and fade this cue.

To get S to produce sounds, bounce him on your knee or pat his back or chest. If he voices any sound, your action will cause its tonal quality to wobble, thus providing a stimulus to experiment with that sound or others. Or, have S hum into a kazoo. Note that all vowels and some consonants are voiced (i.e., require resonance).

Have S practice breath control by blowing out quickly, letting air escape slowly, and then coughing (sharp exhalation). Have S exhale while his mouth is in different positions. Have S blow into party favors or toy instruments.

Once S produces the correct sound, reinforce him for repeating it at different times. Also, have him say it in different ways: loudly, softly, in a whisper, exaggerated.

Part 5:

Present a model for the first sound, then after S says that, give the model for the second (e.g., "Say m"--response--"Say ä"--response). Gradually present the models more quickly so that there is little pause between the models and S's responses. Then present the two models together (e.g., "Say m... ä"--response). Finally combine the two sounds into one model (e.g., "Say mä").

Repeat the model frequently, and gradually shape S's word by reinforcing closer and closer approximations of the combination.

Pair the sounds with actions, such as "m (hands to lips), ä (hands to side of face, palms front)." Have S practice doing both as you model. Then you say the sounds, and S performs the actions. Reverse roles. Always pair the same sound with the same action.

Naming Actions

4/5 Data

Cycle

Skill:

This program teaches a child to name on command common actions that he performs and that he sees other people perform. This skill is taught by using models of the verb less frequently. As the child learns to use words on his own, expressive language emerges. The child can later combine these single words to make simple phrases or sentences, thus expressing to others his feelings or preferences.

Entry Behaviors:

1. S <u>performs actions on command</u> by imitating a model (e.g., Imitating Actions) and/or by following other cues in the situation (e.g., Following Cued Commands). S may or may not be able to perform the action on vocal command alone. Note that S need only follow commands containing those verbs to be named.

2. S consistently <u>produces an approximation (on command) of the verbs</u> to be taught (e.g., Shaping Words), but he does not use the word to describe the action on his own. The purpose of this program is to teach the child to describe an action with a word, not to teach perfect articulation. After the child learns to use some words meaningfully, then you might want to work on articulation. Teach him words that sound distinctly different. If S has a speech impairment, signing may be an appropriate alternative or addition to S's verbal response. Adapt by presenting both symbols (word and sign) where the word is to be presented. Require S to produce both for his response.

3. S <u>hears you say the verbs</u>. If S has a minimal hearing loss, adapt by having S attend to and touch your mouth as you produce the word during the verbal model. Or, teach S to produce the sign for the word, in addition to saying the word.

4. S <u>physically performs the actions to be taught</u>. It is best to use actions you have seen S perform. If S is physically impaired, choose actions S can perform, or adapt the program by performing the actions yourself and asking S to say what you are doing. Choose actions to be labeled that would most benefit S's situation (e.g., If S cannot get food independently when he is hungry, teach the word <u>eat</u>).

5. S <u>sees the action</u> you perform. Or, adapt by giving tactile cues as needed to indicate the action (e.g., perform the action with S, and guide him if necessary).

Objective:

S correctly names two different actions that were performed. S must initiate his response correctly within 5 seconds of the command 4 out of 5 trials for each action, alternated at random.

Cycle:

Record each action S can name. Repeat the program with different actions, and teach two new actions at a time. Remember to choose actions most appropriate to the activities S engages in throughout the day (e.g., run, walk, pull, push, eat, sit, stand). See Actions Chart for suggestions (page 451).

Follow-Up:

During S's daily routines, ask him what he is doing with particular objects, or show him an object and ask him what he would like to do with it (e.g., cookie--"eat"). Reinforce all correct responses. Present models and reinforce when S combines nouns (e.g., "roll" to "roll car"). Have S state his preferences in routine situations (e.g., on the playground--"swing"), then in novel situations (e.g., in a store--"touch"). Always describe your activities to S to present models of different verbs. Reinforce all spontaneous use of verbs.

Program for Expressive Skill 6

Materials:

A variety of objects appropriate to the two target verbs.

Chart:

Actions Chart, page 451.

GENERAL STRATEGY

Action Demonstration:

Perform the action with one or more objects if the action requires objects. Continue the action throughout the trial, and draw S's attention to the action. S may have an object and participate at any time, or you may give S your object.

Cues:

label = say what you are doing, specifically using the verb ("I'm rolling the car").

request S to perform the action = give a command with the verb ("S, roll the car"), and guide S if needed to perform. If S is already performing, simply state what he is doing by using the verb ("S, you're rolling the truck").

verbal model = get S's attention (remove the object if necessary), and tell S to imitate the verb (e.g., "Tell me roll"). Where a verbal model is used as a cue before the command, S must imitate the word before the command is given. If S does not imitate, withhold the object briefly, then begin the trial again. (No error is recorded since no command has been given.) Where the model is presented after the command, the command is repeated with the model ("What are you doing? Tell me roll").

Command:

Give an appropriate command for S to name the action ("S, WHAT ARE YOU DOING?" or "WHAT AM I DOING?").

Latency:

S must initiate his response within 5 seconds of the command or delayed cue.

Correction:

Withhold S's object for a few seconds, and look away from S. Then begin a new trial.

Other Trials:

Repeat the strategy. Vary the trials between the two actions, using a variety of objects.

Modification:

S has not met step criterion after four errors.

	CONDITIONS	BEHAVIOR S names the action...	CRITERIA for each of 2 actions
PRE	Begin the action demonstration (do not use the word). Give the command.	unassisted	4 correct out of 5 trials (each verb)
S/1	Begin the action demonstration. Label the action. Request S to perform the action. Present the verbal model. After S imitates the word, give the command. Immediately present the verbal model, and pause for S to respond. Repeat the verbal model at brief intervals until S repeats the word; terminate after 30 seconds. Correct if needed.	given a label, a request, and repeated verbal models	4 correct out of the last 5 trials for each step (each verb)
S/2	Begin the action demonstration. Label the action. Request S to perform. Present the verbal model. After S imitates the word, give the command. If S does not name the action, present the verbal model (once). Correct if needed.	given a label, a request, a verbal model and, if necessary, one delayed verbal model	
S/3	Begin the action demonstration. Label the action. Request S to perform. Give the command. If S does not name the action, present the verbal model. Correct if needed.	given a label, a request and if necessary, a delayed verbal model	
S/4	Begin the action demonstration. Label the action. Give the command. If S does not name the action, present the verbal model. Correct if needed.	given a label and, if necessary, a delayed verbal model	
S/5	Begin the action demonstration. Give the command. If S does not name the action, present the verbal model. Correct if needed.	given a delayed verbal model if necessary	

Chart (continued)

CONDITIONS	BEHAVIOR	CRITERIA
S/6 Begin the action demon- stration. Give the command. Correct if needed.	unassisted	
POST 1 Same as PRE	unassisted	4 correct out of 5 trials for each test (each verb)
POST 2 New Setting/Objects (same 2 actions)		
POST 3 New Setting/Objects (same 2 actions)		

MODIFICATIONS

Use a peer model who can name the actions. Ask the peer to model immediately before you give S the command. For example, during the action demonstration, have the peer, then S, imitate the word after the verbal model. Give the command to the peer; then after the peer responds, immediately give the command to S. Gradually have the peer participate less by asking him to model less often.

Change the pre-command strategy. Saturate S's environment with objects and materials for performing the target verb. Before each trial, present a 30-second interval in which you label the action and request S to perform it. Then discontinue the action demonstration (rather than conducting it throughout the trial). Require S to respond to the verbal model (if specified) and command before you allow him to continue the action. Gradually reintroduce the ongoing action demonstration, and require S to respond as he participates.

Naming Objects

4/5 Data

Cycle

Skill:

This program teaches the child to name common objects in his environment when requested to do so. This skill is taught by reducing the number of models of the noun that are given during and after interactions with an object. As the child learns to use words on his own, expressive language emerges. The child can later combine these single words to make simple phrases or sentences and thus express his feelings or preferences.

Entry Behaviors:

1. S uses objects appropriately on command by imitating (e.g., Imitating Actions) and/or by following other cues in the situation (e.g., Following Cued Commands). Note that S need only follow commands on those nouns to be taught. S may or may not be able to identify the object when someone else names it (e.g., Identifying Objects).

2. S consistently produces an approximation of the nouns to be taught (e.g., Shaping Words), but he does not use the words to describe the object on his own. This program teaches the child to describe the object with a word, not perfect articulation. Select nouns that sound distinctly different, and accept approximations. After the child can use some nouns meaningfully, then you might want to work on articulation. If S is speech impaired, signing may be an appropriate alternative or addition to his verbal response. Adapt by presenting both symbols (word and sign) where the word is to be presented. Require S to produce both for his response.

3. S hears you say the noun. Or, if S has a minimal hearing loss, adapt by having S attend to and touch your mouth as you say the word. You may also teach S to produce the sign for the word, in addition to saying the word.

4. S sees the object. Or, adapt by giving additional tactile cues if needed to indicate the object (e.g., have S feel the object).

Objective:

S correctly names two different objects. S must initiate his response correctly within 5 seconds of the command 4 out of 5 trials for each object, alternated at random.

Cycle:

Record each object S can name. Repeat the program with different objects, and teach two new objects at a time. Remember to choose objects most appropriate to S's needs. See the Common Objects Chart (page 457).

Follow-Up:

Continue to ask S to name the objects he has learned to label in a variety of different situations. Generalize S's use of the noun by having him use it to describe other objects of the same category (e.g., tall cups, red cups). Re-inforce when S names objects spontaneously. Require S to state his preferences by combining words (e.g., "want cookie"). Model phrases containing words he knows, and reinforce all approximations (e.g., "car go"). As S learns to name more and more objects, reinforce him when he asks you to name unfamiliar ones (e.g., S asks "What?" or "What's this?" about objects he cannot name). Ask S to confirm the names of objects he knows (e.g., "Is this a doll?" S may say yes or no or name the object correctly).

Program for Expressive Skill 7

Materials:

Two different objects to be taught.

Chart:

Common Objects Chart, page 457.

GENERAL STRATEGY

Object Demonstration:

Interact with S, presenting the objects. Talk about them, and play with them. Do this before each session and between trials as needed to maintain interest. If necessary to maintain S's attention, remove the materials before the beginning of the trial.

Present Object:

Hold up one target, and draw S's attention to it.

Cue:

response practice = say "What is this?" Say "(object)," and have S imitate the word. Since this is used as a cue before the command, S must imitate the word before the command is given. If S does not imitate, withhold the object, then begin the trial again. (No error is recorded since no command has been given.)

Command:

Give an appropriate command to name the object, as described for each step.

Cue:

model = say "Say (object)."

Latency:

S has 5 seconds to say the word after the command or delayed cue.

Correction:

Withhold the object for a few seconds, and look away from S. Then begin a new trial.

Natural Consequence:

Give S the object.

Other Trials:

Repeat the strategy. Vary the trials between the two objects. Note that S must always meet criterion on both.

Modification:

S has not met step criterion after four errors.

	CONDITIONS	BEHAVIOR S names the object...	CRITERIA for each object
PRE	Give the object demonstration, and present the object. Give the command (WHAT IS THIS?). Present the natural consequence.	unassisted	4 correct out of 5 trials (each noun)
S/1	Give the object demonstration, and present the object. Have S <u>practice the response</u>. Immediately after S imitates the word, give the command (WHAT?), followed immediately by the <u>model</u>. Correct if needed. Present the natural consequence.	after practicing; given a model	4 correct out of the last 5 trials for each step (each noun)
S/2	Give the object demonstration, and present the object. Have S <u>practice the response</u>. Immediately after S imitates the word, give the command (WHAT?). If S does not name it correctly, present the <u>model</u>. Correct if needed. Present the natural consequence.	after practicing; given a delayed model if necessary	
S/3	Give the object demonstration, and present the object. Have S <u>practice the response</u>. Immediately after S imitates the word, give the command (WHAT?). Correct if needed. Present the natural consequence.	after practicing	
S/4	Give the object demonstration, and present the object. Give the command (WHAT IS THIS?). If S does not name it correctly, present the	given a delayed model if necessary	

Chart (continued)

CONDITIONS	BEHAVIOR	CRITERIA
model. Correct if needed. Present the natural consequence.		
S/5 Give the object demonstration, and present the object. Give the command (WHAT IS THIS?). Correct if needed. Present the natural consequence.	unassisted	4 correct out of the last 5 trials for each step (each noun)
POST 1 Same as PRE	unassisted	4 correct out of 5 trials for each test (each noun)
POST 2 New Setting		
POST 3 New Teacher		

MODIFICATIONS

Use a peer who can name the objects. Ask the peer to model immediately before you give S the command. For example, give the object demonstration with S and the peer. Present the object and have the peer, then S, practice the response. Give the command to the peer; then after the peer responds, immediately give the command to S. Gradually have the peer participate less by asking him to model less often.

Change the pre-command strategy. Saturate S's environment with objects of the type to be taught (e.g., a variety of books). Give the object demonstration, and have S use the object; then as he is using the object, give the response practice (if specified for the step) and command. Gradually require S to respond when you are holding the object (standard object presentation, response practice, and command).

Focusing Attention

Rate Data

Cycle

Skill:

In this program the child increases the frequency with which he focuses his attention on a single aspect of his environment, looking directly at a particular sound, object, or person. This skill enables the child to respond to a variety of stimulus events and to sustain his attention for longer periods to increase the awareness of his surroundings.

Entry Behaviors:

1. S will <u>look</u> at (1-2 second glance) an identifiable target. Although S has demonstrated that he can attend to an object, he rarely does so. Rather, his usual eye movements appear random or nondirected, and he demonstrates little visual-motor coordination, such as directed reach or movement, and little sustained attention. If S has a visual disability, adapt by using other behaviors in addition to eye contact to define attention; behaviors such as a specific change in body position, head turning, or arm extension. Use only those cycles that are appropriate. Note that the intent of this program is to increase any focused attention at all. For sustained attention (over 2 seconds), refer to programs containing the word <u>attending</u> in their titles.

2. S <u>turns his head</u> slightly. Or, adapt by always keeping the target in a position so that he need only move his eyes (not head) to look at it.

Objective:

S <u>looks at</u> different <u>targets</u>. S must initiate his response correctly to at least five different targets a total of 25 times anytime during a 10-minute session.

<u>looks at</u> = moves eyes to AND fixates 1-2 seconds on a specific point. S may also make other responses (reaching for or holding the target) as long as he fixates.

<u>target</u> = a specific point of focus.

Cycle:

Different cycles increase S's focus on different targets.

1. Varied Targets: S looks at any target.
2. Objects: S looks at objects.

3. Eye Contact: S looks at a person's face, preferably making eye contact. Note that S need only focus on one person rather than on five different targets.

4. Sound: S looks at any target that is making sounds.

Cycles may be taught in any order, although Cycle 1, Varied Targets, usually occurs first.

Follow-Up:

Continue to work on S's attention throughout the day. Give individual trials on a regular basis, taking data to insure that S's performance is or becomes consistent in a variety of natural situations. Demand S's attention whenever presenting a target. This follow-up is extremely important.

Continue to present S with a variety of types of stimulation to increase his awareness. Require S to attend for longer intervals than the brief fixation period that meets the criterion for this program. Later introduce Attending to Voice and Attending to Objects. Encourage S to turn his head to look at different stimulus events. Use the Controlling Head Movements program if S does not have sufficient head and neck control. Later encourage S to look at, then reach for, the target, using Reaching if S does not have sufficient arm and hand control. Also, have S look directly at his hands as he holds or manipulates objects to develop fine motor coordination.

Program for Cognitive Skill 1

Materials:

Select materials appropriate to the cycle.

Chart:

Stimulus Chart (for events), page 467.

GENERAL STRATEGY

Arrangement:

In a play situation, position several objects where S can easily see them.
Include mobiles and pictures, but do not clutter the area. You should be able
to identify the object at which S is looking.

Stimulus Event:

Use suggestions from the Stimulus Chart to structure interactions with S. The
same object may be used in different ways to attract S's attention so that he
will focus (e.g., an object may be held out, shaken, moved, and so on). Conduct
the event in S's range of vision (6 to 36 inches away, to the side, upward,
downward) but not directly in his line of sight. (S must move his eyes and
fixate according to Objective definitions). Continue the stimulus event up
to 30 seconds.

Latency:

None. Anytime S looks at (focuses on) the target, he has made a correct response.

Correction:

Anytime S does not look, bring the target closer, directly in front of his eyes.
Attract S's attention for up to 5 seconds with the target in this position.
Then begin a new stimulus event.

Natural Consequence:

Anytime S fixates on a target, continue the stimulus event until he breaks
attention. After the initial focus (1-2 seconds), you may reinforce S to
sustain his attention. However, this sustained attention is not required and
does not count as a new response. Note: If S usually sustains attention for
more than a brief interval, reconsider the justification for teaching this
program.

Other Trials:

Repeat the strategy. Vary stimulus events during the 10-minute session. Vary
the distance and position of the target (up to 3 feet, to the sides, upward,
downward).

Modification:

S has not met step criterion after four sessions.

Program
Cognitive
Skill 1

	CONDITIONS	BEHAVIOR	CRITERIA
		S moves his eyes and fixates 1-2 seconds on a target...	during a 10-minute session
PRE	Present the stimulus event. Present the natural consequence.	unassisted	25 times, 5 different targets (of the appropriate cycle)
S/1	Present the stimulus event. Correct if needed. Present the natural consequence.	"	5 times, any target
S/2	"	"	10 times, 2 different targets
S/3	"	"	15 times, 3 different targets
S/4	"	"	20 times, 4 different targets
S/5	"	"	25 times, 5 different targets on each of 4 days
POST 1	Same as PRE	unassisted	25 times, 5 different targets for each test
POST 2	New Targets		
POST 3	New Setting		

MODIFICATIONS

Gradually increase the distance and/or direction in which S can focus. At first when the target is a short distance away (6 to 8 inches) and almost in S's line of sight, then, when the target is farther away (12 to 15 inches) and more out of his line of sight, increase S's rate of responding to the target. Gradually S will be moving his eyes/head varied amounts. Continue to increase the distance (up to 3 feet) and direction in which S is to respond, as well as his rate of responding.

Attending to
Objects

Rate Data

Skill:

In this program the child increases the frequency with which he demonstrates
sustained attention to an object or event (object movement or manipulation).
Based on this sustained attention, the child acquires information and experiences
needed to explore and use objects.

Entry Behaviors:

1. S frequently <u>looks in the direction of movement, visual stimuli, and sound</u>
   (e.g., Focusing Attention, cycles for Objects and Sound). Although S does
   respond by looking at the stimulus, this attention is generally very fleet-
   ing (less than 2 seconds).

2. S <u>sees the object</u>. Or, adapt by redefining attention (e.g., S turns his
   head toward the object while it produces sounds).

3. S <u>hears the object's sound</u>. Or, adapt by substituting extra visual or tactile
   cues.

4. S <u>turns his head toward the object</u> (e.g., Controlling Head Movements). Or,
   adapt by positioning the object only within S's range of vision.

Objective:

During a <u>stimulus presentation</u>, S looks at a <u>target</u> for at least 5 seconds. S
responds correctly to at least 5 different targets a total of 25 times during a
10-minute session.

<u>stimulus presentation</u> = actions such as your manipulation of the target, talking
about it, offering and giving it to S, or placing it in his hands.

<u>target</u> = an object no further than 18 inches away from S.

Cycle:

None specified. If you would like to increase the diversity of objects to which
S attends, repeat the program with new objects, excluding ones to which he already
attends. You may also repeat the program to increase the time criterion (e.g.,
from 5 seconds up to 8 or 10 seconds), although regular follow-up activities may
be sufficient to enable S to reach a new criterion.

Follow-Up:

Continue to work on S's attention throughout the day. Give individual trials
on a regular basis. Take data to insure that S's performance is or becomes
consistent in a variety of natural situations. Require S's attention whenever
you show him an object. This follow-up is extremely important.

Continue to present different objects. Reinforce S not only when he looks at
but also when he reaches for, holds, and manipulates the objects (e.g., Grasping, Reaching, Manipulating Objects). Increase the variety of S's experiences
so that he has other sensory input (tactile, kinesthetic, olfactory, auditory)
from objects. Increase the time S will attend to an object.

Program for Cognitive Skill 2

Materials:

Have a variety of objects available.

Chart:

Stimulus Chart (for events), page 467.

GENERAL STRATEGY

Arrangement:

Position S as desired. Use one object at a time, but position other materials close at hand.

Stimulus Event:

Draw attention to the object by dangling it, holding it in front of S, or putting it in his hands. If S shows interest in another object, switch to that one. During the event, give an appropriate command ("LOOK"). Continue to provide a stimulus. If S reaches for the object, give it to him.

Latency:

S must sustain attention as soon as he has focused on the object.

Correction:

None. Go on to a new stimulus event.

Other Trials:

Repeat the strategy. Vary the objects used and the stimuli. Also, vary the distance of the object (up to 18 inches away) and its position relative to S (left, right, ahead, slightly up, down).

Modification:

S has not met step criterion after four sessions.

	CONDITIONS	BEHAVIOR	CRITERIA
		S attends for 5 seconds ...	during a 10-minute session
PRE	Present the stimulus event. As soon as S looks, continue the event.	unassisted	25 times, 5 different targets
S/1	"	"	5 times, any target
S/2	"	"	10 times, 2 different
S/3	"	"	15 times, 3 different
S/4	"	"	20 times, 4 different
S/5	"	"	25 times, 5 different
POST 1	Same as PRE	unassisted	25 times, 5 different targets for each test
POST 2	New Targets		
POST 3	New Setting		

MODIFICATIONS

If S does not look for 5 seconds, increase the amount of time S can sustain attention. At first go through the steps and increase the rate at which S gives attention for 3-second intervals. Then repeat for 4-second intervals. Finally run the program as written (5-second intervals).

Responding to Teacher Model

Rate Data

Skill:

In this program the child increases the frequency with which he makes any response after an action is modeled. This skill is developed in an interactive situation. The child is encouraged to manipulate different objects, as in Manipulating Objects. Once the child performs some action that the teacher imitates, the child is to respond by performing another action. This procedure should increase the probability that subsequent imitation training will be more precise.

Entry Behaviors:

1. S <u>frequently manipulates objects</u>, especially during interactions (e.g., Manipulating Objects). Usually these actions are very simple (e.g., bang, poke, turn) and do not involve an appropriate use of the object. Although S does manipulate various objects, he does not attempt to imitate or even respond to other people's activities or models. Note that in this program, S is responding more frequently to actions that involve objects. The reason is that the objects act as a stimulus to increase attending in most children.

2. S's <u>attention can be drawn to the person interacting with him</u> while a model is given (e.g., Focusing Attention: Varied Targets or Objects and/or Attending to Objects). However, S does not attempt to imitate or respond to the person's actions. S may or may not be able to respond to context cues to follow simple requests (e.g., Following Cued Commands), since both responding to models and responding to cued commands require a similar kind of attentiveness to others.

3. S <u>sees the action modeled</u>. Or, adapt by using other cues, especially auditory and tactile, with the model. Model only the actions S initiates, those he can easily feel or hear you perform. When giving the model, place S's hands on the object or over your hands so that he can feel your model.

4. S <u>performs a variety of actions with his hands and arms</u>. Work only with responses that he is able to perform, adding to the Basic Motor Actions Chart (pages 453-54). Or, adapt by defining the response as an action that does not involve the use of objects or S's hands or arms (e.g., eye blink, open palm, smile).

Objective:

When given a model that is repetitious of an action S just initiated, S produces a <u>response</u>. S must initiate his response within 5 seconds of the model and make at least 15 responses, including five different actions, during a 10-minute session containing as many models as possible.

<u>response</u> = any action with an object, not necessarily an imitation, made after the model. (Do not count disruptive or socially unacceptable actions.)

Cycle:

None specified.

Follow-Up:

Continue to ask S to respond to a variety of your actions. Have others imitate S's actions, and reinforce when S responds to them. As S responds more frequently, initiate the action yourself (i.e., do not wait for S to act first). Simply model an action, and ask S to respond. As described in the Program, continue to give S imitation practice; guide if necessary to shape his response into a copy of the model, a strategy that develops imitative responses (Repeating Teacher Model). Increase S's responding to your actions. Provide physical assistance to enable him to perform the correct action in response to cues (words, commands, gestures). This strategy is developed in Following Cued Commands. Having taught S to respond to actions with objects, require him to respond to actions without objects (clapping).

Interact with S, and imitate his vocal sounds. Reinforce when he responds to these vocal models by making other sounds afterwards. This strategy is contained in Responding Vocally to Model, a program that builds toward verbal imitation and speech. This basic response to another person's sounds and actions is a step in developing imitation (verbal and/or motor).

Program for Cognitive Skill 3

Materials:

Use a variety of objects with duplicates available if needed.

Chart:

Basic Motor Actions Chart, page 453.

GENERAL STRATEGY

Eliciting Stimuli:

In a play situation, present stimuli (about 15 seconds each) for S to perform some action with an object. During each event, <u>demonstrate</u> possible actions with an object, <u>describe</u> what you are doing ("Look, I'm poking"), and physically <u>prompt</u> S to initiate an action (put his hand on the object). Do NOT guide S to perform an action. As soon as S performs an action...

Model:

Draw S's attention to you and the object. Then imitate the action S just performed, and describe what you are doing ("Look, I'm poking").

Command:

Return the object to S. Draw his attention to it. Give a command for S to do what you just did ("S, <u>POKE</u> IT").

Latency:

S must initiate his response within 5 seconds of the command.

Correction:

Guide S to perform the action. Then go to a new eliciting stimulus.

Imitation Practice:

S is correct as long as he performs any action after the model (without assistance). However, if S responds but does not imitate, this is an ideal time to develop imitation. Repeat the model. If S does not imitate, physically assist him to complete a response. Any response S makes during practice is not recorded.

Other Trials:

Repeat the strategy. Vary the eliciting stimulus to encourage S to perform actions for you to model. Present as many models as possible during the 10-minute session. Note that only one response per model is counted.

Modification:

S has not met step criterion after four sessions.

CONDITIONS	BEHAVIOR S produces an unassisted response to the model...	CRITERIA during a 10-minute session
PRE Present stimulus events until S performs an action. As soon as S finishes, present the model and command.	unassisted	15 responses, including 5 different actions
S/1 Present stimulus events until S performs an action. As soon as S finishes, present the model and command. Correct if needed. Give imitation practice if S responds (+) but does not imitate.	"	any 5 responses
S/2 "	"	10 responses, 2 different actions
S/3 "	"	10 responses, 3 different actions
S/4 "	"	10 responses, 4 different actions
S/5 "	"	10 responses, 5 different actions
S/6 "	"	15 responses, 5 different actions
POST 1 Same as PRE	unassisted	15 responses, 5 different actions for each test
POST 2 New Objects		
POST 3 New Setting		

MODIFICATIONS

If S consistently produces no response, add a step. Repeat the model with extra cues (for up to 10 seconds) so that S receives additional cues to respond. Or, add an exaggerated verbal sound to the model to draw S's attention to the action. In successive steps, fade these extra cues by decreasing the number of times you repeat the model, or the extent to which you exaggerate extra sounds, until you are back to the original step with the model presented once in a normal manner.

Add a step where you introduce another child (who can already imitate) to the session. Present stimulus events, and ask the peer to imitate S's actions while you describe this model (e.g., "Look, Johnny's poking the box"). Then you perform the action, and help S to respond, too (e.g., "Let's poke like Johnny").

Gradually over several steps, fade your guidance, and request S to respond to the peer model unassisted but at the same time that you are responding. Trade roles with the peer (i.e., you model, then the peer and S respond at the same time). Have the peer participate for shorter and shorter periods.

Repeating
Teacher Model

Rate Data

Skill:

This program increases the frequency with which the child imitates an action.
After the child spontaneously performs an action, you imitate this action as
a model, and the child is expected to repeat the action after the model. (This
interaction was introduced in Responding to Teacher Model, but there the child
was only required to respond, not imitate.) This game-like interaction is one
early form of imitation that provides experiences helpful to develop the more
sophisticated skill of imitating any action that is modeled.

Entry Behaviors:

1. S frequently performs a variety of actions with objects (e.g., Manipulating
   Objects). Although S uses a variety of objects, he is just beginning to
   combine some basic actions to perform simple tasks (e.g., self-help programs).
   Note that this program is taught using actions performed with objects. The
   reason is that the objects serve as a stimulus for attending in most children.

2. S frequently responds to the actions of others (e.g., Responding to Teacher
   Model and/or Following Cued Commands). Although S usually makes some attempt
   to respond to a command or model, his actual response is not always correct.
   Specifically, S rarely imitates, although he responds to the model.

3. S sees the action modeled. Or, adapt by using other cues, especially auditory
   and tactile, with the model. Model only the actions S initiates, those he can
   easily feel or hear you perform when you present the model. Place S's hands
   on the object or on your hands so that he can feel the model.

4. S performs a variety of actions with his hands or arms. Work only with responses that he is able to perform, supplementing the Basic Motor Actions
   Chart. If S has severely impaired movements and is limited to a very few
   responses (e.g., eye blink, smile), you may use the program to teach S to
   repeat these actions after a model. If necessary, define the response as an
   action that does not involve an object. However, you may need to reconsider
   the practical use of imitation if S has such limited movements.

Objective:

When given a model that is repetitious of an action S just performed, S repeats
that same action. S must initiate his response within 5 seconds of the model and
make at least 15 responses, including five different actions, during a 10-minute
session containing as many models as possible.

<u>action</u> = a motor response involving an object.   See Basic Motor Actions Chart,
pages 453-54.

Cycle:

None specified.

Follow-Up:

Continue to ask S to repeat a variety of your actions. Have others imitate S's
actions, and reinforce S's responding to them. As S becomes more skilled,
initiate the sequence yourself (i.e., do not wait for S to act first). Simply
model an action, and ask S to respond. Assist him if needed. Present a variety
of different models in this way to introduce more generalized imitation, as in
Imitating Actions. Besides asking S to repeat models of actions with objects,
have S repeat models of actions without objects. In addition, ask him to respond
to and imitate vocal models (e.g., Responding Vocally to Model, Shaping Words).

Program for Cognitive Skill 4

Materials:

Use a variety of objects with duplicates available if needed.

Chart:

Basic Motor Actions Chart, page 453.

GENERAL STRATEGY

Eliciting Stimuli:

In a play situation, present stimuli (about 15 seconds each) for S to perform
some action with an object. During each event, demonstrate possible actions
with one object, describe what you are doing ("Look, I'm poking"), and physically
prompt S to initiate an action (put his hand on the object). Do NOT guide S to
perform an action. As soon as S performs an action...

Program
Cognitive
Skill 4

Model:

Draw S's attention to you and the object. Then imitate the action S just performed, and describe what you are doing ("Look, I'm poking").

Command:

Return the object to S. Draw his attention to it. Give a command for S to do
what you just did ("S, POKE IT").

Latency:

S must initiate his response within 5 seconds of the command.

Correction:

Guide S to perform the action. Then go on to a new eliciting stimulus.

Other Trials:

Repeat the strategy. Vary stimulus events to encourage S to perform actions for
you to model. Present as many models as possible during the 10-minute session.
Note that only one response per model is counted.

Modification:

S has not met step criterion after four sessions.

	CONDITIONS	BEHAVIOR	CRITERIA
		S repeats (imitates) the model...	during a 10-minute session
PRE	Present stimulus events until S performs an action. As soon as S finishes, present the model and command.	unassisted	15 responses, including 5 different actions
S/1	Present stimulus events until S performs an action. As soon as S finishes, present the model and command. Correct if needed.	"	any 5 responses
S/2	"	"	10 responses, 2 different actions
S/3.	"	"	10 responses, 3 different actions
S/4	"	"	10 responses, 4 different actions
S/5	"	"	10 responses, 5 different actions
S/6	"	"	15 responses, 5 different actions
POST 1	Same as PRE	unassisted	15 responses, 5 different actions for each test
POST 2	New Objects		
POST 3	New Setting		

MODIFICATIONS

If S consistently produces no response, add a step in which you repeat the model with extra cues (for up to 10 seconds) so that S receives more cues to respond. Or, add an exaggerated sound to the model to draw S's attention to the action. In successive steps, fade these extra cues by decreasing the number of times you repeat the model, or the extent to which you exaggerate any extra sounds. Finally use the original strategy where the model is performed only once, in a normal manner.

Add a step in which you introduce another child (who can already imitate) to the session. Present eliciting stimuli, and have the peer imitate S's action while you describe it (e.g., "Look, Johnny's poking the box"). Then perform the action yourself and assist S (e.g., "Let's poke like Johnny"). Gradually fade your guidance, having S respond to the peer model unassisted but at the same time you are responding. Trade roles with the peer (you model, then the peer and S respond at the same time). Have the peer participate for shorter and shorter periods.

Finding
Hidden Objects

4/5 Data

Skill:

In this program the child searches for and retrieves an object that moves out of
sight while he watches. The skill is taught by fading visual cues indicating
where the object is. With this skill, the child can retrieve objects that have
been put away or search for objects that are missing.

Entry Behaviors:

1. S <u>demonstrates interest in objects</u> (e.g., Attending to Objects, Reaching and/
   or Manipulating Objects). This interest provides natural reinforcement for
   finding the object.

2. S <u>can see</u>. If S is visually impaired, it is still important for him to be
   able to locate objects by using tactile cues (feeling for the object) or
   auditory cues. First teach Finding Source of Sound so that S can locate an
   object that continues to provide an auditory cue as he searches for it (e.g.,
   a radio). Then teach this program by adapting it to include an initial
   auditory cue for locating the object (e.g., turn the radio on, then off).

3. S <u>is mobile</u> and can get to the object (crawl, walk, use a wheelchair). Or,
   adapt the program by hiding objects within S's reach.

4. S <u>makes some motor</u> response to indicate the location of the object (e.g.,
   uncover the object, and pick it up). Select responses appropriate to S's
   capabilities.

Objective:

S retrieves an object that is hidden while he watches. S must initiate his
response within 5 seconds of the command and respond correctly 4 out of 5 trials.

Cycle:

None specified.

Follow-Up:

Continue to play games with S. Hide the objects while he watches, and have him
locate them. Hide objects out of S's reach, and reinforce him when he shows you
in some way (e.g., pointing) that he wants you to get the object for him (e.g.,
Indicating Preferences). Hide the object in several different places before you
allow S to retrieve the object from its last hiding place so that S must pay
attention for a longer period of time. Select an object that makes noise (radio),
and hide it while S is not watching. Then ask S to locate the object by listening
to its sound (e.g., Finding Source of Sound). To improve S's ability to attend
and complete more complex tasks, hide two or three objects, and ask him to find
all of them. Or, have S watch while you hide an object, but do not ask him to
find it until later so that he must remember where it was placed.

Program for Cognitive Skill 5

Materials:

Use a variety of objects S likes (e.g., ball, bag of candy, book, toy car). Teach the program in the classroom or in a playroom where there are at least five possible hiding places (e.g., blanket, box, shelf, chest, wastebasket).

Chart:

None.

GENERAL STRATEGY

Arrangement:

Select an object to hide. Allow S to interact with it. Then get S's attention ("S, look" or "Watch"), and hide the object while S watches. (The amount of the object in view changes from step to step.)

Command:

Give an appropriate command to have S locate the object ("FIND THE DOLL").

Cues:

<u>pointing cue</u> = point to the hiding place, and make an appropriate statement ("There it is").

<u>demonstration</u> = uncover the object, and make an appropriate statement ("Here it is").

Latency:

S must initiate his response within 5 seconds of the command or delayed cue.

Correction:

Use general correction procedures.

Natural Consequence:

Let S interact with the object after he finds it (e.g., play with the doll, look at the book, eat the candy).

Other Trials:

Repeat the strategy. Change the hiding places. Vary the objects and the distance they are hidden from S (within 10 feet).

Modification:

S has not met step criterion after four errors.

CONDITIONS	BEHAVIOR	CRITERIA
	S locates the object...	
PRE Arrange the materials, completely hiding the object. Give the command. Present the natural consequence.	unassisted; the object is completely hidden	4 correct out of 5 trials

S/1 Arrange the materials, hiding half the object. Give the command. If S does not begin to respond correctly, present a demonstration. Then cover half the object again, and repeat the command. Correct if needed. Present the natural consequence.	when the object is half hidden; given a delayed demonstration if necessary	4 correct out of the last 5 trials for each step
S/2 Arrange the materials, leaving only a small portion of the object uncovered. Give the command. If S does not begin to respond correctly, present a pointing cue, and repeat the command. Correct if needed. Present the natural consequence.	when most of the object is hidden; given a delayed pointing cue if necessary	
S/3 Arrange the materials, and hide the object completely. Give the command. If S does not begin to respond correctly, present a pointing cue, and repeat the command. Correct if needed. Present the natural consequence.	when the object is completely hidden; given a delayed pointing cue if necessary	
S/4 Arrange the materials, and hide the object completely. Give the command. Correct if needed. Present the natural consequence.	unassisted; the object is completely hidden	
POST 1 Same as PRE	unassisted; the object is completely hidden	4 correct out of 5 trials for each test
POST 2 New Command (e.g., "WHERE IS THE DOLL?")		
POST 3 New Objects and Hiding Places		

MODIFICATIONS

At first always hide the objects within S's reach; then gradually increase the distance. Finally vary the distance (no more than 10 feet).

Cover the object more gradually. First cover only the tip of the object; then cover 1/4 of the object, 1/2, 3/4, until the object is completely covered.

S may become distracted by all the possible hiding places in a natural setting such as a classroom. If he is distracted, position him at a desk with only one hiding place present. Gradually introduce more hiding places, moving them farther apart, until S can locate the object in a natural setting.

Make a game out of finding the objects. Repeatedly demonstrate to S what you want him to do. For example, hide an object, ask S where it is, then uncover it and show surprise ("There it is!"). Do this several times, and then have S find the object on his own. Gradually fade this extra practice before each trial (e.g., five practices, one trial; three practices, one trial).

Finding
Source of Sound

4/5 Data

Skill:

In this program S listens to the sound an object makes in order to locate it
when it is out of sight. This skill is taught by adding then fading physical
prompts and visual cues that direct S to the current location. This ability to
use sound as a cue is required for such activities as coming when called.

Entry Behaviors:

1. S responds positively to sound; for example, he may turn toward a noise or
    focus on the source of the noise (e.g., Focusing Attention--Sound). This
    reinforcing quality of sound develops S's attention skills. It will enable him
    to continue to search for the sound if he does not locate it immediately.

2. S searches for an object that is out of sight if he has just observed it disappear
    (e.g., Finding Hidden Objects). Although S can search, he usually does so
    only for a short period then loses interest (i.e., S can attend but has a
    short attention span).

3. S hears the sound of the object to be found. If necessary, use only objects
    that make loud noises (e.g., turn up the radio). If S is severely hearing
    impaired, reconsider your rationale for developing attention to sound. Con-
    centrate instead on teaching S to develop his visual skills and ability to
    search for objects (e.g., Finding Hidden Objects--Follow-Up).

4. S sees to search around the room. Or, adapt by placing the object where S
    can contact it easily if he reaches in the correct direction.

5. S is mobile. Or, adapt by placing the object only within his reach.

6. S makes some motor responses that indicate the location of the object (e.g.,
    uncover the object, and pick it up). Select responses appropriate to S's
    capabilities.

Objective:

By listening to its sound, S locates an object positioned out of sight. S must
initiate his response within 5 seconds of the command and respond correctly 4
out of 5 trials.

Cycle:

None specified.

Follow-Up:

Continue to provide S with opportunities to locate objects by listening to their sounds. Develop the skill in new settings, in particular, outdoors. For his own safety, S should be able to locate the direction from which a car is coming (sound of traffic), as well as the direction in which a group or person may be located. This skill will prevent him from being separated from a group and will enable him to avoid dangerous situations (e.g., construction sites, drilling).

While varying the situations in which S is finding objects by their sound, develop his communication skills. Ask him to show you in some way that he wants the object after he has found it. For example, have him point to it (e.g., Indicating Preferences), or attempt to name it (e.g., Producing Sounds on Request, Shaping Words).

Program for Cognitive Skill 6

Materials:

Use a variety of objects that S prefers and that can be wound up or turned on to make noise without requiring you to continue to manipulate them (e.g., radio, music box). Teach the program in the classroom or a playroom where there are at least five possible hiding places (e.g., toy chest, wastebasket, shelf, blanket, box).

Chart:

None.

GENERAL STRATEGY

Arrangement:

Turn on or wind up the object, and hide it while S is not looking (have S hide his eyes, go into another room, and the like). The object may be hidden anywhere within 10 feet of S, except out of his reach. The object should continue to make noise as long as S looks for it.

Attention:

Draw S's attention to the sound ("Listen").

Cue:

position cue = stand or sit next to the hiding place.

Command:

Give an appropriate command to have S locate the object ("FIND THE RADIO").

Cues:

physical prompt = turn S toward the hiding place.
pointing cue = point to the hiding place.

Latency:

S must initiate his response within 5 seconds of the command or delayed cue.

Correction:

Use general correction procedures.

Natural Consequence:

Let S interact with the object after he finds it.

Other Trials:

Repeat the strategy. Change hiding places. Vary the objects and their distance from S (within 10 feet), as well as the objects to be hidden.

Modification:

S has not met step criterion after four errors.

CONDITIONS	BEHAVIOR	CRITERIA
	S locates the object...	

PRE	Arrange the materials. Get S's attention. Give the command. Present the natural consequence.	unassisted	4 correct out of 5 trials
S/1	Arrange the materials. Get S's attention, and use a position cue. Give the command. Correct if needed. Present the natural consequence.	given a position cue	4 correct out of the last 5 trials for each step
S/2	Arrange the materials. Get S's attention, and give the command. If S does not begin to respond correctly, provide the physical prompt with a pointing cue, and repeat the command. Correct if needed. Present the natural consequence.	with a delayed physical prompt and a pointing cue if necessary	
S/3	Arrange the materials. Get S's attention, and give the command. If S does not begin to respond correctly, provide the physical prompt, and repeat the command. Correct if needed. Present the natural consequence.	with a delayed physical prompt if necessary	
S/4	Arrange the materials. Get S's attention, and give the command. Correct if needed. Present the natural consequence.	unassisted	
POST 1	Same as PRE	unassisted	4 correct out of 5 trials for each test
POST 2	New Command (e.g., "Where is the ___?")		
POST 3	New Objects and Hiding Places	unassisted	4 correct out of 5 trials for each test

MODIFICATIONS

At first always hide the objects within S's reach. Then hide the objects about 5 feet away from S. Finally vary the distance of the hiding places, but always within 10 feet of S.

Add steps where the object is not hidden so that when S turns toward the sound, he will see the object. Then partially cover the object. Gradually cover more of the object until it is completely hidden so that S learns to search for it.

Remove the position cue gradually. First walk to the hiding place, and stand next to it. Then walk only part of the way. Next simply turn toward the hiding place or look at it.

If S becomes distracted by all the possible hiding places in a natural setting (e.g., the classroom), teach the program in a relatively empty room with only two or three possible hiding places. Gradually introduce more hiding places until S can locate the object wherever it is hidden in a room with a variety of hiding places.

Imitating Actions

4/5 Data

Cycle

Skill:

In this program the child imitates consistently on command. This skill is developed by adding then fading the physical prompts and guidance given to perform the correct action. Two actions are modeled. The order of presentation is alternated. This imitative behavior can be used to learn new responses from other people, either spontaneously or by direct instruction.

Entry Behaviors:

1. S <u>responds correctly to a variety of simple, routine commands</u> (e.g., Following Cued Commands). Although S can perform commands he has been taught previously, he does not learn new commands (given with words, gestures, models) except with guidance and repeated practice.

2. S <u>imitates a model in a few limited situations</u>, such as in a play setting where the model is the same as the action he just performed (e.g., Repeating Teacher Model). Or, S may respond appropriately when he receives practice on the same action (e.g., Following Cued Commands). Although S occasionally imitates during a game or may imitate one or two actions, he does not consistently imitate each action.

3. S <u>sees the model</u>. Or, adapt by giving extra auditory cues and having S feel the model. Although he cannot see, S can learn to do what others are doing by using cues other than visual cues.

4. S <u>performs a variety of motor actions</u>. In your selection of actions to use as models, select only those that S is able to perform. If S can perform fewer than five observable responses, reconsider teaching imitation since the child will probably not be able to use the skill at this time.

Objective:

S imitates the model of an action when different actions are alternately presented. S must initiate his response within 5 seconds of the command and respond correctly 4 out of 5 trials for each of two different actions.

Cycle:

Record each action S imitates. Two imitated actions constitute one cycle. There are two cycles, each teaching a particular kind of action:

  Cycle A = With Objects
  Cycle B = Without Objects

Although the cycles may be taught in either order, we suggest using actions with objects first since the object serves as an extra cue. After Cycle A is complete and its follow-up is ongoing, teach Cycle B. Continue teaching each cycle of this program with two new actions each time until S passes a pretest on actions that he has never been taught during imitation training (i.e., S has generalized his imitation skills and is imitating new actions).

Follow-Up:

Continue to give S opportunities to imitate, in functional situations to teach appropriate behavior, and in games like Simon Says. Vary the actions you model with any particular object so that S explores many possible uses of the object. Model actions that are more and more difficult to perform. Then have S imitate a sequence. At first model two actions, and have S imitate them in order; then gradually increase the number of actions modeled. Ask S to imitate specific sounds (e.g, Shaping Words). Emphasize the names of the actions modeled to expand S's vocabulary.

Program for Cognitive Skill 7

Materials:

Select two actions to model. <u>Cycle A</u>: Have at least three different objects available, and use each object for both actions. Do this so that S does not pair one action with one object or respond just by performing an appropriate use of the object. <u>Cycle B</u>: None.

Chart:

Actions Chart, page 451.

GENERAL STRATEGY

Setting:

Work in a structured area (e.g., in a chair, at a table). Materials for Cycle A are close at hand but out of S's view.

Cue:

<u>practicing the response</u> = demonstrate the action, ask S to perform the action, and give him guidance if needed. When used, this practice always occurs immediately before the presentation of the model and command for that action.

Model:

Draw S's attention to you, and demonstrate the motor action while you label it ("Look...shake!").

Command:

Draw S's attention to the appropriate place (hand S the object, touch the appropriate body part), and give the command to imitate ("S, DO IT").

Cues:

<u>full guidance</u> = physically assist S to perform the action.

<u>partial guidance</u> = physically assist S, but allow him to do part of the action on his own (e.g., let S start on his own, let S finish on his own, use less pressure when touching him).

Latency:

S must initiate his response within 5 seconds of the command. When guidance cues are presented after the command, S is to respond immediately with that cue.

Correction:

Use general correction procedures.

Other Trials:

Repeat the strategy. Vary the sequence of actions. Note that S must meet criterion on both actions. For Cycle A, vary the object that is used.

Modification:

S has not met step criterion after four errors.

	CONDITIONS	BEHAVIOR	CRITERIA
		S imitates the action modeled...	for each action
PRE	Present the model, then the command.	unassisted	4 correct out of 5 trials (each action)
S/1	Practice the response. After S performs the action, present the model, then the command. Immediately provide full guidance. Correct if needed.	after practice and with full guidance	4 correct out of the last 5 trials for each step (each action)
S/2	Practice the response. After S performs the action, present the model, then the command. Immediately provide partial guidance. Correct if needed.	after practice and with partial guidance	
S/3	Practice the response. After S performs the action, present the model, then the command. If S does not begin to respond correctly, provide partial guidance. Correct if needed.	after practice and with delayed partial guidance if necessary	
S/4	Present the model, then the command. If S does not begin to respond correctly, provide partial guidance. Correct if needed.	with delayed partial guidance if necessary	
S/5	Present the model, then the command. Correct if needed.	unassisted	
POST 1	Same as PRE	unassisted	4 correct out of 5 trials for each test (each action)
POST 2	New Setting		
POST 3	New Teacher		

MODIFICATIONS

Add a step, using a variety of preferred activities such as blowing bubbles or rolling a noisy toy car. Play with S so that both of you perform the actions many times. During this game, intersperse trials (present the model and command) with the preferred activities. Over successive steps, fade out this extra assistance, and present less preferred activities.

Matching

4/5 Data

Cycle

Skill:

This program teaches the child to select identical items, first matching like objects, then later matching like pictures. This skill is taught by adding then fading cues that emphasize particular attributes of the sample items to be matched. Once the child learns to match by appearance and function (e.g., match two spoons or match two pictures of spoons), he can learn to match by secondary attributes of color, shape, and size (e.g., find the matching red sock).

Entry Behaviors:

1. S <u>follows a variety of short commands given with gestures</u> (e.g., Following Cued Commands). Although S may or may not be able to comprehend the specific words of a command, he is usually able to perform the desired action by using your model, gestures, or other cues to understand what is expected of him. Although matching may be taught without this comprehension, it is most functional when the child has some receptive language skills.

2. S <u>uses a variety of common objects</u> with minimal assistance (e.g., self-help skills). Often S can use different objects appropriately on his own, a skill that indicates that he can discriminate between them. Although matching may be taught without this discrimination, it is most functional when it can be combined with other tasks (e.g., find matching socks and put them on, or find another spoon and set the table).

3. S <u>sees the materials</u>. Or, adapt by having S feel the objects to identify them. Note that for matching pictures, S must be able to see the pictures.

4. S <u>hears the command</u> and verbal cues. Or, adapt by substituting other strategies (e.g., signing) to convey the meaning.

5. S has <u>some motor responses</u> that can be used to indicate which item he selects as the match (e.g., touch, point to, pick up). Select a response appropriate to S's capabilities.

Objective:

Given a <u>sample</u>, S indicates its match from a choice of three items. S must initiate his response within 5 seconds of the command and respond correctly 4 out of 5 trials for each of two samples, varied at random.

<u>sample</u> = an item identical to one of the choices.

Cycle:

Record whether S can match objects (all items are objects) and match pictures
(all items are pictures). Teach S to match like objects first. Then as S
develops a functional use for the skill (e.g., S is preparing for an academic
setting), teach him to match like pictures. Note that this program does not
teach S to match the picture to the object it represents, a skill taught in
Identifying Simple Pictures.

Follow-Up:

Continue to have S match a variety of different items. Introduce objects whose
secondary attributes (color, size, shape) are different so that S learns to
generalize the concept of object identity (e.g., a cup may be big or small, red
or blue, tall or short, as long as you drink out of it). However, do not yet
have S match objects by color or other secondary attributes. First teach S to
recognize the name of the objects matched (e.g., Identifying Objects) so that
language clarifies the identity of the object. When S can identify a variety
of objects by name, introduce the word same to describe the matching task. Then
to further develop object identity, have him separate objects by their identity
(e.g., cups from spoons), a task found in Sorting. After S has had many experiences in object identification (e.g., matching, naming, sorting), have him
match the secondary attributes of the objects--color, shape, and size.

Program for Cognitive Skill 8

Materials:

Collect eight items: two different samples, two matches (one identical to each sample), four other choices. Note that for matching objects, all eight items are objects; for matching pictures, all eight are pictures.

Chart:

None.

GENERAL STRATEGY

Arrangement:

Position three items (both matches and one other choice).

Present Sample:

Get S's attention, hold up the sample, and label it ("S, look...ball").
Note: This labeling is a functional, attention-getting strategy. S does not need to respond to the label in order to perform correctly.

Cues:

attribute cue = describe some obvious attribute of the item that identifies it, either by appearance or function (e.g., the roundness of the ball, the fact that it bounces). Add gestures to indicate the attribute (e.g., trace the outside curve of the ball, bounce the ball).

imitative cue = give S the sample, and guide him if needed to make some of the same gestures or motions that you made for the attribute cue.

Command:

(S is holding the sample.) Give an appropriate command ("FIND ANOTHER (ball)" or PUT (ball) WITH (ball).

Latency:

S must initiate his response within 5 seconds of the command or delayed cue.

Correction:

Use general correction procedures.

Other Trials:

Repeat the strategy. Vary the arrangement, but always include both matches and one other choice. Vary trials for the two samples. Note that S must meet criterion on each sample.

Modification:

S has not met step criterion after four errors.

CONDITIONS	BEHAVIOR	CRITERIA
	S indicates the correct match...	for each sample
PRE Arrange the materials and present the sample. Give the command.	unassisted	4 correct out of 5 trials (each sample)

S/1 Arrange the materials. Present the sample. Present the <u>attribute cue, then the imitative cue with the sample.</u> Give the command. If S does not begin to respond correctly, present an <u>attribute cue with the match</u>, and repeat the command. Correct if needed.	given an attribute and an imitative cue with the sample and, if necessary, a delayed attribute cue with the match	4 correct out of the last 5 trials for each step (each sample)
S/2 Arrange the materials. Present the sample. Present the <u>attribute cue, then the imitative cue with the sample.</u> Give the command. Correct if needed.	given an attribute and an imitative cue with the sample	
S/3 Arrange the materials. Present the sample, then present the <u>attribute cue with the sample.</u> Give the command. If S does not begin to respond correctly, present the <u>imitative cue</u>, then repeat the command. Correct if needed.	given an attribute cue with the sample and, if necessary, a delayed imitative cue with the sample	
S/4 Arrange the materials. Present the sample, then present the <u>attribute cue with the sample.</u> Give the command. Correct if needed.	given an attribute cue with the sample	
S/5 Arrange the materials, and present the sample. Give the command. Correct if needed.	unassisted	
POST 1 Same as PRE	unassisted	4 correct out of 5 trials for each test (each sample)
POST 2 New Samples		
POST 3 New Samples		

MODIFICATIONS

Use samples that are markedly different. For example, have as one sample a large red ball and the other a tiny blue block. For other choices, use objects that are neutral in terms of reinforcement value to S. After teaching the program with these materials, repeat the program, using more relevant and functional items, not necessarily with striking differences between them nor of neutral value to S.

If S has difficulty attending, add extra cues. At first hold the sample directly over the correct choice when you give the command. Then position it close to but not directly over the sample. Later, just point to the correct choice. Finally do not use any extra attending cues. Note that these cues assist S to attend but do not necessarily emphasize the attributes by which the objects are to be matched and, thus, are not critical to the task itself.

Identifying
Simple Pictures

4/5 Data

Cycle

Skill:

In this program the child selects the picture that represents a particular object. This skill is taught by adding then fading visual cues emphasizing the similarity between the three-dimensional object and its pictorial representation. With this association between object and picture, the child can perform a variety of tasks where pictures are used to give information and directions.

Entry Behaviors:

1. S <u>uses a variety of common objects</u> with minimal assistance (e.g., self-help skills). S can use common objects appropriately and can name them (e.g., Identifying Objects, Naming Objects). Although this language is not critical to the task itself, a child who can use many objects and who has an immediate, practical use for pictures understands quite a few words. If S cannot use objects because of physical limitations, he should have some response that indicates that he is aware of the names and uses of the objects (e.g., opens his mouth when he sees a spoon or when you say the word <u>spoon</u>).

2. S <u>visually discriminates between different objects</u>. Usually S demonstrates this skill by spontaneously using different objects correctly (e.g., he shows he can tell a sock from a mitten by attempting to put each one on correctly without direction) and by selecting the object that is identical to a sample (e.g., Matching--Objects). S may already be able to select the picture to match a sample picture (e.g., Matching--Pictures), but that skill need not be well developed since this program uses visual cues to emphasize the main attributes of the picture. Although S may not yet discriminate different objects in pictures, he has frequently been shown pictures, picture books, and magazines.

3. S <u>sees the objects and pictures</u>. (S must have visual acuity.)

4. S <u>makes some motor response</u> to indicate which picture he chooses as the correct response. Select an appropriate response for S to use during the program.

Objective:

Given several pictures of familiar objects, S selects the picture of the object presented. S must initiate his response within 5 seconds of the command and respond correctly 4 out of 5 trials for each of two different targets, varied at random.

Cycle:

Repeat the program, using two different targets during each cycle, until S can identify a variety of pictures.

Follow-Up:

Continue to have S identify different pictures he sees during the day. In particular, identify pictures on the labels of cans or boxes so that S learns to tell what is inside without opening the container. Introduce different pictures of the same object, including labels, photographs, and drawings. If S cannot already do so, teach him to match identical pictures (e.g., Matching--Pictures). Introduce S to pictures that have many objects in them, and have him point out or name all the different items. Show S pictures of people performing different actions, and teach him to identify what they are doing. Begin using pictures to give S information or directions for different play and academic activities. After he can recognize a variety of pictures, teach S to recognize pictures of familiar objects that are not present (bridge, truck, house). Finally introduce pictures of objects with which he is completely unfamiliar (giraffe, elephant, tiger).

Program for Cognitive Skill 9

Materials:

Select two targets. For each target, collect one object and one picture that represents that object. Use one-object color pictures with simple lines. If possible, use the picture from the box the object came in, or use magazine pictures so that the object and picture are as similar as possible. Collect several other distractor pictures to be used as possible choices.

Chart:

Common Objects Chart, page 457.

GENERAL STRATEGY

Cues:

object cue = select a visual attribute of the target object that is also found in its picture (the round outline of a ball, the curve of a cup handle). Point out this attribute on the object and describe it ("Look how round the ball is," as you circle the ball with your finger). Let S also trace or touch the attribute on the object and describe it (if he has speech).

picture cue = place the object next to its picture. Using the picture, describe and point out the same attribute as in the object cue. Have S trace or touch the picture.

Arrangement:

Position three pictures (both target pictures and one distractor).

Command:

Hold the object up, or give it to S; and give an appropriate command to find (match) its picture ("FIND THE PICTURE OF THE target" or just "FIND THE PICTURE").

Latency:

S must initiate his response within 5 seconds of the command or delayed cue.

Correction:

Use general correction procedures.

Other Trials:

Repeat the strategy. Vary the arrangement of the pictures. Vary which target is to be identified. Note that S must meet criterion on both targets.

Modification:

S has not met step criterion after four errors.

CONDITIONS	BEHAVIOR S selects the correct picture...	CRITERIA for each target
PRE Arrange the pictures, and give the command.	unassisted	4 correct out of 5 trials (each target)
S/1 Present the object cue. Arrange the pictures. Present the picture cue. Give the command. Correct if needed.	with object and picture cues	4 correct out of the last 5 trials for each step (each target)
S/2 Present the object cue. Arrange the pictures. Give the command. If S does not begin to respond correctly, present the picture cue. Correct if needed.	with an object cue and, if necessary, a delayed picture cue	
S/3 Present the object cue. Arrange the pictures. Give the command. Correct if needed.	with an object cue	
S/4 Arrange the pictures. Give the command. If S does not begin to respond correctly, present the object cue. Correct if needed.	with a delayed object cue if necessary	
S/5 Arrange the pictures, and give the command. Correct if needed.	unassisted	
POST 1 Same as PRE	unassisted	4 correct out of 5 trials for each test (each target)
POST 2 New Pictures (same targets)		
POST 3 New Pictures (same targets)		

MODIFICATIONS

If S selects the real object instead of the picture, add a step. Provide extra visual or verbal cues to help S focus on the pictures ("Where is the picture?"; tap all the pictures, move the object out of sight, and move the pictures closer to S for his selection). Gradually fade the cue(s) so that S learns to select from the pictures, even with the object present.

Putting Objects in Sequence

4/5 Data

Skill:

This program teaches the child to put objects sequentially in/on specified places, by either placing the objects from left-to-right, or from top-to-bottom. This skill is taught by adding then fading visual cues that direct each placement and verbal reminders to continue placement. The concept of sequential placement of objects ("Put one on this place, then this place, then...") is developed, and the child receives concrete experience in the manner in which things are usually ordered in our culture. In addition, the program introduces one-to-one correspondence, since one object corresponds to one place. The placement of objects in a sequence facilitates many pre-academic or workshop tasks such as setting a table (e.g., "This spoon in this place, then one in this place,...") or sorting (e.g., "This bead in this box, then one in this box,...").

Entry Behaviors:

1. S <u>performs a wide variety of tasks</u> with minimal assistance (e.g., self-help skills). S's task repertoire should be large enough to make this particular skill functional and relevant to his needs.

2. S <u>responds correctly to a variety of cued commands</u> for routine tasks (e.g., Following Cued Commands). Although S may or may not be able to comprehend the specific words of a command, he is usually able to perform the desired action by using your model, gestures, or other cues to understand what is expected of him.

3. S <u>sees the objects, the places designated, and the visual cues</u> that direct his placement (pointing). Or, adapt by designating places with tangible boundaries and by having S feel the location of all places before he begins the task. When a pointing cue is to be used, either substitute an auditory cue (tap the place), or guide S's <u>free</u> hand (not the hand placing the object) to touch the place.

4. S <u>positions the object on the place designated</u> (e.g., place a 1-inch cube on a 1-inch square). Or, adapt the materials so that S is able to place the objects (e.g., spread the places farther apart, use boxes or containers as the places, use places significantly larger than the objects). Or, have S indicate to you where to place the objects.

5. S <u>hears the command and verbal cues</u>. Or, adapt by substituting gestures or signs for conveying the meaning.

Objective:

Given five objects, five <u>designated places</u>, and a cued command indicating the place for the first object, S puts each object on one place in sequence. S must initiate his response within 5 seconds of the command and place all five objects correctly (either left-to-right, or top-to-bottom sequencing) 4 out of 5 trials.

<u>designated places</u> = places arranged in a horizontal or vertical row

(e.g. ).

Cycle:

None specified.

Follow-Up:

Continue to present S with functional tasks that require him to place objects
in sequential order (e.g., setting out materials for tasks or snacktime). Whenever you present objects to S or position materials during instruction, do so
from left-to-right or top-to-bottom, and emphasize the concept of next. Position
the designated places farther apart and not directly aligned (but still in a
left-right, top-bottom sequence) so that S has to look more carefully to insure
that he has put only one object on each place. This scanning introduces other
one-to-one correspondence skills, as in Pairing Equal Sets.

Program for Cognitive Skill 10

Materials:

For the places, use an 8 x 1-1/2 inch cardboard strip with five 1-inch solid black squares, evenly spaced: ■ ■ ■ ■ ■ . Have a variety of small objects available that can be easily placed on the squares (only five objects are needed at a time).

Chart:

None.

GENERAL STRATEGY

Arrangement:

Position the strip on the table in front of S. Use either a horizontal or vertical orientation for the strip. Give S one object at a time. Place each one in front of him after the command (or his last placement).

Command:

Give S an appropriate command ("MAKE A ROW") with cues indicating the position of the first object (point to the first square and say "Start here"). If you are sitting opposite S, be sure to cue him to start on his left, not yours.

Cues:

pointing cue = point to the next square in the sequence.

reminder = say "What's next? " "Now what?" or another phrase indicating that S is to continue to place objects, but do not indicate the position of the next object.

Latency:

S must initiate his response within 5 seconds of the command, delayed cue, or last placement.

Correction:

Use general correction procedures if S misplaces any object in the trial.

Review:

After all the objects are placed in sequence, point to the row, emphasize the sequence, and say, "Look, you made a row."

Other Trials:

Repeat the strategy. Alternate horizontal or vertical arrangement of the strip. Note that each trial contains five placements.

Modification:

S has not met step criterion after four errors.

CONDITIONS	BEHAVIOR	CRITERIA
	With an initial pointing cue, S positions all 5 objects in sequence (top-bottom or left-right, with each object at least 3/4 of the way within the boundaries of the place)...	

PRE Arrange the materials, and give the command. Present the review.	unassisted	4 correct out of 5 trials
S/1 Arrange the materials, and give the command. For each placement, present the pointing cue with the reminder. Correct if needed. Present the review.	with the reminder and pointing cue for each placement	4 correct out of the last 5 trials for each step
S/2 Arrange the materials, and give the command. For each placement, present the reminder. For the first 4 placements, if S does not begin to respond correctly to the reminder, present the pointing cue. (Last placement has the reminder only). Correct if needed. Present the review.	with the reminder and, if necessary, the delayed pointing cue for the first 4 placements; the reminder alone for the last placement	
S/3 Same as S/2, but present the delayed pointing cue only on the first 3 placements.	with the reminder and, if necessary, the delayed pointing cue for the first 3 placements; the reminder alone for the last 2 placements	
S/4 Same as S/2, but present the delayed pointing cue only on the first 2 placements.	with the reminder and, if necessary, the delayed pointing cue for the first 2 placements; the reminder alone for the last 3 placements.	
S/5 Arrange the materials, and give the command. If S does not begin to respond correctly, present the reminder for any placement. Correct if needed. Present the review.	with the delayed reminder if necessary for any placement	
S/6 Arrange the materials, and give the command. Correct if needed. Present the review.	unassisted	
POST 1 Same as PRE	unassisted	4 correct out of 5 trials for each test
POST 2 New Materials (cups on saucers, arranged in a row)		
POST 3 New Materials (bowls on place mats, arranged in a row)		

MODIFICATIONS

Make a strip with fewer squares. Add a step using the original step strategy with this shorter strip. Then on successive step(s), teach the step using a longer strip. Finally you will be using a strip with five squares (the progression is from ▮▮▮ to ▮▮▮▮ and then as written ▮▮▮▮▮).

Lining Up
Objects

4/5 Data

Skill:

In this program the child organizes objects into a sequential row, either left-to-right, or top-to-bottom. This skill is taught by adding then fading visual cues that indicate the appearance of the completed row and the placement of each object creating that row. Based on the concept of arranging objects to create order, the child can learn to order objects to make quantity comparisons between different sets (the numerical concepts of more, less, and equal).

Entry Behaviors:

1. S performs a variety of tasks with minimal assistance (e.g., self-help skills). S's task repertoire should be large enough to make this particular skill functional and relevant to his needs.

2. S responds correctly to a variety of cued commands for routine tasks (e.g., Following Cued Commands). Although S may or may not be able to comprehend the specific words of a command, he is usually able to perform the desired action by using your model, gestures, or other cues to understand what is expected of him.

3. S sequences objects when there are designated places to show the arrangement (e.g., Putting Objects in Sequence). Since S can already sequence objects into given places, he can use this experience with arrangements to create an order where there is no predetermined arrangement.

4. S sees the objects, the model row, and the visual cues for placing objects. Or, adapt by having S feel the model row (S/1--S-2). Instead of pointing, guide S to place his free hand (not the one holding the object) on the correct place. Where a cardboard strip is used to provide boundaries to focus his attention for arranging the objects, use a strip of material that S can feel (corrugated paper, felt) and that is firmly attached to the table.

5. S places the objects where you point (next to each other in a straight row). Or, adapt by using larger materials or accepting a less clearly defined row. If you use larger objects, use a larger strip to focus S's attention in S/1--S/2.

6. S hears the command. Or, adapt by substituting other cues (gestures, sign) to convey the meaning.

Objective:

Given five objects and a cued command indicating the position for the first object, S places the objects in a sequential row. S must initiate his response

119

within 5 seconds of the command and place all five objects correctly 4 out of
5 trials, with the cue varied for either left-to-right or top-to-bottom sequencing.

Cycle:

None specified.

Follow-Up:

Continue to present S with frequent opportunities to place objects in rows. Use
a variety of different materials (e.g., blocks, cups, chairs). Emphasize each
object as it is placed (e.g., "This one, now this one,..."). Count as S places
each object, and ask S to imitate you, as an introduction to Counting Rationally.
Ask S to line up one row, then place another row next to it so that the objects
from the two rows are matched. This matching develops one-to-one correspondence,
which was first introduced in Putting Objects in Sequence (one object on each
place) and will be continued in Pairing Equal Sets (each object in one set paired
with the corresponding object from the second set).

Program for Cognitive Skill 11

Materials:

Use a variety of small objects. For S/1--S/2, use two 1 1/2 x 6 inch blank
cardboard strips as noted to help S focus on the task.

Chart:

None.

GENERAL STRATEGY

Cues:

model row = draw S's attention, and make a row with five objects. Place the
objects either vertically or horizontally. The row is made on a blank strip
or on the table as specified. If you are sitting opposite S, be sure that you
make the row from his left or top. Then, draw S's attention to the completed
row ("Look, a row").

strip = a blank cardboard strip placed parallel to the model.

Arrangement:

Give S his five objects, all at one time.

Command:

Give an appropriate command ("MAKE A ROW") with cues indicating the position of
the first object ("Start here." Point).

Cue:

pointing cue = point to the place where S is to position the object and say Here.
To cue S to slide the object carefully up to the preceding object without push-
ing it out of line, you may slide your finger into the correct place before saying
Here.

Latency:

S must initiate his response within 5 seconds of the command, pointing cue, or
last placement.

Other Trials:

Repeat the strategy. Vary trials for either horizontal or vertical rows. Note
that 1 trial = 1 row (all 5 objects).

Modification:

S has not met step criterion after four errors.

CONDITIONS	BEHAVIOR	CRITERIA
	S positions 5 objects in a sequential row, either top-to-bottom, or left-to-right...	
PRE Present the objects to S, then the command.	unassisted	4 correct out of 5 trials

S/1 Make a <u>model</u> row on a strip. Then position another <u>strip</u>, and present the objects to S. Give the command. Present the <u>pointing cue</u> for each placement. Correct if needed.	given a model row, a strip, and a pointing cue for each placement.	4 correct out of the last 5 trials for each step
S/2 Make a <u>model</u> row (not on strip). Present the objects and a blank strip to S, then give the command. Present the <u>pointing cue</u> for each placement. Correct if needed.	given a model row and a pointing cue for each placement on a strip	
S/3 Make a <u>model</u> row, then remove it. Present the objects to S, then give the command. Present the <u>pointing cue</u> for each placement. Correct if needed.	given a model row (later removed) and a pointing cue for each placement	
S/4 Present the objects to S, then give the command. Present the <u>pointing</u> cue for each placement. Correct if needed.	given a pointing cue for each placement	
S/5 Present the objects to S, then give the command. If S does not begin to respond correctly on any placement, present the <u>pointing cue</u>. Correct if needed.	given the delayed pointing cue, if necessary, for any placement	
S/6 Present the objects to S, then give the command. Correct if needed.	unassisted	
POST 1 Same as PRE	unassisted	4 correct out of 5 trials for each test
POST 2 New Materials		
POST 3 New Materials		

MODIFICATIONS

Add a step using the original step strategy but with fewer objects in the row. In successive steps, teach the strategy using more objects (i.e., gradually increase the length of the row) until S can line up five objects.

Present one object to S at a time. Gradually present him with more objects at once.

Sorting

4/5 Data

Skill:

This program teaches the child to sort common objects into separate groups. The child learns to categorize by object identity (e.g., S sorts spoons and forks). This skill is taught by adding then fading cues that emphasize the identity of the objects to be sorted (i.e., verbal cue--name of object; visual cue--sample object to use as a match). Sorting by object identity is used daily in tasks such as putting different clothes or eating utensils in appropriate places. Later the child learns to sort objects by their secondary attributes of color, size, and shape.

Entry Behaviors:

1. S <u>spontaneously uses a wide variety of objects</u> appropriately. This ability indicates that S discriminates objects by their functional identity and, thus, can learn to categorize based on this discrimination. Although S does not sort objects independently, he has had experiences helping someone put objects away or placing each type of object in a different place (e.g., socks in one drawer, pants in another; cups on one side of shelf, plates on the other).

2. S <u>responds correctly to a variety of commands</u> given with or without visual cues (e.g., Following Cued Commands). Frequently, S can either identify objects that are named (e.g., Identifying Objects) or name objects himself (e.g., Naming Objects). Although this object labeling is not required in the sorting task, a child who spontaneously uses a wide variety of objects appropriately typically has some receptive and expressive language.

3. S <u>matches an object to another identical object</u> (e.g., Matching--Objects). But S cannot separate a set of objects without having a sample to illustrate how the objects are grouped.

4. S <u>sees the objects</u> to be sorted. Or, adapt the program by having S sort using <u>tactile cues</u> (feeling each object and sorting by touch). Describe to S what he is feeling.

5. S <u>picks up and moves the objects</u>. Or, adapt by having S indicate where he wants an object to go (e.g., by touching, by looking at the location). Then you place the object for him. At this point, however, reconsider your rationale for teaching this program. The physically impaired child may not need to sort objects in his daily life, but the concepts developed in this program are important for later abstract learning (e.g., visual discriminations by identity, color, size, and shape).

Objective:

Given a set of two different kinds of objects, S sorts the objects into two separate groups. S must initiate his response within 5 seconds of the command and sort all objects correctly 4 out of 5 trials.

separate groups = groups differing by object identity. Each group contains those, and only those, objects with the same function, name, and general appearance (e.g., cups together, saucers together).

Cycle:

None specified. However, you may repeat this program if needed to teach S to categorize other types of objects by using additional but secondary attributes, such as color, shape, or size.

Follow-Up:

Have S sort a variety of different objects throughout the day. In particular, develop daily routines that assist in chores at home (e.g., sorting clothes or silverware, putting dishes away). Have S sort materials used in workshop settings (e.g., screws, nuts), as well as in his school environment (e.g., toys, papers, crayons). Vary the containers where S places the objects, using boundaries or marked off areas on shelves, as well as drawers, closets, and trays.

Once S can easily sort a variety of objects, have him sort by more abstract characteristics (color, shape, size). Have S sort cut-out shapes, then numbers and letters. Describe the relevant characteristics of the objects as S matches and sorts (e.g., object identity "cup," color "red," size "big," shape "round"). This verbalization will help S to categorize on his own.

Program for Cognitive Skill 12

Materials:

Collect four different sets of objects, all within the same category (e.g., "Clothing": four socks, four shoes, four gloves, four ties; or "Food": four oranges, four apples, four bananas, four peaches), and two containers into which the objects may be sorted.

Chart:

None.

GENERAL STRATEGY

Arrangement:

Position the two containers in front of S. Position six objects. Six objects = three each of two different sets (e.g., three cups, three spoons). Note: Only two sets are sorted on any one trial. The combination of sets is specified for each step.

Cues:

sample = hold up an extra object like one S is to sort. Say its name, and place it in one of the containers. Do the same for an extra object from the other set, and place it in the other container. (These samples are not included in the arrangement of the six objects.)

label with pointing cue = point to the appropriate container, and label the type of object it is to hold.

Note: This label is a functional, attention-getting strategy. S does not have to understand the label in order to respond appropriately.

Command:

Give an appropriate command to separate the objects ("S, PUT (spoons) HERE, (cups) HERE") with cues indicating the containers (point to the left one for spoons, the right one for cups).

Latency:

S must initiate his response within 5 seconds of the command, placement of the last object, or delayed cue.

Correction:

Use general correction procedures.

Other Trials:

Repeat the strategy until S meets criterion. Note that 1 trial = S sorts all 6 objects.

Modification:

S has not met step criterion after four errors.

	CONDITIONS	BEHAVIOR S sorts all 6 objects on each trial...	CRITERIA
PRE	Arrange the materials. Vary the combination of sets used for each trial. Give the command.	unassisted (combination of sets varied)	4 correct out of 5 trials
S/1	Arrange the materials. Use the same 2 sets for each trial. Present the samples, then give the command. While S picks up each object, present the label with a pointing cue. Correct if needed.	given samples, then labels with pointing cues (same combination throughout)	4 correct out of the last 5 trials for each step
S/2	Same as S/1, but use 2 new sets of objects throughout.	given samples, then labels with pointing cues (new sets but the same combination throughout)	

S/3 Arrange the materials. Select any 2 sets from S/1 or S/2, but use the same 2 sets on each trial. Present the <u>samples</u>, then give the <u>command</u>. If S does not begin to place each object, present the <u>label with a pointing cue</u>. Correct if needed.	given samples, then, if necessary, delayed labels with pointing cues (same combination throughout)	
S/4 Same as S/3, but vary the combination of sets used for each trial.	given samples, then, if necessary, labels with pointing cues (varied combination)	
S/5 Arrange the materials. Vary the combination of sets used for each trial. Give the command. If S does not begin to place each object correctly, present the <u>label with a pointing cue</u>. Correct if needed.	given delayed labels with pointing cues if necessary (combination varied)	
S/6 Arrange the materials. Vary the combination of sets used for each trial. Give the command. Correct if needed.	unassisted (combination varied)	
POST 1 Same as PRE	unassisted (combination varied)	4 correct out of 5 trials for each test
POST 2 New Sets of Objects		
POST 3 New Sets of Objects		

MODIFICATIONS

If S has difficulty discriminating between sets, make the difference between the
sets more striking. In each set, use objects that are identical or as similar
as possible (e.g., all spoons are the same size and are metal). At the same
time, combine two sets with very different functions that are not from the same
category (e.g., have S sort metal teaspoons and yellow pencils). Gradually
change the materials being sorted so that all four sets are of the same category,
and members of one set are only similar, not identical.

As you give the sample, label the object, giving a pointing cue, and perform
some functional task with the object (e.g., brush--brush your hair; blocks--
build a tower). Gradually reduce the use of this additional demonstration by
presenting it less frequently during a trial or step.

Use a covering cue to prevent S from putting the object in the wrong container
when he is not attending to the task. Place your hand over the container to
prevent S from making an error, thus intercepting the response. Follow this cue
by giving a demonstration of the function of the object, then repeating the
command. Next cover the container, and then allow S to self-correct. Then
give no cue, but allow self-correction as a correct response. Finally as S's
need for self-correction decreases, have him meet the original step criterion.

Pairing
Equal Sets

4/5 Data

Skill:

This program teaches the child to pair the objects from two equal sets. This one-to-one correspondence skill is taught by adding then fading visual and verbal cues to place each object from one set next to the corresponding object in the other set (counting is not required). By pairing objects, the child can later determine whether he has the same number of objects (equality).

Entry Behaviors:

1. S sequences a set of objects into a given series of places (e.g., Putting Objects in Sequence). This sequencing introduces one-to-one correspondence (one object in each place).

2. S performs a wide variety of tasks with minimal assistance (e.g., self-help skills). S's task repertoire should be large enough to make this particular skill functional and relevant to his needs.

3. S responds correctly to a variety of cued commands for routine tasks (e.g., Following Cued Commands). Although S may or may not be able to comprehend the specific words of a command, he is usually able to perform the desired action by using your model, gestures, or other cues to understand what is expected of him.

4. S sees the objects and the visual cues that direct the placement of the objects. Or, adapt and add a procedure that allows S to touch and locate the items you have positioned. Then request him to position his set. Permit S to keep one hand on the first set of objects while he places each object in the second set. Substitute an auditory cue (e.g., tap the table or so on) for the pointing cue.

5. S puts one object next to another. Or, adapt the materials so that S can place the objects (e.g., spread the first set farther apart). Or, have S indicate to you where the objects are to be placed.

6. S hears the command and verbal cue. Or, adapt by substituting other strategies (e.g., gestures, sign) to convey the meaning.

Objective:

When you place a set of three to five objects in front of S and give him an equal set, S places each object of his set in one-to-one correspondence with the first set. S must initiate his response within 5 seconds of the command and place all objects in the set correctly 4 out of 5 trials (1 set = 1 trial).

Cycle:

None specified.

Follow-Up:

Continue to give S opportunities to place equal sets in one-to-one correspondence. Have S apply the skill in daily situations: Set each place at the table; place cups on saucers; arrange classroom materials, such as one crayon for each piece of paper on the table; give each person a pencil. Continue to use a variety of arrangements, not necessarily horizontal or vertical rows, so that S develops scanning skills as well. Introduce counting as part of the task by counting with S as he places each object. Gradually allow S to count without your model (e.g., Counting Rationally). Also, use questions (e.g., "Do you have enough?"; "Do you need more?") to introduce the concepts of equality and inequality (e.g., Selecting Equivalent Amounts). Use language to describe the task (e.g., "more" means to take additional objects and place them).

Program for Cognitive Skill 13

Materials:

Collect a variety of objects.

Chart:

None.

GENERAL STRATEGY

Arrangement:

Position a set of three to five objects in front of S in a horizontal or vertical row. Give S an equal set of objects.

Command:

Give an appropriate command (e.g., "GET ENOUGH") <u>with cues</u> indicating the initial placement ("Start here," and point to the place for the first object).

Cues:

<u>redirection</u> = verbal indication to S that he needs to place more objects (e.g., "What's next?").

<u>pointing cue</u> = point next to an object in the first set and say <u>Here</u> to show S where to place his object.

Latency:

S must initiate his response within 5 seconds of the command, delayed cue, or last placement.

Correction:

Use general correction procedures.

Review Statement:

After S places <u>each</u> object, point first to the object in the original set, then to one S just placed and say, "This one is equal to this one."

Other Trials:

Repeat the strategy. Vary trials for unevenly placed horizontal and vertical rows so that S will arrange objects from top-to-bottom or left-to-right. <u>Note</u>: 1 trial = 1 set.

Modification:

S has not met step criterion after four errors.

CONDITIONS	BEHAVIOR	CRITERIA
	S places each object in his set...	
PRE Arrange the materials. Give the command. Present the review statement for each placement.	unassisted	4 correct out of 5 trials

S/1 Arrange the materials. Give the command. Present the <u>pointing cue</u> for each placement. Correct if needed. Present the review statement after each placement.	given a pointing cue	4 correct out of the last 5 trials for each step
S/2 Arrange the materials. Give the command. If S does not begin to respond correctly, provide <u>redirection</u> and the <u>pointing cue</u>. Correct if needed. Present the review statement after each placement.	given delayed redirection and pointing cues if necessary	
S/3 Arrange the materials. Give the command. If S does not begin to respond correctly, provide <u>redirection</u>. Correct if needed. Present the review statement for each placement.	given delayed redirection if necessary	
S/4 Arrange the materials. Give the command. Correct if needed. Present the review statement for each placement.	unassisted	
POST 1 Same as PRE	unassisted	4 correct out of 5 trials for each test
POST 2 New Materials		
POST 3 New Materials		

MODIFICATIONS

As soon as S places enough objects, remove the materials before he continues to place additional objects. Next in place of removing objects, use only a covering cue (e.g., just place your hand over the set of available objects to prevent S from taking more). Finally use only the cues in the program (i.e., pointing and redirection cues).

Use materials cues. Make a row of five different objects (e.g., cup, spoon, fork, pencil, eraser), then give S five matching objects, one at a time. S will then be matching identical objects as a cue to one-to-one correspondence. Gradually introduce a variety of sets so that S can meet the original criterion with varied objects.

Give S objects one at a time to reinforce placement in one-to-one correspondence. Gradually give S more objects at once so that he can meet the original criterion.

Selecting Equivalent Amounts

4/5 Data

Skill:

This program develops the concept <u>enough</u>, or <u>equal to</u>. The child is given a set of objects and is required to take only the number of objects needed to match the objects in another (smaller) set. This skill is taught by adding then fading cues directing the selection of the correct number (i.e., reminders about one-to-one correspondence, verbal cues, covering cues). Based on previously developed one-to-one correspondence skills, this skill enables the child to learn many tasks involving quantities where he need not recognize the number name, such as "Get this many spoons (showing him the number of place mats)" or "Get enough cups (for the saucers that are out)."

Entry Behaviors:

1. S <u>pairs objects in two equal sets to show one-to-one correspondence</u> (e.g., Pairing Equal Sets). S has previously developed this one-to-one correspondence skill but only when given equal sets.

2. S <u>performs a wide variety of tasks</u> with minimal assistance (e.g., self-help skills). S's task repertoire should be large enough to make this particular skill functional and relevant to his needs.

3. S <u>responds correctly to a variety of cued commands</u> for routine tasks (e.g., Following Cued Commands). Although S may or may not be able to comprehend the specific words of a command, he is usually able to perform the desired action by using your model, gestures, or other cues to understand what is expected of him.

4. S <u>sees the objects and the visual cues</u> that direct the placement of the objects. Or, adapt by adding tactile cues. For the one-to-one correspondence cue, have S touch the objects as you review the correspondence. For the covering cue, let S feel your hand as you cover the objects and prevent him from taking any more.

5. S <u>puts one object next to another</u>. Or, adapt the materials so that S can place the objects (e.g., spread the first set farther apart). Or, have S indicate to you where to place the objects.

6. S <u>hears the command and verbal cues</u>. Or, adapt by substituting other strategies (e.g., gesturing, signing) for conveying the meaning.

Objective:

S selects an equal number of objects from a larger set when a smaller set (from three to five objects) is placed in front of him. S must initiate his response within 5 seconds of the command and place the correct number of objects from the larger set 4 out of 5 trials. <u>Note</u>: 1 trial = 1 set.

Cycle:

None specified.

Follow-Up:

Continue to give S opportunities to select and then place sets of objects in one-to-one correspondence. Change the setting and materials so that S is using the skill in practical situations (e.g., to get enough spoons out of the drawer for each place setting). Continue to use a variety of arrangements so that S develops the skill of scanning a number of objects. Position unequal sets of objects (e.g., six pieces of paper, only two of which have a crayon on top), and have S add to or take away enough to make the sets equal. The use of unequal sets facilitates the introduction of the concepts <u>more than</u> and <u>less than</u>. Before S selects objects, label the number of objects he is to choose (e.g., "five" spoons). As he selects and positions, count with him to introduce rational counting (e.g., Counting Rationally). If he is working with unequal sets, ask him to count not only the objects he selected and positioned but also the total number of pairs. In addition, use descriptive phrases (e.g., "You have <u>enough</u>") to emphasize numerical concepts of <u>equality</u> and <u>inequality</u> (e.g., "Get more"; "Too many").

Program for Cognitive Skill 14

Materials:
Collect a variety of small objects.

Chart:
None.

GENERAL STRATEGY

Arrangement:
Place a set of three to five objects in an unevenly positioned horizontal or vertical row. Give S more objects than needed or an equal set of objects as specified in each step.

Command:
Give an appropriate command ("GET ENOUGH") <u>with cues</u> indicating the position for the first placement ("Start here," and <u>point</u> to the position for the first object).

Cues:

<u>one-to-one correspondence cue</u> = after S places each object, point first to the object in the original set, then to the one S just placed, saying "This one is equal to this one." Do this for <u>each</u> pair.

<u>verbal cue</u> = after S has selected and placed an equal number of objects for the set, say "Enough" or "You have enough" and point to the sets in one-to-one correspondence.

<u>covering cue</u> = after S has placed enough objects, cover the remaining objects in the larger set so that S cannot use them.

Latency:

S must initiate his response within 5 seconds of the command, delayed cue, or last object placed.

Correction:

Use general correction procedures.

Other Trials:

Repeat the strategy. Vary trials for unevenly positioned horizontal and vertical rows and vary the number of objects in the original set and the larger set.
<u>Note:</u> 1 trial = 1 set (all objects).

Modification:

S has not met step criterion after four errors.

CONDITIONS	BEHAVIOR S selects enough objects to make a set equal to...	CRITERIA
PRE Arrange the materials, and give S more objects than needed. Give the command.	a smaller set, unassisted	4 correct out of 5 trials
S/1 Arrange the materials, and give S an equal set. Give the command. Present <u>correspondence cues</u> for each placement. When an equal number of objects is placed, present the <u>verbal cue</u> and <u>covering cue</u>. Correct if needed.	an equal set, given correspondence, verbal, and covering cues	4 correct out of the last 5 trials for each step

S/2 Same as S/1, but give S more objects than needed.	a smaller set, given correspondence, verbal, and covering cues	
S/3 Arrange the materials, and give S more objects than needed. Give the command. Present correspondence cues. If S begins to take more objects than needed, present the verbal cue and covering cue. Correct if needed.	a smaller set, given correspondence cues and, if necessary, delayed verbal and covering cues	
S/4 Arrange the materials, and give S more objects than needed. Give the command. Present correspondence cues. If S begins to take more objects than needed, present the verbal cue. Correct if needed.	a smaller set, given correspondence cues and, if necessary, a delayed verbal cue	
S/5 Arrange the materials, and give S more objects than needed. Give the command. Present correspondence cues. Correct if needed.	a smaller set, given correspondence cues	
S/6 Arrange the materials, and give S more objects than needed. Give the command. Correct if needed.	a smaller set, unassisted	
POST 1 Same as PRE	a smaller set, unassisted	4 correct out of 5 trials for each test
POST 2 New Materials		
POST 3 New Materials		

MODIFICATIONS

If the covering or verbal cues do not prevent S from stopping when he has placed enough objects, remove the pairs as soon as S places them in one-to-one correspondence. Gradually reduce the frequency with which you use this cue. Finally require S to respond with cues specified in the program.

Add any necessary verbal and pointing cues to enable S to take the number of objects he needs. Gradually fade these cues so that S is selecting an equal number of objects without direction.

Substitute materials that cue S to stop placement. For example, use forms printed on a sheet of paper. You place the original set of objects on forms in the top row, then ask S to place objects on forms in the second row, as shown below. Return to the original materials.

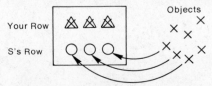

Matching
Equal Sets

4/5 Data

Cycle

Skill:

This program teaches the child to recognize equal sets by placing objects in one-to-one correspondence. The child is given up to five objects and scans a selection of cards to find the one with the equivalent number of forms on it. This selection skill is taught by gradually introducing new cards so that the child is making more difficult visual discriminations. He then places the objects on the forms on the card he has selected; he may self-correct if necessary, using his previously developed one-to-one correspondence skills. By matching equal sets, the child develops visual discrimination of sets before he learns to use the names of numbers.

Entry Behaviors:

1. S <u>places objects in one-to-one correspondence</u> (e.g., Pairing Equal Sets). The more experience he has had with one-to-one correspondence and the more situations and materials he has worked with (e.g., Selecting Equivalent Amounts), the easier the task in this program will be.

2. S <u>sees the objects and the forms on the cards</u>. Or, adapt by changing the materials, either by increasing their size or by adding tactile cues to the forms (e.g., use felt squares on a card). Or, if the child's abilities make material adaptations more difficult than necessary, practice one-to-one correspondence by repeating previous programs with new materials (e.g., Pairing Equal Sets and Selecting Equivalent Amounts) rather than using this program.

3. S <u>hears the command</u>. Note: At this point, S does not have to recognize the number name in the command since he is also given that number of objects. However, this is the first time that the number name is introduced to provide S with experiences that prepare him to count. If necessary, adapt by using either signing (e.g., holding up the number of fingers representative of the number) or introducing numerals as part of the command (e.g., holding up the numeral 3).

4. S <u>picks up or moves the objects</u> as requested. Or, adapt by having S use adaptive equipment or materials (e.g., larger cards or forms, or objects significantly smaller than the form, with the forms spread out considerably). Or, have S indicate the card to you, and you place the objects. Always place the objects and allow S to self-correct since S need not discriminate at first glance but by one-to-one correspondence placement.

Objective:

Given one to five objects (as appropriate to the cycle) and a selection of five cards, S selects the matching card by placing the objects in one-to-one correspondence with the forms on that card. S must initiate his response within 5 seconds of the command and respond correctly 4 out of 5 trials for the new number taught, and 4 out of 5 trials for any numbers previously learned.

Cycle:

Repeat the task for number concepts 2 through 5, and record which sets of objects (one to five) S can match. Each cycle teaches S to recognize one numerical set. The cycles are taught in sequence for sets of increasing quantity so that S learns to recognize one new set at a time.

	New sets recognized	Sets reviewed
Cycle 1:	"one"	
Cycle 2:	"two"	one
Cycle 3:	"three"	one, two
Cycle 4:	"four"	one, two, three
Cycle 5:	"five"	one, two, three, four

The three programs that teach numbers (Matching Equal Sets, Counting Rationally, Selecting a Specified Quantity) can be taught in either of two ways:

1. In order for each cycle (e.g., all three programs for Cycle 1, then all three for Cycle 2, then for Cycle 3, 4, and 5); OR

2. In order separately (e.g., all cycles for Matching Equal Sets, then all for Counting Rationally, then all for Selecting a Specified Quantity).

Follow-Up:

Continue to give S opportunities to find matching sets by using one-to-one correspondence (pairing). As S learns new sets through the cycles of this program, continue to review all previously learned sets. Use situations that incorporate frequently used pairing tasks, such as setting a table. Give S more objects than he needs, and ask him to position a specific number of objects to match those already placed in a set. Use a variety of materials so that S does not lose interest in the activity.

Introduce the concept of equality by using the words equal or same to describe sets of objects. Count as S pairs these sets. This will not only be an introduction to Counting Rationally but also will emphasize the name of the number. Introduce the concepts too many and not enough when determining whether two sets match. As S learns each set in Counting Rationally, combine pairing and counting activities (e.g., "Get enough. Count."). Use functional situations (e.g., one cookie for each child).

Introduce numerals with the number names so that S can perform activities and can use the numerals as cues. Pair the numerals with the materials used in this program (e.g. $\boxed{3}$ with $\boxed{\blacksquare\blacksquare}$). Have S match the numeral to the cards with forms

or to the sets of objects. Introduce worksheets that emphasize the association between numerals and the number of objects in a set (e.g. $\boxed{3 \; \fbox{$\square\square\square$} \atop \times\,\times}$).

Program for Cognitive Skill 15

Materials:

Collect five or more small objects that S can easily handle, and collect five cards with one to five identical shapes on them (e.g. ▪ ⁚ ⋮ ⁖ ⁛)

Chart:

None.

GENERAL STRATEGY

Arrangement:

Position the cards on the table in random order (the number of cards is specified for each step). Give S the number of objects specified for the step.

Command:

Give an appropriate command to find the matching card ("S, PUT (number) ON (number)" or "FIND (number)") with cues (point to the display of cards).

Latency:

S must initiate his response within 5 seconds of the command or last object placed. S also has 5 seconds in which to initiate self-correction after placing all of the objects.

Self-Correction:

If S places the objects on the wrong card, allow him to complete this response. Then wait up to 5 seconds (latency) for S to initiate correction of his error by moving the objects to the correct card. If S initiates self-correction within 5 seconds of the placement of the last object, the response is counted as a "+." If S does not initiate self-correction within 5 seconds after he has placed the objects, record a "-" and provide correction.

Correction:

Use general correction procedures. Note: When you correct S, include the following information: Tell S "too many," or "not enough," depending on his error, and point to the empty forms or the remaining objects.

Consequence:

When the objects have been correctly placed, give the request, "S, give me (number placed)." Hold out your hand. Give S assistance if needed to select and hand you each object as you count.

Other Trials:

Repeat the strategy until S meets criterion. Randomly vary the objects and the positions of the cards for each trial. On the tests and last step where S must meet criterion on both the new number taught and on reviewed numbers from previous cycles, vary the number requested in the command.

Modification:

S has not met step criterion after four errors.

CONDITIONS	BEHAVIOR	CRITERIA
X = the number concept being taught in the cycle (e.g., for Cycle 3, X = "three")	S selects the correct card unassisted...	
PRE Position all 5 cards. Present X, or less than X, objects and the command for that number. Present the consequence.	from 5 cards; S may self-correct	4 correct out of 5 trials for X, and 4 correct out of 5 trials for numbers less than X (total of 8 out of 10 trials)

S/1 Position the X card. Present X objects and the command for X. Correct if needed. Present the consequence.	from a choice of 1 card	4 correct out of the last 5 trials (X only) for each step
S/2 Position the X card and one other (total = 2 cards). Present X objects and the command for X. Correct if needed. Present the consequence.	from a choice of 2 cards; S may self-correct	
S/3 Position the X card and 2 others (total = 3 cards). Present X objects and the command for X. Correct if needed. Present the consequence.	from a choice of 3 cards; S may self-correct	
S/4 Position the X card and 3 others (total = 4 cards). Present X objects and the command for X. Correct if needed. Present the consequence.	from a choice of 4 cards; S may self-correct	
S/5 Position the X card and 4 others (total = 5 cards). Present X objects and the command for X. Correct if needed. Present the consequence.	from a choice of 5 cards; S may self-correct	
S/6 Position all 5 cards. Present X, or less than X, objects, and give the command for that number. Correct if needed. Present the consequence.	from a choice of 5 cards; S may self-correct	4 correct out of 5 trials for X, and 4 correct out of 5 trials for numbers less than X (total of 8 out of 10 trials)
POST 1 Same as PRE	from a choice of 5 cards; S may self-correct	4 correct out of 5 trials for X, and 4 correct out of 5 trials for numbers less than X (total of 8 out of 10 trials) for each test
POST 2 New Cards (Different shapes or colors)		
POST 3 New Command (e.g., "FIND X").		

MODIFICATIONS

If S is not scanning the cards scattered randomly in front of him, place the cards in a row(s) so that S can look from left-to-right and top-to-bottom. Provide S with this structure for the entire program. Then go back and execute the steps with the cards positioned as originally described.

If S is making persistent errors even after using self-correction, change your materials so that the other cards use shapes different from those on the X-concept card. Gradually make the shapes look more and more like those on the X-card.

If S is making errors when the concepts X, and less than X, are reviewed (S/6), alternate trials for these concepts. Present several trials for X, then several for one concept less than X, then for another concept less than X. Gradually alternate by presenting fewer trials for each concept. Finally present fewer consecutive trials randomly to meet criterion.

Counting Rationally

4/5 Data

Cycle

Skill:

This program teaches the child to count objects as he touches or places each one. (The pairing of each object with the number name in sequence is "rational counting," whereas reciting the names in sequence without an object referent is "rote counting.") This rational counting skill is taught by adding then fading verbal models and cues for the number names. With this skill, the child can count objects to find out how many are in a set or to select the amount requested.

Entry Behaviors:

1. S <u>selects the set that matches one he is given</u>. For example, S selects a card with the same number of forms on it as the number of objects held in his hand (e.g., Matching Equal Sets). <u>Note</u>: See Cycle information. If S has skipped matching sets because of a visual impairment, he needs to have many other one-to-one correspondence experiences using tactile cues, such as putting cups on saucers or matching one set of objects with another set (e.g., Pairing Equal Sets, Selecting Equivalent Amounts).

2. S <u>responds correctly to a variety of cued commands</u> for routine tasks (e.g., Following Cued Commands). Although S may or may not be able to comprehend the specific words of a command, he is usually able to perform the desired action by using your model, gestures, or other cues to understand what is expected.

3. S <u>picks up or moves objects</u> as requested. Or, adapt by having S use adaptive equipment. Or, have S count as you place the objects so that his vocal response accompanies an object referent.

4. S <u>sees the objects</u>. Or, adapt by adding tactile cues (e.g., use felt squares on which objects may be placed). Or, place objects in a row, and have S touch and count rather than place and count.

5. S <u>hears and imitates the number name</u> (e.g., Shaping Words) so that he may count aloud. Or, adapt by using either signing (e.g., holding up the correct number of fingers while counting) or introducing numerals (e.g., having S point to the correct numeral instead of saying the word). Either of these adaptations should have previously been introduced in Matching Equal Sets.

Objective:

Given from one to five objects (as appropriate to the cycle), S places and counts the objects in sequence. S must initiate his response within 5 seconds of the command and respond correctly 4 out of 5 trials. 1 trial = 1 set of objects counted.

Cycle:

Record how far S can count <u>as</u> he picks up, places, or touches each object. Each cycle teaches S to count a specific number of objects. The cycles are taught in sequence for number values of increasing quantity so that S learns to count to one new number at a time.

	<u>New number counted</u>	<u>Numbers automatically reviewed</u>
Cycle 1:	"one"	
Cycle 2:	"two"	one
Cycle 3:	"three"	one, two
Cycle 4:	"four"	one, two, three
Cycle 5:	"five"	one, two, three, four

The three programs teaching numbers (Matching Equal Sets, Counting Rationally, Selecting a Specified Quantity) can be taught in either of two ways:

1. In order for each cycle (e.g., all three programs for Cycle 1, then all three for Cycle 2, then for Cycles 3, 4, and 5); OR

2. In order separately (e.g., all cycles for Matching Equal Sets, then all cycles for Counting Rationally, then all cycles for Selecting a Specified Quantity).

Follow-Up:

Continue to provide opportunities to count and place objects. Vary the task requests to include "S, how many? Count," as an introduction to Selecting a Specified Quantity. Combine the "count" task request with daily routines and commands, such as "S, get me four spoons. Count to four." Note that as S counts up to a number, he automatically reviews the previous cycle(s).

Reinforce S if he counts silently after he has had plenty of experience counting aloud. Counting silently is a valuable skill when S begins independent worksheet assignments in a classroom setting. Present worksheets that require him to cross out or circle a particular number of objects or to circle the numeral that represents the number of objects pictured. Since S has been introduced to numerals during follow-up activities for Matching Equal Sets, you may use numerals to enable him to complete tasks instead of only giving verbal directions.

Program for Cognitive Skill 16

Materials:

Collect a variety of small objects that may be easily handled (at least five).

Chart:

None.

GENERAL STRATEGY

Arrangement:

Position the objects (the number being taught) in front of S. Give an appropriate task request (e.g., "Put (number) here") and indicate that S is to put the objects in a line as he positions them (e.g., "Make a row here," while you point).

Cue:

count = you count each object as S places it, and assist him to line up the objects as necessary.

Command:

Give an appropriate command for S to count ("S, COUNT") with cues (point to the first object to be counted). Note that the command is always for the new number being taught in the cycle.

Cues:

pointing cue = point to each object in sequence.
model = say the number name in sequence.

Latency:

S must initiate his response within 5 seconds of the command or last cue.

Correction:

Use general correction procedures.

Other Trials:

Repeat the strategy until S meets criterion. Randomly vary the objects used for each trial.

Modification:

S has not met step criterion after four errors.

CONDITIONS	BEHAVIOR S counts...	CRITERIA
PRE Arrange the materials. Give the command.	as he places each object, unassisted	4 correct out of 5 trials
S/1 Arrange the materials. Count. Give the command, then present the pointing cue and model for each object. Correct if needed.	each object, given a pointing cue and model; after having placed all the objects while you counted	4 correct out of the last 5 trials for each step

S/2 Arrange the materials. <u>Count</u>. Give the command. Present the <u>pointing cue</u> for each object. If S does not begin to count each object correctly, present the <u>model</u>. Correct if needed.	each object, given a pointing cue and, if necessary, a delayed model; after having placed all the objects while you counted	
S/3 Arrange the materials. <u>Count</u>. Give the command. If S does not begin to count each object correctly, present the <u>pointing cue</u> and <u>model</u>. Correct if needed.	each object, given a delayed pointing cue and model if necessary; after having placed all the objects while you counted	
S/4 Arrange the materials. Give the command. If S does not begin to count each object correctly, present the <u>pointing cue</u> and <u>model</u>. Correct if needed.	as he places each object, given a delayed pointing cue and model if necessary	
S/5 Arrange the materials. Give the command. Correct if needed.	as he places each object, unassisted	
POST 1 Same as PRE	as he places each object, unassisted	4 correct out of 5 trials for each test
POST 2 New Materials		
POST 3 New Materials		

MODIFICATIONS

Physical guidance is a useful strategy to enable S to synchronize his counting with the placement of the objects. Use extra pressure on S's hand as he places an object, and present the model with emphasis. Coordinate your model and S's response with your physical guidance.

Begin the session with a warm-up in which you ask S to imitate the number names without counting any specific objects. Make a game out of this imitation practice. Then begin your trial(s). Gradually reduce the amount of time spent practicing vocal imitation.

Provide an extra cue to enable S to place each object. Present an auditory cue (e.g., tap the table), and count as S places each object. Or, if S does not readily place an object to be counted, add an auditory cue (e.g., hit a drum once) before he is to place an object. Gradually fade the additional auditory cues.

Use functional materials (e.g., cups and saucers, spoons and bowls, straws and glasses) instead of small objects if you feel S is making unnecessary errors due to lack of interest. Position one set of objects (e.g., saucers, bowls, or glasses) in a row as the placement cue, and give S the second set (e.g., cups, spoons, or straws) to be placed in or on the first set as he counts. Gradually fade the use of the first set. At first ask S to place only the second set within some general boundary (e.g., an area on the table using colored tape as a boundary). Then give S only the objects to count.

Use additional materials to structure the counting skill. Use the number cards from Matching Equal Sets: five 3 x 5 inch white cards, with from one to five 1-inch squares ▆ ▆ ▆ ▆ ▆ . Have S place objects on each shape as you

count. Then use the strategies in this program. Later use only a blank card and finally only the materials (objects) listed in the original program.

Selecting a
Specified
Quantity

4/5 Data

Cycle

Skill:

This program teaches the child to <u>count and place</u> the requested number of objects from those available. Verbal cues to count and to place the specified number of objects are gradually faded until the child can select the correct number without assistance. This skill is an application of rational counting that enables the child to respond to a variety of functional commands that include numbers up to five (e.g., "Get three cups," "Bring two forks," "Put out four pencils").

Entry Behaviors:

1. S <u>counts or states the number of objects in a set</u> for the numbers to be used in this program (e.g., Counting Rationally). S may count silently, count aloud, or visually recognize a set and state the number of objects in it. If S cannot identify the quantity by name, reconsider your rationale for teaching this program; review Counting Rationally or its prerequisites.

2. S <u>responds correctly to a variety of cued commands</u> for routine tasks (e.g., Following Cued Commands). Although S may or may not be able to comprehend the specific words in a command, he is usually able to perform the desired action by using your model, gestures, or other cues to understand what is expected of him.

3. S <u>picks up or moves objects</u> as requested. Or, adapt by having S use adaptive equipment. Or, have S count out the objects as you select them, and tell you to stop when the correct quantity has been counted. If no adaptive equipment is possible, reconsider your rationale for teaching this program since S might have more use for other math skills.

4. S <u>sees the objects</u> to be counted. Or, adapt by adding tactile cues (e.g., S first feels the objects, then places them inside a container or boundary).

5. S <u>hears and imitates the number name</u> (e.g., Shaping Words) so that verbal counting may be used as a teaching strategy. Or, adapt by using either signing or written numerals to substitute for speech. Either of these adaptations should have previously been introduced in Matching Equal Sets and Counting Rationally.

Objective:

When more objects than needed are present, S selects the specified number of objects and makes a new set. S must initiate his response within 5 seconds of the command and respond correctly 4 out of 5 trials for the new number, and 4 out of 5 trials for all numbers smaller than this number (total: 8 out of 10 trials).

Cycle:

Repeat the task for number concepts <u>2</u> through <u>5</u>, and record which sets of objects (one to five) S can match. Each cycle teaches S to select a specified number. The cycles are taught in sequence with numbers of increasing quantity so that S learns one new number at a time.

Cycle 1:   S selects <u>one</u> object

Cycle 2:   S selects one or <u>two</u> objects

Cycle 3:   S selects one, two, or <u>three</u> objects

Cycle 4:   S selects one, two, three, or <u>four</u> objects

Cycle 5:   S selects one, two, three, four, or <u>five</u> objects

The three programs that teach numbers (Matching Equal Sets, Counting Rationally, Selecting a Specified Quantity) can be taught in either of two ways:

1. In order for each cycle (e.g., all three programs for Cycle 1, then all three for Cycle 2, then for Cycles 3, 4, and 5); OR

2. In order separately (e.g., all cycles for Matching Equal Sets, then all cycles for Counting Rationally, then all cycles for Selecting a Specified Quantity).

Follow-Up:

Continue to review each of the numbers S has been taught. Use a variety of task requests to enable S to select a number of objects from a larger set. Vary the number in the larger set.

Present a sheet with pictures, and have S cross out the number of objects specified as an introduction to worksheets. Begin using the numerals to represent the number of objects in a set. Again, use worksheets, and have S practice writing numerals.

Expand the strategies in this program to cover the number concepts <u>5</u> through <u>10</u>. See previous math program strategies, as well as those contained here for ideas.

Use materials found throughout the classroom to have S select and then distribute specified numbers of objects. When S can recognize numerals and pictures (Identifying Simple Pictures), present pictorial directions for different activities, such as setting the table or retrieving materials (e.g., 4 ✎ , 5 ━━━).

Program for Cognitive Skill 17

Materials:

Collect at least six small objects that S can easily handle.

Chart:

None.

GENERAL STRATEGY

Arrangement:

Seat S at a table or desk. Position in front of S the number of objects specified in the step.

Command:

Give an appropriate command ("S, PUT (number) HERE") with cues indicating where to place the objects (point to the area or container). Note: As specified in the step, the command may be either for the new number for the cycle or for any number smaller than that.

Cues:

count cue = say count, then count with S if necessary.

review cue = as soon as S has placed the correct number of objects, review the number name by saying "Look, (number). How many?" Prompt S as needed to repeat the number.

Latency:

S must initiate his response within 5 seconds of the command or last object placed.

Correction:

Use general correction procedures.

Consequence:

Have S perform a task with the selected objects (e.g., count them again, put them in one-to-one correspondence with another set of materials, or put the objects in a specific place where they are needed, such as crayons on a work table).

Other Trials:

Repeat the strategy until S meets criterion. Randomly vary the objects used, as well as the number presented and the quantity requested in the command. S must meet criterion on varied quantities as noted in each step.

Modification:

S has not met step criterion after four errors.

CONDITIONS	BEHAVIOR	CRITERIA
$\underline{X}$ = The number taught in the cycle (e.g., for Cycle 3, "three")	S selects the correct number of objects...	
PRE Present more than $\underline{X}$ objects. Give the command for $\underline{X}$, or less than $\underline{X}$ (vary). Present the consequence.	unassisted	4 correct out of 5 trials for $\underline{X}$, and 4 correct out of 5 trials for numbers smaller than $\underline{X}$ (total: 8 out of 10 trials)
S/1 Present $\underline{X}$ objects. Give the command for S, followed immediately by the count cue. Correct if needed. After the response, present the review cue. Present the consequence.	given $\underline{X}$ objects, a count cue, and a review cue	4 correct out of 5 trials for $\underline{X}$
S/2 Present more objects than needed. Give the command for $\underline{X}$, followed immediately by the count cue. Correct if needed. After the response, present the review cue. Present the consequence.	given a count cue and a review cue	4 correct out of 5 trials for $\underline{X}$, and 4 correct out of 5 trials for less than $\underline{X}$ for each step
S/3 Give S more objects than needed. Give the command for $\underline{X}$, or less than $\underline{X}$. If S does not begin to place and count objects correctly, present the count cue. Correct if needed. After the response, present the review cue. Present the consequence.	given a review cue and, if necessary, a delayed count cue	"
S/4 Present more objects than needed. Give the command for $\underline{X}$, or less than $\underline{X}$. If S begins to place more objects than necessary, present the review cue. Correct if needed. Present the consequence.	given a delayed review cue only if necessary	"

S/5 Present more objects than needed. Give the command for X, or less than X. Correct if needed. Present the consequence.	unassisted	"	
POST 1 Same as PRE	unassisted		4 correct out of 5 trials for X, and 4 correct out of 5 trials for numbers smaller than X for each test
POST 2 New Materials			
POST 3 New Command (e.g., "Give me")			

MODIFICATIONS

If S is having trouble selecting the correct quantity, add steps where you use 3 x 5 inch white cards to focus S's attention on his selection. Place a set of objects on one card, and have S select and place the specified number of objects on the second card. Fade the use of one card, then the other, by using only marked boundaries on the table. Finally present the objects without any placement cues.

If S makes errors when the command varies, or when the number of objects available varies, execute the steps but present only one set of objects (e.g., always present six objects and request the number being taught in the cycle). Gradually increase the number of objects presented, and vary the number requested. Repeat the steps as written.

Neither physical guidance to place the objects nor a covering cue to discontinue placement should be necessary since S has previously performed using verbal cues alone. However, S may need practice with one of these cues. Physically guide S to place each object as you and he count. Once enough objects have been placed, cover any extra objects and say "enough." Gradually fade the physical guidance, then the counting cue. Gradually fade the covering cue, then the verbal cue enough. Finally execute the steps as designated.

Reaching

Skill Analysis

Skill:

In this program the child develops eye-hand coordination and the arm strength
necessary to reach purposefully and contact something that attracts his attention
(e.g., objects, people). The child is taught to reach when he is placed in a
variety of different positions. This directed reaching is the beginning of the
child's exploration of his environment. His fine motor development is refined
as he learns to perform a variety of actions with objects once he contacts them.

Entry Behaviors:

Overview
Fine Motor
Skill 1

1. S demonstrates many voluntary arm and hand movements (e.g., jerks and flails
   arms) and also purposefully moves his arms to bring his hand(s) to his mouth
   or to bring his hands in contact with each other. If S's arms are physically
   impaired, consult with a physical therapist to determine if it is appropriate
   to teach the program. Then adapt the program to compensate for S's physical
   impairments (e.g., require S to reach with only one hand, limit the positions
   in which S must reach).

2. S automatically stretches his arm(s) out to his side when he sees someone he
   knows or his favorite toy (bilateral reaching reflex). Or, S has exhibited
   this reflex in the past. However, he does not purposefully reach for an
   object. S may also automatically close his fingers around an object placed
   in his hand (grasp reflex), or has exhibited this reflex in the past. However,
   S probably cannot hold an object without support.

3. S follows the movement of an object or person with his eyes when either is within
   a few feet of him and moves slowly (vertical, horizontal, or circular movements). If S is visually impaired, he should be able to move his head toward
   the sound of an object as it produces noise. Adapt the program by using only
   toys which produce sound.

4. S observes an object or person for several seconds during stimulus events
   (e.g., Focusing Attention).

Objective:

From a variety of positions, S moves his hand/arm/upper torso to contact objects
placed 1-2 inches out of arm's reach.

positions = lying on stomach, back, side, or sitting.

arm's reach = the full extension of S's arm (straight at elbow, or as straight
as possible for S's physical condition). Objects should be placed in front of
S, to his side, above his head.

Cycle:

None specified.

Follow-Up:

Prompt S to reach for a variety of different objects. Teach him to wiggle on
his stomach to move toward and contact objects out of his reach. Provide many
kinds of stimulus events to prompt S to hold objects (e.g., Grasping Objects)
or to perform other actions with objects, such as throwing, dropping, squeezing
(e.g., Manipulating Objects). Repeat all the actions you see S perform, and
prompt him to perform the action again (e.g., Responding to Teacher Model).
Reinforce when S looks at objects for longer periods of time as he plays with
them to further develop eye-hand coordination and attending skills (e.g.,
Attending to Objects). Always describe the object and what S is doing to model
vocalization during these play activities (e.g., Making Sounds).

Program for Fine Motor Skill 1

Materials:

Collect a variety of toys that will "do something" when S contacts them (toys with moveable parts, toys that make noise, and the like).

Chart:

Stimulus Chart: See sections entitled "Sight" and "Sound" for suggested toys, pages 467-68.

GENERAL STRATEGY

Stimulus Event:

Place S in different positions. Provide as much support as needed but leave him free to move in the desired direction. Note that all parts require S to move his hand, arm, and/or upper torso to reach for the object.

On His Side  On His Stomach

On His Back 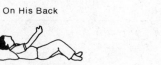 Sitting

Program Fine Motor Skill 1

Position:

Attract S's attention to the object by shaking, moving it, touching S with it, and the like. Then position it as described for the part, but always keep it within S's range of vision.

Command:

Give an appropriate command ("GET IT") <u>with cues</u>, and continue the stimulus event, maintaining S's attention to the object.

Latency:

S must initiate his response within 5 seconds of the command.

Correction:

Use Suggestions listed for each part.

Natural Consequence:

Allow S to interact with the object as long as he continues to respond. Help him to feel and grasp the object.

Other Trials:

Repeat the strategy. Vary the objects and the stimulus event. Require S to reach with both hands, one at a time. 1 trial = 1 opportunity to perform 1 part. Note that S must meet criterion for each arm.

Modification:

S has made no gains in <u>average parts completed</u> after two successive probes (2 weeks).

CONDITIONS	BEHAVIOR	CRITERIA
PRE Test *5 only. Position S as desired. Present a stimulus event, and place the target 1-2 inches past S's arm reach. Give the command. Present the natural consequence.	*5. Target--from a variety of positions, S moves his hand/arm/ upper torso to con- tact objects placed 1-2 inches out of arm's reach.	4 correct out of 5 trials for each arm

---

DAILY INSTRUCTION/WEEKLY PROBES

Position S as desired. Present a stimulus event, and place the object at the distance specified for each part. Give the command. Assist if needed. Present the natural consequence. Always vary S's position so that he reaches from different positions.		Continue daily instruc- tion/weekly probes until S performs *5 correctly 4 out of the last 5 trials

---

1. Position the object within 2 inches of S's hand. Vary the position of the object to require S to use different hand movements (up, down, sideways).	1. S <u>moves his hand</u> to contact an object.	at least 5 times for each hand

---

2. Position the object far enough from S's hand that he must move his forearm (at least 5 inches) to contact it. Vary the position of the object to require S to move his arm in different directions (up, sideways, down).	2. S <u>moves his forearm</u> and hand to contact an object.	at least 5 times for each arm

---

3. Position the object far enough away from S's hand so that he must move his entire arm to contact it. Vary the position of the object to require S to extend his arm in different directions (up, forward, sideways, down).	3. S <u>moves his whole arm</u> to contact an object.	at least 5 times for each arm

4. Position the object in front of S, 1-2 inches out of his reach, so that he must extend his arm and shift forward slightly to reach it. Vary the position of the object to require S to reach forward from different positions. Insure that if S is sitting upright, he is positioned so that his shift in weight will not cause him to fall over.	4. S <u>shifts his upper torso</u> slightly forward and <u>extends his arm</u> to contact an object positioned just out of his reach (forward only). 	at least 5 times for each arm
*5. Position the object 1-2 inches out of S's reach so that he must move his hand/arm/upper torso to contact it. Vary the position of the object to require S to reach in different directions (up, down, forward, sideways).	*5. Target--from a variety of positions, S moves his hand/arm/upper torso to contact objects positioned 1-2 inches out of arm's reach.	4 correct out of the last 5 trials for each arm
POST 1 Same as PRE	*5. Target--from a variety of positions S moves his hand/arm/upper torso to contact objects positioned 1-2 inches out of arm's reach.	4 correct out of 5 trials on each test for each arm
POST 2 New Setting		
POST 3 New Setting (different from POSTS 1 and 2)		

SUGGESTIONS

Part 1:

Require S to move his hand through different substances that provide resistance (water, sand, styrofoam chips) in order to increase strength in S's hand, fingers, and wrist.

At first place the object so that it touches S's fingertips. Gradually increase the distance so that S must move his fingers or wrist to contact the object.

Hold S's hand in yours, and move his fingers to rotate his wrist and provide a stimulus for him to move his hand. <u>Note</u>: Do not force S's hand; use gentle movements.

Tickle the back of S's hand and fingers to stimulate him to raise his hand to contact an object placed above it.

Have S tap objects that make noise (drums, balls).

Part 2:

Grasp S's forearm and guide him to move it in all possible directions to contact an object (raise it, move it sideways, and the like). Gradually fade your guidance. <u>Note</u>: S's elbow may remain resting on a surface.

Present stimuli to elicit arm movements. Stroke his forearm with ice, lotion, a feather, your hand, or use a blow dryer.

"Tease" S with the object. Place it at his fingertips. Then as he reaches for it, slowly move it back so that S has to extend his arm to get it. Gradually increase the distance you move the object before you allow S to have it.

Have S pat or bounce objects. Or, tie an elastic string (about 4 inches long) to S's wrist with a ball attached. Prompt S to retrieve the ball as it rolls, or have S pull the ball around by moving his forearm.

Part 3:

At first position S's arm, resting it on a surface. Place the object on the surface also, so that S must move his arm sideways and forward. Then suspend the object in different positions (to S's side, at midline, and the like), so that he must also raise his whole arm to contact the object. Gradually increase the number of directions in which S can reach.

Guide S to raise and extend his arm to contact the object when it is placed in a variety of different positions. Gradually fade your guidance.

Hold S's Hand   Hold S's Shoulder   Hold S's Elbow

OR   OR

Hang mobiles or other objects in areas where S spends time (crib, chair, play-pen). Encourage S to bat at the hanging objects.

To increase S's arm strength, have him hold his arms outstretched. Provide physical assistance if needed. Gradually increase the length of time he holds his arms out unassisted.

To increase S's shoulder or arm strength, have him move his arms under water (in a swimming pool or tub).

To develop S's shoulder movements, have him swing his arms forward and back, then sideways and back. At first you raise S's arm, then let it swing. Prompt S to control this movement (i.e., to move his arm slowly). Also, prompt S to raise his arm in a controlled manner rather than just swinging it upward. Gradually have S swing his arms more slowly as he learns to control his motions.

Part 4:

Place S on his side, and position the object just out of his reach. As S starts to reach, gently push his back or pull his arm to cause him to roll forward onto his stomach to reach the object. Gradually fade your guidance as S learns that he must shift his weight to contact the object.

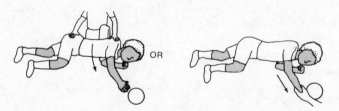

OR

To develop S's balance as he shifts forward, tip S slightly forward by holding his shoulder and rocking him forward and back gently. Practice this movement from all positions (in a chair, sitting on the floor, lying on his stomach over a bolster, on his side, on his back). Reinforce S when he performs more of the movement on his own. Insure that any shift in position will not cause him to fall over and injure himself.

At first prompt S to extend his arm. Then place the object at his fingertips. Slowly move the object a little farther away so that S has to shift slightly forward to get it. Gradually increase the distance. When S can shift after his arm is already extended, start him from a position where his arm is not already extended. He then must both extend his arm and shift forward to obtain the object.

Grasping Objects

Skill Analysis

Cycle

Skill:

This program develops finger, thumb, and wrist coordination, as well as the strength needed for grasping small, lightweight objects. The child is required to pick up and hold an object without support for a few seconds. He may do this by placing his whole hand over the object with his fingers curled around it, or by grasping the object with his thumb and finger(s). (The size of the object determines which grasp he must use, but both grasps are taught.) However, the program does not develop the arm or hand strength necessary for lifting or holding heavier objects.

Entry Behaviors:

1. When an object contacts his palm, S's fingers automatically curl around it (grasp reflex). However, S's hands should frequently be open and relaxed. If S keeps his hands in a tight fist, consult a physical therapist to determine if this program is appropriate to teach. It may be necessary to use relaxation exercises for S's hands prior to using this program (e.g., rub S's forearm; stroke the back of S's hand and fingertips; or to keep the hand unclenched for periods of time, sew an elastic band to a bean bag and fit this over S's hand so that the bean bag rests in his palm with his fingers curled around it).

2. S voluntarily moves his thumb and fingers in some way. When an object is placed within his reach and range of vision, he may contact it by batting at it with his arms or hands, or by moving his hands and fingers toward the object. However, S is unable to pick up an object placed near his hand. If S is unable to move his thumb, adapt the program, using only Parts 1-4. Use materials S can pick up and hold with his fingers and palm, or support between two fingers.

3. S moves his wrist in some way to bring his hand in contact with the object (e.g., moves his wrist up and down or rotates it). If S is unable to move his wrist, adapt the program by requiring him to grasp an object while support is provided for his arm and wrist.

4. S <u>sees objects</u> placed within his reach and range of vision and <u>visually</u> <u>tracks</u> them if they are moved slowly. If S is visually impaired, he should be able to turn his head toward objects that produce sounds as they are moved slowly within his range of vision. Adapt the program by having S feel the object so he will know where it is in order to grasp it.

5. S <u>responds positively</u> to some kinds of stimuli (e.g., Responding to Social Interaction, Focusing Attention, Making Sounds, or Reaching).

Objective:

When an object is placed within 2-3 inches of his hand, S picks up and <u>grasps</u> the object for 3 seconds. S must initiate his response within 5 seconds of the command and respond correctly 4 out of 5 trials.

<u>grasp</u> = hold the object free of support, either with his whole hand, fingers curled around the object, OR with his thumb and finger(s), depending upon the size of the object.

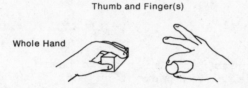

Thumb and Finger(s)

Whole Hand

Cycle:

Each cycle teaches S to grasp with one hand (left or right). Repeat the program for each hand. You may also repeat the program to focus on a particular grasp that is not well developed (e.g., thumb and finger(s) grasp).

Follow-Up:

Continue to have S grasp different objects. Vary the size, shape, and weight of the objects. If one grasp is more difficult for S to learn, increase opportunities for practicing that grasp. Present smaller objects to develop the pincer grasp (thumb and forefinger), and present larger objects for the hand grasp. Gradually increase the length of time S must hold an object. Introduce heavier and larger objects that require two hands. Reinforce when S looks at the object as he holds it, a strategy to develop his eye-hand coordination and attending skills (e.g., Focusing Attention--Objects, Attending to Objects). Position the object farther and farther away to develop S's reaching skills (e.g., Reaching). Then ask S to explore objects by performing simple actions with them (e.g., Manipulating Objects). Label the objects and actions to expand S's vocabulary.

Program for Fine Motor Skill 2

Materials:

Collect a variety of lightweight objects: Hand-size for the hand grasp (cup, ball, doll, toy car, ball of yarn) and smaller than 1 inch in diameter or length for the thumb and finger(s) grasp (blocks, raisins, pencils and crayons, spoons, rattles).

Chart:

None.

GENERAL STRATEGY

Position:

Position S comfortably with support if needed, but leave his wrist and fingers free to move.

Stimulus Event:

Attract S's attention to the object by shaking, sounding, moving it, or touching S with it. Then position it near S's hand as described for the part.

Command:

Give an appropriate command ("GET IT") with cues, and continue the stimulus event to maintain S's interest in the object.

Program
Fine Motor
Skill 2

Latency:

S must initiate his response within 5 seconds of the command.

Correction:

Use Suggestions listed for each part.

Natural Consequence:

Allow S to interact with the object as long as he continues to respond.

Other Trials:

Repeat the strategy. Vary the shape, size, and texture of the objects within the guidelines for each part. Also vary stimulus events. 1 trial = 1 opportunity to perform 1 part. Note: Always have S grasp with the same hand.

Modification:

S has made no gains in average parts completed after two successive probes (2 weeks).

CONDITIONS	BEHAVIOR	CRITERIA
PRE Test *7 only. Position S. Present a stimulus event. Then position an object no more than 2-3 inches from S's hand. Give the command. Present the natural conse-quence. Vary objects so that S must use both the hand grasp and thumb and finger(s) grasp.	*7. Target--when an object is placed within 2-3 inches of his hand, S picks up and grasps it for 3 seconds.	4 correct out of 5 trials

DAILY INSTRUCTION/WEEKLY PROBES

CONDITIONS	BEHAVIOR	CRITERIA
Position S. Present a stimulus event. Then position an object as described for the part, and give the command. Assist if needed. Pre-sent the natural consequence.		Continue daily instruc-tion/weekly probes until S performs *7 correctly 4 out of the last 5 trials
1. Position an object on the surface (table, floor, and the like), directly under S's fingertips. Do not touch his palm since this activates the grasp reflex. Vary the objects, but do not use anything that rolls easily.	1. S <u>curls his fingers</u> around an object placed inside his fingertips. Whole Hand 	at least 5 times
2. Position an object(s) on the surface within 2-3 inches of S's hand. Vary the posi-tion and distance of the object(s) from S's hand. Vary the ob-jects, but do not use anything that rolls easily.	2. S <u>rakes or scoops</u> objects toward him with his fingers. 	at least 5 times
3. Position an object in S's hand. (Object is on a surface with S's hand over it; OR, S's palm is facing up with the object resting in it.) Vary the objects,	3. When an object is placed in his hand, S <u>curls his fingers around it and main-tains a grasp</u> for at least 3 seconds (keeps his fingers curled	at least 5 times

but always use hand-
size ones, preferably
rounded to make it
easier for S to curl
his fingers around
them.

around the object).

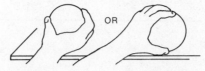

---

4. Position an object on the surface within 2-3 inches of S's hand. Vary the position and distance of the object from S's hand. Vary the objects, but always use ones small enough to fit in S's palm so that he does not have to use his thumb.	4. S <u>picks up and holds an object with his palm and fingers</u> (S does not have to use his thumb). 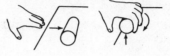	at least 5 times
5. Position an object on the surface within 2-3 inches of S's hand. Vary the position and distance of the object from S's hand. Vary the objects, but always use ones so large that S has to curl his fingers <u>and</u> thumb around them to pick them up (cup).	5. S <u>picks up and holds an object with his palm, fingers, and thumb</u>. 	at least 5 times
6. Position an object on the surface within 2-3 inches of S's hand. Vary the position and distance of the object from S's hand. Vary the objects, but always use ones so small that S uses only his thumb and finger(s) to grasp (1-inch blocks, raisins).	6. S <u>picks up and holds an object with his thumb and finger(s)</u>. 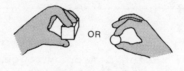	at least 5 times
*7. Position an object on the surface within 2-3 inches of S's hand. Vary the position and distance of the object from S's hand. Vary objects so that S must use both the hand grasp and thumb and finger(s) grasp.	*7. Target--when an object is placed within 2-3 inches of his hand, S picks up and grasps it for 3 seconds.	4 correct out of the last 5 trials
POST 1 Same as PRE	*7. Target--when an object is placed within 2-3 inches of his hand, S picks up and grasps it for 3 seconds.	4 correct out of 5 trials for each test

SUGGESTIONS

Part 1:

Present stimuli for S's fingers. Pull yarn or string across the inside of his fingers or between his fingers. Gradually decrease the time period and amount of stimuli needed before S curls his fingers.

Place your hand over S's wrist and squeeze to cause his fingers to curl. Gradually decrease your pressure.

Use a cylinder or some other object that will roll into S's palm as soon as his fingers touch it or close over it. When S has had practice with several objects that roll, return to materials that do not roll.

To increase strength in hands, fingers, and wrist, guide S to push his hand through water or sand. Gradually decrease your guidance so that S is making more movements on his own. Prompt S to sift through the sand or water and to make grasping motions (extending, curling fingers).

Part 2:

Guide S to move his hand in a raking motion through a pile of objects. Present a variety of objects: styrofoam pieces, marbles, jacks, and the like. Practice with different types of objects, and gradually fade your guidance. When S begins to rake without assistance, present objects such as cotton balls that will not slip through his fingers easily.

Position objects at S's fingertips. Gradually increase the distance so that S must extend his fingers or move his hand farther.

Use objects such as a piece of cloth that can be easily pulled if S moves only one or two fingers. Then present solid objects that require S to use all his fingers to rake the object toward him.

Guide S to make raking motions through finger paints or similar substances that provide tactile stimuli. (Try mixing sand in the paints to make a gritty substance.) Gradually fade your guidance.

Part 3:

Guide S to hold onto the object by placing your hand over his and applying pressure. Gradually decrease the amount of pressure you exert.

Use objects with sticky surfaces (e.g., put double-backed tape on them). Then return to original materials.

To increase the number of times S closes his fingers around the object, use objects S can squeeze (nerf balls, play dough, silly putty, small stuffed balls, bean bags). Then use more solid objects (blocks, cups, hard rubber balls).

Attach a plastic bag filled with rice, cereal, or shaving cream over S's hand. Prompt S to squeeze the material to strengthen muscles needed for a grasp of longer duration.

Part 4:

Hold S's hand at the wrist, then guide him to move his hand to the object to pick it up. Gradually fade your guidance.

Gradually increase the distance the object is placed from S, as well as the direction in which it is placed (forward, to each side, above, and the like). Note that an object placed to the side of S's hand requires wrist rotation to contact it, while one placed in front or above the hand requires elbow and shoulder movements to contact it.

Place a cylindrical block in S's hand with his fingers curled over it. Rotate the block so that S must exert pressure on the block to hold it in place. Guide S if necessary to do this. Gradually fade your guidance.

Part 5:

Place your hand over S's, and guide him to pick up and hold the object. Gradually fade your guidance.

Attach a string to the object. After S makes contact with the object and begins to grasp it, pull on the string. Prompt S to grasp more firmly, using his thumb and fingers.

Part 6:

Guide S to move his thumb and finger(s) together in a pinching motion to select a sticky object (e.g., hard candy). Gradually fade your guidance and provide a variety of objects for S to select.

Use toy clickers. Guide S to push the clicker with his thumb and finger(s) to make noise.

Put tape or a sticky substance (e.g., rubber cement) on the tips of S's thumb and forefinger. Guide S to press and pull his fingers apart. Have S practice this activity to increase the strength of his fingers.

Manipulating Objects

Rate Data

Skill:

This program increases the frequency with which the child spontaneously manipulates objects. Along with practicing his existing motor skills, the child may also perform actions in new combinations and produce new actions, possibly at random. Although the actions are simple (e.g., poking, turning, shaking) and are not necessarily appropriate uses of the object, this experimentation is important for learning how objects can be used, a cognitive, as well as a motor, skill.

Entry Behaviors:

1. S responds to stimuli and can briefly focus his attention on his environment (e.g., Responding to Social Interaction, Focusing Attention--Objects, and/or Attending to Objects). Although S does emit some responses, he usually sits unoccupied or wanders when unattended, even when surrounded by a variety of toys or other objects. If S is visually impaired, it is very important to reinforce S's exploration of his environment. Concentrate on stimulus events containing tactile, kinesthetic, and auditory cues, and have S feel your hands as they manipulate the object (no adaptations required).

2. S has some arm and hand movements that allow him to contact and manipulate an object (e.g., Grasping Objects and Reaching). Although S may occasionally contact an object, he does this infrequently and rarely uses objects appropriately on his own. If S has limited arm and hand movements, insure that the objects are appropriate to his ability and are within his reach. The Basic Motor Actions Chart, page 453, suggests actions and materials that may be expanded to be more appropriate to S.

Objective:

During social interactions providing stimuli with objects, S manipulates the objects in some way without physical guidance. S makes at least 20 separate responses, including at least five different actions, anytime during a 10-minute session.

manipulate = perform an action with the object (see the Basic Motor Actions Chart for suggestions). Each action and/or episode is counted separately (e.g., if S pokes, then bangs a toy car twice, this counts as three separate responses). The responses should be deliberate, not uncontrolled (e.g., if S continually moves one arm and happens to push a ball that is placed next to that arm, this is not counted; however, if S must move toward the ball before pushing it, this response counts). Do not count destructive or unacceptable social behavior.

Cycle:

None specified. However, you may repeat the program to increase the number of
different responses S produces. If you would like to work on eye-hand coordination, you may repeat the program and require S to look at the object as he
manipulates it.

Follow-Up:

Continue to reinforce S's manipulation of different objects. Always have a
variety available when he must amuse himself. Prompt him to look at the object
as he manipulates it. As S spontaneously interacts with toys more frequently,
give a standard command to indicate the onset of free time and help S begin, a
strategy introducing the command Play in Following Cued Commands.

Whenever S performs some action with an object, prompt him to watch as you
imitate him, then guide him to perform the action again. This interaction
introduces S to imitation, a skill more fully developed in Responding to and
Repeating Teacher Model, as well as Imitating Actions.

As S's fine motor coordination improves, present objects with fitted parts, an
introduction to Placing In/On. Collect a variety of functional objects that S
may play with and explore. While S experiments (plays) with these objects,
demonstrate their use.

Program for Fine Motor Skill 3

Materials:

Collect a variety of toys or other stimulus objects with duplicates as needed (see Stimulus Event).

Chart:

Basic Motor Actions Chart, page 453.

GENERAL STRATEGY

Stimulus Event:

Select one toy and perform some action with it as a stimulus. During this event, demonstrate possible actions with the toy, describe what you are doing ("Look, I'm pulling"), and prompt S to respond (place his hand on the object). Do NOT guide S to complete the response. Continue presenting different objects and events for 10 minutes, and change stimuli frequently. Anytime S manipulates an object on his own, imitate him. You may need a duplicate object available if you cannot use a particular object at the same time.

Latency:

S may respond anytime during the 10-minute session.

Correction:

Anytime S is not responding, guide him to perform an action. Then go on to a new activity.

Modification:

S has not met step criterion after four sessions.

	CONDITIONS	BEHAVIOR	CRITERIA
		S manipulates an object...	during a 10-minute session
PRE	Present a stimulus event. Continue to present different objects and events.	unassisted	20 responses, including 5 different ones
S/1	Present a stimulus event. Correct if needed, then begin another event.	"	any 5 responses
S/2	"	"	10 responses, 2 different actions
S/3	"	"	10 responses, 3 different actions
S/4	"	"	10 responses, 4 different actions
S/5	"	"	10 responses, 5 different actions
S/6	"	"	15 responses, 5 different actions
S/7	"	"	20 responses, 5 different actions
POST 1	Same as PRE	unassisted	20 responses, 5 different actions for each test
POST 2	New Objects		
POST 3	New Teacher		

MODIFICATIONS

If S responds infrequently, add steps before S/1 to review basic arm and hand movements. During each session, present basic stimulus activities from the Stimulus Chart, page 467. Gradually increase the rate of any arm and hand movements, and note how often S produces a response meeting the definition of manipulate. When S manipulates an object at least three to five times during each session for a week, begin again at S/1. However, before each session, provide stimuli for a few minutes. Do this throughout the program if needed.

Placing In/On

Chain

Cycle

Overview
Fine Motor
Skill 4

Skill:

This program shapes a chain of motor responses required to: grasp an object, move it to another position, and place it in a container. This skill requires fine motor coordination and enables S to increase the appropriate use of a larger number of objects.

Entry Behaviors:

1. S grasps, picks up, and manipulates objects in some way (e.g., Grasping Objects, Manipulating Objects). Although S manipulates objects in random or nondirected ways (banging, poking, shaking, pulling), he demonstrates little appropriate use of toys or objects that require some precision to fit parts together. If S cannot perform simple manipulations, review the basic skills of grasping, squeezing, rotating the wrist, as well as other actions in the Basic Motor Actions Chart, page 453, for Manipulating Objects. In addition, consider teaching the command "PUT IT HERE" in Following Cued Commands to place and release an object without the requirement that it be fitted into place. If S has an impaired grasp, adapt by redefining grasp to use adaptive devices to secure the object. If S has an impaired release, use materials that stick together once fitted (e.g., bristle blocks).

2. S sees the container or place in which the object goes. Or, adapt by allowing S to feel the target instead of looking at it. Note that materials used with the visually impaired should have the necessary tactile boundaries. Without these boundaries, some cycles of the program will be nonfunctional for that child.

Objective:

S fits an object in or on a specific target. S must initiate his response within 5 seconds of the command and respond correctly 4 out of 5 trials.

fit = adjust as needed to put the object competely within the container; OR put the object at least 3/4 of the way on a target defined by a flat marked surface.

object = a small, easily held item that S can grasp.

target = an area or a container that is large enough to contain the object in only one position and that is delineated by sides, rims, edges, or by outlines, cutout shapes, or other flat boundaries. The target is clearly indicated by the teacher.

Note: The intent of this program is the motor skill of fitting, not the cognitive skill of selecting the appropriate target.

Cycle:

This program is repeated, using different sets of materials of increasing difficulty. Record the objects S can place or fit for the following sets:

Set 1: Individual containers--the container will hold one object which requires little adjustment (e.g., soap in soapdish, spoon in silverware tray, plastic bowl in a larger bowl, sandwich in sandwich box).

Set 2: Marked surfaces--a card or other flat surface marked with the exact shape of the object to be placed on it (e.g., a 1-inch cube is placed on a card with a 1-inch square drawn on it).

Note: Set 2 introduces the use of standard materials in Cognitive Skills 5 through 11.

Set 3: Fitted containers--the container will hold the object in only one position (e.g., key in lock, plastic ring on ring-stack pole, toothbrush in toothbrush rack, puzzle piece in puzzle, plastic cup in identical cup, coin in piggybank, soda bottle in carton).

The sets are taught in order, although Set 2 may be omitted if there is no immediate use for the skill. During any one cycle, materials may be varied to include similar items from the same set. Any set or cycle may be repeated with new materials.

Follow-Up:

Continue to develop S's fine motor coordination by presenting smaller and smaller objects that are more difficult to fit together. Combine with matching and visual discrimination skills that require S to select the correct container, such as finding the correct puzzle part by fitting several different ones. Although there are many toys that are readily available and can be used with this program, focus on functional objects that require coordination, especially with older students. In addition, develop teaching materials that use marked surfaces that cue the placement of objects for other tasks. For example, to teach S to set a table, make plastic place mats with the outline shapes of the forks, knives, spoons, plates, and cups to cue each placement.

Program for Fine Motor Skill 4

Materials:

Collect objects, targets, and containers appropriate to the materials set to be taught.

Chart:

None.

GENERAL STRATEGY

Arrangement:

Position the target and the object in front of S within his reach.

Attention:

Draw S's attention to the target, and hand him the object, or position it for him to pick up.

Command:

Give an appropriate command to place the object ("S, PUT____ IN/ON____"), with cues indicating the correct target (e.g., point to the target, tap it).

Latency:

S must initiate his response within 5 seconds of the command (or last part completed).

Correction:

Use general correction or Suggestions on any part that S does not perform correctly. After you assist him, allow him to continue the trial on his own. Correct him only if needed.

Natural Consequence:

Perform an appropriate activity with the materials. Note that 1 trial = fitting 1 object.

Other Trials:

Repeat Trial 1 strategy as often as appropriate. Vary the use of similar materials of the same set. You may set up the situations to practice the skill if desired.

Modification:

S has made no gains in average parts completed after two successive probes (2 weeks).

CONDITIONS	BEHAVIOR	CRITERIA
		for *7 only
PRE Get S's attention, and give the command. Present the natural consequence.	*7. Target--S fits the object unassisted.	4 correct out of 5 trials

DAILY INSTRUCTION/WEEKLY PROBES

Get S's attention, and give the command. Correct each part if needed. Present the natural consequence.	1. S grasps the object that you bring to his hand.	Continue daily instruction/weekly probes until S performs *7 correctly 4 out of the last 5 trials
	2. S looks at the target indicated (may occur anytime prior to Part 4).	
	3. S brings the object directly over the target.	
	4. S lowers the object, touching the target.	
	5. S turns the object and and target as needed to fit the object in/on.	
	6. S releases the object, leaving it correctly placed.	
	*7. Target--S fits the object unassisted.	
POST 1 Same as PRE	*7. Target--S fits the object unassisted.	4 correct out of 5 trials for each test
POST 2 New Materials (same set)		
POST 3 New Setting		

SUGGESTIONS

Part 1:

Note: A refusal to grasp is often a behavioral rather than skill problem. Use reinforcement to increase S's task behavior.

Begin with large objects that S can grasp easily. Gradually present smaller objects of the same materials set.

Request S to grasp objects. Put a sticky substance (e.g., adhesive tape) on the objects to be held (See Suggestions in Grasping Objects).

Part 2:

Prompt S to trace the edges or boundaries of the target. Do this before each trial. Gradually decrease the use of exploration as a cue.

If S frequently looks away from the target while trying to position the object, remind or guide him to look. Reinforce all appropriate attending. Gradually fade the reinforcement so that S attends on his own. Gradually fade your reminders and guidance.

Part 3:

If S has a poor aim, at first bring his hand very close to the target (within 1 inch). Gradually shape his aim by extending the distance he is required to bring the object.

Prompt S to practice eye-hand coordination activities. Have S follow with his eyes (track) as you slowly guide his hand to a specific target.

Move the target to S's hand, which is already holding the object. Gradually move the target less to increase the distance S must move the object to touch the target.

Part 4:

Require S to look at and touch small targets, but do not require him to hold an object. After this practice, return to the original part.

Combine with Part 3 to shape the aim-touch response. Gradually require greater precision (smaller targets) and greater distance.

Part 5:

Require S to look at the target (See Suggestions for Part 2).

Reinforce when S works slowly and makes continued attempts. Gradually fade the amount of guidance and reinforcement required.

Provide assistance: nearly fit the object, but allow S to finish the task. Gradually perform less of the task so that S completes more of it.

Have S work on easier, then more difficult, tasks. Gradually fade the difference between the size of the object and the target until they are almost the same size. Specifically for Set 2, use the following:

Object	Target
1" cube	large--all black 3" x 5" index card
	smaller--3" x 5" card with 2" x 4" black rectangle
	smaller--3" x 5" card with 2" x 2" black square
	exact--3" x 5" card with 1" x 1" black square
	(The size of the black part may be changed even more gradually.)

Part 6:

Hold the object in place; then gradually fade your pressure as S gains precision. Prompt S to move very slowly to prevent jostling the materials.

Give verbal cues or guide S to release carefully. Gradually fade your guidance and reminders.

Controlling
Head
Movements

Skill Analysis

Skill:

This program provides the child with a variety of activities that will strengthen his neck and upper shoulder muscles and prompt him to move his head in different directions. This head control is needed to develop trunk control and mobility.

Entry Behaviors:

1. S exhibits <u>some voluntary responses</u>, such as eye movements or reaching. However, S must be propped or supported most of the time to prevent his head from dropping forward, backward, or to the sides. Select stimulus events that are commensurate with S's abilities and that he is known to respond to.

2. S has the <u>necessary physiological capacity for moving his head</u>. If you are not sure if S is able to move his head, consult a physical therapist before you begin this program.

Objective:

When sitting with his shoulders supported, S lifts his head and maintains or regains an erect head position for 1 minute when tipped in any direction. S must initiate his response within 5 seconds and respond correctly 4 out of 5 trials.

Cycle:

None specified.

Follow-Up:

Place S in a variety of situations and positions where he must hold his head up. Increase the time that he must hold his head up. Gradually give S's shoulders less support when he is in a sitting position in order to develop more balance and trunk control for Sitting. Gradually increase the distance S raises his head when lying on his stomach so that he develops arm strength to push up and support his weight on his forearms, a skill to be developed in Crawling on Stomach and Crawling on Hands and Knees. Prompt S to use head movements in other tasks. For example, call S or manipulate an object, and have him turn to see what is happening, an introduction to Attending to Voice and Attending to Objects. Prompt S to look down at his hands (a controlled movement, not lag), and then turn his head to continue to look as he reaches, or as you move his hands, an introduction to better fine motor coordination and aim required for Reaching.

Program for Gross Motor Skill 1

Chart:

Stimulus Chart, page 467.

GENERAL STRATEGY

Position:

Set up a play situation with a variety of toys S prefers. S always has support at his back, sides, and shoulders (propped with pillows or similar objects).

Stimulus Event:

Hold a toy in S's sight. Then move it so that he can see it only if he lifts or maintains an erect head position. Attract S's attention to the object, and tell him to lift or hold up his head. Cue S to reach for it while you hold it above his head or at his side. Continue the stimulus event up to 30 seconds.

Latency:

S has 5 seconds to move his head (Parts 1, 2, 3, 4, 5, 6, 7) and, once his head is up, he must keep it up for the criterion time (Parts 3, 4, 6, 7).

Correction:

Use Suggestions for each part.

Other Trials:

Vary the stimulus event. 1 trial = 1 opportunity to perform 1 part.

Modification:

S has made no gains in <u>average parts completed</u> after two successive probes (2 weeks).

CONDITIONS	BEHAVIOR	CRITERIA
PRE Test *7 only. Position S, and present the stimulus event. During the event, engage S in activities that cause him to change his center of gravity (e.g., reaching, turning, moving); OR tip S slightly sideways, backward, and forward.	*7. Target--S lifts his head and maintains or regains an erect head position for 1 minute when tipped in any direction--unassisted.	4 correct out of 5 trials

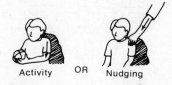

Activity   OR   Nudging

DAILY INSTRUCTION/WEEKLY PROBES

Place S in a position described for the part. Present the stimulus event. Assist if needed.

Continue daily instruction/weekly probes until S performs *7 correctly 4 out of the last 5 trials

1. Position S on his back.

1. S <u>turns his head from side to side</u> when lying on his back.

at least 5 times

Topview

---

2. Position S on a cushion roll to support his chest so that he is at a 45° angle but his head is down (fore-arms resting on floor).

2. S <u>lifts his head up</u> while on his stomach with chest raised and supported.

at least 5 times

Supported at the Chest

---

3. Position S on his stomach with his weight on his fore-arms. If necessary, you may support S at the shoulders.

3. S <u>lifts his head up and turns it</u> from side to side while on his stomach and leaning on his forearms (keeps head erect for 1 minute).

at least 5 times

---

4. Position S on his back. <u>Slowly</u> pull S into a sitting posi-tion by pulling him in a circle sideways, then up, never straightforward. (Work on this part only after S exhibits some head control.)

4. S <u>keeps his head in line with his body</u> (no head lag) when pulled up.

at least 5 times

<u>Note:</u> This skill is not required to meet the target but is in-cluded as an appropriate skill to work on at this time.

3-to-5 Seconds Only during Pulling

---

5. Position S in an erect sitting position with support at his upper chest, sides, and back if needed. (His head lags forward, to the side, or back).

5. S <u>lifts his head while in a supported sitting position.</u>

at least 5 times

From the Front   From the Side
or Back

6. Same as Part 5.	6. S <u>lifts and turns his head from side to side while in a supported sitting position</u> (keeps head erect for 1 minute).	at least 5 times
*7. Position S in a sitting position. After S lifts his head, tip him gently sideways, backward and forward, or engage him in activities that cause him to move naturally in these ways.	*7. Target--S lifts his head and maintains or regains an erect head position for 1 minute when tipped in any direction--unassisted (keeps head erect for 1 minute).	4 correct out of the last 5 trials
POST 1 Same as PRE	*7. Target--S lifts his head and maintains or regains an erect head position for 1 minute when tipped in any direction--unassisted.	4 correct out of 5 trials for each test
POST 2 New Teacher		
POST 3 New Setting		

SUGGESTIONS

Part 1:

Guide S to turn his head. Hold S's head between your hands, or gently push one side of S's head toward the desired direction. Gradually fade the pressure used.

Part 2:

Raise S's head by putting pressure on his forehead or chin. Or, use a chinstrap. Fade this pressure and guidance gradually.

Chinstrap

Guidance—You May Use His Shoulder for Leverage

Gradually increase the distance S lifts his head. At first place the toy where S barely has to lift his head to see it. Gradually hold the toy higher so that S raises his head higher.

Position S on his stomach on a large beach ball with his arms bent under his chest. (Stabilize the ball against the wall or have another person help.) Cue him to raise his head by rolling the ball. After he can raise his head with this kind of stimulus, return to the original position for the part.

Position S on a wedge that raises his chest and slants down to his feet. After S can lift his head in this position, use the original position.

Part 3:

Guide S to turn his head. Gradually fade your guidance, and increase the distance S can turn his head while continuing to center it between his shoulders.

Use a wedge or cushion roll as described in Part 2. After S can turn his head in that position, decrease the size of the support until S is on his forearms with you holding his shoulders if needed.

Part 4:

Note: Always pull S in a circular motion toward one side, never directly forward.

Position S on his back on a wedge so that he has less distance to come when you pull him. Gradually increase the distance by using a smaller wedge or pillow until he is pulled up from the floor.

Put your hand behind S's head to catch him if he falls back. Fade the pressure you use to help him regain his head position.

Place S in an upright position. Tip him back slightly, and catch him if necessary. Then pull him back upright. Gradually increase the distance you tip him and the pressure you exert.

Part 5:

Gradually increase the distance S can lift his head unassisted.

Place one hand on each of S's shoulders, and push his shoulders back. This will cause S's head to raise slightly. Then lift his chin the rest of the way. Fade your guidance gradually.

Part 6:

By moving S's arms (straightening, lifting, or lowering the shoulders; or moving his arms up and out), you can help S to balance his head. (S must already exhibit some head control for this to be of assistance.) Gradually fade the use of these additional movements.

Gradually increase the amount of time S can raise his head and look forward; then work on turning his head.

Guide S to turn. Gradually fade the assistance. At first hold S's head in your hands. Then place only one hand under his chin. Next push on his cheek with one hand or finger. Finally provide no assistance. Or, use a chinstrap, and fade the support you provide.

Part 7:

Increase the length of time S can maintain an erect head position when not tipped.

At first move S's shoulders only slightly. Gradually increase the forcefulness of your movements to increase the distance he is pushed off balance.

Support S's head if he loses control. But gradually decrease the pressure you exert to assist him in regaining an erect head position.

Sitting

Skill Analysis

Skill:

This program contains a variety of activities to develop the neck and shoulder muscles, trunk control, and balance needed to remain sitting upright. The muscle strength and coordination developed here are also needed when the child learns to sit up, crawl, stand, and walk.

Entry Behaviors:

1. S <u>controls his head movements</u> to lift his head and maintains an erect head position while sitting with support for his back and shoulders (e.g., Controlling Head Movements). However, S needs support to sit upright (pillows at his back and side, someone holding his shoulders, and the like). Note that this program teaches S to <u>maintain</u> a sitting position; for moving into a sitting position, see Sitting Up.

2. S <u>uses his arms</u> to bear weight for balance and support. If it is questionable whether S has this ability, consult a physical therapist. It is possible for S to balance without using his arms; however, this requires more trunk control. In this program the use of arms is recommended but not required.

Overview
Gross Motor
Skill 2

Objective:

When placed in a sitting position (on the floor), S sits for 1 minute, using his hands <u>if needed</u> for support and balance when he falls or leans forward and sideways. S must initiate his response immediately and respond correctly 4 out of 5 trials.

<u>if needed</u> = S may either support his trunk weight with his hands and arms, OR he may use only his trunk muscles to prevent himself from falling.

<u>Note</u>: In this program, S learns to support his weight as it shifts forward and sideways. He is not required to maintain or regain a sitting position if his weight has shifted backward since that skill is more difficult. That skill is taught in Sitting Up, where the child learns to push and pull up from the floor into a sitting position.

Cycle:

None specified. However, you may repeat the program to teach a specific sitting position. Do this if S can sit in one or two positions but has great difficulty in another one that is appropriate to his needs.

Follow-Up:

Place S in a variety of situations where he must sit unsupported for longer
periods of time. Position S on rocking boards or other tilting objects (swings,
rocking horse, rocking chair) where he must hold on and work harder to maintain
his balance. Seat S in a chair without arms. Require him to sit unsupported for
a variety of activities (watching television, eating). To introduce Sitting Up,
encourage S to get up from a lying position. To begin work on Standing and
Standing Up, teach S to sit with his feet tucked beneath him. Encourage him to
pull from a tucked sitting position to a kneeling position. As a preparation
for Crawling on Hands and Knees, assist S to move from a tucked sitting position
to a crawl position.

Tucked Position

Crawl Position

Kneeling Position

Program for Gross Motor Skill 2

Chart:

None specified.

GENERAL STRATEGY

Position:

Set up a play situation with a variety of toys S prefers. Position S in a sitting position on the floor, and provide support as specified for the part.
Always place S's hands on the floor either in front of him or to either side to
allow him to support his weight with his hands.

Legs Crossed   '4' Shape   'V' Shape   Legs Bent

Avoid any position where S's knees are turned in or his back is very rounded.

Stimulus Event:

Provide a stimulus for S to remain sitting. For example, talk to S, hold up a
toy in his sight, or place it on the floor near him. Attract his attention to
it. Continue the event up to 30 seconds. Whenever possible, sit in front of S
during the event.

Latency:

S must initiate his response immediately to maintain his balance.

Correction:

Use Suggestions listed for each part.

Other Trials:

Vary the stimulus event. Present trials throughout the day rather than consecutively. 1 trial = 1 opportunity to perform 1 part.

Modification:

S has made no gains in <u>average parts completed</u> after two successive probes (2
weeks).

CONDITIONS	BEHAVIOR	CRITERIA
PRE Test *8 only. Place S in a sitting position. Present the stimulus event for S to reach forward and to his sides to obtain an object; OR gently tip S forward and sideways to require him to use his hands for support and balance.	*8. Target--S sits for 1 minute using his hands as needed for support and balance when he falls or leans forward and sideways. 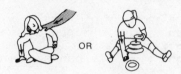 Nudged OR Learning (to Reach)	4 correct out of 5 trials

DAILY INSTRUCTION/WEEKLY PROBES

Place S in a sitting position. Provide support at his shoulders.		Continue daily instruction/weekly probes until S performs *8 correctly 4 out of the last 5 trials
1. Place S in a sitting position. Provide support at his shoulders.	1. S <u>sits for 1 minute with his head erect when supported at the shoulders.</u>	at least 5 times
2. Place S in a sitting position. Provide support at his waist.	2. S <u>sits for 1 minute with his head and trunk erect when supported at the waist.</u> OR Towel	at least 5 times
3. Place S in a sitting position. Provide support at his hips.	3. S <u>sits for 1 minute with his head and</u>	at least 5 times

trunk erect when
supported at the hips.

OR

Booster Chair

| 4. | Place S in a sitting position with a bar, handle, or similar object that he can hold onto; or hold out your hands for S to grasp in the front or to the side). | 4. | S sits for 1 minute with his head and trunk erect while holding onto something. | at least 5 times |

S Holds a Stationary Object

OR

S Grasps Your Hands

| 5. | Place S in a sitting position. | 5. | S sits for 1 minute, using his hands as needed for support (see drawings under Position in General Strategy). | at least 5 times |

| 6. | Place S in a sitting position. Provide a stimulus to reach forward; or gently tip him forward so that he uses his hands to catch his weight. | 6. | S sits for 1 minute, using his hands as needed to catch his weight when he falls or leans forward. | at least 5 times |

Reaching

OR

Nudged

| 7. | Place S in a sitting position. Provide a stimulus to reach sideways; or gently tip him sideways so that he uses his hands to catch his weight. | 7. | S sits for 1 minute, using his hands as needed to catch his weight when he falls or leans sideways. | at least 5 times |

*8. Place S in a sitting position. Provide a stimulus to reach sideways and forward; or gently nudge him in these directions.	*8. Target--S sits for 1 minute, using his hands as needed for support and balance when he falls or leans forward and sideways.	4 correct out of the last 5 trials
POST 1 Same as PRE	*8. Target--S sits for 1 minute, using his hands as needed for support and balance when he falls or leans forward and sideways.	4 correct out of 5 trials for each test
POST 2 New Teacher		
POST 3 New Setting		

SUGGESTIONS

Part 1:

Move S's arms and shoulders as necessary (pushing back, pulling forward, straightening, lifting, and lowering) to assist him to keep his head erect. Fade this extra assistance gradually.

Have someone else hold S's head erect by placing pressure on his forehead or chin. Fade this guidance gradually.

Support S's trunk from his hips to his shoulders (with pillows or similar objects). Gradually remove the extra props until you are holding him just at his shoulders.

Part 2:

Provide S with more support by holding him firmly around his chest, under the arms. Gradually reduce the pressure and support until you hold him just at the waist.

Give S support by wrapping a wide towel around his chest, and by holding the ends of the towel behind him. Gradually reduce the amount of support until the towel is just at his waist.

Part 3:

Sit close behind S with your legs straddling him. Give support by holding his hip and thigh area. Gradually reduce the amount of support until you hold him only at the hips.

Prop pillows around S at his buttocks and sides. Hold the pillows firmly against
S's hips. Gradually reduce the amount of pressure until S is supported only at
his hips.

Use a seat belt or cloth strapped around S to hold him in a booster chair.
Loosen the seat belt or cloth gradually to fade the use of the support.

Part 4:

Hold S's arms at the elbows to provide more support. Gradually move your hands
down his arms until finally he is grasping your hands or thumbs. (You are not
helping him to grasp.)

Place S's hands on a bar, chair seat, or other sturdy object that does not tip
and is easy to grasp. Place your hands over his, and gradually reduce the amount
of pressure until he can hold alone.

Part 5:

Assist S to place his hands flat on the floor. Place your hands over S's to
keep them steady. Or, grasp his arms below the elbow, and push down to keep
S's hands flat on the floor. Gradually exert less pressure until S can support
his weight on his own.

Gradually lower the support used in Part 4 so that S is no longer hanging on but
rather is supporting his own weight. Use boxes of varying heights so that S
gradually supports more of his body weight.

Parts 6 and 8:

Position S on his stomach over the top of a large ball so that his feet and arms
do not touch the floor. (The ball must be large, such as 3 feet in diameter.)
Roll the ball forward so that S must reach out with his hand(s) to catch his
weight. Continue to roll it back and forth, and physically assist S to catch
his weight. Gradually fade your guidance. When S can catch his weight this
way, return to the original position.

Gently tip S forward, then grasp his arms. Guide S to move his hands from the
side to place them flat on the floor in front of him. (You may want to sit with
S between your legs.) Gradually fade the amount of assistance you provide.

Gradually increase the forcefulness with which you nudge S or the distance that
he must lean forward to get the toy.

Place cushions under S's arms to catch part of his fall. Push him gently forward.
Reduce the size of the pillows so that S will fall forward a greater distance
until he can catch his weight without any props.

Parts 7 and 8:

Gently tip S sideways, then grasp his arm on the side that is falling toward the floor
Place that hand flat on the floor to catch his weight. Gradually increase the
forcefulness with which you push. When necessary, push S's opposite knee or
leg slightly up in the air. Fade your guidance gradually.

Have S practice on a rocking board. Rock S back and forth. Guide if necessary,
and fade this assistance.

Crawling on Stomach

Skill Analysis

Skill:

In this program the child develops the muscle strength and coordination necessary to move forward on his stomach, using his arms and legs. From this skill he develops the ability to creep on his hands and knees and eventually, to walk upright.

Entry Behaviors:

1. S exhibits <u>head control</u> in a variety of ways. For example, he can keep his head erect for at least one minute, turn it from side to side while sitting, lift his head for a few seconds while he lies on his stomach, and keep his head in line with his body while being pulled up to a sitting position from lying down (e.g., Controlling Head Movements).

2. S has <u>some arm strength</u> and can support his weight on his forearms for a few seconds while lying on his stomach. However, his arm and shoulder muscles are not strong enough for him to maintain the position any longer.

3. S has <u>purposeful movements</u>. For example, he reaches for familiar people or toys; rolls over from back to stomach or stomach to back; and kicks and wiggles as if to move toward something he wants, although he cannot propel himself for any distance. If S's arms or legs are impaired, reconsider teaching this program. Consult a physical therapist to determine a more appropriate skill to teach at this time. (Some children learn to stand and walk without crawling because leg braces make crawling impossible.)

Objective:

S crawls forward 5 feet on his stomach unassisted. S must initiate his response within 5 seconds of the command and respond correctly 4 out of 5 trials.

<u>Note</u>: Reciprocal arm and leg movements (moves arm on one side with opposite leg, then alternates) are not required for S to pass this program. He must simply move his arms and legs to crawl. However, the alternation of arms and legs is a skill necessary for the child to learn in order to crawl on hands and knees and then to walk. Therefore, exercises are included in this program to develop the alternation of arm and leg movements.

Cycle:

None specified.

Follow-Up:

Provide S with a variety of opportunities to crawl, and increase the distance
you require him to crawl. Provide him with different reasons for wanting to
move (e.g., to get a toy, to come to you). Place toys at his side or behind
him so that S learns to move his body around and then crawl. Place him on
his hands and knees (with support) to prepare him for learning to creep (e.g.,
Crawling on Hands and Knees). Hold S in a standing position frequently to
assist him in developing the muscle strength and coordination needed for
Standing and Walking.

Program for Gross Motor Skill 3

Chart:

None

GENERAL STRATEGY

Position:

Always position S on his stomach, leaning on his forearms.

Stimulus Event:

Attract S's attention, and provide him with a reason for moving into the desired position (hold up a toy, move away from him).

Command:

Give an appropriate command ("LOOK AT ME"... "COME GET THE TOY") with cues, and continue the stimulus event to attract S's attention.

Latency:

S must initiate his response within 5 seconds of the command.

Correction:

Use Suggestions listed for each part.

Natural Consequence:

Allow S to interact with you and the toy as long as he continues to respond.

Other Trials:

Repeat the strategy. Vary the objects and the stimulus events. Present trials throughout the day rather than consecutively. 1 trial = 1 opportunity to perform 1 part.

Modification:

S has made no gains in average parts completed after two successive probes (2 weeks).

CONDITIONS	BEHAVIOR	CRITERIA
PRE Test *6 only. Position S, and present the stimulus event. Give the command. Continue the stimulus event. Present the natural consequence.	*6. Target--S crawls forward 5 feet on his stomach unassisted.	4 correct out of 5 trials

DAILY INSTRUCTION/WEEKLY PROBES

Position S (always on his forearms). Present the stimulus event. Give the command. Continue the stimulus event. Assist if needed. Present the natural consequence.
Note: S must be able to lift his head and keep it erect for each part.

Continue daily instruction/weekly probes until S performs *6 correctly 4 out of the last 5 trials

---

1. Provide stimuli so that S continues to support his weight on his forearms to maintain his position.

1. S supports his weight on his forearms (chest on floor) for 1 minute.

at least 5 times

---

2. Provide stimuli so that S raises his chest and straightens his arms (e.g., hold a toy at eye level, and move it above S's head so that he raises his head to see it, thus raising his chest and arms).

2. S straightens his arms and raises his chest to support his weight on his hands for 1 minute.

at least 5 times

---

3. Provide stimuli so that S reaches forward (e.g., place a toy just out of reach in front of S's arm). Repeat for the other arm. Give trials for each arm alternately.

3. S scoots slightly forward by reaching.

at least 5 times for each arm

---

4. Provide stimuli so that S moves forward. S will scoot forward by alternating his arms.

4. S pulls himself forward about 2 feet, using his arms (pull first with one arm, then the other; OR pull with both arms at once).

at least 5 times

---

5. Provide stimuli so that S moves forward at least 2 feet. S will push himself forward with his feet. (Tap his feet as a cue to get him started.) Assist S to move his arms only if necessary.

5. S pushes himself forward about 2 feet, using his legs.

at least 5 times

---

*6. Provide stimuli for S to move forward at least 5 feet, using his arms and legs.

*6. Target--S crawls forward 5 feet on his stomach unassisted.

4 correct out of the last 5 trials

POST 1 Same as PRE	*6. Target--S crawls for-ward 5 feet on his stomach unassisted.	4 correct out of 5 trials for each test

POST 2 New Setting

POST 3 New Setting (different from POST 2)

SUGGESTIONS

Part 1:

Place S on his stomach, leaning on his forearms at a slight elevation (cushion roll, wedge, or similar object) to help support his chest. Gradually decrease the height of the elevation, and increase the amount of time S can support his weight.

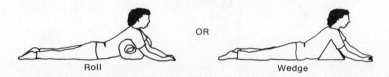

Hold S's forearms firmly to assist him to keep his balance. Gradually apply less pressure until S can support his weight unassisted.

Position yourself behind or beside S and hold his shoulders. Pull them back slightly so that S will be bearing less weight on his forearms. Gradually fade your guidance.

Part 2:

Guide S to raise his chest off the floor by holding and supporting his arms at the elbow and straightening them. (Insure that S's hands are flat on the floor.) Hold S's arms in this position, and gradually fade your guidance until S is able to support his weight unassisted.

Hold S's shoulders and pull them up and back to raise S's chest off the floor, thus straightening his arms. Hold him in this position. Gradually decrease the amount of support you provide until S can raise himself and keep the position unassisted.

Position yourself behind or beside S and place your hands under his chest. Pull S's body up, causing him to straighten his arms. Hold him in this position. Gradually decrease the amount of support you provide until S can raise himself and maintain the position unassisted.

Place S over a cushion wedge large enough for him to straighten his arms and support his weight. Assist S to keep his arms straight. Decrease the size of the wedge so that he must push himself higher to straighten his arms. Gradually remove your guidance.

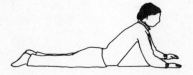
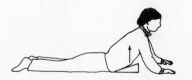

191

Place S on his stomach, leaning on his forearms over a small cushion wedge. Stroke S's back from the neck down to provide a stimulus to raise his head, arch his back, and straighten his arms. Stroke his legs or feet also. Then remove the wedge, and try this exercise without it.

If S is small enough, try this exercise for strengthening the back and neck muscles. Hold S out from you with one hand on his chest and one on his legs. Hold him in this position. Or, slowly move S back and forth to prompt him to arch his back, lift his head, and wiggle his arms.

Hold S as previously described. Place him over the floor, a table, or a large beach ball so that his arms are touching the surface. Lower S and prompt him to push against the surface to support his weight on straightened arms.

Part 3:

Give S practice in reaching by placing him over your lap. Hold a toy slightly in front of S above his eye level. Prompt S to reach for the toy, arch his back, and lift his head and shoulders.

Place the toy right at S's fingertips so that he must move his arm only slightly to contact the toy. Gradually place the toy farther away so that he must move his arm more to reach the toy.

Guide S to move his arm forward to reach a toy. Do this exercise with each arm. Gradually fade your guidance.

Pull S's Hands   OR   Pull Forearms   OR   Move Shoulders

Place S on his stomach over a cushion roll. Put a toy in front of S. Roll the cushion slightly forward to move him closer to the toy. Once S imitates using his arms to reach for the toy, roll the cushion less. Then require S to roll the cushion himself as he reaches.

Part 4:

Guide S to use his arms to pull his body forward. Alternate arms. Gradually fade your guidance and increase the distance S must move without your guidance. Position yourself behind S, then lift his shoulder and move it forward. Do the same with the other shoulder. Repeat until S reaches the toy.

Position yourself in front of S. Grasp his arm, and move it forward. Repeat with his other arm. Continue until he reaches the toy. Gradually fade your guidance.

Position S on his stomach, on his forearms. Position yourself in front of S, and grasp his hands. Scoot or lift one of S's arms, and pull it forward. Repeat with his other arm. Gradually decrease your assistance until S is holding your hands but pulling himself forward.

To build arm strength, place S on his forearms over a wedge slanting downward. Place a toy in front of S, and guide him to alternate his arms and hands to move toward the toy. Then return to the original position (on the floor, on his stomach).

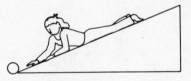

Place each of S's arms on a piece of cardboard. Pull one piece forward a few inches, and help S to scoot his body forward. (Hold the piece in place so that it does not scoot away.) Then do the same with the other arm. After S can pull forward this way, use guidance without the cardboard.

Place S on a roller crawl board. Guide S to reach for a toy in front of him by moving first one arm and then the other. Gradually fade your guidance. Then return to placing S on the floor. Have S practice this exercise on the crawl board frequently.

Part 5:

Use any of the following exercises to help S strengthen his leg muscles:

a. Place S on his back. Raise his legs, and guide them to move as if he were riding a bicycle.

b. Place S on his back. Grasp S's foot with one hand and his knee with your other hand to keep his leg straight. Then push against S's foot with your hand. This will prompt S to push his foot against your hand.

c. Place S on his back. Place a kick panel or some flexible object (e.g., foam rubber square attached to the wall) in front of S. Guide S to kick or push against the object with his feet. Gradually fade your guidance. As the object gives under the pressure of S's kicks, it should stimulate him to kick and push more. (Insure that the object will not fall or scoot when S pushes it.)

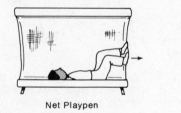

Net Playpen

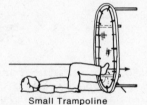

Small Trampoline

Place S on his stomach. Tickle his foot, or otherwise provide a stimulus for him to pull one leg up to bend at the knee. Alternate feet.

Lift S's hip up sharply, which will pull his leg up. Gradually fade the pressure you exert. Alternate hips.

Place S on his stomach on the floor. Place your hands against the soles of his feet. First push against one foot. S's knee will bend, and he will scoot forward. Do the same with the other foot. Gradually push less, and simply hold your hand against S's foot to provide something to push against.

Place S on his stomach with his feet flat against the wall and his knees bent out. Provide a stimulus so that S pushes against the wall to reach a toy. When S can do this without assistance, place him on the floor away from the wall, and prompt him to push against the floor to move forward.

Place S on a roller crawl board. Help him to alternately move his feet. Prompt him to use his arms, as well as to move forward. Have S practice this frequently.

Sitting Up

Chain

Skill:

In this program the child learns to pull or push up to a sitting position from a position lying on his back or stomach. This requires muscle strength in the legs, torso, and especially the arms. It also requires coordination to rotate the hips to move into a sitting position. All these skills are also necessary to develop the strength and coordination needed for crawling, standing up, and walking.

Entry Behaviors:

1. S sits unsupported with his head erect for at least 1 minute, using his hands for support and balance (e.g., Sitting). If S has very little arm strength or his arms are physically impaired, reconsider teaching this program. Or, develop your own task analysis to teach S to sit up using only his leg and trunk muscles, a far more difficult skill similar to a "sit-up."

2. S keeps his head in line with his body (no head lag) as you pull him up from lying on his back to a sitting position (e.g., optional exercise in Sitting). S tries to pull himself up as you grasp his hands.

3. S raises his head and pushes himself up using his forearms, although he may not be able to keep this position long. This position requires S to bend his arms at the elbow. If S is physically impaired, preventing him from bending his arms, reconsider teaching this program. Or, develop your own task analysis for sitting up, focusing on leg and trunk muscles.

4. S performs leg movements (e.g., lifting and lowering legs, moving legs from side to side, kicking, bending knees). If S's leg movements are very limited, adapt this program by omitting parts that require S to use his legs. Then require him to simply pull or push himself up to a sitting position using his arms. If S cannot bend his knees, reconsider using this program, and consult a physical therapist for other motor skills to work on, such as Standing.

5. S is capable of rolling over from his back to his stomach and stomach to back, although he may not have exhibited this skill often. If S can only roll from one position (either stomach or back), adapt the program so that S is required to sit up from only one position.

Objective:

When placed on his back or stomach, S pushes or pulls to a sitting position un-assisted, using furniture to hold onto if necessary. S must initiate his response within 5 seconds of the command and respond correctly 4 out of 5 trials.

Cycle:

None specified. However, you may repeat the program to teach S to sit up from more difficult positions.

Follow-Up:

Provide S opportunities to pull up on a variety of furniture (table leg, foot stool, bar or rail, crib bars). Once he is sitting, assist him to use the furniture to pull himself up to a standing position (introduction to Standing Up). If S has more trouble sitting up from one position than another (e.g., lying on his back), provide more opportunities with assistance, if necessary, to sit up from that position. Provide S with a variety of reasons for wanting to sit up (to touch a mobile, to play with you). During every activity, talk to S constantly, and prompt him to vocalize. Describe what he is doing ("You're sitting up!"). Also, teach S to lie back down from a sitting position without hurting his head.

Program for Gross Motor Skill 4

Chart:

None.

GENERAL STRATEGY

Arrangement:

Place S on the floor on his back or stomach. Collect a variety of toys to use as stimuli for S to sit up. Insure that some object is available for S to hold onto if necessary (bar, table leg).

Attention:

Draw S's attention to a toy. Place it so that S must sit up to obtain it. Talk about the toy, and manipulate it.

Command:

Give an appropriate command ("SIT UP"; "GET THE TOY") <u>with cues</u> indicating what you wish S to do (e.g., motion with your arms, shake the toy).

Latency:

S must initiate his response within 5 seconds of the command (or last part completed).

Correction:

Use general correction or Suggestions on any part that S does not perform correctly. After you assist him, allow him to continue the trial on his own. Correct him only if needed.

Natural Consequence:

After S sits up, allow him to play with the toy, and interact with him for as long as he continues to respond.

Other Trials:

Repeat the strategy. Present trials throughout the day rather than consecutively. Alternate trials between sitting up from back or stomach. Note that 1 trial = S sits up once.

Modification:

S has made no gains in <u>average parts completed</u> after two successive probes (2 weeks).

CONDITIONS	BEHAVIOR	CRITERIA
		for *6 only
PRE Get S's attention, and give the command. Present the natural consequence.	*6. Target--S pushes or pulls up to a sitting position unassisted, using furniture to hold onto if necessary.	4 correct out of 5 trials

DAILY INSTRUCTION/WEEKLY PROBES

Get S's attention, and give the command. Correct each part if needed. Present the natural consequence.	1. S rolls to his side from his back or stomach.	Continue daily instruction/weekly probes until S performs *6 correctly 4 out of the last 5 trials
	2. S pushes or pulls his chest up to a 45° angle with the floor (1 and 2 may occur simultaneously).	
	3. S repositions his legs as necessary to balance his weight.	
	4. S rotates his hips to shift weight from his side to his buttocks (occurs simultaneously with 5).	
	5. S straightens his body until he is sitting upright, using his arms to push or pull if necessary.	
	*6. Target--S pushes or pulls up to a sitting position unassisted, using furniture to hold onto if necessary.	
POST 1 Same as PRE	*6. Target--S pushes or pulls up to a sitting position unassisted, using furniture to hold onto if necessary.	4 correct out of 5 trials for each test
POST 2 New Setting		
POST 3 New Setting (different from POST 2)		

SUGGESTIONS

Part 1:

Assist S in rolling to his side. Gradually fade your guidance as S builds the strength needed to move his body by himself.

<u>From Stomach:</u>

Guide S to push against the floor with one hand and leg to move his body backward and onto his side.

OR

Guide S to push against the furniture with one arm to move his body backward and onto his side.

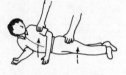   

<u>From Back:</u>

Guide S to swing one arm and leg to move his body forward and onto his side.

OR

Guide S to hold the furniture with one arm and pull to move his body forward and onto his side.

Provide S with a lot of practice in rolling over from all positions: back, side, and stomach. Guide S to position his legs so rolling over will be easier. Gradually fade the amount of assistance.

Part 2:

Assist S to push or pull his body upright. Place S's arms so that he may push or pull with them while you assist him to raise his body off the floor. Gradually fade your guidance as S gains more strength in his arms.

Both Arms and Hands Pushing   OR   One Arm Resting on the Floor,
from the Floor   One Pulling Up on Furniture

Part 3:

Assist S in positioning his legs so that he will be able to balance his weight and move more easily into a sitting position. You will be able to help S position his legs by bending the knee of his lower leg. You may also want to help S support his weight on his hands by holding and supporting his arms at the elbow. Gradually fade your guidance.

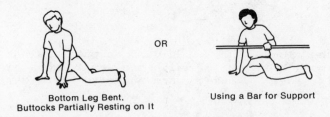

Bottom Leg Bent.
Buttocks Partially Resting on It

OR

Using a Bar for Support

Parts 4 and 5:

Assist S to shift his weight from his side to his buttocks. Gradually fade your guidance.

Guide S to push against the floor with his arms and to scoot his legs around.

Move Top Leg Up
and Around

Scoot Bottom Leg Out
trom Underneath
OR

Final Position

Guide S to pull with one arm while he holds and scoots.

 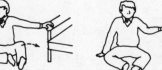

Pull with His Arm

Move His Top Leg Up and His Bottom
Leg Out from Underneath His Top Leg

Final Position

Place S's arms correctly, either both hands flat on the floor or one holding onto furniture. Then hold S's shoulders, and pull him up sideways to sit upright. Reposition his legs if necessary. Gradually fade your guidance.

If S is using his arms correctly but having trouble repositioning his legs, get behind and hold S around his waist or hips. Guide him to rotate his hips and sit erect. Then move his bottom leg out from under his other leg. Gradually fade your guidance.

Hold one of S's hands, and pull him up to an erect sitting position. Gradually pull with less force as S uses more arm strength and rotation to pull himself up, grasping your hand.

Standing

Skill Analysis

Skill:

In this program the child develops the muscle strength and coordination needed to maintain a standing position, using furniture for balance if necessary. The trunk control and leg strength developed here are also necessary for walking and standing up.

Entry Behaviors:

1. S maintains a sitting position, unassisted (without back support) for at least 1 minute (e.g., Sitting). S uses his arms and/or back and torso muscles to bear weight for balance and support. If S is not yet sitting, reconsider your rationale for teaching him to stand.

2. S has some arm and length strength typically demonstrated by crawling. However, some children may learn to stand and walk without learning to crawl due to their physical impairment (e.g., leg impairments requiring braces). Consult a physical therapist before using this program if you are unsure if S is physically capable of standing.

Objective:

When placed in a standing position, S stands for 1 minute and grasps furniture if needed for balance. S must initiate his response as soon as he is placed in the standing position and respond correctly 4 out of 5 trials.

Cycle:

None specified.

Follow-Up:

Provide more opportunities for S to stand. Vary the object he holds onto (your hand, a bar, furniture). Have him stand for increasingly longer periods of time. To develop balance, have S take part in activities while he is standing (e.g., throwing a ball). Provide opportunities for S to practice standing without anything nearby on which to hold. Prompt him to take steps away from the furniture toward you or to begin cruising along furniture (introduction to Walking). Assist S if needed to stand up from a sitting position (Standing Up). Talk to S, and describe his activities. Prompt him to vocalize what he is doing.

Program for Gross Motor Skill 5

Chart:

None.

GENERAL STRATEGY

Position:

Assist S to get into a position appropriate for the part. Place furniture in front of S (e.g., table) that he can hold onto for balance. Place toys that S prefers on the table to amuse him as he stands.

Stimulus Event:

Encourage S to continue to maintain his balance in position. Attract his attention to the toys. Prompt him to play with a toy. Move it around occasionally so that S must shift his weight, and use his arms and legs to maintain his balance. Continue the event as long as S is supporting his weight.

Latency:

S must initiate his response immediately to maintain his balance and keep from falling.

Correction:

Use Suggestions listed for each part.

Other Trials:

Repeat the strategy. Present trials throughout the day rather than consecutively. Vary the toys used. Note that 1 trial = 1 opportunity to perform 1 part.

Modification:

S has made no gains in <u>average parts completed</u> after two successive probes (2 weeks).

Program
Gross Motor
Skill 5

CONDITIONS	BEHAVIOR	CRITERIA
PRE Test *5 only. Assist S to stand up in front of furniture. Present the stimulus event.	*5. Target--when placed in a standing position, S will stand for 1 minute, using furniture if needed for balance.	4 correct out of 5 trials

DAILY INSTRUCTION/WEEKLY PROBES

Place S in a position appropriate for the part. Present the stimulus event, and assist if needed.		Continue daily instruction/weekly probes until S performs *5 correctly 4 out of 5 trials
1. Place S at a standing table, and fasten the door.	1. S stands in a stand-table for 5 minutes.	at least 5 times
2. Select furniture that reaches S's elbow when he is kneeling (low table, foot stool, chair, sofa). Assist S to a kneeling position with his forearms or hands on the furniture. Note: Many children learn to stand without first balancing their weight on their knees. If this task causes difficulty for S, omit this part.	2. S kneels at furniture for 1 minute.	at least 5 times
3. Select furniture that reaches S's elbow when he is standing. Assist S to a standing position with his hands or elbows resting on the furniture. Provide support around the trunk of his body. If S tries to take steps,	3. S stands for 1 minute with support around his trunk (for balance)	at least 5 times

allow him to do so
with your support, but
do not count this as a
correct response. <u>Note</u>:
This part is for bal-
ance, not weight support;
do not pull up to keep
S standing. Simply
assist him to balance
so that he does not
lean too much in one
direction.

Hands

Towel

Harness

4. Assist S to stand in front of furniture as in Part 3. When S leans too much in one direction, place your hands at his back and/ or shoulders.	4. S stands for 1 minute with support at his back and shoulders when necessary for balance.	at least 5 times

5. Assist S to stand in front of furniture with his hands or elbows resting on it.	*5. Target--when placed in a standing posi- tion, S will stand for 1 minute, using furniture if needed for balance.	4 correct out of the last 5 trials
POST 1 Same as PRE	*5. Target--when placed in a standing posi- tion, S will stand for 1 minute, using furniture if needed for balance.	4 correct out of 5 trials for each test
POST 2 New Setting		
POST 3 New Setting (different from POST 2)		

SUGGESTIONS

Part 1:

S may not have the leg and trunk strength to stand at a standing table. Some
children can scoot or slide down from the table even with the door closed. If
S is particularly small, assist him into a standing position, and provide support
for his entire trunk. Allow S to lean slightly forward or backward against you.
Prompt S to keep both feet on the floor. When S can do this, use the standing
table again without your support.

Pad the standing area with pillows to provide a tighter fit to prevent S from scooting down. Remove the amount of padding gradually until S can stand at the standing table without it.

Place S on a prone board with straps at the knees, buttocks, and waist. Use extra straps, if needed, for support. (Make sure S does not fall backward.) Gradually increase the time S can stand this way; then use the standing table again.

Encourage S to bear more of his own weight while standing. Hold him under his arms, and bounce him up and down slightly. Keep his feet on the floor. Do NOT do this if S raises his legs off the floor.

Part 2:

Assist S to a kneeling position between your knees. Place a toy on one knee, or hold it for S. Move your legs closer together, or press one leg against S's buttocks if he begins to sit down. Gradually provide less support.

Assist S into a kneeling position with a large beach ball, pillows, or similar object behind his knees to prevent him from sitting down. Provide less and less support behind his knees until he can kneel without assistance.

Assist S to a kneeling position with a large beach ball or roll in front of him. The ball or roll should be large enough for S to rest his elbows on it when he is kneeling in front of it. At first experiment with different positions for S's arms on the beach ball until you find one that is most comfortable and offers the most support for S. Then roll the beach ball slightly, and help him to hold onto the ball. Gradually roll the ball farther and farther from S until he can kneel without the support of the beach ball.

Place S in the tucked sitting position with his hands flat on the floor. When he can keep this position for at least 30 seconds, place a chair or low stool in front of him, and place his forearms on the furniture. When he can balance himself in the tucked position, begin to push his buttocks up so that he is in the kneeling position. Hold him in this position for longer periods of time, and gradually reduce your support until he is kneeling at furniture without additional support.

Place S in the tucked sitting position with his arms resting on a chair or couch. Assist S to support his weight for a few seconds while he is on his knees with his forearms on the chair or couch. Then allow him to sit back. Gradually increase the length of time S can support his own weight on his knees and arms.

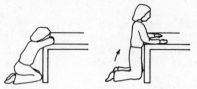

Place S in the tucked sitting position, having him hold onto your hands. Pull him up slowly so he is balancing on his knees. Gradually hold S for longer periods.

Place S on a board in a kneeling position with straps at his buttocks and chest. Place S at a table where he can play, and place the board at an angle to the table. Gradually decrease the angle of the board until S can kneel upright at the table without support.

Part 3:

Hold the ends of the towel, harness, or similar object so firmly at first that S cannot move sideways or forward. Gradually release your pressure, and allow S more room to shift his weight as he gains more control over his balance.

Have S lean, half sitting, on a low desk or table with both feet on the floor. Push S up and forward to a standing position. Provide support at the torso as necessary. Encourage S to lean less and less on the table, and to use more leg strength for support.

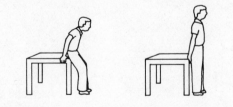

Part 4:

Hold S's shoulders firmly as he stands. Gradually reduce the amount of pressure you exert. Then release your hold altogether, and place your hands on S's back or sides (shoulders) only when he begins to fall.

Place an extra large beach ball or similar object in front of S. It should be
large enough for S to rest his elbows on when he is standing. Assist S to lean
against the beach ball, and then roll the ball slightly. Once S is leaning against
the ball, you may want to provide further assistance by putting pressure at the
opposite side of the ball so that it does not move very far at one time. Continue
to roll the ball in different directions farther and farther from S until he can
stand, using the beach ball only when necessary to catch his balance.

Allow S to stand with his hands remaining flat on the table. Increase the length
of time S can stand, and use the table for support. Then prompt S to lift one or
both hands to play with a toy and to shift his weight as necessary to keep his
balance. Always provide support at S's back and shoulders when necessary. Gradually fade your assistance.

Crawling on
Hands and
Knees

Skill Analysis

Skill:

In this program the child develops the muscle strength and coordination necessary to move forward on his hands and knees. As the child becomes more mobile, he learns to pull himself up to a standing position and then to walk.

Entry Behaviors:

1. S <u>crawls on his stomach at least 5 feet</u> (e.g., Crawling on Stomach). Although S can push or pull with both arms and legs, he may not be using alternate arm and leg movements as he crawls on his stomach.

2. S <u>sits unsupported</u> for at least 1 minute (e.g., Sitting). While sitting, S has the arm strength to support part of his weight on his hands while he participates in an activity.

Objective:

S crawls forward 5 feet on his hands and knees* unassisted. S must initiate his response within 5 seconds of the command and respond correctly 4 out of 5 trials.

*<u>Note</u>: Reciprocal arm and leg movements are required for S to pass this program.

Cycle:

None specified.

Follow-Up:

Provide S with a variety of opportunities to crawl. Increase the distance you require him to crawl. Place toys at his side or behind him so that he learns to move his body around and then crawl toward the object. Teach S to crawl up and down a few steps or on a hill outside. Guide S to use furniture to pull himself up to a standing position; then hold him up. Once he is standing, release him and allow him to fall toward you so that he will take his first steps.

Program for Gross Motor Skill 6

Chart:

None.

GENERAL STRATEGY

Position:

Position S as described for the part.

Stimulus Event:

Attract S's attention, and provide him with a reason for moving into the desired position (hold up a toy, move away from him).

Command:

Give an appropriate command ("COME TO ME" or "GET THE TOY") <u>with cues</u>, and continue the stimulus event to maintain S's attention.

Latency:

S must initiate his response within 5 seconds of the command.

Correction:

Use Suggestions listed for each part.

Natural Consequence:

Allow S to interact with the toy (and you) as long as he continues to respond.

Other Trials:

Repeat the strategy. Vary the objects and the stimulus events. Present trials throughout the day rather than consecutively. 1 trial = 1 opportunity to perform 1 part.

Modification:

S has made no gains in <u>average parts completed</u> after two successive probes (2 weeks).

CONDITIONS	BEHAVIOR	CRITERIA
PRE Test *7 only. Assist S into a sitting position with his feet tucked underneath. Present the stimulus event. Give the command, and continue the stimulus event. Present the natural consequence.	*7. Target--S crawls forward 5 feet on his hands and knees unassisted.	4 correct out of 5 trials

DAILY INSTRUCTION/WEEKLY PROBES

Position S as described for the part. Present the stimulus event. Give the command. Continue the stimulus event. Assist if needed. Present the natural consequence.		Continue daily instruction/weekly probes until S performs *7 correctly 4 out of 5 trials
1. Assist S into a sitting position with his feet tucked (supporting his weight on his hands, his buttocks resting on his legs). Provide a stimulus to encourage S to maintain this position.	1. S supports his weight in a tucked position 1 minute.	at least 5 times
2. Assist S into a crawl position on his hands and knees (arms and legs spread slightly and hands flat on the floor, with fingers spread). Provide a stimulus so that S maintains this position.	2. S supports his weight on his hands and knees 1 minute.	at least 5 times
3. Assist S into a tucked sitting position. Provide a stimulus so that S will push up on his hands and knees (e.g., manipulate a toy in front of him, slightly above eye level).	3. S pushes up from a tucked position to support his weight on his hands and knees.	at least 5 times
4. Assist S into a tucked sitting position. Provide a stimulus so that S pushes up on his hands and knees. Then provide a stimulus so that S reaches forward. Repeat the strategy for his other hand. Alternate trials for each arm.	4. S reaches forward with one arm when supporting his weight on his hands and knees.	at least 5 times for each arm

Chart (continued)

CONDITIONS	BEHAVIOR	CRITERIA
5. Assist S into a tucked sitting position. Provide a stimulus so that S moves forward 5 feet. Position yourself behind S, and guide him to scoot one leg forward, then the other. (S must move first one arm forward, then the other, unassisted.)	5. S moves forward 5 feet, alternating his arms.	at least 5 times
6. Assist S into a tucked sitting position. Provide a stimulus so that S moves forward 5 feet. (S must move first one leg, then the other, unassisted.) If S does not alternate his arms, assist if needed.	6. S moves forward 5 feet, alternating his legs. Right leg and left arm move forward, then left leg and right arm.	at least 5 times
*7. Assist S into a tucked sitting position. Provide a stimulus so that S crawls forward 5 feet.	*7. Target--S crawls forward on his hands and knees 5 feet unassisted.	4 correct out of the last 5 trials
POST 1 Same as PRE	*7. Target--S crawls forward on his hands and knees 5 feet unassisted.	4 correct out of 5 trials for each test
POST 2 New Setting		
POST 3 New Setting (different from POST 2)		

SUGGESTIONS

Part 1:

Help S into a tucked sitting position. Position yourself behind S (or in front of him, whichever is easier for his size), and hold his legs steady with your hands over his knees. Increase the length of time S maintains this position with your support, and then gradually fade your assistance.

Assist S into a tucked position but with the upper part of his body resting on the floor. Guide S to use his arms to push up and support his weight on his hands, thus building arm strength. Gradually move your support up S's arms until you are holding him at the shoulders, and then not at all.

Place S in the tucked sitting position. Assist him to extend his arms to the front or sides for support. Hold S's arms at the elbows to prevent his arms from buckling. Increase the length of time S maintains this position with your support, and then gradually fade this support.

Part 2:

Help S into a tucked position. Stand behind S, and place a blanket or strip of cloth under his stomach. Hold the ends of the cloth, and pull S by his waist to bring him to a crawl position. Gradually relax your hold on the ends of the cloth as S begins to support his weight on his hands and knees. Later, offer support only by tugging at his waistband as a cue to maintain the position.

Place S in a crawl position. From behind, place your hands under S's stomach to support him on his hands and knees. Gradually support S less. Give a tug on his waistband as a cue to maintain the position.

To develop balance, as well as strength, place S on his hands and knees over a cushion roll. Move the roll back and forth slightly (or push S's buttocks forward) to require S to place weight on his hands, then on his knees, to strengthen his muscles. Remove the cushion roll when you feel S supporting his own weight, and use other supports (e.g., towel at waist). Finally remove all supports.

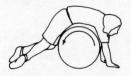

Make sure that S's legs and hands are spread slightly, with his hands flat on the floor. Repeat the exercise with the cushion roll placed lengthwise between S's arms and legs. Roll it gently sideways. Use this to develop balance and strength.

Part 3:

Kneel behind S. Push S's buttocks forward and up. Hold him in the crawl position.
Then allow S to relax and fall back to the tucked position. Gradually support S's
buttocks less so that he must support his own weight. Then only push S's buttocks
when he begins to fall back. If S's arms buckle and he falls forward, allow him
to relax for awhile; then try again.

If S is small and needs to increase arm strength, place him on his stomach on the
floor. Kneel behind him, and hold his legs around his thighs, then lift so that
he must push up to support his weight on his arms. As S gains more arm strength,
place him in the tucked position again.

Part 4:

Help S into a crawl position over a cushion roll. Then push S forward or sideways
slightly so that he must move his hands and replace them to maintain his balance.
Encourage S to rock back and forth. Guide S to replace his hands, if necessary,
and gradually fade your guidance. When S balances himself in this position, remove the roll, and prompt him to reach for the toy again.

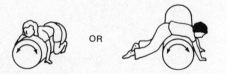

Assist S into a tucked sitting position, and prompt him to reach for a toy held
in front of him. When S can do this with each arm (one at a time), have him
reach while on his hands and knees in a crawl position.

Place S in a tucked position. Gently rock him back and forth, and prompt him to
shift his weight on his hands and knees. Gradually fade your guidance. Encourage
S to perform this rocking motion on his own.

Place S on his stomach over a cushion roll. Place a toy in front of S on the
floor. Then lift S's legs, roll him forward, and prompt him to reach for the
toy. Gradually decrease your guidance until S can reach forward on his hands
and knees for the toy. Then remove the roll.

Guide S to lift his hand and move it to a toy a few inches in front of him on
the floor. Repeat for his other hand. Gradually fade your guidance, and increase the distance of the toy from S.

Part 5:

Help S into a tucked sitting position. Have an aide or another teacher kneel
behind S to move his legs forward. Position yourself at S's side or in front
of him. Grasp his arms, and guide S to pick up one arm and place it back on
the floor, palm flat, then the other arm. Gradually provide less assistance.

Place a towel or strip of cloth around S's middle. Stand over and slightly
behind S with one foot on each side. Pull up on the ends of the cloth, to
support S in the crawl position. Do not try to work with S's legs, but move
him forward. Pull first on one end of the cloth, then the other. When you
pull on the end of the cloth, this should swing one of S's hands off the floor,
and replace it forward. Gradually decrease this assistance as S learns to move
his arms.

Assist S into a tucked sitting position on a ramp, facing downward. Gravity will
help S to move his arms forward. Help S to alternate arms, then gradually decrease this assistance.

Part 6:

Kneel behind S, grasp his legs around the calves or ankles, and move one leg forward, then the other. Have another person support S's weight, or use an adjustable
crawler if S is just beginning to alternate his arms. Gradually fade your guidance.

Place a towel or strip of cloth around S's middle. Stand over S with one foot
on each side. Pull up on the ends of the cloth, supporting S in the crawl position. Place your bare feet behind S's feet, and push one of his feet forward,
then the other. Gradually fade your guidance.

Stand behind S. Pull up on S's waistband, or place a towel, cloth, or similar
object under S's stomach and pull up. Then walk forward. Pull S with you, but
allow him to move his arms and legs without assistance. Gradually fade your
assistance.

Standing Up

Chain

Skill:

In this program the child learns the sequence of pushing or pulling himself from a sitting position on the floor to a standing position. The child has already learned to stand but has not yet developed the leg strength, coordination, and balance necessary for moving into a standing position.

Entry Behaviors:

1. S makes <u>simple leg movements</u> (e.g., lifting and lowering legs, moving legs from side to side, kicking, bending knees). If S cannot bend his knees or has very limited leg movements, reconsider the use of this program, and consult a physical therapist for other motor skills to teach.

2. When S is placed in a standing position, he <u>remains standing for a short while</u> (e.g., Standing), although he may need to hold onto furniture or your hands to maintain his balance.

3. S <u>uses his arms and hands for balance and support</u>, usually demonstrated during sitting (e.g., Sitting). If S has very little arm strength or if his arms are physically impaired, reconsider the use of this program. Instead, develop a task analysis for standing up that uses only the leg and trunk muscles, such as standing up from sitting in a chair.

4. S <u>has the arm strength</u> to pull or push himself up to sit from a prone or supine position (e.g., Sitting Up). If S has very little arm strength, he will need well-developed trunk and leg strength in order to stand up. In this case, develop your own task analysis.

5. S <u>sits unsupported in a variety of positions</u> on the floor (e.g., Indian style, legs straight in front of him, legs extended and bent upward at the knees). If S sits only in one position, adapt this program by omitting the requirement that S must stand up from a variety of sitting positions.

Objective:

When placed in a <u>sitting position</u>, S pushes or pulls up to a standing position unassisted, using furniture to hold onto if necessary. S must initiate his response within 5 seconds of the command and respond correctly 4 out of 5 trials.

<u>sitting position</u> = sitting erect on the floor unsupported. (The position varies between trials.)

Cycle:

None specified. Repeat the program if needed to teach a particular sitting position that is very difficult for S.

Follow-Up:

Encourage S to stand often by pulling up on any furniture nearby. Also, have S stand up without something to hold on to. Once he is standing, assist S to cruise (step sideways, along furniture) or to walk toward you. Have S stand for longer and longer periods of time, sometimes without holding onto something for balance. Have S stand up from different positions (from squatting, lying down, sitting on a tricycle or wagon). Provide S with a variety of reasons for standing up (e.g., to play with a toy on the table, to look out the window). Whenever S stands up, talk to him, and encourage him to vocalize what he is doing ("You're standing up!"). Use a variety of commands to stand (e.g., "S, stand up and get your toy!").

Program for Gross Motor Skill 7

Chart:

None.

GENERAL STRATEGY

Arrangement:

Place S in a sitting position on the floor. Choose a position that is comfortable
for him. Place something within S's reach so that he grasps it while pulling
himself up if necessary (bar, table). To encourage S to stand up, provide a
variety of toys he prefers.

Attention:

Draw S's attention to a toy, and talk about it; or show S why he might want to
stand.

Command:

Give an appropriate command ("STAND UP"; "GET THE TOY") <u>with cues</u> indicating what
you wish S to do (e.g., stand up yourself, motion with <u>your arms</u>, shake the toy).

Latency:

S must initiate his response within 5 seconds of the command (or last part
completed).

Correction:

Use general correction or Suggestions on any part that S does not perform correctly.
After you assist him, allow him to continue the trial on his own. Correct him only
if needed.

Natural Consequence:

After S stands up, allow him to play with the toy. Interact with him for as long
as he continues the activity.

Other Trials:

Repeat the strategy. Present trials throughout the day rather than consecutively.
Vary the sitting positions in which S is placed.

Modification:

S has made no gains in <u>average parts completed</u> after two successive probes
(2 weeks).

Program
Gross Motor
Skill 7

CONDITIONS	BEHAVIOR	CRITERIA
		for *6 only
PRE Get S's attention, and give the command. Present the natural consequence.	*6. Target--S pushes or pulls up to a standing position unassisted, using furniture to hold onto if necessary.	4 correct out of 5 trials

DAILY INSTRUCTION/WEEKLY PROBES:

Get S's attention, and give the command. Correct each part if needed. Present the natural consequence.	1. S <u>positions his hands</u> on the floor or holds onto furniture.	Continue daily instruction/weekly probes until S performs *6 correctly 4 out of the last 5 trials
	2. S <u>positions his legs into a tucked</u> position (feet under buttocks).	
	3. S <u>pushes or pulls into</u> a kneeling position.	
	4. S <u>pulls one leg up into a half-kneeling</u> position.	
	5. S <u>pushes or pulls</u> the <u>rest of the way</u> to stand.	
	*6. Target--S pushes or pulls up to a standing position unassisted, using furniture to hold onto if necessary.	
POST 1 Same as PRE	*6. Target--S pushes or pulls up to a standing position unassisted, using furniture to hold onto if necessary.	4 correct out of 5 trials for each test
POST 2 New Setting		
POST 3 New Setting (different from POST 2)		

SUGGESTIONS

Part 1:

Guide S to position his hands. For example, place your hands firmly over S's, either flat on the floor or holding onto the furniture. Choose whichever method seems easier for S. As he becomes used to positioning his hands, gradually fade your guidance, and apply less pressure.

Hands Flat on the Floor

Hands on the Furniture

Combination
(One Hand on the Floor, One Holding the Furniture)

Have S shift arm positions when sitting. Prompt him to reach out to bars or stationary objects and to reach forward, and put more weight on his arms. (He will need to support and balance much of his weight on his arms as he shifts his legs in Part 2.)

Part 2:

Guide S to push or pull himself into a tucked sitting position. Move S's legs together, and bend his knees so that he is sitting on his legs. Gradually fade this guidance.

Wrap a towel around S's waist, or hold him there to provide support for his weight as he shifts his legs. Gradually support less weight until S supports all of it on his arms as he shifts his legs around.

Place S in a tucked sitting position but with one leg not quite in place. Have S pull this leg around into the tucked position. Practice with the other leg, also. Gradually position S with more of his buttocks resting on the floor so that he has to bring his legs further beneath his buttocks to move into the tucked position.

Part 3:

Guide S to push or pull up to a kneeling position. Sit behind him, and push his buttocks up if needed. Gradually push less, and decrease the amount of guidance you give as S gains more strength in his arms and legs to pull himself up.

Pushes against the Floor and Pulls   Pulls, Holding onto the Furniture

Grasp S's hands, and pull him into a kneeling position. Gradually pull less as S pulls more.

Position a toy on a table or shelf at S's waist height (when kneeling), and encourage S to kneel to reach the toy. Raise the height of the toy, and have S practice reaching higher and higher until he kneels erect to get it.

Part 4:

Guide S to pull himself into a half-kneeling position. Place your hand on top of or behind S's knee and raise his leg until his foot is resting flat on the floor. You might also want to hold S's other leg steady with your other hand. Gradually provide less leverage as S uses more of his own strength to raise his leg.

Raises One Leg Up So Foot Is Flat on the Floor

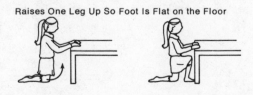

Part 5:

Hold the ankle or foot of S's leg that is bearing the weight as he pulls himself up. This will help him keep his balance. Gradually apply less pressure.

Stand in front of S, and grasp his hands. Pull S to a standing position. Gradually exert less pressure until S can grasp your hands and pull himself up. Then have S grasp furniture to pull himself up.

Kneel behind S, and push up on his buttocks as he pulls himself up to stand. Gradually exert less force until S can pull himself up without the assistance.

To develop S's leg strength, place him in a sitting position with his knees bent, feet flat on the floor. Kneel in front of S, and place his toes under your knees or feet to stabilize his feet. Grasp both of S's hands, and pull him toward you into a squatting position; then hold your hands stable in front of and slightly above S's shoulders. Have S pull up on your hands to move to a standing position. Allow S to continue to grasp your hands when he is in a standing position. Gradually exert less force as he pulls himself up, holding onto your hands. Then have S resume practice on standing from the half-kneeling position.

You may kneel or stand in front of S, depending on S's height and weight.

Use the same strategy, but have S pull or push up on a stationary object. Then have S resume practice on standing from the half-kneeling position.

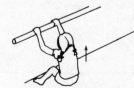

Feet Up to the Wall   Holding onto the Bar, and Pushing against the Floor

Walking

Skill Analysis

Skill:

This program develops a child's muscle strength, balance, and the coordination needed to take his first few steps unassisted. With this beginning, the child can expand his mobility to walk up and down steps, run, jump, and perform a variety of other gross motor activities.

Entry Behaviors:

1. S <u>stands</u> (or is learning to stand) while holding onto furniture for balance (e.g., Standing). Sometimes S is able to let go and stand for a few seconds unsupported.

2. S <u>moves his legs</u>. If S cannot bend his knees, reconsider teaching this program. Consult with a physical therapist to determine if this is an appropriate skill to teach at this time.

3. S <u>controls movement of his arms and legs</u>. If S experiences involuntary movements of his arms or legs (e.g., a child with cerebral palsy), consult a physical therapist to determine if this is an appropriate skill to teach at this time.

Objective:

From a standing position, S walks forward 5 feet unassisted. S must initiate his response within 5 seconds of the command and respond correctly 4 out of 5 trials.

Cycle:

None specified.

Follow-Up:

Provide S with a variety of opportunities to walk (e.g., in the park, through the house). Also, provide different reasons to walk (e.g., to come to you, to eat a meal, to go outside). Gradually increase the distance you require S to walk. Help S develop even more balance and coordination by walking up and down steps, running, jumping, going down a slide, climbing. Talk to S frequently about what he is doing, and encourage him to respond vocally to develop speech skills. Use a variety of commands for walking (e.g., "Come and get your toy"). Have S perform tasks that require him to walk around (e.g., putting objects away, setting the table). Continue to combine these tasks as S walks with more facility.

Program for Gross Motor Skill 8

Chart:

None.

GENERAL STRATEGY

Position:

Assist S to stand with something nearby to hold for balance (chair, table). S's feet should be spread slightly, pointed forward.

Stimulus Event:

Attract S's attention, and provide him with a reason to move forward (play with a toy, place it on a table in front of him, talk to him).

Command:

Give an appropriate command ("WALK TO THE TOY" or "COME TO ME") with cues. Continue the stimulus event to attract S's attention.

Latency:

S must initiate his response within 5 seconds of the command.

Correction:

Use Suggestions listed for each part.

Natural Consequence:

Allow S to interact with the toy (and you) as long as he continues to participate.

Other Trials:

Repeat the strategy. Vary the stimulus events. Present trials throughout the day rather than consecutively. 1 trial = 1 opportunity to perform 1 part.

Modification:

S has made no gains in average parts completed after two successive probes (2 weeks).

Program
Gross Motor
Skill 8

CONDITIONS	BEHAVIOR	CRITERIA
PRE Test *5 only. Position S, and present the stimulus event and command. Continue the stimulus event. Present the natural consequence.	*5. Target--S walks forward 5 feet unassisted.	4 correct out of 5 trials

DAILY INSTRUCTION/WEEKLY PROBES:

Position S as described for the part. Present the stimulus event. Give the command, and continue the stimulus event. Assist if needed. Present the natural consequence.		Continue daily instruction/weekly probes until S performs *5 correctly 4 out of the last 5 trials
1. Place furniture 1/2 to 1 foot apart in a row about 10 feet long. Assist S to stand by the first piece of furniture. Provide a stimulus for S to sidestep to the end of the row (e.g., place a toy on the last chair, stand at the end of the row).	1. S sidesteps 10 feet, moving from one object to another.	at least 5 times
2. Provide a stimulus for S to walk forward 5 feet. Walk behind S to provide support at his waist.	2. S walks forward 5 feet with support at his waist. Hands Towel (Ends Crossed in Back)	at least 5 times
3. Provide a stimulus for S to walk forward 5 feet. Assist S to stand behind a chair, walker, or a piece of furniture that he can easily push forward.	3. S walks forward 5 feet by pushing a chair or walker. Chair Walker Push-Toy	at least 5 times

Chart (continued)

CONDITIONS	BEHAVIOR	CRITERIA
4. Provide a stimulus for S to walk forward 5 feet. Walk beside S, and hold his hand. Note: Do not assist S by pulling him. Make sure S does not have to raise his arm very high to hold your hand, as this could affect his balance.	4. S walks forward 5 feet by holding your hand.	at least 5 times
*5. Provide a stimulus for S to walk forward 5 feet.	*5. Target--S walks forward 5 feet unassisted.	4 correct out of the last 5 trials
POST 1 Same as PRE	*5. Target--S walks forward 5 feet unassisted.	4 correct out of 5 trials for each test
POST 2 New Setting		
POST 3 New Setting (different from POST 2)		

SUGGESTIONS

Part 1:

Position S in front of a long table with a toy at the end. Stand behind S, and assist him to slide his hands along the table and to move his feet sideways to reach the end of the table. Gradually fade your guidance. Then return to using furniture spaced 1/2 to 1 foot apart.

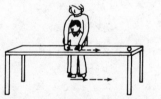

Position S in front of a long table as shown above. Move one of S's hands along the table as far as he can reach, so that he must also move his feet to maintain his balance. Again, encourage S to take a few independent steps when he reaches the end of the table. Gradually fade your guidance, and use pieces of furniture spaced apart.

Place furniture in a row as described for the part. Guide S to move along the furniture. Help him to raise his hand and place it on the next piece of furniture. Move his foot at the same time. Gradually fade your guidance.

Use the strategy suggested, but place the chairs so that they are almost touching. Gradually move the pieces of furniture farther apart, and fade your guidance.

Part 2:

Stand behind S, and allow him to lean against your body. Continuously nudge him forward. Hold S in a convenient position (e.g., your hands held over his shoulders and chest). Gradually move farther from S with your hands placed on his shoulders or waist, and catch him when he falls backward. When S's balance has improved, stand behind him, and hold his waist with your hands or a towel or harness.

If S is having trouble bending his knees and alternating his feet to walk forward, tie long strips of cloth on S's feet. Wrap them around S's knees so that by pulling the ends of the strips, you can help him lift his feet and take steps forward. Gradually fade your pressure. Then discontinue using the strips, and support S only at the waist.

Position S behind a large cushion roll or beach ball. Place his hands on the roll. Move the roll forward slightly so that S must take steps to keep his balance.

Stand behind S, and hold him around his waist. Turn the upper part of his body slightly, first to one side and then the other, to teach him to move his body as he takes steps.

Have S "knee walking" if he is having trouble alternating his legs or balancing himself while standing. Position S on the floor in a tucked sitting position. Prompt him to push or pull himself to a kneeling position, and assist him if necessary. Then help S to walk forward on his knees. You might have to hold S in the kneeling position and help him knee walk by lifting and moving one side of his body forward, then the other. Gradually fade your guidance.

Note: Knee walking is a good exercise to teach a child to balance his weight and to alternate his legs to move forward. However, many children learn to walk without knee walking. If knee walking proves to be difficult for your child, do not try it.

Use the harness or towel wrapped around S's middle (or use your hands) to guide one side of his body forward, then the other. In addition, place your feet behind S's, and slide one foot forward, then the other, if S is not moving his feet. Gradually fade your guidance, and hold S less firmly so that he is walking with assistance only to keep his balance.

Part 3:

Position S behind the chair or walker as described. Stand behind him, and push gently against his back or buttocks to prompt him to walk forward. Gradually fade your guidance.

Position S behind the chair or walker as described. Then stand in front of the chair, and pull it forward so that he must walk forward to maintain his balance.

Play "choo-choo." Have S hold another child's waist as you hold S's waist (or switch positions with the other child so that S follows you). Move around the room. Then return to using the chair or walker.

Guide S to push against the chair or walker with his hands to move it forward. Gradually fade your guidance.

Stand in front of S. Each of you should hold onto a bar. Walk backward, and pull S with you. Gradually provide less support with the bar. Have S walk without this support when his balance improves.

Hold one side of a Hoola Hoop, and have S hold the other side. Pull the hoop toward you to prompt S to take steps. Try positioning your hands in different places on the hoop to find a position that works the best (or try using different size hoops). Gradually fade the amount of support you give.

Part 4:

Stand in front of S, and grasp his hands. Pull him forward to take several steps. Gradually pull less, but let him grasp your hand(s) as he walks forward. Then return to having S hold your hand as he walks beside you.

Help S to stand up next to a bar, long table, or a similar object. Then prompt him to walk forward with one hand resting on the bar or table. When S can walk 5 feet with this support, return to having S hold your hand as he walks beside you.

Chewing

Skill Analysis

Skill:

This program develops S's lip, tongue, and jaw movements to teach him to chew a variety of different foods. This skill is an important step to learn prior to feeding oneself independently. In addition, the development of lip, tongue, and jaw control frequently improves the ability to produce different sounds for speech.

Entry Behaviors:

1. S swallows liquids and soft foods. Although S eats strained baby foods or pudding, he gags on junior or other foods that require chewing to break them down before swallowing.

2. S moves his tongue, lips, and jaws and exhibits the sucking reflex. Although S moves his mouth, he does not coordinate these actions to chew. Rather, these actions are random and uncontrolled. If the actions appear to be involuntary, consult an occupational therapist.

Objective:

When a bite-size piece of food is held to his mouth, S opens his mouth, (you place the food on his tongue) chews, and swallows without assistance. S must initiate his response within 5 seconds of the presentation of food and respond correctly 4 out of 5 trials.

food = edible that requires some chewing or mashing before swallowing. See Medium Textures on the Foods Chart, page 461. Vary the foods within that one set.

Note: In this program S is not required to chew with his mouth closed. However, that skill is developed in one of the parts, even though it is not part of the target skill.

Overview
Eating
Skill 1

Cycle:

None specified. The program may be repeated if desired to teach different or specific foods within the Medium Textures category on the Foods Chart, page 461.

Follow-Up:

Continue to expand the variety of foods S can chew. As S becomes proficient at chewing, gradually introduce small pieces of food that require extensive chewing, as represented by the Hard Textures on the Foods Chart, page 461. Whenever you feed S, guide him to hold the food or the spoon as you bring the food to his mouth to introduce the self-feeding skills of Eating Finger Foods and Eating with a Spoon. In addition, present larger pieces of food so that S is required to bite off a portion, a skill that is developed in Eating Finger Foods. As S develops control of mouth movements, encourage him to produce different sounds as an introduction to Making Sounds.

Program for Eating Skill 1

Chart:

Foods Chart, Medium Textures only, page 461.

GENERAL STRATEGY

Setting:

Work with S at any time during the day. Initially, choose times other than mealtime since the assistance you provide to S may be aversive.

Position:

Seat S in an upright position with his feet flat on the floor for support. His head should be erect with his neck supported if necessary. Do not allow S's head to fall back at any time during feeding, since it is usually impossible to swallow in this position.

Attention:

Draw S's attention to the piece of food. (It may be a single bite-size piece or a single mouthful on a spoon.)

Present Food:

Hold the food to S's mouth, and gently touch it to his lips. Tell him to eat ("S, EAT THE FOOD.") After S opens his mouth, place the food as described in the parts. If you use a spoon, do not remove it until S closes his lips. NEVER scrape food off by bringing the spoon against his front teeth. Always have him use his lips to retain the food..

Latency:

S must initiate his response within 5 seconds of the presentation of the food.

Correction:

Use Suggestions for each part.

Other Trials:

Always allow plenty of time between trials to swallow the food. Vary the foods within the category of Medium Textures. Present trials at different times during the day rather than consecutively. Note that 1 trial = 1 opportunity to perform 1 part.

Modification:

S has made no gains in average parts completed after two successive probes (2 weeks).

CONDITIONS	BEHAVIOR	CRITERIA
PRE Test *6 only. Position S. Get his attention, and present the food. Place it in the center of S's mouth.	*6. Target--S opens his mouth, chews, and swallows one bite unassisted.	4 correct out of 5 trials

DAILY INSTRUCTION/WEEKLY PROBES:

Position S. Get his attention, and present the food. Place it as directed for the appropriate part. Assist if needed.		Continue daily instruction/weekly probes until S performs *6 correctly 4 out of 5 trials
1. Present the food. After S opens his mouth, place the food, and assist him to chew if needed.	1. S opens his mouth for food.	at least 5 times
2. Place the food between his teeth (either side) or on his tongue. After S closes his lips, assist him to chew if needed.	2. S closes his lips when food is placed in his mouth. If a spoon is used, S must close his lips to retain the food as the spoon is removed.	at least 5 times
3. Place the food between S's teeth (alternate between sides) or on his tongue if he can move the food as described in Part 4.	3. S moves his jaws up, down, and sideways, to chew the food.	at least 5 times
4. Place the food on the center of S's tongue. After S moves the food to the side, assist him to chew if needed.	4. S uses his tongue to position food between his teeth to chew.	at least 5 times
5. Place the food in the center of S's mouth on his tongue. Assist him to chew if needed.	5. S keeps his lips closed while chewing and swallowing. Note: This skill is not required to meet the target, although it has been included as an appropriate skill to work on.	at least 5 times

Chart (continued)

CONDITIONS	BEHAVIOR	CRITERIA
6. Present the food. Place it in the center of S's mouth.	*6. Target--S opens his mouth, chews, and swallows one bite unassisted.	4 correct out of the last 5 trials
POST 1 Same as PRE	*6. Target--S opens his mouth, chews, and swallows one bite unassisted.	4 correct out of 5 trials given for each test
POST 2 New Setting		
POST 3 Different Foods (Medium Textures)		

SUGGESTION

Part 1:

Use jaw control (any of the three methods listed below):

a. forefinger on side of jaw; thumb on chin; middle finger under jaw.

b. thumb on side; finger on chin; middle finger under chin.

c. forefinger between nose and upper lip; thumb on side of jaw; third finger on chin; fourth finger under chin. (This method provides the most control.)

With the middle finger, press with firm, upward strokes until S's mouth opens. Do this often whenever S is eating. Gradually fade this physical prompt.

If S refuses to open his mouth, begin feeding with soft, highly preferred foods. Gradually introduce other foods, in particular those that require more chewing. Do this only as S becomes more proficient at chewing, specifically Parts 4 and 5.

Part 2:

Gradually fade any of the following physical prompts:

a. Stroke S's lower lip gently upward with forefinger. Stroke from the middle of his chin to his lip to enable his lips to touch.

b. Pull out S's lower lip, then release it; S's lip will close, and this will stimulate the muscles that are needed to close the lips on his own.

c. Place your forefinger between S's upper lip and nose. Apply firm and continuous pressure downward until his lips touch.

Press S's lips closed between your thumb and forefinger. Gradually fade your guidance.

Stroke around the area of S's mouth with a paint brush to stimulate him to close his mouth.

Stroke the area around S's mouth with ice. <u>Caution:</u> This may not be appropriate for a child prone to seizures.

Place a drop of lemon juice on the tip of S's tongue to stimulate S to pucker his mouth. This automatically closes it.

When wiping S's mouth, always wipe upward from the chin so that his mouth will close.

Part 3:

Stimulate chewing by applying firm, continuous pressure to S's mouth and jaws, using jaw control, either the front or side method. Do not try to move S's jaw or mouth. Gradually fade this pressure. (For methods, see Part 1.)

Provide S with practice in chewing. Place one end of a strip of raw beef (seasoned for taste) in S's mouth, and grasp the other end. Apply pressure, using jaw control to encourage S to chew the meat. S will not be able to break off any pieces and will receive practice chewing. Provide this practice often.

Place a very small piece of food in one side of S's mouth. Hold S's mouth and jaws, using either front or side jaw control, and gently help S to move his jaws up, down, and sideways. Gradually fade your guidance. Then gradually increase the size of the food until it is bite-size so that S is required to move his jaws with more force.

Use a metal spoon coated with plastic (commercially available) to press down on S's bottom side teeth. This will stimulate the biting motion.

Wrap a softened piece of chewing gum in gauze, and place it between S's side teeth to provide him with practice chewing. Grasp one end of the gauze to prevent S from swallowing the gum.

Part 4:

Provide S with practice on tongue movements. Place a sticky, good tasting substance (peanut butter, marshmallow cream) at different places inside S's mouth (roof of mouth, the sides, on the side teeth S uses to chew). Encourage S to lick the food.

Place the food between the chewing surfaces of the side teeth so that S will learn where the food must be in order to chew.

Try using a plastic coated spoon to keep S's jaws open to see if he is moving the food to the side of his mouth with his tongue.

<u>Note:</u> Do not work on Part 4 until S can move food with his tongue. Otherwise, it is likely that he will simply swallow the food when it is placed on his tongue.

Part 5:

Guide S by holding his lips closed between your thumb and forefinger. Do this only for short periods and only if S can breathe sufficiently through his nose. Gradually fade your guidance.

Part 6:

Use very small pieces of food at first. Gradually increase the size of the food until it is bite-size and requires moderate chewing.

Eating
Finger Foods

Chain

Skill:

In this program the child learns to pick up food with his fingers, place it in his mouth, bite off a piece if necessary, then eat it. This skill is needed for many common foods not eaten with utensils, such as sandwiches, potato chips, candy, and cookies.

Entry Behaviors:

1. S <u>picks up</u> the food with one or both hands. If S cannot use a pincer grasp adequately, do not use foods such as small raisins while teaching this program. If S has an impaired grasp, teach Eating with a Spoon or Eating with a Fork, where adaptive equipment or materials can be used.

2. S <u>reaches for the food and brings it to his mouth</u> by bending his arm at the elbow. If S cannot bring the food to his mouth, reconsider your rationale for teaching any of the self-feeding programs. You may need to develop an alternate task analysis with special equipment.

3. S <u>chews and swallows</u> whatever food is to be used (e.g., Chewing). If S is not chewing properly or is just learning to chew, use soft finger foods that are easily digestible: small pieces of hot dog, cheese, soft fruit slices (see the Foods Chart, page 461).

Objective:

S picks up the food, places it in his mouth, bites off a piece if necessary, and eats the food unassisted. S must initiate his response within 5 seconds of the command and respond correctly 4 out of 5 trials. 1 bite = 1 trial.

Cycle:

None specified. However, you may repeat the program to teach specific foods that cause S particular difficulty.

Follow-Up:

Continue to provide S with practice in eating a variety of finger foods, both larger portions from which S must bite off a portion (sandwiches, cookies), and smaller bite-sized pieces, which may be picked up with the thumb and finger (miniature marshmallows). Provide a wide variety of foods, preferably those with some nutritional value, such as carrot sticks, crackers, and cheese. Present candy and sweets less frequently. Provide S practice in using a cup as well (e.g., Drinking from Cup).

Program for Eating Skill 2

Chart:

Foods Chart, page 461.

GENERAL STRATEGY

Setting:

Work with S at any time during the day. Initially, choose times other than mealtime since the assistance you provide to S may be aversive.

Arrangement:

Seat S in an upright position with his feet flat on the floor for support. His head should be erect with support if necessary. Do not allow S's head to fall back at any time during feeding, since it is almost impossible to swallow in this position. Place a finger food S prefers in front of him within his reach.

Attention:

Draw S's attention to the food on the table, and talk about it.

Command:

Give an appropriate command ("EAT THE CRACKER") with cues indicating what you wish S to do.

Latency:

S must initiate his response within 5 seconds of the command (or last part completed).

Correction:

Use general correction or Suggestions on any part that S does not perform correctly. After you assist him, allow him to continue the trial on his own. Correct him only if needed.

Other Trials:

Allow S time to swallow the food between trials. Vary the foods that are used. Repeat the strategy as often as appropriate. You may set up situations to practice the skill if desired, but limit sessions to 10 minutes. Note that when it takes more than one bite to eat the food (sandwich, cookies), each bite = 1 trial. After the first trial, S may continue to hold the food so that Parts 1 and 2 need not be repeated.

Modification:

S has made no gains in average parts completed after two successive probes (2 weeks).

CONDITIONS	BEHAVIOR	CRITERIA
		for *7 only
PRE Get S's attention, and give the command.	*7. Target--S picks up the food and eats one bite unassisted.	4 correct out of 5 trials

DAILY INSTRUCTION/WEEKLY PROBES:

Get S's attention, and give the command. Correct each part if needed.	1. S <u>extends his hand(s)</u> to the food. 2. S <u>picks up the food</u>. 3. S <u>raises the food</u> to his mouth. 4. S <u>opens his mouth</u> and places the food in it. 5. S <u>breaks off a bite</u> of food if needed (S may continue to hold the remainder, such as a cookie, or replace it on the table). 6. S <u>chews and swallows</u> the food. *7. Target--S picks up the food and eats one bite unassisted.	Continue daily instruction/weekly probes until S performs *7 correctly 4 out of the last 5 trials
POST 1 Same as PRE	*7. Target--S picks up the food and eats one bite unassisted.	4 correct out of 5 trials for each test
POST 2 New Setting		
POST 3 New Teacher		

SUGGESTIONS

Part 1:

Guide S to reach for the food. Place your hand over his, and guide him to extend it to the food. Or, exert pressure with one hand just above and behind S's elbow, and place your other hand in opposition on the forearm. Gradually decrease the amount of pressure you exert.

Use backward chaining. At first guide S's hand all the way to the food. Then guide halfway, and let him finish. Gradually provide less assistance so that S must bring his hand farther to the food on his own.

Have S reach for different toys, food, and the like. Vary the distance and position of the objects. Gradually decrease the amount of assistance you give S.

Part 2:

At first use only sticky and easy-to-grasp foods (e.g., marshmallows, fresh bread). Gradually introduce others.

Provide practice in grasping a variety of objects. At first use foods that can be easily grasped, such as sandwiches sliced in quarters, bread sticks, french fries, or peanut butter and crackers.

If S tries to squeeze the food in his hands, at first use only foods that cannot be mashed, such as apple slices, whole pickles, carrot or celery sticks. If S refuses to bite such foods, put peanut butter or cream cheese on the fruit or vegetable. Gradually introduce a wider variety of foods with different textures.

Part 3:

Use backward chaining. Guide S's hand all the way to his mouth. Then guide his hand part of the way, and allow him to finish. Gradually provide less guidance so that S is bringing his hand to his mouth unassisted.

Part 4:

Touch the food to S's lips, using, for example, a popsicle that would melt enough for S to taste, even if his lips were closed. As soon as S opens his mouth, prompt him to handle the food. Release or relax your grasp. Allow S to complete the task on his own (putting the food in his mouth).

Use backward chaining for Parts 2, 3, and 4. First guide S to grasp the food, raise it to his mouth, and place it in. Then guide S through grasping and raising the food, but have him place the food in his mouth. Next only guide S to grasp the food, and have him complete the rest. Finally remove your guidance altogether.

At first use highly reinforcing foods. After S learns to place some of these foods in his mouth, gradually introduce others.

Part 5:

Note: S may break off a piece of food with his teeth, gums, or lips. If you are using bite-sized pieces (e.g., miniature marshmallows), omit this part.

At first use foods that are already in bite-sized pieces that can be put into the mouth whole. Then present pieces of food that can be easily broken off with the front teeth or lips, such as a piece of bread or banana. Introduce other foods in larger portions that are more difficult to bite, such as carrot sticks, hamburgers, and the like.

Use foods like a breadstick or sandwich that you can hold by one end. Pull the food with an upward or downward movement as S holds it in his mouth to help him to break off a piece. Gradually fade your assistance.

Part 6:

Review the Suggestions from the Chewing program (pages 235-36) if S is having any difficulty chewing and swallowing.

Drinking
from
a Cup

Chain

Skill:

In this program the child learns to pick up a cup and to bring it to his mouth to drink. This task chain involves the use of a whole-hand grasp and eye-hand coordination to pick up the cup, bring it to his mouth, and return the cup to the table without spilling.

Entry Behaviors:

1. S <u>picks up</u> the cup with one or both hands by grasping the handle with one hand, wrapping his hand(s) around the cup, or holding the cup between his palms. If S has an impaired grasp, adapt by using adaptive equipment or materials that enable him to secure the cup in his hand(s).

2. S <u>reaches for the cup</u> and <u>brings it to his mouth</u>. If S cannot bring the cup to his mouth, reconsider your rationale for teaching any of the self-feeding programs. You may need to develop your own task analysis with special equipment.

3. S's <u>hand(s) is steady</u> enough to hold the cup without spilling. If S has cerebral palsy or another disability that causes shaking, partially fill the cup or use a special cup with spillproof features.

4. S <u>swallows liquids</u>. When teaching this program, choose liquids that S prefers.

5. S has <u>experience drinking from a cup</u> with assistance (e.g., you hold the cup as he drinks). This program teaches S to handle the cup on his own, not to swallow liquid from the cup.

Objective:

Given a cup with liquid, S picks it up, brings it to his mouth, and drinks unassisted without spilling. S must initiate his response within 5 seconds of the command and respond correctly 4 out of 5 trials. 1 trial = S drinks one or more swallows, then replaces the cup.

Cycle:

None specified. However, you may repeat the program for cups that are difficult to use (e.g., paper cups that crush).

Follow-Up:

Provide S the opportunity to drink from a variety of cups, glasses, mugs, paper cups, with and without handles. Present him with a variety of drinks, both hot and cold. Introduce S to drinking liquids through a straw. Combine feeding skills (e.g., Eating Finger Foods, Drinking from a Cup) so that S is feeding himself. Allow him to do as much as possible on his own. Work on table manners, such as wiping his face (e.g., Using a Napkin), or cleaning up a spill. Expand S's vocabulary. Name the drink and encourage him to tell you what he is drinking (e.g., Naming Objects).

Program for Eating Skill 3

Chart:

Foods Chart, page 461.

GENERAL STRATEGY

Setting:

Work with S at any time during the day. Initially, choose times other than mealtime since the assistance you provide to S may be aversive.

Arrangement:

Seat S in an upright position with his feet flat on the floor for support. His head should be erect with support if necessary. Do not allow S's head to fall back at any time during feeding, since it is almost impossible to swallow in that position. Place a cup with liquid S prefers in front of him, within his reach.

Attention:

Draw S's attention to the cup. Talk about it if desired.

Command:

Give an appropriate command ("DRINK YOUR MILK") with cues indicating what you wish S to do.

Latency:

S must initiate his response within 5 seconds of the command (or last part completed).

Correction:

Use general correction or Suggestions on any part that S does not perform correctly. After you assist him, allow him to continue the trial on his own. Correct him only if needed.

Other Trials:

Always allow S to drink as much as he wants before he sets the cup down. However, insure that S does not gulp the liquid. Allow plenty of time between trials. Vary the liquids that are used. Repeat the strategy as often as appropriate. Note that 1 trial = S drinks one or more swallows, then replaces the cup.

Modification:

S has made no gains in average parts completed after two successive probes (2 weeks).

CONDITIONS	BEHAVIOR	CRITERIA
		for *8 only
PRE Get S's attention, and give the command.	*8. Target--S picks up the cup, drinks from it, and replaces the cup unassisted without spilling.	4 correct out of 5 trials

DAILY INSTRUCTION/WEEKLY PROBES:

Get S's attention, and give the command. Correct each part if needed.	1. S <u>extends his hand</u> to the cup.	Continue daily instruction/weekly probes until S performs *8 correctly 4 out of the last 5 trials
	2. S <u>picks up</u> the cup.	
	3. S <u>brings the cup to his mouth</u>.	
	4. S <u>places the rim</u> of the cup between his lips.	
	5. S <u>tilts his cup</u> and head slightly to pour liquid into his mouth.	
	6. S <u>swallows the liquid</u>.	
	7. S <u>replaces the cup</u> on the table.	
	*8. Target--S picks up the cup, drinks from it, and replaces the cup unassisted without spilling.	
POST 1 Same as PRE	*8. Target--S picks up the cup, drinks from it, and replaces the cup unassisted without spilling.	4 correct out of 5 trials for each test
POST 2 Different Cup		
POST 3 Different Setting		

SUGGESTIONS

Part 1:

Use backward chaining to develop S's aim. First guide S's hand all the way to the cup; then guide his arm 3/4 of the way, halfway, and finally have S extend his hand to the cup the whole way without assistance.

Use a weighted cup to prevent spills when S is first learning to extend his hand to the cup. Then when S's aim is better, return to a regular cup, but do not fill it very full. Finally fill the cup about 3/4 full.

Part 2:

Guide S to hold the cup in any one of the following positions, and gradually
fade this assistance.

(If S Cannot
Use His Fingers)

Use plastic place mats under the cup so it does not slide around when S
tries to pick it up.

At first place only a little bit of liquid in the cup to make the cup
lighter and to prevent spilling. Gradually pour more liquid into the cup.

Parts 3 and 4:

Use backward chaining. Guide S's hand(s) holding the cup all the way to
his mouth. Then guide it almost to his mouth. Gradually provide less
assistance until S is bringing the cup to his mouth unassisted.

Have S feed himself crackers and other finger foods to develop his aim
(bringing hand to mouth).

Part 5:

Fill the cup almost full so that S does not have to tilt the cup very far
for the liquid to flow into his mouth. As S drinks more liquid, he will
have to tilt the cup farther, and this will gradually develop this skill.

Vary the amount of liquid in the cup. Place your finger under S's chin,
and apply gentle pressure to prompt S to tilt his head slightly. Gradually
apply less pressure until S tilts his head back on his own. (Be careful
not to tilt S's head back so far that it is difficult for him to swallow.)

Use a small cup at first, and fill it at least 1/4 full of liquid so that
S will not have to tilt his head or the cup very far. Then provide practice
drinking from larger glasses holding less liquid, so that he must tilt his
head and the glass farther back.

Place your finger on the bottom of S's cup, and tilt it slightly. Gradually
apply less pressure until S can tilt his cup without assistance.

Use a training cup that has a covered top with a small opening from which
S may drink. When S is able to use the training cup, introduce a regular
cup or small glass that has very little liquid in it.

Note: This type of training cup is preferable to those with spouts, which
sometime encourage sucking.

Part 6:

Review Suggestions from the Chewing program if S is having difficulty
swallowing.

Gently compress S's lips over the rim to keep the liquid in his mouth before swallowing. Gradually apply less pressure.

Part 7:

Fill the cup with only a small amount of liquid, and teach S that every time he replaces the cup on the table, it will be filled with liquid again (only enough for one or two swallows). Gradually put more in the cup each time as S learns to replace the cup without spilling any liquid.

Use a weighted cup that will not tip over easily when S replaces it. When S can replace the weighted cup without spilling, introduce a regular cup or glass.

Have S carry, hold, and set down cups. At first use cups with tops and/or ones with very little liquid. As S becomes more proficient, fill the cup with more liquid, and remove the top if one has been used.

Eating with a Spoon

Chain

Skill:

In this program the child learns to complete the sequence of scooping food onto a spoon and putting it into his mouth. Although S is able to chew and swallow common foods and will feed himself with his fingers, he does not yet use utensils.

Entry Behaviors:

1. S chews and swallows the food being used. If S does not chew properly or is just learning to chew, use semi-solid foods, such as pudding, which dissolve easily and may be swallowed without chewing.

2. S reaches for the spoon and brings it to his mouth by bending his arm at the elbow. S previously used this reach when feeding himself finger foods (e.g., Eating Finger Foods). If S cannot get the spoon to his mouth, reconsider your rationale for teaching any of the self-feeding programs. You may need to develop an alternate task analysis.

3. S holds the spoon. If S has an impaired grasp, adapt by using equipment or materials that enable S to secure the spoon in his hand.

Objective:

Given a bowl of food and a spoon, S uses the spoon to feed himself without assistance. S must initiate his response within 5 seconds of the command and respond correctly 4 out of 5 trials. 1 spoonful = 1 trial.

Overview
Eating
Skill 4

Cycle:

None specified. However, the program may be repeated if desired to teach foods that are more difficult to scoop (e.g., soup).

Follow-Up:

Continue to increase the variety of foods S can eat with a spoon. As S becomes more proficient with a spoon, slowly introduce more difficult foods (e.g., soups). Make eating with a spoon part of the daily routine so that S learns to feed himself without requiring a command. During meals, combine the use of a spoon with S's other eating skills (e.g., Eating Finger Foods, Drinking from a Cup). Introduce the use of a fork to spear certain foods (e.g., Eating with a Fork). Expand S's vocabulary by naming the foods he is eating so that he can request those on his own.

Program for Eating Skill 4

Chart:

Foods Chart, page 461.

GENERAL STRATEGY:

Setting:

Work with S at any time during the day. Initially, choose times other than mealtime since the assistance you provide to S may be aversive.

Arrangement:

Seat S in an upright position with his feet flat on the floor for support. His head should be erect with his neck supported if necessary. Do not allow S's head to fall **back** at any time during feeding, since it is almost impossible to swallow in this position. Place a bowl of food S prefers in front of him within his reach. Place the spoon beside or in the bowl of food.

Attention:

Draw S's attention to the bowl of food and the spoon. Talk about each, if desired.

Command:

Give an appropriate command ("USE THE SPOON") <u>with cues</u> indicating what you wish S to do.

Latency:

S must initiate his response within 5 seconds of the command (or last part completed).

Correction:

Use general correction or Suggestions on any part that S does not perform correctly. After you assist him, allow him to continue on his own. Correct him only if needed.

Other Trials:

Always allow plenty of time between trials for S to swallow the food. Vary the foods used, but present only those of the same consistency when teaching the program the first time. Limit sessions to 10 minutes. Repeat the strategy as often as appropriate during the session. 1 trial = 1 spoonful. <u>Note</u>: After the first trial, S may continue to hold the spoon so that Part 1 need not be repeated.

Modification:

S has made no gains in <u>average parts completed</u> after two successive probes (2 weeks).

CONDITIONS	BEHAVIOR	CRITERIA
		for *8 only
PRE Get S's attention, and give the command.	*8. Target--S uses the spoon to feed himself one bite unassisted.	4 correct out of 5 trials

DAILY INSTRUCTION/WEEKLY PROBES:

Get S's attention, and give the command. Correct each part if needed.	1. S <u>grasps the spoon handle</u>. 2. S <u>raises the spoon</u> and positions it over the bowl. 3. S <u>scoops the food</u> onto the spoon. 4. S <u>raises the spoon (food) to his mouth</u>. 5. S <u>opens his mouth and inserts</u> the spoon (food). 6. S <u>closes his mouth</u> over the food and <u>slides the spoon out</u> (without scraping the spoon on his teeth). 7. S <u>chews and swallows</u> the food if necessary. *8. Target--S uses the spoon to feed himself one bite unassisted.	Continue daily instruction/weekly probes until S performs *8 correctly 4 out of the last 5 trials
POST 1 Same as PRE	*8. Target--S uses the spoon to feed himself one bite unassisted.	4 correct out of 5 trials for each test
POST 2 New Setting		
POST 3 Different Textured Food		

SUGGESTIONS

Part 1:

Guide S to use any one of several grasps. Gradually fade your physical assistance and/or extra directions.

Part 2:

Guide S to position the spoon before making a scooping motion (Part 3).
Gradually fade this assistance and extra directions.

Position the spoon at the back
of the bowl to scoop forward
with the side of the spoon.

Position the spoon to the side of
the bowl to scoop with the top of
the spoon toward the other side of
the bowl.

Part 3:

Place S's free hand on the side of the bowl to hold it steady while he
scoops. Gradually fade your guidance. Or, use a suction cup on the bottom
of the bowl. Decrease the use of this assistance. Have S use only his
free hand to steady the bowl. (S may meet criterion holding the bowl on
his own.)

Provide practice in scooping, using a larger spoon on which the food is
more likely to stay. S may also scoop such materials as sand. S may use
a small hand shovel or a large spoon to develop the scooping motion.

Parts 4 and 5:

Use backward chaining for Parts 2 through 5. Guide S to position the spoon
over the bowl, scoop, raise it to his mouth, and then insert it in his
mouth. Next guide S only to position the spoon, scoop, and raise it to
his mouth. Allow him to insert it on his own. Then guide S only to position the spoon and scoop. Allow him to raise and insert it unassisted.
Finally guide S only to get the spoon to the bowl, and allow him to finish.
After that point, remove all guidance.

Use highly reinforcing foods, since S has already demonstrated that he can
insert food in his mouth by hand (e.g., Eating Finger Foods). If S does
not put the spoon in his mouth, it is probably a reinforcer problem rather
than a lack of physical skill.

If S has trouble controlling the spoon and keeping it level so that the food
does not fall off, use only sticky foods (pudding, oatmeal, mashed potatoes,
fruit). In addition, use physical guidance to keep the spoon upright.
Gradually fade the guidance, and introduce other foods.

Part 6:

Gently put pressure on S's jaws as a reminder to close his mouth over the
food. If S has consistent problems keeping his mouth closed, review the
exercises suggested in the Chewing program.

Compress S's lips by using your thumb and forefinger, one above, one below
each lip. Gradually fade your guidance. Make sure that S uses his lips
to keep the food in his mouth and does not scrape the spoon against his
teeth.

Part 7:

If S is having trouble chewing and swallowing, refer to Suggestions in
the Chewing program (pages 235-36).

Eating with a Fork

Chain

Skill:

In this program the child learns to pick up a fork, spear food, and bring the food to his mouth to eat it. Eye-hand coordination is developed.

Entry Behaviors:

1. S picks up the fork. If S has an impaired grasp, adapt the program by using adaptive equipment or materials that enable S to secure the fork in his hand.

2. S reaches for the fork and brings it to his mouth. If S cannot bring the fork to his mouth, reconsider your rationale for teaching any of the self-feeding programs. You may need to develop your own task analysis with special equipment.

3. S feeds himself with a spoon (e.g., Eating with a Spoon). This skill is usually taught before using a fork since more coordination is often required to spear or scoop food with a fork.

4. S chews and swallows the food. If S is not chewing properly or is just learning to chew, reconsider your rationale for teaching this program at this time. Almost any food that S could spear with a fork would require thorough chewing to prevent him from choking.

Objective:

Given a bowl or plate of food and a fork, S uses the fork to eat by spearing each bite of food unassisted. S must initiate his response within 5 seconds of the command and respond correctly 4 out of 5 trials. 1 trial = 1 bite.

food = small, bite-sized pieces of food that can be easily speared (not too tough). For example: pieces of meat, ravioli, green beans, beets, and the like (S is not required to cut the food).

Cycle:

None specified.

Follow-Up:

Provide S with a variety of foods he can eat with a fork. Teach him to cut his food (e.g., cake) with the side of the fork, to scoop or spear the food, and then to eat it. Also, teach S to use a knife and fork together by spearing the meat with the fork and then using the knife to cut the meat. Allow S to feed himself as much as possible using utensils (spoon, fork, cup), and give him assistance only if necessary. Work on table manners. Require S to keep his face clean while he eats. Also require him to clean up food he spills. Expand his vocabulary. Name the food he is eating.

Program for Eating Skill 5

Chart:

Foods Chart, page 461.

GENERAL STRATEGY:

Setting:

Work with S at any time during the day. Initially, choose times other than mealtime since the assistance you provide to S may be aversive.

Arrangement:

Seat S in an upright position with his feet flat on the floor for support. His head should be erect with support if necessary. Do not allow S's head to fall back at any time during feeding, since it is almost impossible to swallow in this position. Place a bowl or plate of food S prefers in front of him within his reach. Place the fork beside or on the plate of food.

Attention:

Draw S's attention to the plate of food and fork. Talk about them if desired.

Command:

Give an appropriate command ("EAT YOUR MEAT") <u>with cues</u> indicating what you wish S to do.

Latency:

S must initiate his response within 5 seconds of the command (or last part completed).

Correction:

Use general correction or Suggestions on each part that S does not perform correctly. After you assist him, allow him to continue the trial on his own. Correct him only if needed.

Other Trials:

Always allow plenty of time between trials to swallow the food. Vary the foods. Always use small pieces that can be speared. Limit sessions to 10 minutes. Repeat the above strategy as often as appropriate. 1 trial = 1 forkful. <u>Note</u>: After the first trial, S may continue to hold the fork so that Part 1 need not be repeated.

Modification:

S has made no gains in <u>average parts completed</u> after two successive probes (2 weeks).

CONDITIONS	BEHAVIOR	CRITERIA
		for *8 only
PRE Get S's attention, and give the command.	*8. Target--S uses a fork to feed himself one bite unassisted.	4 correct out of 5 trials

DAILY INSTRUCTION/WEEKLY PROBES:

Get S's attention, and give the command. Correct each part if needed.	1. S <u>picks up the fork</u>. 2. S <u>positions the fork</u> over the food, with the prongs pointing toward the food. 3. S <u>spears a piece</u> of of food. 4. S <u>raises the fork</u> (food) to his mouth. 5. S <u>opens his mouth</u> and <u>inserts the fork</u> (food). 6. S <u>closes his mouth</u> over the food and <u>slides the fork</u> out. 7. S <u>chews and swallows</u> the food. *8. Target--S uses a fork to feed himself one bite unassisted.	Continue daily instruction/weekly probes until S performs *8 correctly 4 out of the last 5 trials.
POST 1 Same as PRE	*8. Target--S uses a fork to feed himself one bite unassisted.	4 correct out of 5 trials for each test
POST 2 New Setting		
POST 3 New Materials		

SUGGESTIONS

Part 1:

Guide S to hold the fork in any one of several positions, and gradually
fade your guidance.

 OR  OR

<u>Note</u>: It is usually easier to spear food using the third grasp pictured
because the prongs will already be pointing down toward the food.

Parts 2 and 3:

Have S hold a pencil, stick, or fork and touch the tip end downward on specific targets. Vary the distance and the size of the targets.

Use a bowl with high sides so that as S spears the food, it will not slide as much as if it were on a plate. Position the bowl on a plastic place mat to keep it from sliding. When S can spear this way, switch to a bowl with lower sides or to a plate.

Guide S to push the fork farther into the food if he is having trouble keeping the food on the fork. Gradually fade this guidance.

For a while, try placing only one piece of food on the plate, then gradually add more.

Hold the piece of food for S as he spears it, and gradually fade your assistance. Or, use pieces of food without sauce on them, such as a plain piece of meat that does not slide around on the plate. When S can spear this food, begin using a variety of foods again.

Position the plate on a plastic place mat or use a suction cup on the bottom of the plate if S is moving the whole plate as he tries to spear the food.

Parts 4 and 5:

Use backward chaining. Hold S's hand when he moves the fork all the way to his mouth. Then guide it almost to his mouth. Provide less guidance until S can bring the fork all the way to his mouth unassisted.

Use highly reinforcing foods since S has already demonstrated that he can insert food in his mouth in Eating Finger Foods. If S does not put the fork in his mouth, it is most likely a reinforcer problem rather than lack of a physical skill.

Guide S to place the food in his mouth to prevent him from hurting himself with the prongs. Gradually fade this guidance.

Part 6:

Gently put pressure on S's jaws as a reminder to close his mouth over the food. If S has consistent problems keeping his mouth closed, review the exercises suggested in the Chewing program, pages 235-36.

Gently put pressure on S's lips or jaws so that his lips will stay together and the food will stay in his mouth when he slides the fork out. Gradually apply less pressure.

Part 7:

Use Suggestions from the Chewing program (pages 235-36) if S is having trouble chewing or swallowing.

Pulling Off

Chain

Cycle

Skill:

In this program the child learns to reach, grasp, and pull off simple clothing articles, such as hats, scarves, mittens, and socks. With this skill, the child can learn more complex and refined chains (e.g., to unfasten, then pull; to insert, then pull on).

Entry Behaviors:

1. S <u>extends his arm</u> far enough to reach the article to be removed (e.g., Reaching). If S has impaired arm movement, teach only for articles that he can reach, and position him for his best reach. If S cannot reach the article with his hand, you may adapt by allowing S to "grasp" and pull with either his toes or teeth. If this adaptation is impractical, reconsider the rationale for this particular skill, and teach S alternative strategies for the grasp-pull chain (e.g., stabilizing the article, then moving his body away).

2. S <u>grasps (whole-hand or pincer)</u> the article securely and maintains a grip during gentle pulling (e.g., Grasping Objects). Or, adapt by using adaptive equipment or materials that enable S to secure the article.

3. S <u>cooperates in dressing</u> by attending (looking at the clothing, body part, or adult) or attempting to assist (moving his body to facilitate dressing). Preferably, S does not resist physical guidance.

Objective:

When wearing clothing that can be removed by pulling, S pulls the article completely off without assistance. S must initiate his response within 5 seconds of the command and respond correctly 4 out of 5 trials.

Cycle:

Select one type of clothing (e.g., hat <u>or</u> scarf <u>or</u> sock) to teach at a time, since each type involves reaching to a different body part and pulling in a different direction: stretch-knit hats, mittens, woolen neck warmers (untied), short stretch socks, pull-on shoes, belts (unbuckled). Repeat the program to teach other clothing as appropriate for S. You may also use this program to teach a component of a more complex skill, such as grasping a sleeve (at the cuff) and pulling his arm out.

Follow-Up:

Continue to have S remove articles at appropriate times. Set up routines
at school for times and places for appropriate undressing. For example,
always have S take off his hat after recess and put it on his hook in the
closet. Maintain routines so that S learns to predict what is to happen
and thus learns to take off the article at appropriate times without your
reminders. During teaching and as a follow-up, emphasize the name of the
body part involved, the article, and the activity (<u>hand</u>, <u>mitten</u>, <u>pull</u>).
Encourage S to practice this pulling skill on more complex tasks, even if
he cannot perform the rest of the task yet. For example, help S pull his
arms out of a pullover sweater. Or encourage him to pull off a T-shirt
after you have removed it so that S need only pull with a brief motion to
free it. Or, have S pull the tie ends of his shoelaces, and then you untie
them (see other Dressing Skills).

Program for Dressing Skill 1

GENERAL STRATEGY

Arrangement:

Place S in a comfortable position (with support if needed) in which he can remove the article.

Attention:

Draw S's attention to the article to be removed. Talk about the object as desired.

Command:

Give an appropriate command ("HAT OFF") <u>with cues</u> indicating what you wish S to do.

Latency:

S must initiate his response within 5 seconds of the command (or last part completed).

Correction:

Use general correction or Suggestions on any part that S does not perform correctly. After you assist him, allow him to continue the trial on his own. Correct him only if needed.

Natural Consequence:

After S has removed the article, have him put it in an appropriate place. 1 trial = the removal of 1 article.

Other Trials:

Repeat the strategy as often as appropriate. You may set up situations to practice the skill if desired.

Modification:

S has made no gains in <u>average parts completed</u> after two successive probes (2 weeks).

CONDITIONS	BEHAVIOR	CRITERIA
		for *6 only
PRE Get S's attention, and give the command. Present the natural consequence.	*6. Target--S pulls the article off unassisted.	4 correct out of 5 trials

DAILY INSTRUCTION/WEEKLY PROBES:

Get S's attention, and give the command. Correct each part if needed. Present the natural consqeuence.	1. S <u>extends</u> his hand(s) to the article, re-positioning himself if needed to reach the article.	Continue daily instruction/weekly probes until S performs *6 correctly 4 out of the last 5 trials.
	2. S <u>grasps</u> the article at an appropriate place.	
	3. S <u>pulls</u> the article <u>1 inch off</u> (initial tug).	
	4. S <u>adjusts his body and/or loosens the article</u> if needed.	
	5. S <u>pulls the article</u> until it comes off.	
	*6. Target--S pulls the article off unassisted.	
POST 1 Same as PRE	*6. Target--S pulls the article off unassisted.	4 correct out of 5 trials for each test
POST 2 New Setting		
POST 3 Different Articles (same type)		

SUGGESTIONS

Part 1:

For socks or shoes, have S lean forward while maintaining his balance and reach for his foot. Guide S if needed; then gradually fade this assistance.

Sitting with His Back Supported (Chair or Floor), S Brings One Leg Up in the Air to Hold His Foot.

Sitting (Chair or Floor), S Crosses One Leg over the Other Knee.

For a hat or scarf, have S raise his arm(s) to the top of his head and touch his head.

For mittens, have S put his hands together and bring them to his midline and to his left or right.

Part 2:

Suggested points for grasping:

At the Top of His Mittens   At the Toe of His Socks   At the Heel and Toe of His Shoe

At the Top of Hat   OR   At the Cuff (His Thumb Inside)

Have S point to the correct place to grasp. Color code these parts if necessary to help S remember where to grasp. Later remove these cues.

Part 3:

Have S hold objects while you pull in the opposite direction to strengthen his grip (i.e., play tug-of-war). Have S pull things away from you.

Use loose (one-size too large) articles so that S can pull more easily until he has learned the grasp-pull chain. Then return to his own articles.

Part 4:

To loosen tight articles, prompt S to stretch the cuff or move his hand or foot while pulling. Practice Parts 3 and 4 simultaneously.

Show S where to change his grip to allow for easier removal. Practice grasp-pull-release, regrasp-pull if necessary.

Part 5:

Require S to pull off more of the article. First arrange it so that it comes off with a short pull or tug. Then do less so that he must pull longer and/or harder to remove it.

Unsnapping

Chain

Skill:

In this program the child learns to grasp a garment at the appropriate position so that it may be unsnapped (grasp--pull). This skill involves a generalized type of pulling (as in Pulling Off) but requires a more refined grasp to hold the material near the snap and a more controlled pull to unsnap without tearing the garment.

Entry Behaviors:

1. S <u>reaches the snap</u> with both hands at the same time. If S can reach with only one hand, use Velcro snaps. These may be pulled apart with one hand. To adapt this program, delete the parts that refer to actions with the second hand.

2. S <u>grasps (palmar or pincer) and holds the material</u> while he pulls gently. Or, allow S to use adaptive equipment or materials that enable him to secure the article.

Objective:

When wearing a garment that is snapped, S pulls the snap apart without tearing the garment, unassisted. S must initiate his response within 5 seconds of the command and respond correctly 4 out of 5 trials. 1 trial = 1 snap.

Cycle:

None specified. However, the program may be repeated if needed to teach snaps located in different places. For example, S may be able to unsnap his jacket but not his pants. You may repeat to teach him to unsnap his pants.

Overview
Dressing
Skill 2

Follow-Up:

Continue to require S to unsnap his clothing at appropriate times. Establish routines so that he learns to unsnap only at appropriate times and without waiting for your command. Combine unsnapping with other tasks needed to remove a garment. For example, S unsnaps his pants, unzips them (e.g., Unzipping Pants), then pulls them down or off (e.g., Taking Off Pants) to undress himself. When having S unsnap, repeat the word <u>snap</u> often to expand S's vocabulary.

Program for Dressing Skill 2

GENERAL STRATEGY

Arrangement:

S is wearing his garment snapped. If the snap is above the waist, S may be sitting or standing with support as long as his hands or arms are free to reach the snap. If the snap is at the waist (e.g., for pants), S should be standing, if possible, so that the snap is easy to grasp. Alternately, he may be lying down or sitting with his back extended as far as possible to straighten his waist.

Attention:

Draw S's attention to the snap. Talk about why the garment needs to be unsnapped, or make other relevant comments.

Command:

Give an appropriate command ("UNSNAP YOUR COAT") with cues indicating what you wish S to do.

Latency:

S must initiate his response within 5 seconds of the command (or last part completed).

Correction:

Use general correction or Suggestions on any part that S does not perform correctly. After you assist him, allow him to continue the trial on his own. Correct him only if needed.

Natural Consequence:

Have S finish removing the garment with your help if needed. Or, if the garment has several snaps, have S go on to the next trial(s) to finish unsnapping the garment. 1 trial = unsnapping 1 snap.

Other Trials:

Repeat the strategy as often as appropriate. You may set up situations to practice the skill if desired.

Modification:

S has made no gains in average parts completed after two successive probes (2 weeks).

Program
Dressing
Skill 2

CONDITIONS	BEHAVIOR	CRITERIA
		for *5 only
PRE Get S's attention, and give the command. Present the natural consequence.	*5. Target--S pulls one snap apart without tearing the garment, unassisted.	4 correct out of 5 trials

DAILY INSTRUCTION/WEEKLY PROBES:

Get S's attention, and give the command. Correct each part if needed. Present the natural consequence.

1. S <u>grasps the top</u> flap of the material.
2. S <u>grasps the bottom</u> flap of the material.
3. S <u>presses</u> the bottom snap and material to his body (holds it in place).
4. S <u>pulls the top of the snap</u> and material away from his body until the snap opens.
*5. Target--S pulls one snap apart without tearing the garment, unassisted.

Continue daily instruction/weekly probes until S performs *5 correctly 4 out of the last 5 trials.

POST 1 Same as PRE

*5. Target--S pulls one snap apart without tearing the garment, unassisted.

4 correct out of 5 trials for each test

POST 2 New Setting

POST 3 Different Garment (with snaps)

SUGGESTIONS

Parts 1 and 2:

Guide S to grasp in one of the following ways; then gradually fade your guidance.

Waist snap: S's hand holding the bottom of the snap, his thumb inside the waistband, with his top hand as in either <u>a</u> or <u>b</u>.

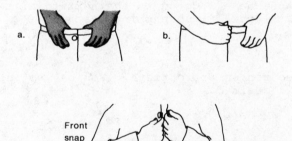

Have S grasp the material and open snaps on garments positioned in front of him (on a table). After S can unsnap in that position, return to the original position with the garment on him.

Parts 3 and 4:

Place your hand over S's to hold the material in place while he pulls with the other hand. Gradually fade your pressure.

Have S pull apart Velcro or adhesive tape strips so that he learns to pull gently but firmly. Gradually introduce more difficult snaps to pull apart.

Place your hand about 3 inches above S's top hand so that when he pulls, your hand stops him from pulling too far and tearing the garment. Gradually hold your hand farther away so that S learns to control his own movement.

Have S push and pull separately. For example, you hold and S pulls, then S holds and you pull. Also, use S's toys to develop his push and pull strength. Then have him perform both actions together.

Putting Hat On

Chain

Skill:

In this program the child learns to grasp his hat appropriately, position it on his head, and pull it on securely. Although this is a general motor chain, it requires coordination to position and adjust the hat.

Entry Behaviors:

1. S <u>raises both arms to his head</u>. Frequently, S can pull his hat off before he learns to pull (put) it on since it can be removed with one hand and no adjustment is required. If S can only raise one arm, use hats that can be adjusted by grasping and pulling several times with the same hand. Adapt by adding parts to the task analysis to allow this method.

2. S <u>grasps the hat with both hands</u> and retains it during gentle pulling (e.g., Pulling Off: Hat). Or, adapt by allowing S to use adaptive equipment or materials that enable him to secure the hat. Or, adapt by adding parts to the task analysis to allow S to grasp and adjust the same hand.

Objective:

S pulls his hat completely on his head and adjusts it if necessary without assistance. S must initiate his response within 5 seconds of the command and respond correctly 4 out of 5 trials.

Cycle:

None specified. However, you may repeat the program for specific hats that cause S difficulty.

Follow-Up:

Continue to have S put on a variety of different hats appropriate to the weather (slicker hat for rain, woolen hat for cold, baseball or other cap for sun). Establish routines so that S learns to put his hat on at appropriate times without your command. Combine with other tasks so that S performs all tasks for getting ready to go outside. For example, S puts on his coat (e.g., Putting On Shirt), hat, and mittens (e.g., Putting Mittens On). When S puts his hat on, repeat the word <u>hat</u> to emphasize it to expand S's vocabulary.

Program for Dressing Skill 3

Arrangement:

S may sit or stand if desired, with support if needed. Both of his hands or arms should be free to manipulate the hat.

Attention:

Hold out the hat to S, and draw his attention to it. Talk about the hat if desired.

Command:

Give an appropriate command ("HAT ON") <u>with cues</u> indicating what you wish S to do.

Latency:

S must initiate his response within 5 seconds of the command (or last part completed).

Correction:

Use general correction or Suggestions on any part that S does not perform correctly. After you assist him, allow him to continue the trial on his own. Correct him only if needed.

Natural Consequence:

Once S is ready (coat, hat, mittens), go outside.

Other Trials:

Repeat the strategy as often as appropriate. You may set up situations to practice the skill if desired.

Modification:

S has made no gains in <u>average parts completed</u> after two successive probes (2 weeks).

CONDITIONS	BEHAVIOR	CRITERIA
		for *6 only
PRE Get S's attention, and give the command. Present the natural consequence.	*6. Target--S pulls his hat on, and adjusts it if necessary without assistance.	4 correct out of 5 trials

DAILY INSTRUCTION/WEEKLY PROBES:

Get S's attention, and give the command. Correct each part if needed. Present the natural consequence.	1. S <u>grasps</u> the hat. 2. S <u>raises</u> the hat to his head. 3. S <u>positions the hat</u> on his head, and pulls it if needed. 4. S <u>pulls the hat down</u> securely on his head. 5. S <u>adjusts the hat</u> if needed to fit properly. *6. Target--S pulls the hat on, and adjusts it if necessary without assistance.	Continue daily instruction/weekly probes until S performs *6 correctly 4 out of the last 5 trials.
POST 1 Same as PRE	*6. Target--S pulls the hat on, and adjusts it if necessary without assistance.	4 correct out of 5 trials for each test
POST 2 New Setting		
POST 3 Different Hat		

SUGGESTIONS

Part 1:

Guide S to grasp the hat in one of the following ways; fade the amount of guidance you provide.

Soft Hat:

thumbs on the inside of the visor.

Baseball Cap:

Thumb on the inside of the visor, and other thumb (optional) inside the back of the cap to keep it from buckling.

Hat with a Hard Band:

Whole-hand grasp on
the top part of the hat.

Part 2:

Guide S to raise the hat in one of the followoing ways; fade the amount
of guidance provided.

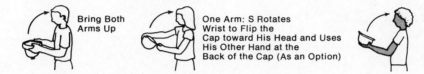

Bring Both Arms Up

One Arm: S Rotates Wrist to Flip the Cap toward His Head and Uses His Other Hand at the Back of the Cap (As an Option)

One Hand

Use backward chaining (with Part 3). At first guide S to bring the hat
all the way up, and have him pull it into position. Then guide him to
bring it almost all the way, as he aims and pulls it into position.
Gradually decrease your assistance, and require S to bring it farther
each time, thus improving his aim.

Part 3:

Guide S to position the hat correctly on his head. Fade your guidance.
Then fade your verbal cues to reposition it when he places it incorrectly.

At first use only hats with hard hatbands (straw hats, cowboy hats) that
automatically fit around S's head. Then use hats that have soft bands
(knit caps, soft caps), which S must stretch to fit on his head.

Part 4:

Assist S to pull the hat down. Gradually require him to perform more of
the movement.

If S has a weak grip, play tug-of-war to increase his strength.

Have S place a knit cap on your head and pull it down if necessary. Then
use S's own hat again.

Part 5:

Have S practice in front of a mirror. Demonstrate how to adjust the hat,
and give verbal cues as he imitates you. Fade the demonstration and your
verbal cues.

Have S practice on large hats that require little adjustment. Then introduce smaller hats with a more difficult fit.

Unzipping Jacket

Chain

Skill:

In this program the child combines fine motor grasping with pulling to
pull the zipper tab down on his own jacket. This skill is an extension
of pulling but requires more fine motor coordination to locate, grasp,
and hold the tab, as well as to pull the zipper along the track.

Entry Behaviors:

1. S <u>moves one arm</u> as needed to unzip the jacket (up and down at midline).
   S <u>brings his other arm to midline</u> to grasp the material near the zipper
   to stabilize it as he pulls. If S has use of only one arm, adapt by
   deleting the part that refers to stabilizing the zipper with the other
   hand.
2. S <u>grasps the zipper tab</u> and retains it while he pulls (e.g., Pulling
   Off). Use only garments with tabs large enough that S can grasp them
   or add larger tabs. Or, adapt by allowing S to use adaptive equipment
   or materials that enable him to secure the article.

Objective:

When wearing a garment with a front (neck-to-waist) zipper that detaches,
S unzips the garment completely and separates the two sides without assistance. S must initiate his response within 5 seconds of the command and
respond correctly 4 out of 5 trials.

Cycle:

None specified.

Follow-Up:

Continue to have S use this skill at all appropriate times. Set up a
routine so that S arrives, unzips and removes his coat, and hangs it up.
This routine will help S to learn to unzip at appropriate times without
your command. Prompt S to pull up the zipper to zip his jacket after you
have put the zipper tab in its track, introducing Zipping Jacket. When
working with S, use the words <u>zip</u> and <u>zipper</u> frequently to expand S's
vocabulary.

Program for Dressing Skill 4

GENERAL STRATEGY

Arrangement:

S is wearing the garment with the zipper completely zipped, but any other fastenings are open (hooks, snaps). S is standing if possible, with support if needed. If S cannot stand, have him lie down or stretch out so that the garment is not gathered up at the waist.

Attention:

Draw S's attention to the zipper. Talk about it if desired.

Command:

Give an appropriate command ("UNZIP JACKET") with cues indicating what you wish S to do.

Latency:

S must initiate his response within 5 seconds of the command (or last part completed).

Correction:

Use general correction or Suggestions on any part that S does not perform correctly. After you assist him, allow him to continue the trial on his own. Correct him only if needed.

Natural Consequence:

After the jacket is unzipped, help S take off the jacket and hang it up.

Other Trials:

Repeat the strategy as often as appropriate. You may wish to set up situations to practice the skill.

Modification:

S has made no gains in average parts completed after two successive probes (2 weeks).

CONDITIONS	BEHAVIOR	CRITERIA for *6 only
PRE Get S's attention, and give the command. Present the natural consequence.	*6. Target--S unzips the garment completely and separates the two sides unassisted.	4 correct out of 5 trials

DAILY INSTRUCTION/WEEKLY PROBES:

Get S's attention, and give the command. Correct each part if needed. Present the natural consequence.	1. S grasps the zipper tab with his dominant hand.	Continue daily instruction/weekly probes until S performs *6 correctly 4 out of the last 5 trials
	2. S lifts the tab to unlock the zipper.	
	3. S stabilizes the jacket with his free hand, holding it secure (this may occur anytime before Part 4 is complete).	

<table>
<tr><td></td><td>4. S <u>pulls the tab
down</u> the track to
the end.
5. S <u>separates the
zipper</u> at the bottom.
*6. Target--S unzips the
garment completely
and separates the two
sides unassisted.</td><td></td></tr>
</table>

POST 1 Same as PRE	*6. Target--S unzips the garment completely and separates the two sides unassisted.	4 correct out of 5 trials for each test

POST 2 New Setting

POST 3 Different Jacket

SUGGESTIONS

Part 1:

Pull S's zipper partly down so that he can see the tab. Have him grasp
in this position. Gradually move the zipper up each time so that S must
grasp at higher positions until the tab is at his neck.

Have S grasp very small items. Guide if needed for a pincer grasp, and
gradually fade your guidance. Use Suggestions in Grasping Objects, (pages
155-61).

Part 2:

As in Part 1, unzip the zipper partly, and guide S to grasp and lift up to
unlock it. Gradually fade your guidance and/or move the starting point up
until it is at S's neck.

Part 3:

Guide S to grasp. Point to the correct positions for grasping. Gradually
fade your guidance and pointing cue.

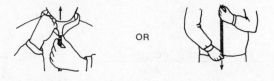

OR

Part 4:

Combine with Parts 1, 2, and 3 for backward chaining. Unzip the zipper
partly. Have S grasp, unlock, and finish unzipping. Gradually start at
higher positions until the tab is at his neck.

Part 5:

Guide S to pull <u>down</u> the zipper tab at the bottom and <u>up</u> on the other
side of the jacket. Gradually fade your guidance.

Have S grasp and hold with one hand while pulling away with the other (up
and down pulling, NOT side to side, which would break the zipper). Separate
practice on <u>grasping</u> and <u>holding while pulling</u> should precede the completion
of the task.

Putting
Mittens On

Chain

Skill:

In this program the child learns to grasp one mitten, insert his hand, and
adjust his thumb while he pulls the mitten on. This skill is an extension
of pulling but requires fine motor coordination to insert and adjust his
hand and thumb.

Entry Behaviors:

1. S <u>brings his hands together</u> in front of him. Frequently, S pulls his
   mittens off (e.g., Pulling Off: Mittens) before he pulls them on
   because the removal requires little adjustment (simple grasp and pull)
   and less thumb control (for positioning the thumb).

2. S <u>grasps the mittens,</u> one hand on each mitten, and retains each while
   gently pulling. Or, adapt to allow use of adaptive equipment or
   materials that enable S to secure the mitten.

Objective:

S pulls his mittens onto his hands with his thumbs properly adjusted
without assistance. S must initiate his response within 5 seconds of
the command and respond correctly 4 out of 5 trials. 1 mitten = 1 trial.

Cycle:

None specified.

Follow-Up:

Continue to have S put on his mittens. Establish routines so that he
learns to put them on at appropriate times without your command. Combine
this with other tasks so that S performs all tasks for getting ready to
go outside. For example, S puts on his coat (e.g., Putting On Shirt),
hat (e.g., Putting Hat On), and mittens. When S puts on his mittens,
repeat the word <u>mittens</u>, and emphasize it to expand S's vocabulary. As
S develops more control over his finger movements, teach him to put on
gloves.

Program for Dressing Skill 5

GENERAL STRATEGY

Arrangement:

S may sit or stand with support if needed. Both hands or arms should be free to work at midline.

Attention:

Hand S his mittens or position them in front of him. Draw attention to the mittens, and talk about them if desired.

Command:

Give an appropriate command ("MITTEN ON") with cues indicating what you wish S to do.

Latency:

S must initiate his response within 5 seconds of the command (or last part completed).

Correction:

Use general correction or Suggestions on any part that S does not perform correctly. After you assist him, allow him to continue the trial on his own. Correct him only if needed.

Natural Consequence:

If this trial was for the first mitten, present the next trial to put on his other mitten (1 trial = 1 mitten). When S has on his mittens and other outdoor garments, go outside.

Other Trials:

Repeat the strategy as often as appropriate. You may set up situations to practice the skill if desired. Whenever you use the program, always have S put on both mittens. 1 trial = 1 mitten.

Modification:

S has made no gains in average parts completed after two successive probes (2 weeks).

Program
Dressing
Skill 5

CONDITIONS	BEHAVIOR	CRITERIA
		for *5 only
PRE Get S's attention, and give the command. Present the natural consequence.	*5. Target--S pulls one mitten on and adjusts it if needed unassisted.	4 correct out of 5 trials

DAILY INSTRUCTION/WEEKLY PROBES:

Get S's attention, and give the command. Correct each part if needed. Present the natural consequence.	1. S grasps the mitten with the opposite hand for which it is intended (he may reposition it if needed to grasp).	Continue daily instruction/weekly probes until S performs *5 correctly 4 out of the last 5 trials.
	2. S inserts his fingers and thumb into the mitten.	
	3. S pulls the mitten all the way on.	
	4. S adjusts the mitten if his thumb is not positioned in the mitten thumb (this may be concurrent with Part 3).	
	*5. Target--S pulls one mitten on and adjusts it if needed unassisted.	
POST 1 Same as PRE	*5. Target--S pulls one mitten on and adjusts it if needed unassisted.	4 correct out of 5 trials for each test
POST 2 New Setting		
POST 3 Different Mittens		

SUGGESTIONS

Part 1:

Demonstrate how to hold the mitten so that S can insert his hand correctly (for Part 2). Reduce the number of times you cue S to hold the mitten correctly.

a. Match hand to mitten, palm up.

b. Match hand, palm down.

Left Hand

Left Hand

After S positions his hand as needed, help him grasp the cuff firmly with the other hand. Gradually fade your guidance.

Left Hand

Grasp the inside of
the cuff to insert
hand, palm up.

OR

Grasp the backside of
the cuff to insert
hand, palm down.

Left Hand

Part 2:

Guide S to press his thumb next to his palm or fingers. Gradually decrease your pressure.

Have S spread his thumb and fingers apart; then bring them all tightly together with his fingers straight. This practice will increase his fine motor skills.

Prompt S if necessary to insert his hand (in position) into a bag or larger mitten than needed. After S can insert his hand into this larger opening, return to the original mitten.

Part 3:

Guide S to aim his thumb and fingers toward the mitten (Part 4). Then pull the mitten almost all the way on. Have S complete the pull movement. Leave more for him to do until he pulls the mitten all the way on unassisted (backward chaining).

If S can control his thumb, have him adjust the mitten thumb by wiggling his thumb while he pulls (depends on S's manual dexterity).

Put the mitten half way on; then adjust the thumb. Have S pull the mitten the rest of the way on. Continue to require S to pull more, but have him stop part way to allow you to position his thumb.

Part 4:

Have S put on mittens that are one-size too large so that it is easy for him to slip his thumb in or move it around to the mitten thumb once his hand is in. Then have S put on his own mittens.

Guide S to grasp the mitten thumb, and pull it so that he can slip his thumb into it. (This may be done during Part 3 when S has the mitten partly on.) Fade your guidance.

Putting Shoes On

Chain

Skill:

In this program the child puts on his shoes by stretching the opening, sliding the shoe on, and then adjusting the fit. (This sequence insures that the shoes are put on the correct feet.) This skill is an extension of pushing or pulling but requires the child to recognize and adjust an improper fit.

Entry Behaviors:

1. S <u>moves his arms or legs and bends his trunk to reach his foot</u>, either to hold the shoe while pulling it on (S is sitting, holding his foot) or to place the shoe next to his foot to step into it (S is sitting or standing and moves his leg to insert his foot).

   a. <u>Step-in method</u>: S can <u>move his leg to insert his foot</u> into the shoe. The step-in method requires less fine motor coordination but requires S to <u>sit or stand with minimal support</u>. This method is functional only if S wears shoes that slip on easily; many tie shoes require the pull-on method.

   b. <u>Pull-on method</u>: S can <u>sit with minimal support and reach his foot</u> comfortably. This is the same position used in pulling off his shoe (e.g., Pulling Off: Shoe). Frequently that skill is acquired first, since it involves a simple pull without inserting the foot or adjusting.

2. S <u>grasps the shoe</u> to stretch it open for an easier fit. If S cannot grasp, use slip-on shoes with the step-in method. Adapt by omitting the optional part that refers to stretching the opening.

Objective:

When given his shoes, S puts each on the correct foot and adjusts the fit if necessary without assistance. S must initiate his response within 5 seconds of the command and respond correctly 4 out of 5 trials. 1 shoe = 1 trial.

Overview
Dressing
Skill 6

Cycle:

None specified. You may teach either method (step-in, pull-on) through the same task analysis. If you have taught S the step-in method, you may repeat the program later for the pull-on method when S's fine motor skills are more developed. If necessary, repeat the program to teach S to put his boots on.

Follow-Up:

Continue to have S put on his own shoes in a variety of appropriate situations. Introduce different (new) shoes that are more difficult to put on, such as sneakers. Have S put on boots. In particular, if S learned the pull-on method, encourage him to pull on his socks (e.g., Putting Socks On), then pull on his shoes in the same position. While S is working with his shoes, use the word shoe frequently to expand his vocabulary. Establish routines during the day so that S puts his shoes and socks on at appropriate times without your command.

Program for Dressing Skill 6

Arrangement:

S may have his socks on. The laces of the shoes are untied and loosened. S may be sitting (chair, floor) or standing with support if needed. If he is sitting in a chair, his feet should be supported or on the floor, not hanging above the floor.

Attention:

Hand the shoes to S. (Do not indicate left-right.) Draw attention to the shoes, and talk about them if desired.

Command:

Give an appropriate command ("SHOE ON") with cues indicating what you wish S to do.

Latency:

S must initiate his response within 5 seconds of the command (or last part completed).

Correction:

Use general correction or Suggestions on any part that S does not perform correctly. After you assist him, allow S to continue the trial on his own. Correct him only if needed.

Natural Consequence:

When S has his shoes on, have him go to some place or do something that emphasizes the concept that by wearing his shoes, he can engage in certain preferred activities (e.g., walking outside).

Other Trials:

Repeat the strategy as often as appropriate. You may set up situations to practice the skill if desired. Whenever using the program, always have S put on both shoes. 1 trial = 1 shoe.

Modification:

S has made no gains in average parts completed after two successive probes (2 weeks).

**Program
Dressing
Skill 6**

CONDITIONS	BEHAVIOR	CRITERIA
		for *7 only
PRE Get S's attention, and give the command. Present the natural consequence.	*7. Target--S puts one shoe on the correct foot, and adjusts the fit if necessary, unassisted.	4 correct out of 5 trials

DAILY INSTRUCTION/WEEKLY PROBES:

Get S's attention, and give the command. Correct each part if needed. Present the natural consequence.	1. Optional--S picks up the shoe(s) and stretches the opening if needed (Parts 1 and 2 may occur in either order).	Continue daily instruction/weekly probes until S performs *7 correctly 4 out of the last 5 trials
	2. S positions himself and/or the shoe(s).	
	3. S points his toes and places them in the correct shoe.	
	4. S slides the shoe onto his foot (or his foot into the shoe).	
	5. S pushes his heel all the way in the shoe.	
	6. S adjusts the fit if needed.	
	*7. Target--S puts one shoe on the correct foot and adjusts the fit if necessary, unassisted.	
POST 1 Same as PRE	*7. Target--S puts one shoe on the correct foot and adjusts the fit if necessary, unassisted.	4 correct out of 5 trials on each test
POST 2 New Setting		
POST 3 Different Shoes		

SUGGESTIONS

Part 1: (optional)

Note: If S has slip-on shoes, this part need not be performed.

Begin by using old slip-on shoes that are a size too large. After S has learned the rest of the parts with those shoes, work on this part with tighter shoes.

Guide S to grasp and stretch the opening; then fade your guidance.

S grasps the sides and stretches the shoe apart.	OR	S grasps the tongue and the heel and stretches the opening (particularly good for tie-up shoes).

For the pull-on method, S may change his grasp if necessary after he stretches the shoe. Guide S for the following (optional) grasp, then fade your guidance.

Part 2:

Try different positions to determine the easiest for S, and then select one to teach. Guide S if needed to get into that position (after he stretches the shoes, if necessary). Gradually fade your guidance.

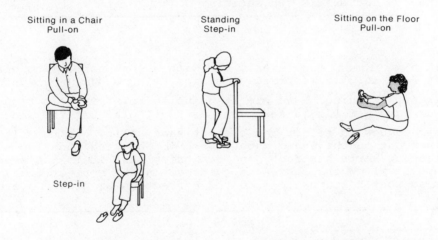

Sitting in a Chair
Pull-on

Standing
Step-in

Sitting on the Floor
Pull-on

Step-in

You may have S practice separately the placement of his shoes next to his feet so that he will pick the correct one for Part 3. (Note: S is not required to place the shoes in any particular way but only to place them near his feet.)

Part 3:

Guide S's toes by pulling his heel up (not pushing his toes down). Gradually fade this guidance.

Run your finger along the bottom of S's foot to prompt him to point his toes. Gradually fade this cue.

If S has difficulty selecting the correct shoe, use the suggestion in Part 2
about teaching S to position the shoes side by side in front of his feet.
Or, paint the outside sole of each shoe red. Teach S to position the shoes
on the floor so that the marks are on the outside. He can then place his
feet beside or behind the shoes to make a correct selection. Fade your
verbal cues.

Use the shape of the shoe (i.e., how it curves more on the side) as a cue
to placement, as pictured above. Exaggerate this cue, in addition to
any visual cues. Gradually fade the use of any added cues.

Parts 4 and 5:

Use backward chaining with Part 3. Pull S's shoe almost all the way on,
and allow him to finish the rest. Gradually pull the shoe on less so that
S pulls or pushes more of the shoe, until he can insert his foot all the
way.

Provide practice with a shoe a size too large so that S's heel slips in
easily. Then have S put on his own shoes.

Part 6:

Teach S to hold a shoehorn (preferably one with a long handle) to enable
him to slip his foot in. (S may meet criterion using a shoehorn unassisted.

If S is not already standing, have him stand up to make sure his foot is
completely in or have him wiggle and push his foot to adjust the shoe.

After S has learned how to select the correct shoe, allow him to select
incorrectly, then put on the wrong shoe. Describe how the shoe looks funny
on the wrong foot or hurts his foot, and emphasize that it is the wrong
shoe. Then have S switch the shoes and put them on the correct feet. Fade
your reminders so that S learns to make the correction on his own (i.e.,
self-correct).

Putting Socks On

Chain

Skill:

In this program the child learns to grasp his sock, insert his foot, pull up the sock, and adjust it if needed. This skill is an extension of pulling but requires the child to maintain his position with his foot within reach and, at the same time, grasp and adjust the sock.

Entry Behaviors:

1. S can <u>reach his feet</u> by extending his arms and bending at the waist. S balances in this position while he manipulates his sock. This position is the same one S uses to pull off his sock. Frequently, that skill is taught first (e.g., Pulling Off: Socks), since it involves a simple pull rather than maneuvering the sock.

2. S <u>grasps the sock</u> with both hands and retains it during gentle pulling (e.g., Pulling Off). Or, adapt to allow S to use adaptive equipment or materials that enable him to secure the sock. If S grasps with only one hand, add components that require S to grasp more frequently with one hand.

Objective:

When given his socks, S pulls each sock completely on, inserts his foot, and adjusts the fit unassisted. S must initiate his response within 5 seconds of the command and respond correctly 4 out of 5 trials. 1 trial = 1 sock.

Cycle:

None specified. However, you may repeat the program specifically for knee socks if necessary.

Follow-Up:

Continue to have S put his socks on at appropriate times. Vary the type and style of socks and introduce knee socks after S can put on crew (ankle) socks. Set up a routine with Putting Shoes On so that S puts on his shoes and socks at appropriate times without your command. Repeat the words <u>sock</u> or <u>pull</u> to expand S's vocabulary.

Program for Dressing Skill 7

GENERAL STRATEGY

Arrangement:

S is sitting on the floor against a wall or in a chair with back support. You may assist S to move into a sitting position.

Attention:

Hand S his socks or place them in front of him. Draw S's attention to them, and talk about them if desired.

Command:

Give an appropriate command ("SOCK ON") with cues indicating what you wish S to do.

Latency:

S must initiate his response within 5 seconds of the command (or last part completed).

Correction:

Use general correction or Suggestions on any part that S does not perform correctly. After you assist him, allow him to continue the trial on his own. Correct him only if needed.

Natural Consequence:

When S has put on his socks, help him put on his shoes.

Other Trials:

Repeat the strategy as often as appropriate. You may set up situations to allow S to practice the skill if desired. Whenever you use this program, always have S put on both socks. 1 trial = 1 sock. If the first trial was for the first sock, present the next trial to put on his other sock.

Modification:

S has made no gains in average parts completed after two successive probes (2 weeks).

CONDITIONS	BEHAVIOR	CRITERIA
		for *7 only
PRE Get S's attention, and give the command. Present the natural consequence.	*7. Target--S pulls one sock completely on and adjusts the fit unassisted.	4 correct out of 5 trials

DAILY INSTRUCTION/WEEKLY PROBES:

Get S's attention, and give the command. Correct each part if needed. Present the natural consequence.	1. S <u>grasps the cuff</u> of his sock and stretches the opening if needed (this may occur before or after Part 2).	Continue daily instruction/weekly probes until S performs *7 correctly 4 out of the last 5 trials
	2. S <u>repositions</u> himself if needed to bring his foot within reach (bends or crosses his leg and leans forward).	
	3. S <u>brings the sock to his foot</u>.	
	4. S <u>inserts his toes</u> into the opening (at least 1 inch).	
	5. S <u>pulls the sock</u> as far on as possible.	
	6. S <u>adjusts the sock heel</u> so that it is in position.	
	*7. Target--S pulls one sock completely on and adjusts the fit unassisted.	
POST 1 Same as PRE	*7. Target--S pulls one sock completely on and adjusts the fit unassisted.	4 correct out of 5 trials for each test
POST 2 New Setting		
POST 3 Different Socks		

SUGGESTIONS

Part 1:

Guide S to grasp the cuff and stretch it slightly. You may have S stretch
the sock lengthwise before grasping the cuff.

If the sock has a fairly long band or section that goes up the leg, you may demonstrate how to insert your thumbs into the sock. Then gather it up to the heel, or even the toe. Fade your cues.

Have S grasp and pull stretchy material, using both hands.

Part 2:

Assist S to move his leg into an appropriate position (legs crossed or leg bent). You may need to guide him to raise his leg with his hands if he has poor leg control. Fade your assistance.

Have S practice leg positions by imitating you. Use varied positions during recreation and physical activities.

Part 3:

Use backward chaining with Part 4. At first guide the sock all the way until S's toes are in. Then guide the sock to within 2 inches of his toes, and have S insert his toes. Gradually guide S's arms less and less until he brings the sock all the way to his foot and inserts his toes.

Part 4:

Guide S to bring the sock to his toes. You may have S point or raise his toes and leave his heel on the floor. Fade your assistance gradually.

Have S insert his foot in a bag or over-sized sock. Gradually have S use practice materials with smaller openings until S can insert his toes into his own sock.

Part 5:

If S can control his leg movements, have him extend his leg while he pulls the sock so that his leg action helps move the sock on. Place your hand(s) over S's, and help him grasp the sock, and/or push down on his knee to help him extend his leg. Gradually fade the pressure you use.

Use backward chaining. At first pull S's sock all the way on. Then pull it only as far as his ankles, then his heel, then the ball of his foot. Gradually leave more for S to do.

Provide S with practice with a sock that pulls on very easily, such as one that is a size too large or that is made of cotton rather than stretch material. After S can pull easily using the large sock, have him use his own sock.

If S has difficulty getting his heel in, have him grasp the sock at his heel with one hand and pull it from that position. Fade your cues to do this.

Part 6:

Show S the heel of the sock and how it should be at his own heel. Guide S to pull it around. Gradually fade your assistance.

Use a shorter cuffed sock that enables S to move the heel more readily into place. When S can put on this kind of sock, use his own sock.

Taking Off Pants

Chain

Skill:

This program teaches S to push down and remove long or short pants that are already unfastened. This skill requires fairly good balance and is usually initiated after the child can stand and/or when you teach him to push his pants to his knees for self-toileting.

Entry Behaviors:

1. S balances upright, holding for support if needed. This balance is extremely important not only in learning the pants-down or pants-off chain but also in the rest of self-toileting:

   a. Standing only: S can stand by holding for support. While standing, he can lean over to reach below his knees with one or both hands and balance on one leg to step out of the pants. (This position requires the most highly developed balance.)

   b. Standing or sitting: S can stand by holding for support. While standing, he can reach down past his hips to push the pants part way. He can then move into a sitting position (on a chair or the floor) and bend forward to push or pull his pants off all the way.

   c. Kneeling or sitting: Same as position b except that S kneels rather than stands. (This position requires the least developed balance but is generally less useful than position a or b unless S cannot stand.)

2. S grasps the pants and either grasps and pulls (e.g., Pulling Off) or moves his legs or feet to get the pants off his ankles and feet. Or, adapt to allow S to use adaptive equipment or materials that enable him to secure the pants.

Objective:

When his pants are unfastened, S pulls his pants down and removes them completely without assistance. S must initiate his response within 5 seconds of the command and respond correctly 4 out of 5 trials.

Cycle:

None specified. However, you may use the first part of the chain (pants-down) to teach the child to pull his pants down far enough when you are teaching self-toileting. The program may be repeated later to teach the complete chain (pants-off).

Follow-Up:

Continue to have S take off his pants at appropriate times. Have S do this only at routine times, such as before bathing or swimming, so that he learns to do this without your command (and not do it at other inappropriate times). During the routine, combine tasks such as unfastening his pants (e.g., Unsnapping, Unzipping), as well as other undressing skills. As S develops coordination and can take off his pants, help him pull them up, thus beginning instruction on Putting On Pants. During instruction, repeat the words <u>pants</u> and <u>off</u> to expand S's vocabulary.

Program for Dressing Skill 8

GENERAL STRATEGY

Arrangement:

S is standing or kneeling. He may grasp something for support. If S will sit in a chair to remove his feet from the pants, the chair should be just behind S so that he does not have to walk to it. S's pants are unfastened, and his shoes are off.

Attention:

Draw S's attention to his pants. Talk about them if desired.

Command:

Give an appropriate command ("PANTS OFF") with cues indicating what you wish S to do.

Latency:

S must initiate his response within 5 seconds of the command (or last part completed).

Correction:

Use general correction or Suggestions on any part that S does not perform correctly. After you assist him, allow him to continue the trial on his own. Correct him only if needed.

Natural Consequence:

After S has his pants off, help him hang them up or put them away.

Other Trials:

Repeat the strategy as often as appropriate. You may wish to set up situations for S to practice the skill.

Modification:

S has made no gains in average parts completed after two successive probes (2 weeks).

CONDITIONS	BEHAVIOR	CRITERIA
		for *9 only
PRE Get S's attention, and give the command. Present the natural consequence.	*9. Target--S pushes his pants down and removes them completely, unassisted.	4 correct out of 5 trials

DAILY INSTRUCTION/WEEKLY PROBES:

Get S's attention, and give the command. Correct each part if needed. Present the natural consequence.	1. S positions his hands at the sides of his pants.	Continue daily instruction/weekly probes until S performs *9 correctly 4 out of the last 5 trials.
	2. S pushes or pulls the pants over his hips.	
	3. S pushes or pulls the pants past his knees.	

4. S <u>repositions</u> (sits, leans) if needed to be able to free his feet (Parts 5 and 6, or 7 and 8 may occur in either order).

5. S <u>removes his right foot</u> from the pants leg.

6. S <u>puts his right foot</u> down.

7. S <u>removes his left foot</u> from the pants leg.

8. S <u>puts his left foot down, free</u> of the pants.

*9. Target--S pushes his pants down and removes them completely, unassisted.

POST 1 Same as PRE	*9. Target--S pushes his pants down and removes them completely, unassisted.	4 correct out of 5 trials for each test
POST 2 New Setting		
POST 3 Different Pants		

SUGGESTIONS

Part 1:

Select one of the following procedures to position S's hands. He should grasp at the sides of his pants, NOT the front. Gradually fade your guidance.

Thumb Inside at the Sides   OR   Hold the Material at the Sides   OR   Slip His Hands Inside the Waistband

If S has to support himself with one hand, have him hold his pants with his free hand at one side as shown in the pictures. Fade your guidance.

Part 2:

Assist S by pulling with him until the pants are over his hips. Gradually fade the pressure that you use. Have S push farther and farther down without assistance until he can push the pants over his buttocks.

If S has to support himself with one hand, have him tug the pants, then grasp on the other side. Alternate sides until he completes Parts 2 and 3.

At first use pants that are a size too large so that S can slip them over his hips more easily. (Make sure that S's belt is removed and that the zipper is all the way down.) Then when S can pull down loose pants, have him work on his regular pants.

Part 3:

Use forward or backward chaining. (Forward chain--S pushes his pants down, and you help him push them when he can push no farther.) (Backward chain-- You assist S to start the push-off chain. Then allow him to finish it.)

Part 4:

Assist S to sit in one of the following positions. Gradually fade your cues or guidance.

Have S practice sitting down in the same spot where he was standing.

Parts 5 and 7:

Guide S to lift his leg, point his toes, shake his foot, and push the pants with his hands to free his foot. Gradually fade your guidance.

Use backward chaining. Assist S to get his foot almost all the way out, and have him complete the chain on his own. Gradually provide less assistance while S pulls his leg out, so that he has to remove more of it without your assistance.

Have S pull on and push off an extra large tube sock to get the idea of pulling or pushing material over his heel. Practice with an extra large sock until S can perform the task. Then go back to using his own sock.

Parts 6 and 8:

Guide S to place his foot back down on the pants so that his foot holds the pants down while he pulls the other foot out (for standing and chair positions only). Fade your cues to put his foot on his pants.

Guide S to place his foot completely free of the pants so that it is out of the way when he is pulling his other leg free. Fade your cues to keep his foot away.

Taking Off Shirt (Coat, Jacket)

Chain

Cycle

Skill:

This program teaches the child to remove a front-opening shirt or other garment (already unfastened) by pulling it back over the shoulders, then removing one's arms from the sleeves. Although the task involves simple pulling, its difficulty lies in the balance and maneuvering needed to free the first arm from the garment.

Entry Behaviors:

1. S <u>reaches the front collar</u> of his shirt with one or both hands and <u>reaches the opposite sleeve cuff</u> with at least one hand. S <u>raises or shrugs</u> the other shoulder <u>while he bends that arm</u> and holds it close to his body. Note that for Set 1 garments (See Cycle information), S need only free his shoulders and straighten his arms so that the shirt slips off. S has enough balance to <u>remain upright</u> (sitting or standing) and hold himself steady if needed during these maneuvers. If S does not have this balance or maneuverability, you can develop your own program based on S's physical capabilities.

2. S <u>grasps</u> the shirt at the collar or elsewhere with both hands and retains the grasp during gentle pulling (e.g., Pulling Off). Or, adapt to allow S to use adaptive equipment or materials that enable him to secure the shirt. If S grasps with only one hand, adapt by adding parts that require S to change his grasp more frequently to pull with one hand.

Objective:

When his front-opening shirt or other garment is unfastened, S removes the shirt completely and frees both arms without assistance. S must initiate his response within 5 seconds of the command and respond correctly 4 out of 5 trials.

Cycle:

There are two cycles, taught in order, to allow for different garments:

<u>Set 1</u>: Heavy or lined coats, short-sleeve shirts, or other garments that slip off once S's shoulders are free.

<u>Set 2</u>: Long-sleeve shirts, sweaters, or other garments that require S to pull the sleeves to free his arms.

The first set uses only the first part of the task chain, whereas the second uses several additional parts for pulling the sleeves.

Follow-Up:

Combine skills to require S to take off a variety of different front-opening shirts or garments. As S develops fine motor skills, have him unfasten his garment (e.g., Unsnapping, Unzipping Jacket, Unbuttoning), then remove it. Combine the unfasten-remove garment chain, and require S to respond to a single command. Establish routines so that S learns to remove the garment at appropriate times without a command. In the routine, require S to take off his hat and mittens, then unfasten and remove his coat. When you work with him, use the word <u>coat</u> (or the name of the garment) frequently to expand S's vocabulary.

Program for Dressing Skill 9

GENERAL STRATEGY

Arrangement:

S sits, or stands if the garment is so long that he would be sitting on part of it. S may have back support if needed while sitting. If he needs support, position something in front of S so that he may pull forward to remove the shirt from his back. S is wearing the garment, but it is already unfastened completely.

Attention:

Draw S's attention to the shirt. Talk about it if desired.

Command:

Give an appropriate command ("SHIRT OFF") with cues indicating what you wish S to do.

Latency:

S must initiate his response within 5 seconds of the command (or last part completed).

Correction:

Use general correction or Suggestions on any part that S does not perform correctly. After you assist him, allow him to continue the trial on his own. Correct him only if needed.

Natural Consequence:

After S removes the garment, help him hang it up or put it away.

Other Trials:

Repeat the strategy as often as appropriate. You may set up situations to practice the skill if desired.

Modification:

S has made no gains in average parts completed after two successive probes (2 weeks).

CONDITIONS	BEHAVIOR	CRITERIA for *9 only
PRE Get S's attention, and give the command. Present the natural consequence.	*9. Target--S removes the shirt completely by pulling both arms out without assistance.	4 correct out of 5 trials

DAILY INSTRUCTION/WEEKLY PROBES:

Get S's attention, and give the command. Correct each part if needed. Present the natural consequence.	1. S grasps the front of his shirt. 2. S pulls his shirt open in front. 3. S pulls his shirt over both shoulders as far down as possible.	Continue daily instruction/weekly probes until S performs *9 correctly 4 out of the last 5 trials

4. S _shakes or maneuvers his arms_ to free the shirt as much as possible. _Note:_ For Set 1 materials, use only Parts 1-4 and the target. For Set 2 materials, continue on for Parts 5-8 and the target.

5. If needed to free his right arm, S _grasps that sleeve_ with his left hand.

6. S _pulls his sleeve off_ his right arm.

7. If needed to free his left arm, S _grasps his left sleeve_ with his right hand.

8. S _pulls his sleeve off_ his left arm.

*9. Target--S removes the shirt completely by pulling both arms out without assistance.

POST 1 Same as PRE	*9. Target--S removes the shirt completely by pulling both arms out without assistance.	4 correct out of 5 trials for each test
POST 2 New Setting		
POST 3 Different Shirt		

SUGGESTIONS

Part 1:

Guide S to grasp the shirt. Gradually fade your guidance and reminders.

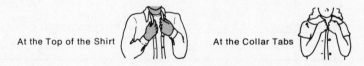

At the Top of the Shirt   At the Collar Tabs

Demonstrate where to grasp. Use clothing cues already on the garment (e.g., button, buttonhole), or add cues to the garment (e.g., safety pins). After S learns to grasp the correct place, remove any extra cues on the garment, and gradually fade out your reminders.

Part 2:

(With Part 3) Use forward chaining. Have S pull his hands up and apart; then guide him to completely open the shirt and free his shoulders. Gradually have S pull farther and farther on his own before you help, until he can free his shoulders (Part 3) unassisted.

Pull upward slightly, then outward and downward.

Have S use a coat that is one size too large and that fits loosely at the shoulders. After S can successfully remove the large coat, return to his own clothing.

Part 3:

Guide S to pull the shirt down as far as possible. Gradually fade your guidance.

Part 4:

Guide S to straighten his arms behind his back and shrug his shoulders. Gradually use less pressure. Note that for Set 1, the garment should slide off at this point.

Parts 5, 6, 7, 8:

Guide S to grasp the sleeve cuff either in front or in back.

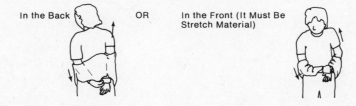

In the Back   OR   In the Front (It Must Be Stretch Material)

Use backward chaining for Parts 5 and 6 or 7 and 8. Help S pull almost all the way; then let him make the final tug on his own to free his arm. Gradually help him less to perform of the task, and have him pull farther on his own to free his arm until he can do it all unassisted, including grasping at the cuff. Reverse hands to free the second arm if necessary.

Have S transfer objects from hand-to-hand behind his back. This practice will teach him the position involved in tugging at the sleeve behind his back.

Putting On Pants

Chain

Skill:

In this program the child learns to insert one, then the other leg into his pants, and then pull them up. Although it requires little fine motor skill, it takes considerable balance for the child to be able to stand while he pulls. In addition, it requires the child to move his legs independently to insert them into the pants legs while he sits or stands.

Entry Behaviors:

1. S <u>bends or leans to reach his feet</u> in one of the following positions:

   a. <u>Standing</u>: S <u>stands</u>, holding for support. S <u>balances while leaning</u> over to insert his feet one at a time in the pants. (This position requires more balance.)

   b. <u>Sitting then standing</u>: S sits, holding for support while <u>bending over</u> to insert his feet. S then <u>stands up and remains standing</u> while pulling up the pants.

   These two positions are the same as in Taking Off Pants. Although the two skills (off-on) may be taught concurrently, usually S can <u>take off</u> before he can <u>put on</u> his pants unassisted because the latter requires him to also insert his feet. S may learn to toilet himself independently when he begins to learn the end of the pants-on chain (pulling up the pants from the knees).

2. S <u>moves his legs independently</u> to insert his feet into the pants legs without assistance, although he may aim or lift his own leg with his hands. Preferably, S can point his toes or at least <u>extend his foot</u> enough to fit it through the leg opening.

3. S <u>grasps</u> the pants and holds them during gentle pulling (e.g., Pulling Off). Or, adapt to allow S to use adaptive equipment or materials that enable him to secure the pants.

Objective:

S inserts his feet into his pants appropriately and pulls the pants up completely without assistance. S must initiate his response within 5 seconds of the command and respond correctly 4 out of 5 trials.

Cycle:

None specified. However, if S has difficulty on particular garments such as long pants, you may repeat the program specifically for those garments. Or, you may repeat this program to teach S to pull up his pants in another position (i.e., either Standing or Sitting then Standing).

Follow-Up:

Continue having S put on his pants at appropriate times. Have him put on different types of pants, including underwear, as well as outer garments. Establish routines at dressing time so that S learns to perform without waiting for your command. Combine this skill with other tasks involved in wearing pants (e.g., Zipping Pants, Snapping) and in completely dressing oneself (e.g., Putting On Shirt, Socks, and Shoes). When you work with S, use the word pants frequently to expand his vocabulary.

Program for Dressing Skill 10

Arrangement:

Have S either stand (if he is going to stand while inserting his feet) or sit on a chair or bench (if he is going to sit to insert his feet, then stand to pull the pants up). Provide something nearby for S to hold onto for balance if needed. The pants should be unfastened.

Attention:

Hold or position S's pants, and draw S's attention to them. Talk about them if desired.

Command:

Give an appropriate command ("PANTS ON") <u>with cues</u> indicating what you wish S to do.

Latency:

S must initiate his response within 5 seconds of the command (or last part completed).

Correction:

Use general correction or Suggestions on any part that S does not perform correctly. After you assist him, allow him to continue the trial on his own. Correct him only if needed.

Natural Consequence:

After S's pants are on, have him finish dressing. Then allow him to leave the dressing area.

Other Trials:

Repeat the strategy as often as appropriate. You may set up situations to practice the skill if desired.

Modification:

S has made no gains in <u>average parts completed</u> after two successive probes (2 weeks).

Program
Dressing
Skill 10

CONDITIONS	BEHAVIOR	CRITERIA
		for *10 only
PRE Get S's attention, and give the command. Present the natural consequence.	*10. Target--S inserts his feet appropriately and pulls his pants on completely unassisted.	4 correct out of 5 trials

DAILY INSTRUCTION/WEEKLY PROBES:

Get S's attention, and give the command. Correct each part if needed. Present the natural consequence.	1. S grasps his pants at the waistband and positions the pants (S may self-correct anytime if needed to get the front in the correct place).	Continue daily instruction/weekly probes until S performs *10 correctly 4 out of the last 5 trials.
	2. S positions himself (bends or leans) to bring the waist open-ing to his feet (S may position first, then grasp his pants if he is sitting).	
	3. S inserts one foot into the waist open-ing.	
	4. S pushes or pulls his leg through the appro-priate pants leg until his foot is free.	
	5. S inserts his other foot (as in Part 3).	
	6. S pushes his leg through (as in Part 4).	
	7. S repositions (stands up) if needed.	
	8. S pulls the pants to his hips.	
	9. S pulls the pants to his waist.	
	*10. Target--S inserts his feet appropriately and pulls his pants on completely unassisted.	
POST 1 Same as PRE	*10. Target--S inserts his feet appropriately and pulls his pants on completely unassisted.	4 correct out of 5 trials for each test
POST 2 New Setting		
POST 3 Different Pants		

SUGGESTIONS

Part 1:

Guide S to grasp the sides of the waistband with the front away from him.
Gradually fade your support, but continue to point out where to grasp.
Finally fade these cues so that S positions the pants with the front placed
correctly. Allow S to self-correct by putting the pants on backward, then
correcting himself.

Front

Have S hold the pants up to his waist to check for the front, turning them
around if necessary. Provide this practice until S self-corrects without
assistance.

Part 2:

Guide S to bend, lean, and/or bring his foot up so that the waistband is
at his foot. Help S hold for support if necessary. Gradually fade your
guidance. Note that the farther S bends, the less he has to move his leg,
but the more he has to balance.

 Brings His Leg Up with
His Heel Resting
on the Edge of a
Chair   OR

 Raises His Leg Up and
Bends over While Balancing
on One Leg

If S has poor leg control, guide him to raise his own leg and rest his heel
on the edge of the chair. Fade your guidance.

Parts 3 and 5:

Guide S to place his foot in the opening next to his hand (the same side)
to insure that his leg goes into the correct pants leg. If necessary,
pull up on S's heel slightly to help him point his foot. Fade your
guidance.

Parts 4 and 6:

Use forward or backward chaining. For forward chaining, allow S to push his leg a short way into the pants. Then assist him to pull the pant leg up until his foot is out. Gradually have him push farther on his own. For backward chaining, assist S to push his foot almost through, then have him do the final push or pull alone. Gradually have him do more alone, and withdraw your assistance. Make sure that S's foot is completely through the pants cuff on long pants.

For long pants, guide S to grasp his pants farther down (e.g., at the knee) as he pushes his leg in. Gradually fade your guidance.

Use pants that are a size too large, and have S put in his feet. Also, cut off the legs of his pants so that he has less length to push his leg through. Gradually decrease the size of the pants, and increase the leg length until the pants are normal size.

Part 7:

Provide extra directions and assistance for S to stand up if he inserts his legs while sitting. S may release the pants to stand and then grasp them again if he needs to hold for support. Gradually fade your cues or reminders. (If S is already standing, this part is omitted.)

Put your arm around S's waist, and stand up when he does to support him. Fade this assistance.

Parts 8 and 9:

Use forward chaining if the pants fit tightly at the hips. Have S start to pull on his own, then assist him in particular to pull the pants over his hips. Gradually assist less and less, and allow him to pull farther on his own.

At first use pants that are a size too large so that they pull over S's hips more easily. After S can pull these up, have him use his regular pants.

Putting On Shirt
(Coat, Jacket)

Chain

Skill:

This program teaches the child to insert arms into sleeves and pull on a
front-opening shirt or other garment. Although little fine motor coordination is required, the child needs shoulder and arm coordination and maneuverability to insert his arms into the shirt and to adjust the shoulder fit.

Entry Behaviors:

1. S maneuvers his shoulders and arms to insert them into the sleeves (e.g.,
    extending, raising, straightening, bending, and rotating the shoulders
    and arms). In the task chain, S may either bring the shirt around his
    back or raise it over his head to insert his arms. Frequently, S can
    already take off his shirt (e.g., Taking Off Shirt) since that task re-
    quires less maneuverability.

2. S balances (sitting or standing) and holds himself steady if needed dur-
    ing these maneuvers. If S does not have this balance and maneuverability,
    consider developing your own program specifically for S's physical
    capabilities.

3. S grasps the shirt to bring it to an appropriate position to insert his
    arms. Or, adapt to allow S to use adaptive equipment or materials that
    enable him to secure the shirt.

Objective:

When given his shirt or other front-opening garment, S inserts his arms into
the sleeves and pulls the shirt completely on without assistance. S must
initiate his response within 5 seconds of the command and respond correctly
4 out of 5 trials.

Cycle:

None specified. However, you may repeat the program to teach specific
garments that are particularly difficult for S to put on (e.g., long-
sleeved shirts, tight sweaters).

Follow-Up:

Continue to have S put on his shirts and all other garments of this type.
Combine with other dressing skills so that S can put on and fasten the shirt
(e.g., Zipping Jacket, Snapping), as well as put on other garments).
(e.g., Putting On Hat, Mittens, Pants). Establish daily routines so that
S learns to predict when to put on the garment without your command. As
you work with S, use the word coat (or the name of the garment) frequently
to expand S's vocabulary.

Overview
Dressing
Skill 11

Program for Dressing Skill 11

GENERAL STRATEGY

Arrangement:

S may sit or, if the garment is full-length, stand. Provide something for S to hold onto if he needs support for balance.

Attention:

Hold or position the garment and draw S's attention to it. Talk about it if desired. (Do not hold out the garment for S to insert his arms.)

Command:

Give an appropriate command ("SHIRT ON") with cues indicating what you wish S to do.

Latency:

S must initiate his response within 5 seconds of the command (or last part completed).

Correction:

Use general correction or Suggestions on any part that S does not perform correctly. After you assist him, allow him to continue the trial on his own. Correct him only if needed.

Natural Consequence:

After S's garment is on, help him fasten it and finish dressing.

Other Trials:

Repeat the strategy as often as appropriate. You may wish to set up situations to allow S to practice the skill.

Modification:

S has made no gains in average parts completed after two successive probes (2 weeks).

CONDITIONS	BEHAVIOR	CRITERIA
		for *7 only
PRE Get S's attention, and give the command. Present the natural consequence.	*7. Target--S inserts his arms into the sleeves and pulls the garment completely on, unassisted.	4 correct out of 5 trials

DAILY INSTRUCTION/WEEKLY PROBES:

Get S's attention, and give the command. Correct each part if needed. Present the natural consequence.

Note: For Methods 1, 2, or 3, see the pictures that follow this chart. Select only one method listed under Suggestions.

1. S takes the garment and positions it to insert his right or left arm.

Continue daily instruction/weekly probes until S performs *7 correctly

	2. S <u>inserts one arm</u> into the correct sleeve.	4 out of the last 5 trials
	3. S <u>repositions the garment</u> if needed for the other sleeve (Parts 2, 3, and 4 may occur in any order).	
	4. S <u>inserts his right or left</u> arm into the correct sleeve.	
	5. S <u>slides his arms into the sleeves</u> all the way.	
	6. S <u>adjusts the fit</u> if needed.	
	*7. Target--S inserts his arm into the sleeves and pulls the garment completely on, unassisted.	
POST 1 Same as PRE	*7. Target--S inserts his arms into the sleeves and pulls the garment completely on, unassisted.	4 correct out of 5 trials for each test
POST 2 New Setting		
POST 3 Different Garment		

SUGGESTIONS

Method 1:

| S <u>positions</u> the garment (flat on a table or his lap). | S <u>inserts</u> each arm | S repositions the garment (swings it over his head). | S <u>slides</u> both arms in. |

Method 2:

| S <u>positions</u> the coat. | S repositions the garment (swings it in a circle up over his head). | S <u>inserts</u> each arm. | S <u>slides</u> both arms in. |

Method 3:

S <u>positions</u> the coat.	S <u>inserts</u> one arm (pushes his arm as far in as possible).	S <u>repositions</u> the garment (brings it around his back and over his shoulders).	S <u>inserts</u> his other arm.	S <u>slides</u> both arms in.

Parts 1 and 3:

Demonstrate how to position the garment. At first hold the garment so that S can insert his arms. After he can insert his arms, gradually fade your assistance.

Use color tabs or stitching as a cue to show S where he is to grasp the garment. When S can put on the garment on his own, remove these extra cues.

Provide practice in front of a mirror. (This, however, may confuse S since the reflection is in reverse.

Parts 2 and 4:

Have S insert his hands into bags or other openings. In particular for Method 3, have S insert his hand when he cannot see the opening. Guide S to feel for the opening, and fade your guidance. After the practice, return to using S's garment.

Guide S's hand to the opening. Use backward chaining. First guide S's hand until it nearly touches the opening. Then withdraw your support as his hand approaches the opening. Eventually require S to move his hand on his own.

You hold the garment, and have S put his arms in. When S can put the garment on as you hold it, guide him to position it himself. Fade your assistance.

Parts 5 and 6:

Guide S to move his arms to the side. This action causes him to fit the garment over his arms. Then have S adjust the garment by shaking his arms or moving his shoulders. Gradually fade this assistance.

First use heavy coats with a smooth lining since the weight and finish help to slide the coat on. Then use other garments, such as sweaters or stretchy garments. These are more difficult since they usually require S to pull to get the sleeves all the way on and to adjust the fit.

Taking Off
T-Shirt

Chain

Skill:

In this program the child completes the task chain required to pull a
shirt off over his head. This task requires coordination to maneuver
arms, shoulders, and head to pull the shirt off.

Entry Behaviors:

1. S <u>moves his shoulders and arms</u> to pull the garment off (e.g., extending,
   raising, straightening, bending, rotating). In the task chain, S pulls
   the shirt over his head first and then removes it from his arms; or pulls
   his arms out of the sleeves and then pulls the shirt over his head. (<u>Note</u>:
   Four alternate methods to remove the shirt are described under Suggestions.)
   S may be able to take off a front-opening garment already (e.g., Taking
   Off Shirt), since this task has some similar motions but does not require
   that S pull the shirt off over his head. If S's arm(s) is physically
   impaired, reconsider teaching this program. You may want to develop
   your own task analysis.

2. S <u>balances himself</u> (either sitting or standing) so that his hands are
   free to pull off his shirt. If S cannot keep his balance, reconsider
   teaching the program at this time.

3. S <u>holds the shirt firmly with both hands</u> to pull it off. Or, adapt to
   allow him to use adaptive equipment or materials that enable him to
   secure the shirt. If S can hold with only one hand, reconsider teaching this program since it is difficult to take off a pullover shirt
   using only one hand.

Objective:

S pulls a T-shirt (pullover) completely off over his head without assistance.
S must initiate his response within 5 seconds of the command and respond
correctly 4 out of 5 trials.

Cycle:

None specified. However, you may repeat the program to teach garments more
difficult to remove (turtlenecks, long sleeves) or to teach another one of
the alternate methods shown under Suggestions in the Program.

Follow-Up:

Have S pull off a variety of pullover garments: sweaters, knit tops,
and T-shirts that are long-sleeved, short-sleeved, or sleeveless. Set
up a routine to incorporate the skill during the day (e.g., before physical
activity, in preparation for washing face). Pullovers are often turned
inside out in the process of being taken off. Point to the label as a cue,
and help S turn his shirt right side out as he removes it. Talk to S as
he is removing his shirt, and use specific task requests (e.g., "PULL UP/
DOWN"). Encourage S to describe what he is doing to expand his vocabulary.

Program for Dressing Skill 12

GENERAL STRATEGY

Arrangement:

Before you start, assist S into a comfortable position (with support if needed) for removing his shirt.

Attention:

Draw S's attention to the shirt. Talk about it if desired.

Command:

Give an appropriate command ("SHIRT OFF") <u>with cues</u> indicating what you wish S to do.

Latency:

S must initiate his response within 5 seconds of the command (or last part completed).

Correction:

Use general correction or Suggestions on any part S does not perform correctly. After you assist him, allow him to continue the trial on his own. Correct him only if needed.

Natural Consequence:

After S has removed the article, have him put it in an appropriate place.

Other Trials:

Repeat the strategy as often as appropriate. You may set up situations to practice the skill if desired.

Modification:

S has made no gains in <u>average parts completed</u> after two successive probes (2 weeks).

Program
Dressing
Skill 12

CONDITIONS	BEHAVIOR	CRITERIA
		for *6 only
PRE Get S's attention, and give the command. Present the natural consequence.	*6. Target--S pulls T-shirt off unassisted.	4 correct out of 5 trials

DAILY INSTRUCTION/WEEKLY PROBES:

Get S's attention, and give the command. Correct each part if needed. Present the natural consequence.

Note: For Methods 1, 2, 3, or 4, see the pictures that follow this chart. Select only one method listed under Suggestions. However, Parts 3-5 may occur in a different order.

1. S positions his hands if needed.

2. S grasps the T-shirt.

3. S pulls the T-shirt over his shoulders.

4. S pulls the T-shirt over his head.

5. S frees his arms.

*6. Target--S pulls the T-shirt off unassisted.

Continue daily instruction/weekly probes until S performs *6 correctly 4 out of the last 5 trials

POST 1 Same as PRE	*6. Target--S pulls the T-shirt off unassisted.	4 correct out of 5 trials for each test
POST 2 Different Shirt (pullover)		
POST 3 Another Shirt (different from POST 2)		

SUGGESTIONS

Try any of the methods described below. Choose one to teach that is most appropriate for S.

Method 1:

(best for garments with loose necklines and short sleeves)

S positions his hands.	S grasps the T-shirt.	S pulls it over his shoulders.	S pulls it over his head.	S frees his arms (shakes).

Method 2:

S positions his hands.	S grasps the T-shirt (as far down as possible).	S pulls it over his head and shoulders.	S frees his arms.

Method 3:

S positions his hands.	S grasps the T-shirt.	S pulls it over his head.	S pulls it over his shoulders.	S frees his arms (shakes).

Method 4:

(best for garments with loose bodice or tight neckline)

S positions his hands.	S grasps the T-shirt.	S frees his arms.	S pulls it over his shoulders.	S pulls it over his head.

Part 1:

Use cues (e.g., tag, tape) on S's clothing to indicate where to grasp. If you add something to the garment, remove it after S learns to grasp correctly.

Play games such as Simon Says or other imitation games to provide practice getting his arms into position (crossed for Method 1, behind his shoulders for Method 2, at the neckline for Method 3, or at one sleeve for Method 4).

Part 2:

Use large, loose garments that stretch well and have an abundance of material to grasp (e.g., pullover sweater, nylon pullover). Gradually use smaller and smaller shirts until S can grasp a close-fitting undershirt.

Have S grasp and pull cloth or rope that you hold, as in a tug-of-war. As you practice with S, increase your resistance to S as he pulls.

Have S grasp and pull off other garments besides shirts (e.g., mittens, socks, gloves, scarf, hat). Practice using these easier garments before going back to using a shirt.

Parts 3, 4, and 5:

Use backward chaining for Parts 3, 4, and 5. For example, for Method 1, guide S to pull the shirt off his shoulders, head, and arms. Then guide S to pull the shirt off his shoulders and head, but have him pull or shake the shirt off his arms unassisted. Next assist S to pull the shirt off his shoulders, but have him pull it off his head and arms unassisted. Finally have S take off the shirt without your assistance.

Use loose-fitting garments at first that are easier to pull off (e.g., a V-neck shirt with short sleeves or a T-shirt several sizes too large). When S can easily remove this shirt, use a tighter-fitting pullover with a regular neckline.

Use only short-sleeved shirts at first, as they will be easier to pull over the shoulders.

Putting On T-Shirt

Chain

Skill:

This program teaches the skill required to insert the head and arms into
a pullover shirt to pull it on. The child needs shoulder and arm coordination and strength to pull the shirt down over his head and fit his arms
in properly.

Entry Behaviors:

1. S moves his shoulders and arms to insert them into the sleeves (extending, raising, straightening, bending, rotating). In the task chain, S
   pulls the shirt over his head first and then inserts his arms, or inserts
   his arms first and then pulls it over his head. S is able to take off a
   T-shirt or put on a front-opening shirt with little or no assistance
   since these tasks have many similar motions. They do not, however, require that S insert his arms or pull the shirt over his head (e.g., Taking
   Off T-Shirt, Putting On Shirt).

2. S balances himself (either sitting or standing) with his hands free to
   pull off his shirt.

3. S holds the shirt firmly with both hands while pulling it. Or, adapt by
   allowing him to use adaptive equipment or materials that enable him to
   secure the shirt. If S can hold with only one hand, reconsider teaching
   this skill. It is very difficult to put on a pullover shirt using only
   one hand.

Objective:

S pulls a T-shirt (pullover) over his head, inserts his arms into the sleeves,
and adjusts the shirt on his body without assistance. S must initiate his
response within 5 seconds of the command and respond correctly 4 out of 5
trials. Note: In this program S does not have to discriminate between front
and back since many pullovers are reversible. Teach this discrimination
skill as a follow-up.

Cycle:

None specified. However, you may repeat the program to teach specific garments that are particularly difficult for S to put on (long-sleeved or tight-
fitting shirts, shirts with a turtleneck).

Overview
Dressing
Skill 13

Follow-Up:

Have S put on a variety of pullover shirts and other garments that must be pulled over the head (ponchos, dresses, skirts). Also, have S put on pullovers that must be zipped or fastened in some other way. Set up a routine so that S dresses and undresses himself (shirt, pants, socks) each day at appropriate times, and provide assistance when necessary. Give S opportunities to discriminate the back of his shirt from the front: Place a tab on the back of the shirt, or use pullovers on which the front is easily distinguishable (e.g., V-necks). Talk to S as he is dressing, and use specific task requests (e.g., "PULL UP/DOWN"). Encourage S to describe what he is doing to expand his vocabulary.

Program for Dressing Skill 13

GENERAL STRATEGY

Arrangement:

S may sit or stand. Have something available for S to hold onto for balance.
Place the shirt flat in front of S on a table or hold it out with the back
of the shirt facing up. S will not have to discriminate the back and front
of a T-shirt in this program.

Attention:

Draw S's attention to the shirt. Talk about it if desired. Do not hold
the garment open for S to insert his arms.

Command:

Give an appropriate command ("SHIRT ON") <u>with cues</u> indicating what you wish
S to do.

Latency:

S must initiate his response within 5 seconds of the command (or last part
completed).

Correction:

Use general correction or Suggestions on any part that S does not perform
correctly. After you assist him, allow him to continue the trial on his
own. Correct him only if needed.

Natural Consequence:

After S's garment is on, help him to finish dressing.

Other Trials:

Repeat the strategy as often as appropriate. You may set up situations to
practice the skill if desired.

Modification:

S has made no gains in <u>average parts completed</u> after two successive probes
(2 weeks).

CONDITIONS	BEHAVIOR	CRITERIA
		for *9 only
PRE Get S's attention, and give the command. Present the natural consequence.	*9. Target--S pulls the T-shirt over his head, inserts his arms into the sleeves, and adjusts the fit unassisted.	4 correct out of 5 trials

DAILY INSTRUCTION/WEEKLY PROBES

	Note: For Methods 1 or 2, see the pictures that follow this chart. Select only one method listed under Suggestions. However, several of the parts may occur in a different order, depending on the method selected.	
Get S's attention, and give the command. Correct each part if needed. Present the natural consequence.	1. S takes the garment and positions it if needed.	Continue daily instruction/weekly probes until S performs *9 correctly 4 out of the last 5 trials
	2. S inserts one arm into the correct sleeve.	
	3. S inserts the other arm into the correct sleeve.	
	4. S repositions the garment if needed.	
	5. S inserts his head into the neck opening.	
	6. S pulls the neck opening over his head.	
	7. S slides his arms into the sleeves all the way.	
	8. S adjusts the fit by pulling down the shirt.	
	*9. Target--S pulls the T-shirt over his head, inserts his arms into the sleeves, and adjusts the fit unassisted.	
POST 1 Same as PRE	*9. Target--S pulls the T-shirt over his head, inserts his arms into the sleeves, and adjusts the fit unassisted.	4 correct out of 5 trials for each test
POST 2 Different Shirt (pullover)		
POST 3 Another Shirt (different from POST 2)		

SUGGESTIONS

Try any of the methods described below. Choose <u>one</u> to teach that is most appropriate for S.

Method 1:

<u>S takes the garment and positions it</u> (grasps the bottom hem at the back of the shirt and gathers up as much material as possible).

<u>S inserts his head into the neck opening.</u>

<u>S pulls the neck opening over his head.</u>

<u>S repositions the garment</u> (turns it so that the sleeves are on the side).

<u>S inserts one arm</u> into the correct sleeve.

<u>S inserts the other arm</u> into the correct sleeve.

<u>S slides both arms</u> into sleeves.

<u>S adjusts the fit</u> by pulling down.

Method 2:

<u>S takes the garment and positions it</u> (grasps the bottom hem at the back of the shirt).

<u>S inserts one arm</u> into the correct sleeve.

<u>S inserts the other arm</u> into the correct sleeve.

<u>S repositions the garment</u> if needed.

<u>S inserts his head</u> into the neck opening.

<u>S pulls the neck opening over his head.</u>

<u>S slides his arms into both sleeves.</u>

<u>S adjusts the fit</u> by pulling down.

Part 1:

Method 1: S takes the garment and positions it. Guide S to gather up the shirt with his hands or help him to hold the shirt open so the neck hole is accessible. Gradually fade your guidance.

Method 2: Guide S to hold the shirt open with one hand so he will be able to insert his other arm into the sleeve. Gradually fade your guidance.

Parts 2 and 3:

S inserts his arms into the sleeves. Have S insert his arms into another garment that is less confining than a T-shirt (e.g., coat). After the practice, have S go back to using a T-shirt.

Assist S to hold the shirt open so that it is easier for him to insert his arms. Gradually fade your guidance.

Use an over-sized pullover shirt to make it easier for S to insert his arms into the sleeves. When S can insert his arms into the sleeves of this shirt, go back and use his T-shirt.

Part 4:

Method 1: S repositions the garment if needed. Assist S to turn the T-shirt so that the sleeves are resting on his shoulders. Gradually fade your guidance.

Method 2: Assist S to raise his arms and lower his head so he will be able to insert his head into the neck opening. Gradually fade your guidance.

Part 5:

S inserts his head into the neck opening: Use over-sized garments with larger neck openings to make it easier for S to insert his head. When he can pull these on, have S pull on his own T-shirt.

Assist S to hold the shirt open so that it is easier for him to insert his head. Gradually fade your assistance.

Part 6:

S pulls the neck opening over his head. Use backward chaining to have S insert and pull the shirt over it. First guide S to position the shirt over his head, to insert his head into the neck opening, and then to pull the shirt completely over his head. Next assist S to position the shirt and insert his head, but only pull the neck opening partially over his head. Require S to pull the shirt the rest of the way over his head. Assist S less until he can position the shirt, insert his head, and pull the shirt over his head unassisted.

Part 7:

S slides his arms into the sleeves. Guide S to move his arms in various ways (straightening, extending, and the like) in order to push them through the sleeves. Gradually fade your guidance.

Assist S to put on stretchy garments with loose, short sleeves. When S can insert his arms into these garments, have him put on tighter garments, those with longer sleeves, and so forth.

Part 8:

S adjusts the fit. Use backward chaining. First guide S to pull the shirt all the way down his body to adjust the fit. Next guide S to pull the shirt part of the way down, and have S finish on his own. Finally have S pull the shirt down unassisted.

Unhooking

Chain

Skill:

This program teaches the child to grasp his garment and pull in opposite directions to separate the hook and eye. Although the task chain is short, it requires fine motor coordination and the ability to pull. As the child develops fine motor skills and more complex chains, he is able to unfasten snaps (simple pull), hooks (pull to release), then more difficult fastenings, such as laces, buttons, and buckles.

Entry Behaviors:

1. S reaches the hook with both hands (e.g., Reaching for Objects). Use hooks only on garments that he can reach, and position him for his best reach. If S has use of only one arm, adapt by deleting parts that refer to the hand that holds the eye of the hook in place, and add parts if needed to grasp and maneuver with only one hand.

2. S grasps the material around the hook and holds on during gentle pulling (e.g., Unsnapping). Or, adapt to allow S to use adaptive equipment or materials that enable him to secure the sides of the hook.

Objective:

When wearing a garment fastened by a hook, S pulls in opposite directions to separate the hook unassisted. S must initiate his response within 5 seconds of the command and respond correctly 4 out of 5 trials. 1 hook = 1 trial.

Cycle:

None specified.

Follow-Up:

Continue to have S unhook a variety of different garments at appropriate times. Establish routines with other tasks that occur together naturally, such as unhook, unzip, and pull down his pants for toileting (e.g., Unzipping Pants, Taking Off Pants), or unhook and pull off a coat (e.g., Taking Off Shirt). Combine these tasks under a single command (e.g., for "Put your coat away," S has to unzip it, remove it, then hang it up). Encourage S to unhook the garment at appropriate times without waiting for your command. When you work with S, emphasize specific words like hook to expand his vocabulary.

Program for Dressing Skill 14

GENERAL STRATEGY

Arrangement:

S is wearing the garment hooked. If the hook is above the waist, S may sit
or stand with support if needed as long as his arms are free to maneuver.
If the hook is at the waist (e.g., on pants), S should stand, lie down, or
be positioned so that his torso is extended to make grasping easier.

Attention:

Draw S's attention to the hook. Talk about it if desired.

Command:

Give an appropriate command ("UNHOOK PANTS") <u>with cues</u> indicating what you
wish S to do.

Latency:

S must initiate his response within 5 seconds of the command (or last part
completed).

Correction:

Use general correction or Suggestions on any part that S does not perform
correctly. After you assist him, allow him to continue the trial on his
own. Correct him only if needed.

Natural Consequence:

If there are more hooks on the garment, present the trial(s) to finish unhooking it. After the garment is unfastened, help S remove it and hang it up.
1 trial = 1 hook.

Other Trials:

Repeat the strategy as often as appropriate. You may set up situations to
practice the skill if desired.

Modification:

S has made no gains in <u>average parts completed</u> after two successive probes
(2 weeks).

Program
Dressing
Skill 14

CONDITIONS	BEHAVIOR	CRITERIA
		for *5 only
PRE Get S's attention, and give the command. Present the natural consequence.	*5. Target--S separates the hook unassisted.	4 correct out of 5 trials

DAILY INSTRUCTION/WEEKLY PROBES

Get S's attention, and give the command. Correct each part if needed. Present the natural consequence.	1. S <u>grasps</u> the material next to the <u>hook</u>.	Continue daily instruction/weekly probes until S performs *5 correctly 4 out of the last 5 trials
	2. S <u>grasps</u> the material next to the <u>eye</u> (Parts 1 and 2 may occur in either order).	
	3. S <u>holds the eye</u> in place or moves it toward the open end of the hook.	
	4. S <u>pulls the hook</u> to separate the hook from the eye (Parts 3 and 4 are concurrent).	
	*5. Target--S separates the hook unassisted.	
POST 1 Same as PRE	*5. Target--S separates the hook unassisted.	4 correct of 5 trials for each test
POST 2 New Setting		
POST 3 Different Garment		

SUGGESTIONS

Parts 1 and 2:

Guide S to grasp the material. Gradually fade your guidance and extra directions.

Pants

OR

Shirt

Use visual and/or tactile cues (e.g., pieces of tape or Velcro) near the hook and/or eye to enable S to locate and grasp the hook. Gradually fade these cues.

Parts 3 and 4:

Have S practice the parts separately. At first hold the eye in place, and guide S to unhook. Gradually fade your assistance. Then guide S to hold the eye in place and you unhook. Again, fade your assistance.

Make sure that S looks at the hook to see which way to pull it open. At first have S practice when the garment is flat on the table so that he can see the hook. (The garment should be turned so that the hook opens as it would when S is wearing it.) After S can unhook in this position (or with hooks mounted on a board), return to the original arrangement where the garment is on S. Gradually fade your reminders to look at the hook while pulling.

Untying

Chain

Skill:

In this program the child learns to pull out the bow, then uncross the
laces of his shoes. This requires considerable attending skill and fine
motor coordination to keep from knotting the laces instead of untying them.

Entry Behaviors:

1. S reaches his feet and shoes with one or both hands. Usually, S is
   already able to pull his shoes off once they are untied (e.g., Pulling
   Off--Shoes) since that skill requires basically the same bending position
   but less fine motor skill.
2. S grasps the ends of the laces and pulls with both hands at the same time.
   Or, adapt by adding parts to allow S to use one hand to grasp and pull
   one end, then grasp and pull the other one.

Objective:

When wearing his shoes with laces tied in a simple bow, S pulls the bow out
and uncrosses the laces without assistance. S must initiate his response
within 5 seconds of the command and respond correctly 4 out of 5 trials.
1 shoelace = 1 trial.

Cycle:

None specified.

Follow-Up:

Continue to have S untie different bows on garments or other materials,
as well as shoes. Combine several tasks into a routine under one command
(e.g., say "Take off your shoes and socks," and have S untie his shoes,
take them off, then pull off his socks). Encourage S to untie his shoes
at appropriate times without your command. Emphasize different words
(shoe, lace, untie) as you work with S to expand his vocabulary.

Program for Dressing Skill 15

GENERAL STRATEGY

Arrangement:

S is wearing the shoe with laces tied in a simple bow (not in a knot or double bow). The ends of the laces should extend at least 1 inch from the bow and preferably have plastic tips over the ends of them. S sits in a position where he can reach the shoe to be untied. He may have support if needed as long as his arms are free.

Attention:

Draw S's attention to the shoelace. Talk about it if desired.

Command:

Give an appropriate command ("UNTIE SHOE") with cues indicating what you wish S to do.

Latency:

S must initiate his response within 5 seconds of the command (or last part completed).

Correction:

Use general correction or Suggestions on any part S does not perform correctly. After you assist him, allow him to continue the trial on his own. Correct him only if needed.

Natural Consequence:

After the shoe is untied, have S take it off. 1 trial = 1 shoelace.

Other Trials:

Repeat the strategy as often as appropriate. You may set up situations to practice the skill if desired.

Modification:

S has made no gains in average parts completed after two successive probes (2 weeks).

Program
Dressing
Skill 15

CONDITIONS	BEHAVIOR	CRITERIA
		for *6 only
PRE Get S's attention, and give the command. Present the natural consequence.	*6. Target--S pulls out the bow and uncrosses the laces of one shoe unassisted.	4 correct out of 5 trials

DAILY INSTRUCTION/WEEKLY PROBES

Get S's attention, and give the command. Correct each part if needed. Present the natural consequence.	1. S <u>grasps the tip</u> of one end of the lace. 2. S <u>grasps</u> the other tip end. 3. S <u>pulls the ends</u> until the loops of the bow are gone. 4. S <u>positions his finger(s)</u> under the crossed laces. 5. S <u>uncrosses the laces</u> by pulling up. *6. Target--S pulls out the bow and uncrosses the laces of one shoe unassisted.	Continue daily instruction/weekly probes until S performs *6 correctly 4 out of the last 5 trials
POST 1 Same as PRE	*6. Target--S pulls out the bow and uncrosses the lace of one shoe unassisted.	4 correct out of 5 trials for each test
POST 2 New Setting		
POST 3 Different Shoes/ Other Garment		

SUGGESTIONS

Parts 1 and 2:

Guide S to grasp the ends of the laces. If necessary, teach him to put the left end on the left side, the right end on the right side so that they will not get knotted. Gradually fade your guidance and extra directions.

Have S grasp small objects with just his thumb and index finger. Although S may use another hold besides a pincer grasp, practice developing S's best thumb and finger grasp, using exercises in Grasping Objects.

Paint the tips of the laces as an added visual cue for S to grasp the tips of the laces. Eventually use regular laces. Or, use built-up tips (e.g., wrapped with additional tape) as a cue, then fade this cue.

Part 3:

Guide S to pull one lace, then assist only if needed on the second one. Gradually fade your guidance. S may pull the laces at the same time or one then the other.

Use backward chaining. Pull the laces so that the bow is almost out, and then have S pull the rest of the way. Gradually pull less of the bow out so that S pulls farther and farther until he pulls the bow out unassisted.

Part 4:

Demonstrate where to place your finger, and loosen the lace for S. Then guide S to place his finger(s) there. Gradually fade your guidance. When S can place his finger(s) under the loosened lace unassisted, gradually decrease the amount of lace you loosen (stop demonstrating also). If necessary, teach S to loosen the lace himself as he inserts his finger(s).

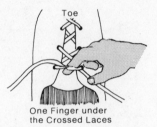

One Finger under the Crossed Laces

OR

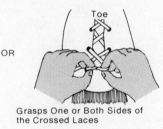

Grasps One or Both Sides of the Crossed Laces

Provide practice on large laces mounted on a sturdy base. When S can untie those laces, gradually use smaller laces until he is untying his shoelaces.

Part 5:

Guide S to pull the crossed part upwards until the laces are uncrossed. If S is grasping the laces, guide him to pull one, then the other side. Alternate until the laces are free. Gradually fade your guidance.

Use backward chaining. Pull the crossed part up almost all the way, and have S make the final pull to uncross them. Pull less of the crossed part so that S must pull more.

Unzipping Pants
(Skirt)

Chain

Skill:

In this program the child learns the sequence of actions to pull down a
zipper that does not separate at the bottom (e.g., on pants or a skirt).
This skill is an extension of other grasp-pull actions, in particular,
unzipping a jacket or other garment that completely separates at the bottom.
However, unzipping pants requires greater fine motor coordination to grasp
and hold the zipper tab while it is pushed to the bottom of the track.

Entry Behaviors:

1. S <u>reaches the zipper</u> and brings both hands to midline (or other location
   of the zipper). If S has the use of only one arm, adapt by deleting
   parts that refer to stabilizing the garment with his other arm and hand.

2. S <u>grasps material with one hand</u> to hold the garment in place and <u>grasps</u>
   <u>and holds the zipper tab</u> with his other hand. (This second grasp is
   often the most difficult part.) Frequently S can already unzip some
   garments (e.g., Unzipping Jacket). Use only garments with zipper tabs
   that S can grasp. If S cannot grasp with one of his hands, have him
   hold the garment in place with that hand while he unzips with the other.
   If S has an impaired grasp, adapt to allow him to use adaptive equipment
   or material to secure the zipper tab.

Objective:

When wearing a garment with a <u>nondetachable</u> zipper that is zipped, S pulls
the zipper tab completely down the track without assistance. S must initiate
his response within 5 seconds of the command and respond correctly 4 out of
5 trials.

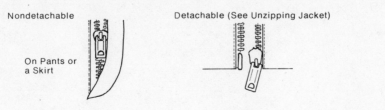

Nondetachable

On Pants or
a Skirt

Detachable (See Unzipping Jacket)

Cycle:

None specified. However, you may repeat the program to teach S to unzip particular garments that are causing difficulty.

Follow-Up:

Continue to have S unzip his garments at all appropriate times. Establish routines so that S learns to unzip his pants at appropriate times (e.g., toileting) but not at other inappropriate times. Combine tasks under one command (e.g., say "Go to the bathroom," and S goes, unzips his pants, pulls the pants down). Have S unzip zippers on other items (e.g., pockets, purses). When you work with S, use the word zipper to expand his vocabulary. Have S zip his pants up also (e.g., Zipping Pants). Encourage S to perform the skill at appropriate times without a command.

Program for Dressing Skill 16

GENERAL STRATEGY

Arrangement:

Preferably, S stands with support if needed as long as his hands and arms are free to operate. Alternately, S may lie down or sit with his back extended as far as possible to keep the zipper track straight. S wears the garment zipped, although any other fastenings are already unfastened.

Attention:

Draw S's attention to the zipper, and make relevant comments if desired.

Command:

Give an appropriate command ("UNZIP PANTS") with cues indicating what you wish S to do.

Latency:

S must initiate his response within 5 seconds of the command (or last part completed).

Correction:

Use general correction or Suggestions on any part that S does not perform correctly. After you assist him, allow him to continue the trial on his own. Correct him only if needed.

Natural Consequence:

Have S take off the garment or pull down his pants, depending on the situation.

Other Trials:

Repeat the strategy as often as appropriate. You may set up situations to practice the skill if desired.

Modification:

S has made no gains in average parts completed after two successive probes (2 weeks).

CONDITIONS	BEHAVIOR	CRITERIA for *5 only
PRE Get S's attention, and give the command. Present the natural consequence.	*5. Target--S pulls the zipper tab all the way down the track unassisted.	4 correct out of 5 trials

DAILY INSTRUCTION/WEEKLY PROBES

Get S's attention, and give the command. Correct each part if needed. Present the natural consequence.	1. S <u>contacts the zipper tab</u> with one hand. 2. S <u>grasps and lifts the zipper tab.</u> 3. S <u>positions his other hand</u> to hold the garment to keep the zipper flat (Parts 2 and 3 may occur in either order). 4. S <u>pulls the tab down</u> to the end of the track. *5. Target--S pulls the zipper tab all the way down the track unassisted.	Continue daily instruction/weekly probes until S performs *5 correctly 4 out of the last 5 trials
POST 1 Same as PRE	*5. Target--S pulls the zipper tab all the way down the track unassisted.	4 correct out of 5 trials for each test
POST 2 New Setting		
POST 3 Different Garment		

SUGGESTIONS

Part 1:

Guide S to reach under the flap of material to locate the zipper tab. Gradually fade your guidance, extra directions, or additional tactile cues.

Part 2:

Guide S to grasp the zipper tab, and lift up slightly so that the zipper unlocks. Gradually fade your guidance.

Pull S's zipper halfway down so that he can see the zipper tab better. Guide S to grasp, raise the tab, and unzip from this position. Gradually unzip the pants a shorter distance so that S grasps the tab when it is higher and harder to see.

Have S grasp small objects. Use strategies out of Grasping Objects, pages 155-61. After S practices grasping a variety of objects, have him again attempt to grasp the zipper tab.

If S has difficulty grasping, guide him to place his index finger under the tab, then squeeze down with his thumb. Gradually fade your guidance.

Part 3:

Guide S to either grasp at the waistband and pull upward, or to grasp at the bottom of the track and pull downward. (Either pull will help keep the zipper track straight for easier unzipping.) Gradually fade your guidance.

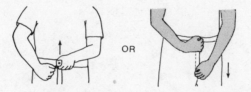

Provide S with practice in pulling. You pull against his pull, as in a tug-of-war.

Alternate with Part 4. You hold while S pulls the zipper, then you unzip as he holds. When S can perform each part separately, have him work on doing both at the same time.

Part 4:

Guide S to pull the zipper down. Gradually reduce your pressure.

Use forward chaining. Have S pull the zipper just a little, then you complete the task. Gradually require S to pull farther before you assist.

Have S pull anything of weight to which a string has been attached. Vary the weight. In particular, practice pulling the string downward. When S has had success with this task, return to pulling the zipper tab down.

Zipping Pants (Skirt)

Chain

Skill:

This program teaches the sequence of actions to pull up a zipper with two
sides permanently connected at the bottom (e.g., pants, skirt). This skill
requires fine motor coordination for grasping the zipper tab when it is all
the way down the track. This is usually more difficult than pulling the
tab down to unzip but easier than zipping a jacket, where the zipper must
be fitted into the track first.

Entry Behaviors:

1. S <u>reaches the zipper</u> and brings back both hands to midline (or other
   location of the zipper). If S has the use of only one arm, adapt by
   deleting parts that require S to stabilize the garment with his other
   arm and hand.

2. S <u>grasps the material with one hand</u> to hold the zipper in place and
   <u>grasps and holds the zipper tab</u> with his other hand. (This second grasp
   is often the most difficult part.) Frequently, S is already able to unzip garments (e.g., Unzipping Jacket and Unzipping Pants). Use only
   garments with zipper tabs that S can grasp. If S cannot grasp with one
   of his hands, have him simply hold the garment in place while he unzips
   with the other. If S has an impaired grasp, adapt to allow S to use
   adaptive equipment or materials to secure the zipper tab.

Objective:

When wearing a garment with a <u>nondetachable</u> zipper, S grasps and pulls the
zipper tab all the way up to lock it into place without assistance. S must
initiate his response within 5 seconds of the command and respond correctly
4 out of 5 trials.

Nondetachable   Detachable (See Zipping Jacket)

Cycle:

None specified. However, you may repeat the program to teach S to zip
specific garments that have difficult zippers. Note that zipping detachable track zippers is covered in Zipping Jacket, pages 377-82.

Follow-Up:

Continue to have S zip his pants at appropriate times. Establish routines
so that S zips his pants appropriately without waiting for your command.
Combine tasks under one command (e.g., say "Put on your pants," and S puts
them on, zips, and snaps them). Have S zip zippers on other items (e.g.,
pockets, purses). When you work with S, use the words zipper, pants, and
zip often to expand his vocabulary. Have S begin to help zip jackets up,
too (e.g., Zipping Jacket).

Program for Dressing Skill 17

Arrangement:

S wears the garment with the zipper completely unzipped. Preferably, S stands with support if needed as long as his hands and arms are free to operate. Alternately, S may lie down or sit with his back extended as far as possible to keep the zipper track flat.

Attention:

Draw S's attention to the zipper. Give relevant comments if desired.

Command:

Give an appropriate command ("ZIP PANTS") with cues indicating what you wish S to do.

Latency:

S must initiate his response within 5 seconds of the command (or last part completed).

Correction:

Use general correction or Suggestions on any part that S does not perform correctly. After you assist him, allow him to continue the trial on his own. Correct him only if needed.

Natural Consequence:

Help S to finish fastening the pants (hook, snap, button).

Other Trials:

Repeat the strategy as often as appropriate. You may set up situations to practice the skill if desired.

Modification:

S has made no gains in average parts completed after two successive probes (2 weeks).

Program
Dressing
Skill 17

CONDITIONS	BEHAVIOR	CRITERIA
		for *6 only
PRE Get S's attention, and give the command. Present the natural consequence.	*6. Target--S pulls the zipper tab all the way up to lock it in place without assistance.	4 correct out of 5 trials

DAILY INSTRUCTION/WEEKLY PROBES

Get S's attention, and give the command. Correct each part if needed. Present the natural consequence.	1. S <u>positions his hand</u> and holds the garment in place to keep the zipper flat.	Continue daily instruction/weekly probes until S performs *6 correctly 4 out of the last 5 trials
	2. S <u>grasps the zipper tab</u> with his other hand (Parts 1 and 2 may occur in either order).	
	3. S <u>holds the garment</u> in place and changes his grasp if needed (concurrent with Part 4).	
	4. S <u>pulls the zipper tab</u> all the way up.	
	5. S <u>pushes the tab flat</u> against the zipper to lock it.	
	*6. Target--S pulls the zipper tab all the way up to lock it in place without assistance.	
POST 1 Same as PRE	*6. Target--S pulls the zipper tab all the way up to lock it in place without assistance.	4 correct out of 5 trials for each test
POST 2 New Setting		
POST 3 Different Pants		

SUGGESTIONS

Part 1:

Guide S to either grasp at the waistband and pull upward, or to grasp at the bottom of the track and pull downward. (Either pull will help keep the zipper track straight for easier zipping.) Gradually fade your guidance.

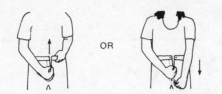

Provide S with practice in pulling. You pull against his pull, as in a tug-of-war.

Part 2:

Guide S to grasp the zipper tab, and lift up slightly so that the tab unlocks. Gradually fade your guidance.

Pull S's zipper halfway up so that he can get a better grasp on the tab. Guide S to grasp and zip from this position. Gradually zip the pants a shorter distance so that S grasps the tab when it is lower and harder to grasp.

Have S grasp small objects. Use strategies out of Grasping Objects, pages 155-61. After S practices grasping a variety of objects, have him again attempt to grasp the zipper tab.

If S has difficulty grasping, guide him to place his index finger under the tab; then squeeze down with his thumb. Gradually fade your guidance.

Parts 3 and 4:

Alternate skills. You hold while S pulls the zipper; then you zip as he holds. When S can perform each part separately, have him work on doing both at the same time.

Guide S to pull the zipper up. Gradually reduce the pressure you exert.

Use backward chaining. Pull the tab almost all the way up, and have S finish. Gradually pull the zipper up a shorter distance so that S pulls farther on his own.

Have S pull anything of weight to which a string has been attached. Vary the weight. In particular, pull the string upward. When S has had success with this task, return to pulling the zipper tab up.

Part 5:

Guide S to push the tab down to lock it. Gradually fade your guidance and extra directions.

Give S a separate request to finish the task (e.g., "Push the tab down"). Delay this extra direction until S finally performs the task without it.

Unbuckling

Chain

Skill:

This program teaches the sequence required to unbuckle a standard belt:
Free the end of the belt, release the tongue from the hole, then pull the
end all the way through the buckle until the sides are separated. This
skill requires attending and fine motor skills to release the tongue, as
well as to perform the actions in sequence in order to unbuckle.

Entry Behaviors:

1. S <u>reaches the belt buckle</u> with one or both hands. It is possible to
   use the task analysis with either or both hands, but the task itself is
   usually easier to perform with two hands.

2. S <u>grasps small objects</u> (e.g., Grasping Objects) and <u>retains while pulling</u>
   gently with at least one hand (e.g., Unsnapping, Unzipping Jacket, or
   Unhooking). Usually the unbuckling skill is not the first unfastening
   skill taught since it requires a longer sequence of actions than some
   other unfastening skills. Or, adapt to allow S to use adaptive equipment or materials to secure the belt. Or, you may need to develop your
   own analysis of the skill specifically for S since there are so many fine
   motor actions involved.

Objective:

When wearing a belt, S unbuckles the belt and completely separates both
belt ends without assistance. S must initiate his response within 5 seconds
of the command and respond correctly 4 out of 5 trials.

Cycle:

None specified.

Follow-Up:

Continue to have S unbuckle his belt at appropriate times. Have S unbuckle
other items, such as shoes with buckles. Combine with other tasks and
establish routines so that S does not need to wait for your command to perform the task at appropriate times (e.g., unbuckle belt, unfasten pants, pull
down pants--for self-toileting). Have S help you buckle his belt to introduce
buckling. Emphasize the words <u>belt</u> and <u>buckle</u> to expand S's vocabulary.

Program for Dressing Skill 18

GENERAL STRATEGY

Arrangement:

S wears a garment with the belt buckled. Preferably, S stands with support if needed as long as his hands and arms are free. Or, have S sit or lie down so that his torso is extended as far as possible for easy access to his waist.

Attention:

Draw S's attention to the buckle. Make relevant comments if desired.

Command:

Give an appropriate command ("UNBUCKLE") with cues indicating what you wish S to do.

Latency:

S must initiate his response within 5 seconds of the command (or last part completed).

Correction:

Use general correction or Suggestions on any part that S does not perform correctly. After you assist him, allow him to continue the trial on his own. Correct him only if needed.

Natural Consequence:

Have S unfasten his pants or continue undressing as appropriate to the situation.

Other Trials:

Repeat the strategy as often as appropriate. You may set up situations to practice the skill if desired.

Modification:

S has made no gains in average parts completed after two successive probes (2 weeks).

CONDITIONS	BEHAVIOR	CRITERIA
		for *6 only
PRE Get S's attention, and give the command. Present the natural consequence.	*6. Target--S unbuckles his belt and completely separates both ends unassisted.	4 correct out of 5 trials

DAILY INSTRUCTION/WEEKLY PROBES

Get S's attention, and give the command. Correct each part if needed. Present the natural consequence.	1. S positions his hands to free the end of the belt.	Continue daily instruction/weekly probes until S performs *6 correctly 4 out of the last 5 trials
	2. S pulls the end of the belt through the first side of the buckle.	
	3. S frees the tongue from the belt hole.	
	4. S holds the tongue out of the way if needed.	
	5. S pulls the end of the belt through the other side of the buckle.	
	*6. Target--S unbuckles his belt and completely separates both ends unassisted.	
POST 1 Same as PRE	*6. Target--S unbuckles his belt and completely separates both ends unassisted.	4 correct out of 5 trials for each test
POST 2 New Setting		
POST 3 Different Belt		

SUGGESTIONS

Part 1:

Guide S to either grasp and hold the end of the belt or to grasp the middle section of the belt. (S may do either or both.)

If the belt end is behind a loop (of the pants), you might want to have S push or pull the end through the loop before he pulls it through the first side of the buckle. Gradually fade your guidance and extra directions.

Add visual cues (e.g., colored tape) and vertical directions to indicate where to hold. Gradually fade first one, then the other.

Part 2:

Guide S to push the belt end and/or pull the middle section up to free the end through the first side of the buckle. Gradually fade your guidance and extra directions.

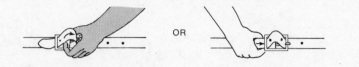

Part 3:

Guide S to pull the belt tighter and/or lift the tongue out. Gradually fade your guidance and extra directions.

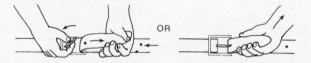

Have S pick up small objects, using a pincer grasp so that it is easy for him to lift and pull the tongue. Also, have S pull the belt tight. Practicing both of these tasks alone will make freeing the tongue from the belthole a simpler task.

Part 4:

Guide S to grasp, cover, or hold down the tongue with his finger(s) or hand. (The hold pictured below is desirable since S can then just pull the buckle up with one hand for Part 5.) Gradually fade your guidance and extra directions.

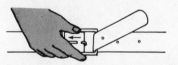

Part 5:

Guide S to pull the buckle away and/or push the tip through. (Make sure that the tongue is out of the way, or cue S to keep pulling it out if it gets caught in the holes.) Gradually fade your guidance and extra directions.

Hooking

Chain

Skill:

In this program the child learns to hold and position a hook and eye, then pull to secure the hook into the eye to fasten his garment. Although the sequence is short, it requires attending and fine motor coordination skills to position the hook.

Entry Behaviors:

1. S <u>reaches the hook</u> with both hands. If S has use of only one hand, delete parts that refer to the second hand, and have S grasp only the flap of material with the hook (not eye) on it.

2. S <u>grasps the material</u> and holds securely during gentle pulling. Usually this fine motor skill is demonstrated when one unhooks the garment (e.g., Unhooking), a task that is usually easier since it requires less attention to the position of the hook. If S's grasp is impaired, adapt by allowing S to use adaptive equipment or materials to secure the garment.

Objective:

S brings the hook and eye together to fasten his garment. S must initiate his response within 5 seconds of the command and respond correctly 4 out of 5 trials. 1 trial = 1 hook.

Cycle:

None specified. However, you may repeat the program to teach hooks located in awkward places (e.g., at the neck).

Follow-Up:

Continue to have S hook a variety of garments and other objects with hooks. Establish routines so that S hooks garments at appropriate times without your command. Combine with other tasks, such as Putting On Pants, Zipping Pants, and Hooking, giving S one command (e.g., "Put on your pants"). Emphasize the words <u>pants</u> or <u>hook</u> to expand S's vocabulary.

**Overview
Dressing
Skill 19**

Program for Dressing Skill 19

GENERAL STRATEGY

Arrangement:

S wears the garment unhooked. If the hook is above the waist, S may sit or stand with support if needed, or lie down. However, if the hook is at the waist, S should stand or be positioned with his torso as straight as possible for easier maneuvering.

Attention:

Draw S's attention to the fastener, and make relevant comments.

Command:

Give an appropriate command ("HOOK PANTS") with cues indicating what you wish S to do.

Latency:

S must initiate his response within 5 seconds of the command (or last part completed).

Correction:

Use general correction or Suggestions on any part that S does not perform correctly. After you assist him, allow him to continue the trial on his own. Correct him only if needed.

Natural Consequence:

If appropriate, help S complete fastening the garment or otherwise complete his dressing.

Other Trials:

Repeat the strategy as often as appropriate. You may set up situations to practice the skill if desired. 1 trial = 1 hook.

Modification:

S has made no gains in average parts completed after two successive probes (2 weeks).

CONDITIONS	BEHAVIOR	CRITERIA
		for *5 only
PRE Get S's attention, and give the command. Present the natural consequence.	*5. Target--S brings one hook and eye together to hook the garment unassisted.	4 correct out of 5 trials

DAILY INSTRUCTION/WEEKLY PROBES

Get S's attention, and give the command. Correct each part if needed. Present the natural consequence.	1. S grasps the material near the hook with one hand (Parts 1 and 2 may occur in either order).	Continue daily instruction/weekly probes until S performs *5 correctly 4 out of the last 5 trials

2. S holds the material
   secure near the eye
   (with the other hand).

3. S brings the hook tip
   to the eye.

4. S pulls the hook into
   the eye until the hook
   and eye are fastened
   securely.

*5. Target--S brings one
   hook and eye together
   to hook the garment
   unassisted.

POST 1 Same as PRE	*5. Target--S brings one hook and eye together to hook the garment unassisted.	4 correct out of 5 trials for each test
POST 2 New Setting		
POST 3 Different Garment w/Hook		

SUGGESTIONS

Parts 1 and 2:

Guide S to grasp the sides of the garment as appropriate. Gradually fade
your guidance and extra directions.

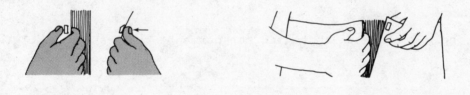

Part 3:

Use backward chaining to develop S's aim. (Make sure he is always looking.)
At first bring the hook and eye almost together, and have him move them
the last 1/4 or 1/8 inch. Gradually move the hook and eye less so that S
increases the distance he must bring them together.

Use an over-sized garment at first, especially for pants, so that S does
not have to pull hard to bring the two sides together. After S can hook
the larger garment, return to his own garment.

Work on S's eye-hand coordination. If the hook is in an awkward or hard-
to-see location, have S watch his hands as he points to the hook and eye.
Also, teach him to fasten hooks that are located in easier places; then
return to the difficult position.

Guide S to bring the hook and eye together, and gradually fade the pressure
you exert on his hands and arms.

Sew large hooks and eyes on S's garments. Gradually replace them with
regular-sized hooks.

Have S practice on a large-hook-and-eye mounted on a board.

Part 4:

Guide S to press the hook down as he pulls it into the eye. Gradually fade
the pressure you exert on his hand or arm.

Have S move each hand separately. You hold the eye secure while he pulls
the hook; then he holds the eye while you hook. Then have S perform both
parts together.

Unbuttoning

Chain

Skill:

This program teaches the child to hold the button and buttonhole appropriately, to insert the edge of the button and to push it all the way through the buttonhole. Although the sequence is short, it requires attending and fine motor skills to position the button correctly.

Entry Behaviors:

1. S <u>reaches the button</u> with both hands. If S has use of only one hand, make this adaptation: delete parts that require S to hold the buttonhole with his other hand. Instead, teach him to manipulate only the button.

2. S <u>fits objects into small places</u> (e.g., Hooking and/or Placing In/On-- Set 3) or has the eye-hand coordination needed to bring one small object (button) in contact with another (buttonhole). Note that S does not have to grasp the button but must be able to manipulate (push, pull) it or the cloth around the buttonhole to position the button.

3. S <u>holds the material</u> around the buttonhole. Or, adapt by allowing S to use adaptive equipment or materials to secure the garment. If S is severely impaired, consider using only Velcro or other easy-to-use fastenings on his garments rather than buttons.

Objective:

S unbuttons his shirt or other garment. S must initiate his response within 5 seconds of the command and respond correctly 4 out of 5 trials. 1 trial = 1 button.

Cycle:

None specified. However, you may repeat the program to teach buttons that are located in awkward places (e.g., at the neck) or that are exceptionally difficult for S to unbutton.

Follow-Up:

Continue to have S unbutton a variety of different garments with different size buttons. Combine with other tasks, and establish routines so that S does not need to wait for a command to perform the task at appropriate times (e.g., unbuckle belt, unbutton pants, pull down pants--for self-toileting). Have S help you button his garments to introduce buttoning. Emphasize the word <u>button</u> to expand S's vocabulary.

Program for Dressing Skill 20

GENERAL STRATEGY

Arrangement:

S wears a garment, buttoned with medium-sized or larger buttons.

Attention:

Draw S's attention to the button(s), and make relevant comments.

Command:

Give an appropriate command ("UNBUTTON") with cues indicating what you wish S to do.

Latency:

S must initiate his response within 5 seconds of the command (or last part completed).

Correction:

Use general correction or Suggestions on any part that S does not perform correctly. After you assist him, allow him to continue the trial on his own. Correct him only if needed.

Natural Consequence:

Help S finish removing the garment.

Other Trials:

Repeat the strategy as often as appropriate. You may set up situations to practice the skill if desired. If there are several buttons on the garment, present trials to finish the unbuttoning task. 1 trial = 1 button.

Modification:

S has made no gains in average parts completed after two successive probes (2 weeks).

CONDITIONS	BEHAVIOR	CRITERIA
		for *5 only
PRE Get S's attention, and give the command. Present the natural consequence.	*5. Target--S unbuttons one button unassisted.	4 correct out of 5 trials

DAILY INSTRUCTION/WEEKLY PROBES

Get S's attention, and give the command. Correct each part if needed. Present the natural consequence.	1. S <u>holds the edge of the material</u> securely near the buttonhole. 2. S <u>repositions the button or buttonhole</u> so that the edge of the button touches the buttonhole. 3. S <u>inserts the edge of the button</u> back into the buttonhole. 4. S <u>pushes the button</u> through the button-hole. *5. Target--S unbuttons one button unassisted.	Continue daily instruction/weekly probes until S performs *5 correctly 4 out of the last 5 trials
POST 1 Same as PRE	*5. Target--S unbuttons one button unassisted.	4 correct out of 5 trials for each test
POST 2 New Setting		
POST 3 Different Garment w/Buttons		

SUGGESTIONS

Part 1:

Guide S to hold the garment near the buttonhole. On pants, make sure that S's thumb is underneath only the flap of material with the buttonhole, not both sides. If possible, have S position his thumb directly underneath the button-hole. (This position facilitates opening the buttonhole wider to guide the button through or to manipulate the buttonhole as the button is pushed through during Part 4.) Gradually fade your guidance and extra directions.

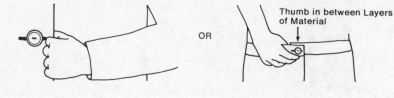

When the garment is unbuttoned, have S hold the garment as shown above and push his thumb out through the hole. Then have him hold and push his thumb while the garment is buttoned, thus pushing the button out away from the buttonhole (facilitates Part 2). Once S has practiced both of these tasks, he will be better able to grasp the garment correctly, as the buttonhole has become a cue for the activity.

Part 2:

Guide S to reposition the button or buttonhole in one of the following ways; then gradually fade your guidance and extra directions:

a. <u>Two hands</u>. Have S use one hand to hold the buttonhole in place. Then with his other hand, have him grasp the button, pull it outward, then turn it flat or horizontal so that it will slip back into the buttonhole.

b. <u>One hand</u>. Have S push the button outward with his thumb (the thumb positioned under the buttonhole, described in Part 1). Then have him use his fingers (same hand) to pull or turn the far side of the button so that its side is at an angle to the hole.

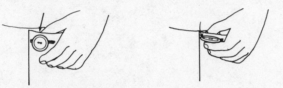

Push the Button, Then Turn the Button

Parts 3 and 4:

Use backward chaining. At first help S to position and push the button almost all the way through; then let him finish on his own. Gradually assist less with positioning, and allow S to complete more on his own until he can position and push the button unassisted.

Have S put buttons through large buttonholes. Then gradually fade the size of the hole by sewing it shut until it is normal for the button.

Have S put pennies in a piggy bank or tokens into a jar with a slot at the top to practice his fine motor skills.

Start by teaching lower-placed buttons or ones that are easy to see and reach. Or, teach with buttons that are mounted on a board. After S can unbutton in this position, then return to those that are more difficult to see (above mid-chest).

Snapping

Chain

Skill:

In this program the child learns to position and push the two sides of a
snap together. Although the chain is short, it requires attention and
fine motor coordination to position the snap.

Entry Behaviors:

1. S reaches the snap with both hands at the same time. Use only snaps that
   are within S's reach. If S can reach with only one hand, use Velcro snaps
   that do not require a second hand to help position the sides. Delete the
   part(s) that refer to actions with the second hand. Usually S is able to
   unsnap the garment (e.g., Unsnapping) before he can snap it since the unfastening skill uses a similar reach and grasp but does not require the
   precision needed to position the sides.

2. S grasps (palmar or pincer) the material around the sides of the snap.
   Or, adapt to allow S to use adaptive equipment or materials to secure
   the sides of the garment.

3. S brings the two sides of the snap in contact with each other (fine motor
   coordination). If S cannot bring them in contact, review this fine motor
   task first (e.g., Placing In/On, Set 3).

Objective:

S snaps his garment unassisted. S must initiate his response within 5
seconds of the command and respond correctly 4 out of 5 trials. 1 trial =
1 snap.

Cycle:

None specified. However, you may repeat the program to teach snaps that
are located in difficult places for S, such as at the neck (top of shirt)
or waist (pants).

Follow-Up:

Continue to have S snap different garments at appropriate times. Establish
routines so that he learns to snap without requiring a command. Combine
snapping with other dressing tasks. For example, he pulls on his pants
(e.g., Putting On Pants), zips them up (e.g., Zipping Pants), then snaps
them. When S snaps, repeat the word snap to expand his vocabulary. Encourage
S to use toys that further develop his fine motor skills (e.g., snapping pop-
beads or other plastic links together).

Program for Dressing Skill 21

GENERAL STRATEGY

Arrangement:

S wears his garment unsnapped. If the snap is above the waist, S may sit or stand with support as long as his hands are free to reach the snap. If the snap is at the waist (e.g., for pants), S should stand, if possible, so that the snap is easy to grasp and bring together. Alternately, he may lie down or sit with his back extended as far as possible so he can grasp the snap more easily.

Attention:

Draw S's attention to the snap, and make relevant comments.

Command:

Give an appropriate command ("SNAP PANTS") with cues indicating what you wish S to do.

Latency:

S must initiate his response within 5 seconds of the command (or last part completed).

Correction:

Use general correction or Suggestions on any part that S does not perform correctly. After you assist him, allow him to continue the trial on his own. Correct him only if needed.

Natural Consequence:

Help S finish getting dressed. Or, if the garment has several snaps, present the next trial(s) to finish snapping the garment. Note that 1 trial = snapping 1 snap.

Other Trials:

Repeat the strategy as often as appropriate. You may set up situations to practice the skill if desired.

Modification:

S has made no gains in average parts completed after two successive probes (2 weeks).

CONDITIONS	BEHAVIOR	CRITERIA
		for *6 only
PRE Get S's attention, and give the command. Present the natural consequence.	*6. Target--S fastens one snap unassisted.	4 correct out of 5 trials

DAILY INSTRUCTION/WEEKLY PROBES

Get S's attention, and give the command. Correct each part if needed. Present the natural consequence.	1. S grasps the material near the top of the snap with one hand. 2. S grasps the material near the bottom of the snap with his other hand.	Continue daily instruction/weekly probes until S performs *6 correctly 4 out of the last 5 trials

	3. S <u>brings the sides of the snap</u> in contact with each other.	
	4. S <u>positions the snap</u> so that the sides are opposite each other.	
	5. S <u>pushes the snap closed.</u>	
	*6. Target--S fastens one snap unassisted.	
POST 1 Same as PRE	*6. Target--S fastens one snap unassisted.	4 correct out of 5 trials for each test
POST 2 New Setting or Position		
POST 3 Different Garment		

SUGGESTIONS

Parts 1 and 2:

Guide S to grasp the garment. Gradually fade your guidance and extra directions. (It is particularly helpful if S has his thumb or fingers directly over the outside material for the top side of the snap and underneath on the bottom side. Then S can use his thumbs to position and close the snap.)

Parts 3 and 4:

Use backward chaining to improve S's aim. Help S to position the snap; then have him push it shut on his own. Then help S place the sides within 1/4 or 1/8 inch, and have him aim the rest of the way. Provide less help until he can bring the sides together on his own.

Have S practice on a snap that is easy to see or on one that is mounted. After S can position the sides when he looks closely, have him return to his own garment. Note that although pant snaps are often easiest to see, they are often the hardest to push closed (Part 5).

Part 5:

Make sure that S has his fingers or thumbs directly over and under the snap as described in Part 1 so that he has something to push against. Guide S to push, and gradually fade the pressure you exert.

Have S push with his thumbs. For example, make a box with a slot just big enough for a fitted object, and have S push the object in with his thumb.

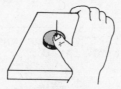

Have S press down to stick tape to his thumb. Or, have S make thumbprints in clay to practice exerting pressure with his thumb.

Zipping Jacket

Chain

Skill:

This program teaches the fine motor actions required to fit a zipper tab
into the track, then pull the tab up the track. The child already pulls
the zipper up and down but has not yet learned to fit the zipper into the
track.

Entry Behaviors:

1. S moves one arm as needed to zip the jacket (up and down at midline). S
   brings his other arm to midline and grasps the material near the zipper to
   stabilize it as he pulls the tab. If S has use of only one arm, reconsider
   the use of this program. Instead, teach S to zip clothing with nondetachable
   zippers (e.g., Zipping Pants), or teach him to fasten jackets and coats that
   have other closings, such as snaps or buttons.

2. S grasps the zipper tab and holds it while pulling (e.g., Unzipping Jacket,
   Zipping Pants, and/or Unzipping Pants). Usually S can perform all zipping
   tasks except fitting the tab into the track. Only use garments with tabs
   large enough that S can grasp them. If S has an impaired grasp, use adaptive equipment or materials that enable him to secure the zipper tab.

3. S fits small objects together (e.g., Placing In/On--Set 3, Snapping and/or
   Hooking). If S has developed some fine motor coordination in skills such
   as these, it will be easier for him to learn to fit the zipper into the
   track.

Objective:

When wearing a garment with a front (neck-to-waist) zipper that is detachable,
S fits the zipper into the track and zips the garment completely without
assistance. S must initiate his response within 5 seconds of the command and
respond correctly 4 out of 5 trials.

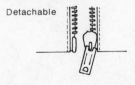

Detachable   Nondetachable
                 (See Zipping Pants)

Cycle:

None specified.

Follow-Up:

Continue to have S use this skill at appropriate times. Set up a routine
so that he puts on his jacket and zips it up when he goes outside for recess
or home after school. This routine will enable S to get his jacket at
appropriate times without your command. Also, provide practice in unzipping
his jacket and taking it off. Require him to zip up a variety of different
garments (jump suits, shirts, coats, sweaters). Talk to S frequently about
the task to encourage him to expand his vocabulary.

Program for Dressing Skill 22

GENERAL STRATEGY

Arrangement:

S wears the garment with the zipper unzipped and the two sides separated.
S may sit or stand as long as the zipper track is fairly straight.

Attention:

Draw S's attention to the zipper, and make relevant comments.

Command:

Give an appropriate command ("ZIP JACKET") <u>with cues</u> indicating what you
wish S to do.

Latency:

S must initiate his response within 5 seconds of the command (or last part
completed).

Correction:

Use general correction or Suggestions on any part that S does not perform
correctly. After you assist him, allow him to continue the trial on his
own. Correct him only if needed.

Natural Consequence:

After the jacket is zipped, present an appropriate consequence, such as
take S outside for recess or go home.

Other Trials:

Repeat the strategy as often as appropriate. You may set up situations
to practice the skill if desired.

Modification:

S has made no gains in <u>average parts completed</u> after two successive probes
(2 weeks).

CONDITIONS	BEHAVIOR	CRITERIA
		for *7 only
PRE Get S's attention, and give the command. Present the natural consequence.	*7. Target--S fits the zipper into the track and zips up the garment completely, unassisted.	4 correct out of 5 trials

DAILY INSTRUCTION/WEEKLY PROBES

Get S's attention, and give the command. Correct each part if needed. Present the natural consequence.	1. S <u>grasps the zipper tab</u> and brings it down to the end of the track.	Continue daily instruction/weekly probes until S performs *7 correctly 4 out of the last 5 trials.
	2. S <u>grasps the other side of the jacket</u> at the bottom next to the zipper track with his other hand (Parts 1 and 2 may occur in any order).	
	3. S <u>positions the zipper tab</u> directly under the end of the zipper track.	
	4. S <u>fits the zipper tab and track together</u> by pushing or pulling separately.	
	5. S <u>holds the bottom of the zipper track secure</u> (now connected) to prevent the two sides of the zipper from coming apart as the jacket is zipped (may occur concurrently with Part 6).	
	6. S <u>pulls the zipper tab up</u> to zip the jacket completely.	
	*7. Target--S fits the zipper into the track and zips up the garment completely unassisted.	
POST 1 Same as PRE	*7. Target--S fits the zipper into the track and zips up the garment completely, unassisted.	4 correct out of 5 trials for each test
POST 2 Different Garment		
POST 3 Another Garment (different from POST 2)		

SUGGESTIONS

Part 1:

At first use garments in which the zipper tab slides down the track very
easily. Guide S to pull the tab to the bottom. Gradually fade your
guidance.

Use backward chaining. First guide S to pull the zipper tab all the way to
the bottom of the track. Then help him to pull the tab halfway, and have
S pull it the rest of the way down the track. Next guide S to pull initially,
and have him pull the zipper tab down the track unassisted. Finally have S
perform the task unassisted.

Have S grasp a variety of small objects between his thumb and finger(s).
After S has had practice with small objects, have him grasp and pull the
zipper tab.

Use garments with unusually large zippers with tabs that are easy to grasp
(parka). When S can easily grasp the larger tabs, have him zip and unzip
garments with regular-sized zippers.

Paint the zipper tab a bright color. Attach a piece of bright yarn or add
a leather strip to the tab. Use garments with brightly colored zipper tabs.
These cues can assist S in locating the tab and grasping it. Gradually fade
these cues (unless they are adaptive materials for S's impaired grasp).

Part 2:

Guide S to hold the other side of the jacket near the bottom of the zipper
track. Gradually fade your guidance.

Part 3:

Guide S to position the zipper tab directly under the track. (Make sure
the zipper tab is all the way down the track.) Gradually fade your guidance.

Have S practice first on a garment placed flat on a table so that the tab and track are easily seen. Then return to the garment that he is wearing.

Use backward chaining for aim. At first bring the sides into position as in the picture above. Then bring them within 1/4 inch, and have S finish positioning them. Provide less guidance until S can bring the two together by himself.

Part 4:

Use backward chaining for Parts 3 and 4. First guide S to position the zipper tab directly under the track, fit it in, and push until the tab is securely in the track. Then help S to position the tab under the track and fit it in, but have S push the tab securely in the track, unassisted. Next give guidance only to position the tab under the track, and have S complete the task unassisted. Finally have S position the zipper tab and fit the two ends of the zipper securely without assistance.

Have S practice on a garment with a very large zipper to make it easier to fit the two ends together at the bottom. Then have him zip garments with regular-sized zippers.

Part 5:

Guide S to hold the bottom of the zipper track together with his thumb and finger(s) to prevent the zipper from coming apart as the jacket is zipped. Gradually fade your guidance.

Practice Parts 5 and 6 separately. You hold the bottom of the zipper track while helping S pull the zipper tab up. Then help S to hold the zipper together at the bottom while you zip the jacket. Gradually fade your guidance, and have S perform both parts at the same time.

Part 6:

Use backward chaining. Pull the tab almost all the way up, and have S finish. Gradually pull the zipper up a shorter distance so that S pulls farther on his own.

Have S pull a string to which an object or weight has been attached. Vary the weight some, but you do not need to develop a great deal of strength here. Rather, practice the pulling motion for zipping.

Guide S to pull the tab up the track as he pulls down with his other hand at the bottom of the zipper. Gradually fade your guidance.

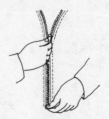

Drying Hands

Chain

Skill:

In this program the child learns to take a towel and rub it over the front
and back of his hands. This chain develops fine motor coordination and wrist
rotation. It is usually initiated with hand washing as a follow-up to self-
feeding and/or independent toileting.

Entry Behaviors:

1. S brings the towel to both hands by bending his arms at the elbow and
   moving one arm toward the other. S can also rotate his wrist so that
   he can move the towel on the front and back of each hand. If S does
   not have these skills, reconsider the use of this program. Or, devise
   your own task analysis to teach the skill.

2. S holds the towel and transfers it from one hand to the other. Or, adapt
   by adding parts to the task analysis to allow S to use adaptive equipment
   or materials as necessary to secure the towel.

3. S cooperates in self-care by attending (looking at materials, body parts,
   or adult) or attempting to assist (moving his body to facilitate washing).
   Preferably, S does not resist physical guidance.

Objective:

When S's hands are wet and a towel is within reach, S takes the towel and
dries his hands unassisted. S must initiate his response within 5 seconds
of the command and respond correctly 4 out of 5 trials.

Cycle:

None specified.

Follow-Up:

Continue to have S use the skill at appropriate times: In the bathroom,
kitchen, utility room; after working or while playing. Vary the type of
towel and/or towel dispenser used. Once S can dry his hands, ask him to
dry other parts of his body (e.g., Drying Face). Establish drying as part
of S's daily routine, and have him use this skill for wiping off sticky
hands. While drying, describe what S is doing so that he associates the words
(e.g., dry) with the action he is performing. As S becomes more proficient,
he may wipe off other surfaces, as well as dry his face and hands.

Program for Grooming Skill 1

GENERAL STRATEGY

Arrangement:

S sits or stands at the sink with the towel dispenser within reach. He is supported if needed as long as his hands and arms are free to operate. S's hands are clean but wet.

Attention:

Draw S's attention to the towel and his hands. Note to S that his hands are wet.

Command:

Give an appropriate command ("DRY YOUR HANDS") with cues indicating what you wish S to do.

Latency:

S must initiate his response within 5 seconds of the command (or last part completed).

Correction:

Use general correction or Suggestions on any part that S does not perform correctly. After you assist him, allow him to continue the trial on his own. Correct him only if needed.

Natural Consequence:

After S dries his hands with the towel, have him put it in/on the appropriate place (wastebasket or rack). 1 trial = drying both hands.

Other Trials:

Repeat the strategy as often as appropriate. You may set up situations for S to practice the skill if desired.

Modification:

S has made no gains in average parts completed after two probes (2 weeks).

CONDITIONS	BEHAVIOR	CRITERIA
		for *5 only
PRE Get S's attention, and give the command. Present the natural consequence.	*5. Target--S takes the towel and dries his hands unassisted.	4 correct out of 5 trials

---

DAILY INSTRUCTION/WEEKLY PROBES:

Get S's attention, and give the command. Correct each part if needed. Present the natural consequence.	1. S takes the towel. 2. S dries one hand. 3. S shifts his grasp and transfers the towel from one hand to the other. 4. S dries his other hand.	Continue daily instruction/weekly probes until S performs *5 correctly 4 out of the last 5 trials

	*5. Target—S takes the towel and dries his hands unassisted.	
POST 1 Same as PRE	*5. Target—S takes the towel and dries his hands unassisted.	4 correct out of 5 trials for each test
POST 2 New Materials		
POST 3 New Setting		

SUGGESTIONS

Part 1:

Guide S to take the towel in any of the following ways. Gradually fade your assistance.

S grasps the towel and brings it free of the holder. (S may use one or both hands.)

S grasps the towel and uses it while it hangs. (S does not have to pull the towel off the rack.)

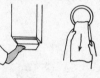 OR

Parts 2 and 4:

Have S rub surfaces that need to be cleaned and dried. This gives him practice with the rubbing motion needed to dry his hands.

Place your hands over S's hand. Physically guide him to exert pressure and to extend the length of his strokes as he rubs. Gradually fade your assistance.

Guide S to complete the task in one of the following positions. Gradually fade your assistance.

Rubs the Opposite Hand with the Towel

Rubs the Palms at the Same Time

If S does not dry his hands well, put soapsuds on his hands so that he can see where to rub. After S can do this, just use water.

Part 3:

Physically guide S to complete the transfer. Gradually decrease the amount of pressure used so that S does not drop the towel. Also, use exaggerated verbal and visual cues, such as pointing and saying "From this hand to this hand." Gradually fade all cues.

Using a Napkin

Chain

Skill:

In this program the child learns to take a napkin and wipe his mouth. This chain develops grasping, releasing, and rubbing skills, which may be used to wash his face and body.

Entry Behaviors:

1. S feeds himself independently or with minor assistance (e.g., Eating Finger Foods and/or Eating with a Fork or Spoon). Use of a napkin is most relevant after the child has done some independent feeding and has experienced the difference between "being clean" and having a dirty face. S can often already dry his hands (Drying Hands), and/or wipe surfaces, or has had other experience in wiping.

2. S brings the napkin to his mouth by bending his arm at the elbow and/or lowering his head. The program may be adapted. Add to or delete parts of the task analysis. Allow S to turn his head to the side to wipe his mouth on a napkin which you have attached to his shirt at his shoulder.

3. S holds the napkin. Or, adapt by using adaptive equipment or materials that enable him to secure the napkin.

Objective:

S brings a napkin to his mouth and wipes his mouth clean. S must initiate his response within 5 seconds of the command and respond correctly 4 out of 5 trials. 1 trial = complete wiping.

Cycle:

None specified.

Follow-Up:

Decrease your verbal cues so that S responds to natural cues to wipe his mouth (e.g., dribbling on the chin). To provide a visual cue, position S in front of a mirror before he eats. Provide tissues, a paper towel, or a washcloth. After he wipes his mouth, have S fold the napkin or dispose of it. Describe to S what he is doing so that he will begin to associate specific words (e.g., wipe) with the response he is to make.

Program
Grooming
Skill 2

Program for Grooming Skill 2

GENERAL STRATEGY

Arrangement:

At snack or mealtime, place a napkin next to S's food (plate) or on his lap.

Attention:

Tell S to wipe his mouth. Then draw attention to the napkin.

Command:

Give an appropriate command ("USE YOUR NAPKIN") with cues indicating what you wish S to do.

Latency:

S must initiate his response within 5 seconds of the command (or last part completed).

Correction:

Use general correction or Suggestions on any part that S does not perform correctly. After you assist him, allow him to continue the trial on his own. Correct him only if needed.

Natural Consequence:

Give S a cue to replace the napkin after he has used it. Then have S continue to eat his food. (Other trials may be given if needed.)

Other Trials:

Repeat the strategy as often as appropriate. You may set up situations to practice the skill if desired.

Modification:

S has made no gains in average parts completed after two probes (2 weeks).

CONDITIONS	BEHAVIOR	CRITERIA for *5 only
PRE Get S's attention, and give the command. Present the natural consequence.	*5. Target--S brings a napkin to his mouth and wipes it clean unassisted.	4 correct out of 5 trials

DAILY INSTRUCTION/WEEKLY PROBES:

Get S's attention, and give the command. Correct each part if needed. Present the natural consequence.

1. S picks up a napkin.
2. S arranges the napkin as necessary (Parts 1 and 2 may occur in either order).
3. S brings the napkin to his mouth.
4. S wipes his mouth with the napkin.

Continue daily instruction/weekly probes until S performs *5 correctly 4 out of the last 5 trials

Overview
Grooming
Skill 2

	*5. Target--S brings a napkin to his mouth and wipes it clean unassisted.	
POST 1 Same as PRE	*5. Target--S brings a napkin to his mouth and wipes it clean unassisted.	4 correct out of 5 trials for each test
POST 2 New Setting		
POST 3 Other Materials		

SUGGESTIONS

Part 1:

Guide S to pick up the napkin. Give additional verbal and visual cues while you fade physical assistance. Finally fade the additional cues.

Pincer grasp at corner
(to shake it open)

Grasp at the side with one or both hands (to wipe)

Have S grasp a cloth that is lying on a flat surface. At first have S grasp a raised portion of the material. Gradually lay the cloth flat on the table without using the bunched-up cloth as a cue.

Part 2: (optional)

Note: This part may be omitted if S just picks up the napkin and wipes. Or, you may teach him to unfold or shake the napkin open if needed.

Guide S to open the napkin in the way you choose. Gradually fade the assistance.

Part 3:

To have S bring the napkin to his mouth, provide physical guidance. Exert pressure at the back of S's neck or head downward and/or on his hand(s) upward toward his face. Gradually decrease this guidance.

Have S imitate actions (e.g., prompt S to touch different parts of his face after you demonstrate) to bring the napkin to his face.

Use backward chaining. At first help S bring the napkin within 1 inch of his mouth, and have him bring the napkin the rest of the way on his own. Gradually have S bring the napkin farther and farther on his own. This helps him to aim the napkin toward his mouth.

Part 4:

Guide S to move the napkin back and forth across his face or to move his head from side to side across the napkin to wipe. Gradually fade the guidance and any extra directions used.

Use a mirror and demonstration so that S sees you perform the task. Have S continue to perform the task in front of the mirror so that he can see where to wipe off the food. Fade your reminders and demonstration. Finally remove the mirror since it would not normally be present during a meal.

Drying Face

Chain

Skill:

In this program the child learns to take a towel, bring it to his face, and wipe his face dry. This chain develops the fine motor coordination and self-care skills needed for independence.

Entry Behaviors:

1. S <u>brings the towel to his face</u> by bending his arm at the elbow and lowering his head or by raising his hands to his head. S can also rotate his wrists or move his head back and forth across the towel. If S does not have these skills, reconsider teaching this program. Or, devise your own task analysis to teach this skill.

2. S <u>holds the towel</u>. Or, adapt by using adaptive equipment or materials that enable S to secure the object. Usually, the child has already grasped a towel or napkin in the initial grooming skills (e.g., Drying Hands and Using a Napkin).

Objective:

When his face is wet and a towel is within reach, S takes the towel and wipes his face dry. S must initiate his response within 5 seconds of the command and respond correctly 4 out of 5 trials.

Cycle:

None specified.

Follow-Up:

Continue to develop S's use of a towel to dry his face, as well as other parts of his body. Establish drying the face as part of his daily routine. Have S use various types of towels and towel dispensers. Get him to incorporate this skill with Washing Face. Have him perform the routine of wash-dry-put away towel for both hands and face. As S is performing the task, have him use the words involved: <u>wash</u>, <u>dry</u>, <u>put away</u>. S may then anticipate the behaviors to follow these words in varied situations.

Program for Grooming Skill 3

GENERAL STRATEGY

Arrangement:

S sits or stands in front of a sink with either a cloth towel hanging on a rack or a towel dispenser within reach. S's face is clean but wet.

Attention:

Draw S's attention to the towel.

Command:

Give an appropriate command ("DRY YOUR FACE") <u>with cues</u> indicating what you wish S to do.

Latency:

S must initiate his response within 5 seconds of the command (or last part completed).

Correction:

Use general correction or Suggestions on any part that S does not perform correctly. After you assist him, allow him to continue the trial on his own. Correct him only if needed.

Natural Consequence:

As soon as S finishes drying his face, present cues to replace or dispose of the towel. Then have him go on to another task.

Modification:

Repeat the strategy as often as appropriate. You may set up situations to practice the skill if desired.

Other Trials:

S has made no gains in <u>average parts completed</u> after two probes (2 weeks).

CONDITIONS	BEHAVIOR	CRITERIA
		for *6 only
PRE Get S's attention, and give the command. Present the natural consequence.	*6. Target--S takes the towel and dries his face unassisted.	4 correct out of 5 trials

DAILY INSTRUCTION/WEEKLY PROBES:

Get S's attention, and give the command. Correct each part if needed. Present the natural consequence.	1. S <u>takes the towel</u>. 2. S <u>positions the towel over one hand</u>. 3. S <u>positions his other hand</u> if needed (optional). 4. S <u>brings the towel to his face</u>. 5. S <u>rubs his face</u> with the towel.	Continue daily instruction/weekly probes until S performs *6 correctly 4 out of the last 5 trials

	*6. Target--S takes the towel and dries his face unassisted.	
POST 1 Same as PRE	*6. Target--S takes the towel and dries his face unassisted.	4 correct out of 5 trials for each test
POST 2 New Setting		
POST 3 Different Towel (new type)		

SUGGESTIONS

Part 1:

Guide S to pull the towel off the rack or from the dispenser. While you fade your assistance, use verbal or visual cues. Gradually fade all cues.

S grasps the towel and brings it free of the holder.

S grasps the towel and uses it while it is hanging (does not pull it off rack)

OR

Parts 2 and 3: (optional)

Provide physical assistance for S to hold the towel with at least one hand so that the towel lays flat. (Second hand is optional.) The towel may lay flat over S's hand. Gradually fade the use of all cues and assistance.

Have S transfer objects from hand to hand to practice using both hands.

Use backward chaining for Parts 2-6 so that S learns to position the towel last. At first you guide S through all parts, but have him rub his face unassisted. Then provide less guidance, and have S bring the towel to his face and rub unassisted. Finally have S position the towel and rub his face unassisted.

Part 4:

Have S cover his face with a towel as in a game situation (e.g., peek-a-boo) or through imitation with a command (e.g., give a model and say "Touch your face"). Use additional verbal or visual cues to assist S to complete the task. Gradually fade these cues during practice.

Use backward chaining. Guide S to bring the towel within inches of his face; then let him bring it the rest of the way on his own. Reduce the distance you guide S so that he brings the towel to his face on his own.

Part 5:

Have S rub surfaces. Put water or powder on the surface so that S can see the result of exerting pressure on the surface. After the practice, have S return to rubbing his face.

Guide S to exert pressure as he rubs his face. Increase the length of the strokes S makes. Then gradually decrease the amount of pressure you use to assist S.

Wiping Nose

Chain

Skill:

In this program the child learns to pick up a tissue or handkerchief and bring it to his face to wipe his nose. This program further develops the child's rubbing skills, also included the program to teach S to wipe his mouth with a napkin.

Entry Behaviors:

1. S <u>brings a tissue to his nose</u> by bending his arm at the elbow and lowering his head or by raising his arm to his face. If S cannot reach his nose, reconsider your rationale for teaching this program.

2. S <u>makes wiping motions</u> either by moving his hand (wrist and forearm) or moving his head back and forth across the tissue. S previously used a similar wiping motion in other self-help skills (e.g., Drying Hands, Using a Napkin, Drying Face). S occasionally wipes his nose on his hands; he does not consistently use a tissue or handkerchief. If S cannot perform a wiping motion, develop your own task analysis to include another motion, such as squeezing the nose.

3. S <u>picks up and releases the tissue.</u> Or, adapt by adding parts to the task analysis to allow S to use adaptive equipment or materials to secure the tissue while wiping.

Objective:

S brings a tissue to his nose and wipes his nose with the tissue unassisted. S must initiate his response within 5 seconds of the command and respond correctly 4 out of 5 trials.

Cycle:

None specified.

Follow-Up:

Require S to wipe his nose whenever it is necessary. To teach S to wipe his nose without your command, have him look in a mirror, and show him that he needs to wipe. Gradually give only occasional reminders until S uses a tissue on his own. As S performs the skill, describe what he is doing (e.g., "S, you're <u>wiping</u> your nose") so that he begins to associate specific words with the activity. Encourage S to describe his own activity. For S's greater independence, have him carry his own handkerchief or tissue (in pocket). Combine wiping nose with other self-care skills (e.g., combing hair) as part of a sequence of activities S completes when he stands in front of a mirror.

Program for Grooming Skill 4

GENERAL STRATEGY

Arrangement:

Position a handkerchief or a tissue box (with one tissue pulled partially out of the box) nearby.

Attention:

Draw S's attention to the tissue or handkerchief, as well as to his nose (which may or may not need wiping). <u>Note</u>: S may be taught the skill without having a "runny" nose. For some children it would be impractical to teach the skill only when they have a runny nose.

Command:

Give an appropriate command ("WIPE YOUR NOSE") <u>with cues</u> indicating what you wish S to do.

Latency:

S must initiate his response within 5 seconds of the command (or last part completed).

Correction:

Use general correction or Suggestions on any part that S does not perform correctly. After you assist him, allow him to continue the trial on his own. Correct him only if needed.

Natural Consequence:

After S finishes wiping his nose with the tissue, help him throw the tissue in the wastebasket or put the handkerchief back in his pocket.

Other Trials:

Repeat the strategy as often as appropriate. 1 trial = S wipes nose area until dry (or completes motor chain vigorously, if "dry nose" practice is executed).

Modification:

S has made no gains in <u>average parts completed</u> after two probes (2 weeks).

CONDITIONS	BEHAVIOR	CRITERIA for *5 only
PRE Get S's attention, and give the command. Present the natural consequence.	*5. Target—S picks up the tissue and wipes his nose unassisted.	4 correct out of 5 trials

DAILY INSTRUCTION/WEEKLY PROBES:

Get S's attention, and give the command. Correct each part if needed. Present the natural consequence.	1. S <u>brings the tissue to his nose.</u> 2. S <u>presses his nose with the tissue</u> (S may blow his nose but this is not required).	Continue daily instruction/weekly probes until S performs *5 correctly 4 out of the last 5 trials.

	3. S moves the tissue across his nose while he presses.	
	4. S continues to wipe if necessary (until the nose is dry).	
	*5. Target--S picks up the tissue and wipes his nose unassisted.	
POST 1 Same as PRE	*5. Target--S picks up the tissue and wipes his nose unassisted.	4 correct out of 5 trials for each test
POST 2 New Setting		
POST 3 New Setting (different from POST 2)		

SUGGESTIONS

Part 1:

Have S pull tissues out of the box. Since the tissue is usually needed immediately when S's nose is running, this part of the task should be completed quickly and practiced separately.

If S is using a handkerchief, have him open or unfold the handkerchief at times other than when needed. S may grasp or position the tissue or handkerchief over his hand:

Grasped to Wipe   Placed on His Hand to Wipe

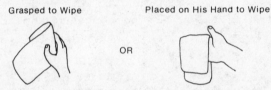

OR

Use backward chaining to teach S to bring the tissue to his nose. At first guide S's hand to within 1 inch of his nose; then require him to touch his nose unassisted. Gradually provide less guidance so that S must bring his hand farther to touch his nose.

Part 2:

Guide S to press his nose by exerting pressure on his fingers. Be careful not to interfere with S's breathing. Gradually fade your guidance and extra directions.

One Hand   Two Hands

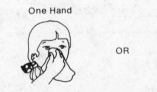

OR

If S tries to blow his nose at this point, have him practice this response when you tell him "S, blow your nose." Demonstrate blowing by breathing deeply, closing your mouth, and blowing air out of your nose. So that S can feel it, place the palm of his hand in front of your nostrils. Have S blow through his nose when it does not need to be wiped.

Parts 3 and 4:

Guide S to move the tissue back and forth (up and down) across his nose or guide him to move his head back and forth (up and down) across the tissue. Gradually fade the amount of guidance given.

Demonstrate in front of a mirror. Then have S watch in the mirror as he wipes his own nose. Fade all cues, including the use of the mirror, since it will not always be available to S when his nose is runny.

Washing Hands

Chain

Skill:

In this program the child learns to lather and rinse his hands. This program builds on previously learned wiping skills such as drying hands but does not require the child to turn on the water or adjust its temperature. The washing procedure can later be applied to other parts of the body.

Entry Behaviors:

1. S <u>clasps and rubs his hands</u>. He has already developed some wrist rotation skills when using a towel to dry his hands (e.g., Drying Hands). If S cannot clasp and rub his hands, develop your own task analysis for washing hands.

2. S <u>holds the soap</u>. Or, adapt by using equipment or materials that enable S to secure the soap.

Objective:

S lathers and rinses his hands unassisted. S must initiate his response within 5 seconds of the command and respond correctly 4 out of 5 trials. 1 trial = washing both hands.

Cycle:

None specified.

Follow-Up:

Continue to have S wash his hands as part of his daily routine. This washing skill may be extended to other body parts (e.g., using soapy hands to wash arms, legs). As S washes, describe what he is doing so that he begins to associate certain words with specific activities. Encourage him to describe the activity he is performing (e.g., "washing"). Continue to have S wash and dry his hands, face, and other body parts. Expand his experience with washing by having him wash out clothing (small articles only) by hand, as well as dishes and other objects. Eventually have S turn on the faucet by himself. He may either place the stopper in the sink to fill the bowl or just let the water run. S can also begin to adjust the water temperature.

Program for Grooming Skill 5

GENERAL STRATEGY

Arrangement:

S stands or sits in front of a sink. A bar of soap and a towel are within reach. The sink may be filled with water, or the faucet may be running. Make sure you adjust the water temperature.

Attention:

Draw S's attention to the soap and his hands. Note to S that his hands need washing.

Command:

Give an appropriate command ("WASH YOUR HANDS") with cues indicating what you wish S to do.

Latency:

S must initiate his response within 5 seconds of the command (or last part completed).

Correction:

Use general correction or Suggestions on any part that S does not perform correctly. After you assist him, allow him to continue the trial on his own. Correct him only if needed.

Natural Consequence:

As soon as S finishes washing his hands, help him turn the faucet off or pull the plug in the sink. Then dry his hands.

Other Trials:

Repeat the strategy as often as appropriate. You may set up situations to practice the skill if desired.

Modification:

S has made no gains in average parts completed after two probes (2 weeks).

CONDITIONS	BEHAVIOR	CRITERIA
		for *7 only
PRE Get S's attention, and give the command. Present the natural consequence.	*7. Target--S lathers and washes his hands unassisted.	4 correct out of 5 trials

DAILY INSTRUCTION/WEEKLY PROBES:

Get S's attention, and give the command. Correct each part if needed. Present the natural consequence.

1. S picks up the soap.
2. S wets his hands and the soap.
3. S lathers his hands.
4. S replaces the soap.
5. S scrubs his hands front and back.

Continue daily instruction/weekly probes until S performs *7 correctly 4 out of the last 5 trials

Program Grooming Skill 5

6. S <u>rinses his hands.</u>

*7. Target--S lathers
and washes his hands
unassisted.

POST 1 Same as PRE	*7. Target--S lathers and washes his hands unassisted.	4 correct out of 5 trials for each test

POST 2 New Setting

POST 3 New Setting (different from POST 2)

SUGGESTIONS

Part 1:

<u>Note:</u> If the bar slips away from S, put it in a soapdish with higher sides. (S may meet criterion with this soapdish).

Have S pick up and grasp objects of various sizes and weights. Provide practice opportunities with both wet and dry objects since soap is particularly slippery.

Initially have S use dry hands to pick up dry soap; then wet hands to pick up dry soap; and finally wet hands and wet soap.

Part 2:

Physically guide S to wet his hands and the soap. S may either hold his hands and the soap under running water or place his hands and the soap in a sink full of water. Fade your guidance and extra directions.

Parts 3 and 5:

Have S hold the soap between his hands. Let him squeeze first one hand, then the other as you help him. Encourage S to rub the soap. Require him to increase his effort while you decrease your assistance.

Practice different rubbing motions (front and back of hand) separately. At first have S rub his palms together with short strokes. Then have him rub the back of each hand, one at a time.

Use a few drops of liquid soap at first so that S does not have to hold the bar of soap while he lathers. When he lathers proficiently, reintroduce the bar of soap.

Use backward chaining to teach S first to rinse his hands; then rub and rinse; then lather, rub, and rinse until he finally has learned the entire sequence.

Part 4:

<u>Note:</u> If the soap slips away from S, have him put it in a soapdish with higher sides. (S may meet criterion with this soapdish.)

Use backward chaining. At first guide S's hand within 1 inch of the target. Gradually increase the distance he is required to bring the object on his own.

Place the soapdish closer to S, and hold it if necessary. Gradually move the dish closer to its usual position. Increase the distance S must move to place the soap.

Part 6:

Guide S to place his hands under the water and to rotate them until rinsed. At first it might be easier for S to put his hands in a bowl of water since they will be thoroughly covered with water without having to rotate his wrists to rinse. Gradually fade your guidance and extra directions.

Demonstrate to S how to rinse his hands by rotating his wrists. Gradually fade the use of the demonstration.

Washing Face

Chain

Skill:

In this program the child learns to lather soap on a washcloth, scrub his face, then rinse the cloth and his face. (He is not required to turn on the water or adjust its temperature.) Although he has already learned to lather and scrub to wash his hands, this program extends these skills by adding the use of a washcloth and by requiring better coordination to keep the soap out of his eyes and mouth.

Entry Behaviors:

1. S raises his hands to his face or lowers his head to contact his hands. If S cannot reach his face, reconsider your rationale for teaching this program.

2. S clasps and rubs his hands and also rubs his face. Through other programs S may be familiar with several rubbing motions, such as scrubbing his hands and lathering (e.g., Washing Hands). If S cannot rub, develop your own task analysis for washing face.

3. S holds the soap. Or, adapt by using equipment or materials that enable S to secure the soap.

Objective:

S uses a washcloth to wash and rinse his face. S must initiate his response within 5 seconds of the command and respond correctly 4 out of 5 trials.

Cycle:

None specified.

Follow-Up:

Continue to have S wash his face as part of his daily routine. Have S use a washcloth for washing all parts of his body except his hands. At first combine this washing skill with other skills that occur at the same time (e.g., Drying Hands and Face). Have S turn on the faucet by himself. (He may either place the stopper in the sink to fill the bowl or just let the water run.) S can also begin to adjust the water temperature.
Develop a morning, mealtime, or bedtime routine of tasks (e.g., undressing, toileting, grooming: Washing Hands and Face, Drying Hands and Face, Brushing Teeth, Brushing Hair). As S performs these actions, describe what he is doing to help him expand his vocabulary. Present him with fewer cues with the task request. As S performs the task, encourage him to describe the activity.

**Overview
Grooming
Skill 6**

Program for Grooming Skill 6

GENERAL STRATEGY:

Arrangement:

S stands or sits in front of the sink with soap, a washcloth, and a towel within reach. The sink may be filled with water, or the faucet may be running with the temperature already adjusted.

Attention:

Draw S's attention to the soap, the cloth, and his face. Note to S that his face needs washing.

Command:

Give an appropriate command ("WASH YOUR FACE") <u>with cues</u> indicating what you wish S to do.

Latency:

S must initiate his response within 5 seconds of the command (or last part completed).

Correction:

Use general correction or Suggestions on any part that S does not perform correctly. After you assist him, allow him to continue the trial on his own. Correct him only if needed.

Natural Consequence:

As soon as S finishes washing his face, help him to turn off the faucet (or pull the plug in the sink). Then put the washcloth away, and dry his face.

Other Trials:

Repeat the strategy as often as appropriate. You may set up situations to practice the skill if desired.

Modification:

S has made no gains in <u>average parts completed</u> after two probes (2 weeks).

CONDITIONS	BEHAVIOR	CRITERIA
		for *8 only
PRE Get S's attention, and give the command. Present the natural consequence.	*8. Target--S uses a washcloth to wash and rinse his face unassisted.	4 correct out of 5 trials

DAILY INSTRUCTION/WEEKLY PROBES

Get S's attention, and give the command. Correct each part if needed. Present the natural consequence.	1. S picks up the soap and cloth.	Continue daily instruction/weekly probes until S performs *8 correctly 4 out of the last 5 trials
	2. S wets the cloth and soap.	
	3. S rubs the soap on the cloth.	
	4. S replaces the soap.	
	5. S closes his eyes and rubs his face.	
	6. S rinses the cloth.	
	7. S rinses his face.	
	*8. Target--S uses a washcloth to wash and rinse his face unassisted.	
POST 1 Same as PRE	*8. Target--S uses a washcloth to wash and rinse his face unassisted.	4 correct out of 5 trials for each test
POST 2 New Setting		
POST 3 Different Time of Day		

SUGGESTIONS

Part 1:

Note: If the bar slips away from S, put it in a soapdish with higher sides. (S may meet criterion with this soapdish.)

Have S pick up and grasp objects of various sizes and weights. Provide practice opportunities with both wet and dry objects since soap is particularly slippery.

At first use dry soap (easier to grasp). Then introduce wet soap.

Part 2:

Assist S to pick up the soap and cloth. Preferably, he should put the soap in his dominant hand so that for Part 3, he will be lathering with that hand. Fade all cues.

Guide S to wet the cloth and soap separately or at the same time, either under the running water or in the filled sink. Gradually fade guidance and extra directions.

Part 3:

Note: S may need to wash his hands thoroughly before washing his face.

Guide S to make short rubbing motions with the soap on the cloth. Preferably, the hand under the cloth is flat, palm up. Gradually decrease the amount of pressure you put on S's hand to get him to rub.

Left Hand under Cloth

Have S practice the rubbing motion at other times (e.g., when using a cloth to wipe a table).

Use liquid soap on the washcloth at first since it lathers up quickly. Then reintroduce the bar of soap.

Part 4:

Use backward chaining. At first guide S's hand to within 1 inch of the target. Gradually increase the distance he is required to bring the soap on his own.

Place a soapdish closer to S, and hold it if necessary. Gradually move the dish closer to its natural position, thus increasing the distance S must move his hand to place the soap.

If the soap continually slips off to the floor, use a soapdish with higher sides. (S may meet criteria with this soapdish.)

Initially have S use dry hands to put down a dry bar of soap; then wet hands to put down dry soap; and finally wet hands and wet soap.

Part 5:

Demonstrate how to close your eyes. Then rub the soap on S's face. Use verbal reminders to have him keep his eyes closed. After S consistently keeps his eyes closed, let him put the soap on his own face.

Guide S to rub his face (cheeks, forehead, chin, nose) in short rubbing motions. Preferably, have S keep his hand(s) that is under the cloth flat so that he rubs with his fingers, not the whole hand. This enables him to avoid his eyes more easily. Gradually fade your guidance.

If desired, have S squeeze out the cloth first so that it is not dripping.

Parts 6 and 7:

Guide S to rinse the cloth and his hands in the filled sink or under running water. Then guide S to either splash his face with water or to rinse his face with the wet cloth. Gradually fade your guidance and extra cues.

Have S rinse when in a swimming or wading pool or in the bathtub where he can practice the task without splashing onto the floor.

Brushing Teeth

Chain

Skill:

In this program the child learns to put toothpaste on his brush and brush his teeth. Although he does not have to remove the cap of the tube, he must hold the brush appropriately to squeeze the paste onto the bristles.

Entry Behaviors:

1. S <u>brings his hand to his face</u> by bending his arm at the elbow and raising his hand to his mouth, or by lowering his head to his hand, as demonstrated by other self-care skills (e.g., Wiping Nose, Eating Finger Foods). If S cannot reach his mouth, reconsider your rationale for teaching this program. You may need to develop your own task analysis for enabling S to assist as you brush his teeth.

2. S <u>rotates his wrist to reach the various areas of his mouth</u> with the brush bristles. S previously used some wrist rotation in other self-care skills (e.g., Washing/Drying Hands, Wiping Nose) but not with the fine motor action needed in this skill. If S cannot rotate his wrist sufficiently, develop your own task analysis for brushing. Require S to reposition the brush in his hand rather than rotate his wrist.

3. S <u>picks up, holds, and releases the toothbrush.</u> Or, adapt by adding parts to the task analysis to allow S to use adaptive equipment or materials if necessary.

Objective:

S squeezes toothpaste onto his toothbrush and brushes his teeth (front, back, top, and bottom) unassisted. S must initiate his response within 5 seconds of the command and respond correctly 4 out of 5 trials.

Cycle:

None specified.

Follow-Up:

Continue to have S brush his teeth as part of a daily routine. Combine brushing teeth with other morning grooming skills, such as washing and drying his face and brushing his hair. Add other activities to the tooth-brushing sequence, such as unscrewing the cap of the toothpaste tube or selecting his own toothbrush from the rack and putting it away. Note that S can pass this program with minimal brushing as long as he brushes front, back, top, and bottom teeth. For good tooth care, S should continue to work on his toothbrushing technique. Present frequent demonstrations and instructions to improve S's brushing methods. This work will also develop his skill in following commands.

Overview
Grooming
Skill 7

Program for Grooming Skill 7

GENERAL STRATEGY:

Arrangement:

S sits or stands in front of a sink with a mirror above it. Place a toothbrush and an open (cap off) toothpaste tube within reach. The tube should be at least half full for easier squeezing.

Attention:

Draw S's attention to the toothbrush, the toothpaste, and his mouth. Note to S that his teeth need brushing.

Command:

Give an appropriate command ("BRUSH YOUR TEETH") <u>with cues</u> indicating what you wish S to do.

Latency:

S must initiate his response within 5 seconds of the command (or last part completed).

Correction:

Use general correction or Suggestions on any part that S does not perform correctly. After you assist him, allow him to continue the trial on his own. Correct him only if needed.

Natural Consequence:

After S finishes brushing his teeth, help him to rinse off his toothbrush, to replace the brush and toothpaste, and to dry his face.

Other Trials:

Repeat the strategy as often as appropriate. You may set up situations to practice the skill if desired.

Modification:

S has made no gains in <u>average parts completed</u> after two probes (2 weeks).

CONDITIONS	BEHAVIOR	CRITERIA
		for *8 only
PRE Get S's attention, and give the command. Present the natural consequence.	*8. Target--S squeezes toothpaste on his toothbrush and brushes his teeth (top, bottom, front, and back) un-assisted.	4 correct out of 5 trials

DAILY INSTRUCTION/WEEKLY PROBES

Get S's attention, and give the command. Correct each part if needed. Present the natural consequence.	1. S grasps the tooth-brush (bristles up).	Continue daily instruction/weekly probes until S per-forms *8 correctly 4 out of the last 5 trials
	2. S grasps the tooth-paste tube.	
	3. S squeezes the paste on the bristles.	
	4. S replaces the tube (may occur here or at the end of the task).	
	5. S puts the brush in his mouth.	
	6. S brushes his teeth (top, bottom, front, and back).	
	7. S rinses his mouth.	
	*8. Target--S squeezes toothpaste on his toothbrush and brushes his teeth (top, bottom, front, and back) unassisted.	
POST 1 Same as PRE	*8. Target--S squeezes toothpaste on his toothbrush and brushes his teeth (top, bottom, front, and back) unassisted.	4 correct out of 5 trials for each test
POST 2 New Setting		
POST 3 Different Time of Day		

SUGGESTIONS

Part 1:

Put a strip of colored tape on the toothbrush handle to indicate the bristle side (e.g., if S's hand covers the tape, he is holding it correctly). Fade this visual cue.

Guide S to pick up the toothbrush (or reposition it after he picks it up) so that the bristles are facing up, ready for the toothpaste. Fade your guidance and/or verbal cues.

Part 2:

Put colored tape near the opened end of the tube as a cue. Fade this visual cue.

Guide S to pick up and/or reposition the tube so that it is ready to be squeezed. Fade guidance and/or verbal cues.

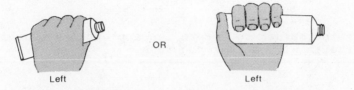

Part 3:

Guide S to apply enough pressure to the tube to squeeze the paste out. Fade your guidance and/or verbal cues.

Prime the tube so that paste will come out with a quick squeeze. Gradually prime it less so that S must squeeze harder and longer.

To build hand strength, have S squeeze tubes or other malleable materials.

Remind S to stop squeezing when enough paste has been placed on bristles. Fade these cues.

To improve S's eye-hand coordination, have him apply toothpaste on a brush or glue on a line. If you apply toothpaste on the brush, repeat the activity. S need not brush his teeth each time.

Use backward chaining to teach S to aim the tube at the bristles. At first assist S to bring the tube all the way to the bristles. Then assist to within 1 inch of the bristles, and allow S to touch the tube to the bristles. Gradually provide less guidance so that S brings the tube the entire distance by himself.

Part 4:

Provide physical guidance for S to put the tube down only if necessary since he has already worked on this skill in other programs (e.g., Following Cued Commands, Placing In/On). Gradually fade your guidance, then your visual and verbal cues (e.g., saying "Put it here" while you point).

Part 5:

Give a demonstration for S to place the brush in his mouth. Provide only minimal physical assistance. Gradually fade all cues.

Review Suggestions in Eating Finger Foods or Eating with a Spoon or Fork to increase his hand-to-mouth coordination (pages 240-41, 252-53, 258-59).

Part 6:

Note: S need only brush top, bottom, front, and back teeth to meet criteria. However, for good hygiene, he needs continued practice. (See Follow-Up, page 409.)

Physically guide S to use back and forth, and up and down, brushing motions. As S gains proficiency with the motions, remind him to brush top, bottom, front, and back teeth. Gradually fade all cues.

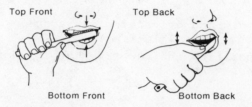

Let S use an electric toothbrush to insure the appropriate brushing motion. He may still meet criteria with this toothbrush.

Part 7:

Have S sip water from a cup or splash his face. S may swallow or spit out the toothpaste. If S uses a cup, review Suggestions in Drinking from a Cup (page 246). Fade all guidance or other cues.

Practice hand-to-mouth coordination through other programs (e.g., Eating Finger Foods).

Brushing Hair

Chain

Skill:

In this program the child learns to use a hairbrush to brush from the top of his head down the sides and back. Brushing is repeated until the hair is smooth.

Entry Behaviors:

1. S brings his hand to his head by bending his arm and/or lowering his head slightly. If S cannot reach his head, consider a different hair-style requiring minimal care by the person responsible for his grooming.

2. S moves his hand to touch different parts of his head, front, back, and sides. He has already developed wrist rotation skills for using a variety of objects, especially in self-care (e.g., Washing/Drying Hands, Wiping Nose, Brushing Teeth). If S cannot move his hand to all parts of his head, develop your own task analysis for brushing hair, or consider a simple hairstyle.

3. S holds his hairbrush. Or, adapt by adding parts to the task analysis to allow S to use adaptive equipment or materials if necessary.

Objective:

S raises the hairbrush to the top of his head and brushes the top, back, and sides of his hair unassisted. S must initiate his response within 5 seconds of the command and respond correctly 4 out of 5 trials. 1 trial = complete brushing. Note: The criterion of "smoothness" is left to your discretion, specific to S's hairstyle.

Cycle:

None specified.

Follow-Up:

Continue to have S brush his hair at appropriate times during the day. As S performs the task, encourage him to expand his vocabulary by telling you what he is doing. Then give S the command to brush his hair without using any additional cues. Encourage him to brush more thoroughly and to arrange his hair more smoothly. Brushing may be combined with other self-care tasks as part of a daily routine: washing face, drying face, teeth, brushing hair. Once a routine has been established, fade the commands so that S performs the tasks with less direction.

Program for Grooming Skill 8

GENERAL STRATEGY:

Arrangement:

S stands or sits in front of a mirror with a hairbrush nearby.

Attention:

Draw S's attention to the hairbrush and his hair. Note to S that his hair needs brushing.

Command:

Give an appropriate command ("BRUSH YOUR HAIR") <u>with cues</u> indicating what you wish S to do.

Latency:

S must initiate his response within 5 seconds of the command (or last part completed).

Correction:

Use general correction or Suggestions on any part that S does not perform correctly. After you assist him, allow him to continue the trial on his own. Correct him only if needed.

Natural Consequence:

After S brushes his hair, have him put the brush away (in a drawer, on a table). Note that 1 trial = smoothing the hair with as many repeated strokes as necessary.

Other Trials:

Repeat the strategy as often as appropriate. You may set up situations to practice the skill if desired.

Modification:

S has made no gains in <u>average parts completed</u> after two successive probes (2 weeks).

CONDITIONS	BEHAVIOR	CRITERIA
		for *6 only
PRE Get S's attention, and give the command. Present the natural consequence.	*6. Target--S raises the hairbrush to the top of his head and brushes the top, back, and sides of his hair unassisted.	4 correct out of 5 trials

DAILY INSTRUCTION/WEEKLY PROBES

Get S's attention, and give the command. Correct each part if needed. Present the natural consequence.	1. S grasps the handle of the brush. 2. S raises the brush to the top of his head. 3. S strokes his hair top to side (on the side of his dominant hand). 4. S strokes his hair top to back. 5. S strokes his hair top to side (opposite side). *6. Target--S raises the hairbrush to the top of his head and brushes the top, back, and sides of his hair unassisted.	Continue daily instruction/weekly probes until S performs *6 correctly 4 out of the last 5 trials
POST 1 Same as PRE	*6. Target--S raises the hairbrush to the top of his head and brushes the top, back, and sides of his hair unassisted.	4 correct out of 5 trials for each test
POST 2 New Setting		
POST 3 Different Brush		

SUGGESTIONS

Part 1:

Guide S to grasp the back of the brush handle so that the bristles point away from the palm. You may add cues to indicate the back of the handle (e.g., put colored tape on the handle so that S's hand covers the tape when he is holding it correctly). Gradually fade all cues.

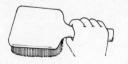

Part 2:

Demonstrate by raising the brush to the top of your head while providing verbal cues. Gradually fade all cues. (Use physical guidance minimally and only if absolutely necessary.)

Have S follow specific commands (e.g., say "Touch your head here" and tap or point to a particular part of his head). While S looks in the mirror, have him bring the brush to his head to develop his eye-hand coordination using the mirror. Fade tactile cues (tapping, guidance), then visual (pointing) cues until S can aim at the top of his own head.

Use backward chaining. Guide S to bring the brush almost to the top of his head. Provide less guidance so that S moves the brush a longer distance by himself.

Parts 3, 4, and 5:

Physically guide S to make any one or all three of the brushing movements. In addition, use tactile and visual cues (e.g., pointing) as necessary. Fade guidance first, then gradually fade all cues.

Dominant Side   Back   Opposite Side

Have S practice the brushing motions. Teach each stroke separately: dominant hand side first, then the back, then the other side (requires crossing midline), and forward if necessary.

Using a mirror, demonstrate brushing. Gradually fade the use of any pointing or verbal cues.

Have S brush your hair, or another's, to practice stroking.

Use backward chaining. Guide S to complete almost the entire stroke. Provide less guidance so that he completes more of the stroke.

Accompanying Materials

Class Observation Record, 421

Data Sheet for 4/5 and Rate Data Programs, 447

Data Sheet for Skill Analysis and Chain Programs, 449

RECEPTIVE LANGUAGE

Skill	Objective	Observation	Cycle	Record
1. Responding to Social Interaction	S makes a *positive response during social interactions.*	Physically interact with S in a playful situation. Record whether he makes any positive movements or sounds (e.g., touches, grasps, gurgles, coos).		
2. Attending to Voice	S maintains eye contact with the speaker for at least 5 seconds.	Talk to S (e.g., change voice intensity, sing, recite rhymes) and record if he looks at you briefly (5 seconds).		
3. Following Cued Commands	Given a *cued command* (a verbal command given with accompanying gestures and context cues), S performs the requested action without assistance.	Point or gesture while you ask S to sit, stand up, hold your hand, give you what he's holding out, and the like, and record if he responds.	Record each different command that S can perform. Each cycle teaches one command. Repeat the program as needed to teach a variety of commands.	

RECEPTIVE LANGUAGE—continued

Skill	Objective	Observation	Cycle	Record
4. Attending to Own Name	S turns his face toward the person who calls his name.	Position yourself anywhere in a quiet room with S (vary your direction relative to him). Call his name during activities, and record if he looks up at you.		
5. Responding to Signal Words	After hearing a *signal word*, S makes an appropriate *anticipatory response* when he hears a word or command that signals the start of an activity or event.	At an appropriate time, give the signal word (e.g., *lunchtime, time to get in the car, let's go outside*) with the appropriate intonation. Record whether S responds without any additional cues.	Record each different command that S can perform. Each command is a cycle. Each cycle teaches one signal word. Repeat to teach S to respond to other signal words.	
6. Identifying Objects	When presented with a choice of three objects, S selects the specified object.	Position some small objects, and ask S to show you the one you name . . . "Show me the *shoe* (cup, doll)."	Record each object S can identify. Each cycle teaches two objects.	

7. Identifying Body Parts	S indicates the specified body part.	Ask S to show you various parts of his body . . . "Show me your hand (arm, leg)."	Record each body part S can identify. Each cycle teaches two body parts. Repeat as needed to teach the names of other body parts.	
8. Identifying People	S points to, or otherwise identifies, a classmate at teacher request.	Ask S to show you various classmates . . . "Which one is Mary?"	Record each person who S can identify. Each cycle teaches the names of two people. Repeat as needed to teach the names of other people, two at a time.	

EXPRESSIVE LANGUAGE

1. Making Sounds	S produces *vocal sounds* when presented with eliciting stimuli.	Play with S, and talk to him. Record any sounds (vowels, consonants, or combinations) that can be clearly distinguished.		
2. Responding Vocally to Model	When presented with a model that is repetitious of a sound elicited from S, S produces a *vocal response.*	As you are playing with S and he makes a sound, imitate that sound. Record if S makes any sound after your imitation.		

EXPRESSIVE LANGUAGE—continued

Skill	Objective	Observation	Cycle	Record
3. Indicating Preferences	S gestures to indicate his preference.	Interrupt an activity S is engaged in, or remove an object S shows interest in, so that it is out of his reach. Ask S what he wants, and record if he uses gestures with or without a vocal sound to specify the object or event.		
4. Producing Sounds on Request	When an object is presented and a command given to imitate the object's name, S makes a vocal response.	Offer S an object such as a toy or a bite of food, and label it. Then ask him to name the object (e.g., "Say cookie."). Record whether he makes any vocal sound (he does not have to imitate).		
5. Shaping Words	S makes a *consistent approximation* of a word within 5 seconds of its model.	Hold up an object, say its name, and record if S attempts to imitate the name in order to get the object.	Record each word S imitates. Each cycle teaches one word at a time. Repeat to teach other words as needed.	

6. Naming Actions	S correctly names two different actions that were performed.	Perform an action encouraging S to participate at anytime. Ask S to name the action (e.g., "What are you doing?").	Record each action S can name. Repeat the program with different actions, and teach two new actions at a time.
7. Naming Objects	S correctly names two different objects.	Interact with S and the objects. Then remove the materials, and present one to S. Ask S what it is (e.g., "What is this?").	Record each object S can name. Repeat the program with different objects, and teach two new objects at a time.
COGNITIVE			
1. Focusing Attention	S looks at different targets.	In a play situation with several objects available, including mobiles and pictures, draw S's attention to a target, and record if he looks at it.	Different cycles increase S's focus on different targets: Varied targets, objects, eye contact, sound (noise-making toys).
2. Attending to Objects	During a stimulus presentation, S looks at a target for at least 5 seconds.	Use one object at a time; draw S's attention to it. If S shows interest in another object, switch objects, and ask S to look . . . "S, Look." Record if he sustains attention.	

COGNITIVE—continued

Skill	Objective	Observation	Cycle	Record
3. Responding to Teacher Model	When given a model that is repetitious of an action S just initiated, S produces a *response*.	As S plays with objects, imitate an action he has just performed. Record if he performs any actions after your imitation.		
4. Repeating Teacher Model	When given a model that is repetitious of an *action* S just performed, S repeats that same *action*.	As S plays with objects, imitate an action he has just performed. Record if he repeats his action (imitates your model).		
5. Finding Hidden Objects	S retrieves an object that is hidden while he watches.	Hide a toy while S watches, and ask him to locate it . . . "Find the car."		

6. Finding Source of Sound	By listening to its sound, S locates an object positioned out of sight.	When S is not looking, hide an object that continues to produce sound (e.g., music box, radio, tape recorder). Draw S's attention to the sound, and ask him to locate the object . . . "Find the radio."	
7. Imitating Actions	S imitates the model of an action when different actions are alternately presented.	Demonstrate an action, and give S a command to imitate . . . "S, do this."	Record each action S imitates. Two imitated actions constitute one cycle.
8. Matching	Given a *sample*, S indicates its match from a choice of three items.	Hold up an object, and label it. Then ask S to find its match from a choice of objects . . . "Find another (*ball*)." Vary the sample presented.	Record whether S can match objects (all items are objects) and match pictures (all items are pictures).
9. Identifying Simple Pictures	Given several pictures of familiar objects, S selects the picture of the object presented.	Position three pictures of common objects, and hold up the object itself. Ask S to find the picture of the object named . . . "Find the picture of the (*target*)." Vary the object presented.	Repeat the program, using two different targets during each cycle, until S can identify a variety of pictures.

COGNITIVE—continued

Skill	Objective	Observation	Cycle	Record
10. Putting Objects in Sequence	Given five objects, five *designated places*, and a cued command indicating the place for the first object, S puts each object on one place in sequence.	Position five squares in a row, and record if S places each of five objects on them in order from left-to-right or top-to-bottom as the squares are laid. Then you point to the first place and tell him to start . . . "Make a row."		
11. Lining Up Objects	Given five objects and a cued command indicating the position for the first object, S places the objects in a sequential row.	Give S five objects, point to a starting place on the table, and ask him to place the objects in order from left-to-right or top-to-bottom . . . "Make a row." Record whether he arranges the objects without any other cues.		
12. Sorting	Given a set of two different kinds of objects, S sorts the objects into two *separate groups*.	Place two containers in front of S along with two different kinds of objects (cups and crayons) mixed in a pile. Point to each container, and ask S to place the objects . . . "Put the *cups* here. Put the *crayons* here." Record whether S sorts the objects correctly.		
13. Pairing Equal Sets	When you place a set of three to five objects in front of S and give him	Position from three to five objects in a row. Give S an equal set of		

	Behavior	Procedure	Teaching Note
	an equal set, S places each object of his set in one-to-one correspondence with the first set.	objects, indicate where the first object is to be placed, and ask S to place the equal set . . . "Get enough." Record if S can place his set in one-to-one correspondence by pairing each object with the objects in the set you positioned.	
14. Selecting Equivalent Amounts	S selects an equal number of objects from a larger set when a smaller set (from three to five objects) is placed in front of him.	Position from three to five objects in a row. Give S more than five objects, indicate where the first object is to be placed, and ask him to pair the sets . . . "Get enough." Record if S pairs only enough objects to make equal sets.	
15. Matching Equal Sets	Given from one to five objects (as appropriate to the cycle) and a selection of five cards, S selects the matching card by placing the objects in one-to-one correspondence with the forms on that card.	Position five cards, each having one, two, three, four, or five squares on them. Give S one object, and ask him to select and then place his object on the "one" card . . . "Put one on one."	Repeat the task for number concepts 2 through 5, and record which sets of objects (one to five) S can match. Each cycle teaches S to recognize one numerical set.
16. Counting Rationally	Given from one to five objects (as appropriate to the cycle), S places and counts the objects in sequence.	Give S five objects, and ask him to count. Have S either pick up, place, or touch the objects as he says the number names in order.	Record how far S can count as he picks up, places, or touches each object. Each number equals one cycle. Each cycle teaches S to count a specific number of objects.

COGNITIVE—continued

Skill	Objective	Observation	Cycle	Record
17. Selecting a Speci-fied Quantity	When more objects than needed are present, S selects the specified number of objects and makes a new set.	Place a pile of objects in front of S, and ask him to give you "one."	Repeat the task for number concepts 2 through 5, and record which sets of objects (one to five) S can give you. Each cycle teaches S to select a specified number.	
FINE MOTOR **1.** Reaching	From a variety of posi-tions, S moves his hand/ arm/upper torso to contact objects placed 1–2 inches out of *arm's reach.*	Place S in a variety of positions (on his side, back, stomach, or sit-ting), and give him head and trunk support if needed. Attract S's attention to an object, and ask him to contact it . . . "Get it." Record in which position S most easily reaches for ob-jects, as well as the distance he reaches. Also, record the objects to which he is attracted.		
2. Grasping Objects	When an object is placed within 2–3 inches of his hand, S picks up and *grasps* the object for 3 seconds.	Position S with head, trunk, and arm support if needed, but allow his wrist and fingers to move freely. Attract his attention to an object, position it near his hand, and ask him to contact		

		it . . . "Get it." Continue to attract his attention to the object, and record how long he grasps each one. Require him to use both a whole-hand and a thumb-finger grasp. Also, record the objects to which he is attracted.	
3. Manipulating Objects	During social interactions providing stimuli with objects, *S manipulates* the objects in some way without physical guidance.	Play with S. Use a variety of toys. Demonstrate, describe, and encourage a variety of basic manipulations (e.g., pick up, turn, put in). Record the responses S makes on his own, as well as the toys to which he responds.	
4. Placing In/On	S fits an object in or on a specific target.	Place an object in front of S, as well as a location. Ask S to place the object . . . "Put *object in/on location.*"	This program is repeated, using different sets of materials of increasing difficulty. Record the objects S can place or fit for the following sets: *Set 1:* Individual containers—The containers will hold one object that requires little adjustment (e.g., soap in a soapdish). *Set 2:* Marked surfaces —A card or other flat surface marked with the exact shape of the object to be placed on it (e.g., a 1-inch cube is placed on a card with a 1-inch square drawn on it).

FINE MOTOR—continued

Skill	Objective	Observation	Cycle	Record
			Set 3: Fitted containers —The container will hold the object in only one position (e.g., key in lock).	
GROSS MOTOR				
1. Controlling Head Movements	When sitting with his shoulders supported, S lifts his head and maintains or regains an erect head position for 1 minute when tipped in any direction.	Hold up a toy at S's eye level, then move it where he can see it only if he lifts or maintains an erect head position. Encourage S to lift and hold up his head. Record the type of support S requires and the length of time S can keep his head erect.		
2. Sitting	When placed in a sitting position (on the floor), S sits for 1 minute, using his hands if needed for support and balance when he falls or leans forward and sideways.	Encourage S to remain seated by interesting him in a toy or an activity. Record the type of support S requires and the length of time he maintains a sitting position.		
3. Crawling on Stomach	S crawls forward 5 feet on his stomach unassisted.	Place S on his stomach, leaning on his forearms. Attract S's attention. Provide him with a reason for moving ahead.		

Record how far S moves forward.

4. Sitting Up	When placed on his back or stomach, S pushes or pulls to a sitting position unassisted, using furniture to hold onto if necessary.	Draw S's attention to a toy to encourage him to sit up to get it. Record how S raises himself to a sitting position and in what position he was originally placed.
5. Standing	When placed in a standing position, S stands for 1 minute, grasping furniture if needed for balance.	Encourage S to continue to maintain his balance in a standing position. Attract his attention to a toy, and encourage him to keep his balance, although he may not need to shift his weight. Record if S shifts his weight, maintains his balance, and how long he continues to stand unassisted.
6. Crawling on Hands and Knees	S crawls forward 5 feet on his hands and knees (reciprocal arm and leg movements required) unassisted.	Place S on his stomach, leaning on his forearms. Attract S's attention. Provide a reason to move ahead. Record how far S moves forward.

433

GROSS MOTOR—continued

Skill	Objective	Observation	Cycle	Record
7. Standing Up	When placed in a *sitting position*, S pushes or pulls up to a standing position unassisted, using furniture to hold onto if necessary.	Draw S's attention to a toy or object, and encourage him to get to it. Record how he stands up and what he uses for support to stand.		
8. Walking	From a standing position, S walks forward 5 feet unassisted.	Draw S's attention to an object or activity, and encourage him to walk forward. Record how far forward he walks without assistance.		
EATING				
1. Chewing	When a bite-size piece of *food* is held to his mouth, S opens his mouth, (you place the food on his tongue) chews, and swallows without assistance.	Seat S in an upright position with his feet flat on the floor for support, his head erect, and with support at his neck if necessary. Draw S's attention to the food, and record if he opens his mouth, chews, and swallows without assistance. Also, record the food(s) used.		

Skill	Criterion	Procedure		
2. Eating Finger Foods	S picks up the food, places it in his mouth, bites off a piece if necessary, and eats the food unassisted.	Seat S in an upright position with his feet flat on the floor for support, his head erect, and with support at his neck if necessary. Position pieces of food, either bite-size or whole. Draw S's attention to the food, and record if he eats it without assistance. Record if he can bite off a piece if necessary and which food(s) are used.		
3. Drinking from a Cup	Given a cup with liquid, S picks it up, brings it to his mouth, and drinks unassisted without spilling.	Seat S in an upright position with his feet flat on the floor. Support his neck if that is necessary. Draw S's attention to the cup, and record if he drinks without spilling. Also, record the liquid used.		
4. Eating with a Spoon	Given a bowl of food and a spoon, S uses the spoon to feed himself without assistance.	Seat S in an upright position with his feet flat on the floor for support, his head erect, and with support at his neck if necessary. Draw S's attention to the food placed in front of him, and record if he feeds himself with the spoon without spilling. Also, record the food(s) used.		
5. Eating with a Fork	Given a bowl or plate of food and a fork, S uses the fork to eat by spear-	Seat S in an upright position with his feet flat on the floor for sup-		

GROSS MOTOR—continued

Skill	Objective	Observation	Cycle	Record
	ing each bite of food unassisted.	port, his head erect, and with support at his neck if necessary. Draw S's attention to the food placed in front of him, and record if he feeds himself with the fork and spears food repeatedly if that is appropriate. Also, record the food(s) used.		
DRESSING				
1. Pulling Off	When wearing clothing that can be removed by pulling, S pulls the article completely off without assistance.	Support S if needed in a position in which he can remove the article. Draw S's attention to the article, and record if he pulls off all or part of it. Also, record the item.	Select one type of clothing (e.g., hat or scarf or sock) to teach at a time, since each type involves reaching to a different body part and pulling in a different direction.	
2. Unsnapping	When wearing a garment that is snapped, S pulls the snap apart without tearing the garment, unassisted.	If the snap is above S's waist, have him sit or stand with support if needed and his arms free. If the snap is at his waist, have S stand or lie down so that he may easily reach the snap. Draw S's attention to the snap, and record if he pulls it apart. Also, record if he unsnaps a jacket or pants, and the position in which he performs the task.		

3. Putting Hat On	S pulls his hat completely on his head and adjusts it if necessary without assistance.	Have S sit or stand with support if needed. Hold out the hat, and draw his attention to it. Record if he takes it from you, puts it on, and completes the task. Also, record the type of hat used.			
4. Unzipping Jacket	When wearing a garment with a front (neck-to-waist) zipper that detaches, S unzips the garment completely and separates the two sides without assistance.	Have S stand with support if needed or alternately lie down so that the garment is not bunched at the waist. With all fastenings open except the zipper, draw S's attention to it, and record if he grasps the tab, pulls it down, and completes unzipping by detaching the zipper at the bottom. Also, record the garment used.			
5. Putting Mittens On	S pulls his mittens onto his hands with his thumbs properly adjusted without assistance.	S may sit or stand with support if necessary. Position or hand S his mittens, and record if he puts them on and completes the task.			
6. Putting Shoes On	When given his shoes, S puts each on the correct foot and adjusts the fit if necessary without assistance.	S may sit or stand with support if necessary. Position or hand S his shoes, and record if he picks each up, puts them on, and completes			

DRESSING—continued

Skill	Objective	Observation	Cycle	Record
		the task. Record the type of shoe used and whether he puts each on the correct foot.		
7. Putting Socks On	When given his socks, S pulls each sock completely on and adjusts the fit unassisted.	Have S sit on the floor against the wall or in a chair with back support. Position or hand S his socks. Record if he picks up each, puts it on, and completes the task.		
8. Taking Off Pants	When his pants are unfastened, S pulls his pants down and removes them completely without assistance.	Have S take his shoes off, and unfasten his pants. He may stand or kneel to begin and hold onto or sit in a chair to complete removing his pants. Draw S's attention to his pants, and record if he pulls them down, changes position if necessary, and completes the task. Record if long or short pants are used.		
9. Taking Off Shirt (Coat, Jacket)	When his front-opening shirt or other garment is unfastened, S removes the shirt completely and frees both arms without assistance.	Have S's garment unfastened. He may sit or stand with support if needed. Draw S's attention to the garment, and record if he frees his	There are two cycles, taught in order, to allow for different garments: *Set 1:* Heavy or lined coats, short-sleeve shirts, or other gar-	

438

	arms and then completely removes the garment. Record the garment used.	ments that will slip off once S's shoulders are free. *Set 2:* Long-sleeve shirts, sweaters, or other garments that require S to pull the sleeves to free his arms.
10. Putting On Pants	S inserts his feet into his pants appropriately and pulls the pants up completely without assistance.	Have S sit or stand near furniture for balance if necessary. Draw S's attention to his unfastened pants as you hold or position them. Record if S picks them up, pulls them on, and then completes the task. Record if long or short pants are used.
11. Putting On Shirt (Coat, Jacket)	When given his shirt or other front-opening garment, S inserts his arms into the sleeves and pulls the shirt completely on without assistance.	Have S sit or stand near furniture for balance if necessary. Draw S's attention to his unfastened shirt (coat, jacket) as you hold or position it. Record if S picks it up, inserts his arm, and then completes the task. Record the garment used.
12. Taking Off T-shirt	S pulls a T-shirt (pullover) completely off over his head without assistance.	S may be in any comfortable position in which he can remove his shirt. Draw S's attention to his shirt, and record if he grasps it, pulls it over his head, shifts his body position if needed, and then completes the task.

DRESSING—continued

Skill	Objective	Observation	Cycle	Record
		Record whether a shirt or sweater is used.		
13. Putting On T-shirt	S pulls a T-shirt (pull-over) over his head, inserts his arms into the sleeves, and adjusts the shirt on his body without assistance.	S may sit or stand with furniture available on which to hold for balance. Place S's shirt flat in front of him or hold it out with the back of the shirt facing up so that S does not have to discriminate front from back. Draw S's attention to his shirt, and record if he picks it up, inserts his arms and head, and then completes the task by adjusting the shirt. Also, record S's position.		
14. Unhooking	When wearing a garment fastened by a hook, S pulls in opposite directions to separate the hook unassisted.	If the hook is above S's waist, have him sit or stand with support if needed with his arms free. If the hook is at his waist, have S stand or lie down so that he may easily reach the hook. Draw S's attention to the hook, and record if he grasps it, separates the hook and eye, and then completes the task. Also, record S's position.		
15. Untying	When wearing his shoes with laces tied in a simple bow, S pulls the	Have S sit in a position with support if needed but with his arms free to		

440

		reach the shoe to be untied. Draw S's attention to the shoelace, which is extended at least 1 inch from the bow. Record if S grasps the lace, pulls it, and then completes the task by uncrossing the laces.
	bow out and uncrosses the laces without assistance.	
16. Unzipping Pants (Skirt)	When wearing a garment with a *nondetachable* zipper that is zipped, S pulls the zipper tab completely down the track without assistance.	Have S's pants zipped but all other fastenings opened. He may stand with support if needed or lie down or sit with his back extended to keep the zipper track straight. Draw S's attention to the zipper, and record if he grasps the tab and pulls it down to complete the task. Also, record the garment used (e.g., pants, skirt) and S's position.
17. Zipping Pants (Skirt)	When wearing a garment with a *nondetachable* zipper, S grasps and pulls the zipper tab all the way up to lock it into place without assistance.	With his pants completely unzipped, have S stand with support if needed or alternately lie down or sit with his back extended to keep the zipper track straight. Draw S's attention to the zipper, and record if he grasps the tab, pulls it all the way up, and locks it to complete the task. Also, record the garment used (e.g., pants, skirt) and S's position.

DRESSING—continued

Skill	Objective	Observation	Cycle	Record
18. Unbuckling	When wearing a belt, S unbuckles the belt and completely separates both belt ends without assistance.	With his belt buckled, have S stand with support if needed or alternately have S lie down or sit to extend his torso for easy access to his waist. Draw S's attention to his belt, and record if he grasps the belt buckle, loosens one end from the other, and then completely separates both belt ends to complete the task. Also, record S's position.		
19. Hooking	S brings the hook and eye together to fasten his garment.	If the hook is above S's waist, have him sit or stand with support if needed and his arms free. If the hook is at his waist, have S stand or lie down so that he may easily reach the hook. With the garment unhooked, draw S's attention to the fastening, and record if he grasps the hook and eye, brings them together, and then hooks them together to complete the task. Also, record S's position.		

20. Unbuttoning	S unbuttons his shirt or other garment.	Have S sit or stand with support if needed, and draw his attention to his buttoned shirt (use medium-sized buttons). Record if S grasps the button, pushes it through the buttonhole, and then completes the task.
21. Snapping	S snaps his garment unassisted.	If the snap is above S's waist, have him sit or stand with support if needed and his arms free. If the snap is at his waist, have S stand or lie down so that he may easily reach the snap. With the garment unsnapped, draw S's attention to the snap, and record if he grasps both parts of the snap, brings them together, and then completes the task by pressing both parts closed. Also, record S's position.
22. Zipping Jacket	When wearing a garment with a front (neck-to-waist) zipper that is *detachable*, S fits the zipper into the track and zips the garment completely without assistance.	Have S sit or stand with support if needed but with the zipper track straight. Draw S's attention to the unzipped zipper, and record if he grasps both sides of the zipper, hooks the ends, pulls the zipper tab up all the way to lock it, and completes the task.

GROOMING

Skill	Objective	Observation	Cycle	Record
1. Drying Hands	When S's hands are wet and a towel is within reach, S takes the towel and dries his hands unassisted.	Have S sit or stand with support if needed as long as his hands and arms are free. After wetting or washing S's hands, draw his attention to the towel and his hands, and record if he grasps the towel, dries each hand, and then completes the drying task.		
2. Using a Napkin	S brings a napkin to his mouth and wipes his mouth clean.	Place a napkin next to S's food or on his lap. Draw S's attention to the napkin and to his mouth when it needs wiping. Record if S picks up the napkin and wipes his mouth clean.		
3. Drying Face	When his face is wet and a towel is within reach, S takes the towel and wipes his face dry.	Have S stand or sit in front of a sink. Draw S's attention to the towel and his wet face. Record if S reaches for and grasps the towel and then dries his face.		

4. Wiping Nose	S brings a tissue to his nose and wipes his nose with the tissue unassisted.	Draw S's attention to the tissue, as well as to his nose (which may or may not need wiping). Record whether S wipes the nose area (he may blow his nose but this is not required).		
5. Washing Hands	S lathers and rinses his hands unassisted.	Have S stand or sit in front of the sink. It may be filled or the water may be left running. You may adjust the water temperature before you draw S's attention to the soap and his hands. Record if S grasps the soap, wets it and his hands, and lathers them. Then record if S cleans and rinses his hands.		
6. Washing Face	S uses a washcloth to wash and rinse his face.	Have S stand or sit in front of the sink. It may be filled or the water may be left running. You may adjust the water temperature before you draw S's attention to the soap and his hands. Record if S grasps the soap, wets it and a washcloth, and lathers the cloth before rubbing his face with it.		
7. Brushing Teeth	S squeezes toothpaste onto his toothbrush and brushes his teeth (front,	Have S sit or stand in front of the sink. Draw his attention to the		

GROOMING—continued

Skill	Objective	Observation	Cycle	Record
	back, top, and bottom) unassisted.	toothbrush, toothpaste (tube already opened), and his mouth. Record if S grasps the toothbrush and squeezes toothpaste on it, brings the brush to his mouth, and brushes his front, back, top and/or bottom teeth.		
8. Brushing Hair	S raises the hairbrush to the top of his head and brushes the top, back, and sides of his hair unassisted.	Have S sit or stand in front of a mirror, and draw his attention to the hairbrush and his hair. Record if S picks up the brush, brings it to his head, and then brushes the top, back, and/or sides of his hair.		

Data Sheet

4/5 AND RATE DATA PROGRAMS

PROGRAM: _____ STUDENT: _____

REINFORCERS: _____ TEACHER: _____

MATERIALS: _____ SESSION TIME: _____

Date	Min.	Step	Responses* $(+, -, \theta)$	Comments

*SYMBOLS + = Correct Response
            − = Incorrect Response
         θ = No response
            = (count as error)

SUMMARY INFORMATION (fill in when applicable):
Total # of Trials: _____

# of Correct: _____

# of Incorrect: _____

% of Correct: _____

Total # of Minutes on Program: _____

447

Data Sheet

SKILL ANALYSIS AND
CHAIN PROGRAMS

PROGRAM: _____   STUDENT: _____

REINFORCERS: _____   TEACHER: _____

MATERIALS: _____   SESSION TIME: _____

Parts					
1. _____	1	1	1	1	1
2. _____	2	2	2	2	2
3. _____	3	3	3	3	3
4. _____	4	4	4	4	4
5. _____	5	5	5	5	5
6. _____	6	6	6	6	6
7. _____	7	7	7	7	7
8. _____	8	8	8	8	8
9. _____	9	9	9	9	9
10. _____	10	10	10	10	10
11. _____	11	11	11	11	11
12. _____	12	12	12	12	12
13. _____	13	13	13	13	13
14. _____	14	14	14	14	14
15. _____	15	15	15	15	15
16. _____	16	16	16	16	16
17. _____	17	17	17	17	17
18. _____	18	18	18	18	18
19. _____	19	19	19	19	19
20. _____	20	20	20	20	20

SUMMARY: PROBE # _____

Date: _____ Min. _____

Average +'s per column _____

Ave. +'s on last probe _____

Ave. parts gained _____

Comments: _____
_____
_____
_____
_____

Instructional days after probe

Date: _____ Min. _____

_____   _____
_____   _____
_____   _____

Parts					
1. _____	1	1	1	1	1
2. _____	2	2	2	2	2
3. _____	3	3	3	3	3
4. _____	4	4	4	4	4
5. _____	5	5	5	5	5
6. _____	6	6	6	6	6
7 _____	7	7	7	7	7
8. _____	8	8	8	8	8
9. _____	9	9	9	9	9
10. _____	10	10	10	10	10
11. _____	11	11	11	11	11
12. _____	12	12	12	12	12
13. _____	13	13	13	13	13
14. _____	14	14	14	14	14
15. _____	15	15	15	15	15
16. _____	16	16	16	16	16
17. _____	17	17	17	17	17
18. _____	18	18	18	18	18
19. _____	19	19	19	19	19
20. _____	20	20	20	20	20

SUMMARY: PROBE # _____

Date: _____ Min. _____

Average +'s per column _____

Ave. +'s on last probe _____

Ave. parts gained _____

Comments: _____
_____
_____
_____

Instructional days after probe

Date: _____ Min. _____

_____   _____
_____   _____
_____   _____

Charts

Actions, 451

Basic Motor Actions, 453

Body Parts, 455

Common Objects, 457

Cued Commands, 459

Foods, 461

Phonemes, 463

Stimulus, 467

Actions Chart

Uses: 1. To select vocabulary words to teach in Naming Actions.
2. To select actions to teach the child to perform on command in Following Cued Commands.

Actions with Objects:

open	push	shake	kick
close	pull	squeeze	pat
pick up	roll	bounce	throw
give	turn	drop	twist
take	rub	dump	fold
hold	touch	raise	hit

Actions without Objects:

sit (down)	turn around	march	stretch
stand (up)	jump	lie down	scoot
walk	hop	sing	
crawl	run	dance	

Basic Motor Actions Chart

Uses:
1. To select materials and responses that increase the child's motor responses for fine motor development (Grasping Objects, Manipulating Objects) or for interactions building imitation (Responding to Teacher Model, Repeating Teacher Model).
2. To select motivational materials for fine motor development.
3. To identify responses that are made by normal children between 6 and 18 months and that are prerequisite for the more complex motor and cognitive tasks usually learned after the age of 18 months.

RESPONSE	SUGGESTED MATERIALS
6–12 months	
Puts object down, then picks it up again.	Small Fisher-Price "people," rattles, squeeze toys, toys with handles.
Bangs one object against another.	Drum and stick, xylophone and stick, blocks, any easily handled object.
Pats an object.	Soft toys, stuffed animals.
Rakes an object to him and picks it up.	Small "people," small blocks, chips, pegs.
Holds onto an object (for 3 seconds) while picking up another.	Small "people," blocks, pegs, rattles, soft rag dolls.
Drops an object after holding onto it (for 3 seconds).	Ball, bean bag, any easily handled object.
Transfers an object from one hand to the other.	Any easily handled object as above.
Pulls an object out of a container.	Any favorite toy that has been placed in a shoebox, toy box, etc., blocks in a box, small items in a plastic can.
Rotates an object at least 90°, using one or both hands.	Any easily held object.
Pokes at an opening with one or two fingers.	Busy box, jack-in-the-box, peg board, toy telephone, doll house.
Takes object off another.	Any objects already mentioned—big object on bottom, little one on top.
Uncovers an object.	Any objects as above, covered by a hanky, napkin, piece of cloth.
Puts an object into a container.	Any object and a container (box) larger than it.
Takes an object out of a container.	Same as above.
Shakes an object.	Objects that make noise and that are easily handled (e.g., bells, bean bags, rattles, tambourines).
12–18 months	
Throws an object purposefully (looks in the direction the object is thrown).	Ball, bean bag, cloth doll, soft objects.
Pushes an object.	String toy, Fisher-Price popper, toy car, sweeper, or any object that has wheels.
Pulls an object.	Same as above.
Opens a container.	Any object with a lid that can be pulled off, raised, or turned.
Closes a container.	Any object with a lid that may be pushed on, lowered, or turned.

Chart *(continued)*

RESPONSE	SUGGESTED MATERIALS
Dumps the objects out of a container.	Any objects in a container.
Turns a knob in one motion.	Busy box, dials on toys, toy stove, door knob.
Turns one page of a book.	Book, magazine, catalogue.
Rolls an object back and forth or to someone.	Ball, toy on wheels.

Body Parts Chart

Uses: 1. To select vocabulary to be taught in Identifying Body Parts.
          2. To suggest motor development and body awareness activities for aides and other volunteers to work on by guidance and/or imitation.

PART	ACTIVITY
Parts Commonly Named in Commands	
arm	Bend, shake, or swing it; reach in all directions; carry, hold, pick up objects of different sizes/weights.
leg	Bend, shake, or swing it; jump, skip, hop; play leap frog; balance on one leg.
hand	Wave, rotate wrist; play pattycake, clap; grasp objects of different sizes/shapes/weights.
foot	Rotate ankle, stamp, march.
head	Nod or shake head; rotate neck slowly.
tummy	Pat tummy; bend and twist at waist.
eyes	Blink or wink; play peek-a-boo; track (follow) an object moving in different directions.
nose	Wiggle it; smell different items (perfume, foods).
mouth	Open and close it, taste different foods (sweet, sour, bitter).
ears	Listen to different tones (high, low, loud, soft); repeat rhythm patterns and tones.
hair	Rub, brush, feel it; shampoo it; brush it in different styles.
Parts Less Frequently Named	
fingers	Wiggle them; point; play finger games (Ten Little Indians); grasp tiny objects.
toes	Wiggle them; walk in sand, mud, thick carpet; play This Little Piggy.
tongue	Extend it; taste different foods.
teeth	Brush them; chew gum or textured foods.
elbow	
neck	
back	
knee	

Common Objects Chart

Uses:
1. To select vocabulary words to teach in Identifying Objects and Naming Objects.
2. To select objects to teach the child to use on command in Following Cued Commands and specific self-help programs.

Clothing/Apparel:	shoe	shirt	mitten	dress	shorts
	sock	pants	sweater	purse	blouse
	hat	coat	jacket	scarf	belt
	button	zipper	snap	hook	lace (for shoe)
Food/Utensils:	fork	plate	bib	juice	
	spoon	glass	napkin	water	
	cup	lunch box	milk	other foods	
				(*see also* Foods	
				Chart, p. 461)	
	bowl	tray	cookie		
Grooming/Bathroom:	soap	sink	wastebasket	mirror	
	towel	toothbrush	hairbrush	tissue	
	toilet	toothpaste	comb	toilet paper	
Furniture/Room Parts:	door	steps	floor	drawer	
	chair	window	lamp	clock	
	table	wall	light	television (TV)	
	closet	shelf	bed	radio	
Toys/Recreation:	doll	truck	ball	box	swing
	book	car	pail	puppet	slide
	wagon	sandbox	bike	record	crayon

Cued Commands Chart

Uses: 1. To select functional commands to teach in Following Cued Commands.
2. To suggest commands for aides and volunteers to use frequently.

COMMANDS	MATERIALS/SITUATION	SUGGESTED CRITERION
SIT (DOWN). (tap/point to place)	S is standing near chair, mat, toilet, swing.	S sits in the indicated place for at least 5 seconds.
STAND (UP). (raise your arms/hands)	S is sitting on floor, in chair, in swing.	S stands up and remains up for at least 5 seconds.
LET'S GO/COME ON. (beckon and start walking)	S is sitting or standing next to you.	S walks with you at least 5 feet without stopping.
GO OVER THERE. (point and nod your head toward place)	S is standing by you.	S walks to the indicated place (10 feet) and stops.
HOLD MY HAND. (stretch out your hand)	S is standing or sitting by you.	S places his hand in/on yours for at least 5 seconds (while walking or balancing).
STOP/NO. (shake index finger)	S is engaging in undesirable behavior.	S stops the behavior for at least 5 seconds.
LOOK. (point to place)	S is near a window or some stimulating target.	S turns his head in the indicated direction for at least 5 seconds.
GIVE ME _____. (hold out your hand and point to object)	S is holding an object.	S releases the indicated object in your hand.
TAKE _____. (hold out object)	S's hands are empty, but you are holding something.	S takes the indicated object and holds it for at least 5 seconds.
GET _____. (point to object)	S is near an object: holding it; it is hanging on a hook or rack.	S goes to and picks up the indicated object.
BRING _____. (beckon to S, and point to object)	S is away from you but is holding something.	S comes to you and releases the indicated object in your hand.
OPEN _____. (point to object/lid)	S is by a closed: door, box, drawer.	S pulls the indicated door or lifts the lid at least halfway open.
CLOSE _____. (point to object/lid)	S is by an open: door, box, drawer.	S pushes the indicated door shut or lowers the lid all the way.
PUT _____ HERE. (point to container or area)	S is holding an object in/near a container (box, drawer, can) or an area with boundaries (sheet of paper, shelf).	S puts the object in/on the place indicated.
TAKE ONE. (gesture to choices)	Offer S choices (plate of cookies, tray with cups of juice).	S selects one item (does not grab or snatch).

Chart *(continued)*

COMMANDS	MATERIALS/SITUATION	SUGGESTED CRITERION
GIVE _____ to _____ . (hold out object to S and point to someone else)	S's hands are empty and he is near another person.	S takes the object and gives it to the indicated person.
LET'S TRADE. (hold out object to S and point to his object)	S is holding an object.	S gives you his object and takes the indicated one.
GO PLAY. (point to toy area)	S is unoccupied.	S goes to the indicated area and picks up a toy.
WIPE _____ . (point to rag and spill)	S is by a spill or dirty area and the rag is near.	S takes the rag and rubs it back and forth on the indicated place.
PULL _____ . (point to object/part)	S is near or has an object with a string or part to pull: pull-toy, talking doll, light with pull string.	S pulls the string/part until the toy/object is activated or stops.
PUSH _____ . (point to object/part)	S is near or has an object with a button or part to push: doorbell, elevator button, on-off buttons.	S pushes the button until the object is activated.
TURN _____ . (point to object and indicate correct direction)	S is near or has an object with a handle or top: doorknob, faucet, jars, tubes, thermos bottle.	S turns/screws or unscrews as indicated, as far as needed.
POUR _____ . (point to pitcher then to empty container(s))	S is near a light pitcher (containing sugar, sand, salt, water) and large empty cups or bowls to receive the contents from the pitcher.	S pours all of the contents into the indicated containers.
WRITE.	S has a large piece of paper and markers: felt tip pen, pencil, crayon.	S makes at least one mark on the paper without marking the table.
(command appropriate to the object)—point to the object and model or gesture its use	S is holding or is near a particular object: *see* Common Objects Chart for suggested objects.	S uses the object as indicated.

Foods Chart

Uses: 1.   To select appropriate foods to use to teach eating skills.
           2.   To select vocabulary words to teach in Identifying or Naming Objects.

* = easily digested by most children

LIQUIDS

fruit juices
hot chocolate (warm)
iced tea
koolaid
milk
milk shakes
soda pop
water

FINGER FOODS	SPOON FOODS	FORK FOODS
SET 1 **SOFT TEXTURES**		
*popsicles	*applesauce *baby foods *cream pies *ice cream *jello *oatmeal *pudding *yogurt	
SET 2 **MEDIUM TEXTURES**		

bacon
bread
*cheese
cherry tomatoes
cream candies, fudge
doughnuts/sweet rolls
hamburgers
*hot dogs
*ice cream bars
meat slices (ham, bologna, turkey)
French fries
pickles
soft cookies (short bread)
*marshmallows
*soft fruit (plums, peaches, straw-
   berries, apricots, bananas)
*some sandwiches (peanut butter
   and jelly)
	*apricots, peaches
	*baked beans
	*rice
	cereal
	cooked vegetables (broccoli, car-
	   rots, corn, peas)
	*cup-up spaghetti
	*eggs
	*macaroni and cheese
	*potato salad
	*fruit salad
	   (bananas)
	tomatoes
	ravioli
	pie/cobblers
		french fries
		green beans
		hot dog slices
		meatloaf
		pancakes
		ravioli
		salads
		sausage
		waffles

SET 3 **HARD TEXTURES**		
tacos pretzels	fresh apple slices uncooked vegetables	steak pork chops

461

FINGER FOODS	SPOON FOODS	FORK FOODS
SET 3 HARD TEXTURES		
corn chips	cauliflower, carrots, peas	baked chicken
graham crackers	some cereals (Grape Nuts, Granola)	ham
potato chips		
peanut brittle		
cookies (ginger, chocolate chip)		
radishes		
celery		
cucumbers		
carrots		
melba toast		
nuts		
toast		
cereals		

Phonemes Chart

Uses:
1. To select stimulus events that increase the likelihood that the child will produce a specific sound (Making Sounds, Responding Vocally to Model, Shaping Words).
2. To select activities for increasing vocalization in general.
3. To select vocabulary words containing specific phonemes.
4. To identify the phonemes with their orthographic symbols.

The phonemes have been listed in approximate order of development:

VOWELS   front vowels—ă, e, ĭ, u, ē, ā
           back vowels—ä, ô, ō, oŏ, ōō
           others and diphthongs—ûr, ẽr, ī, ou, oi, (diphthongs with ẽr are omitted)

CONSONANTS   early sounds—b, p, m, t, d, n, k, g, ng
                    later sounds—h, w, f, v, l, r, s, sh
                    difficult combinations—th, t͡h, hw, y, ch, j, zh

FRONT VOWELS:	EVENTS-GAMES	VOCABULARY
ă black	Pretend to sneeze. ("A-a-choo!") Pretend to be scared. ("A-a-a!") Quack like a duck.	can, hat, mat, banana, apple, candy, hand
ĕ deck	Make a machine gun sound. ("E-e-e!") Pretend you can't hear and cup your ear. ("Eh?")	egg, leg, elbow, elephant
ĭ inch	Pretend something tastes bad. ("Ick!")	hit, lip, sink, crib, bib
ŭ cup	Pretend not to understand. ("Huh?") Swing S in the air. ("U-u-p!") Have S exhale sharply. ("Huh")	up, umbrella, cup, fun, tummy, run
ē eat	Pretend to be scared. ("Eek!") Swing S. ("Whee") Laugh. ("Hee hee")	eat, treat, seat, bean
ā ate	Call to S. ("Hey!") Be excited. ("Yea!")	tray, cake, play, clay, plate, face

BACK VOWELS	EVENTS-GAMES	VOCABULARY
ä farther	Uncover something. ("A-ha!") Laugh. ("Ha ha")	pot, top, map, hot, sock, clock
ô lawn	Pretend to be sad or disappointed. ("Aw!")	ball, faucet, dog, call
ō coat	Pretend to be surprised. ("Oh!") Pretend S is in trouble. ("Uh-oh" or "Oh-oh")	go, boat, coat, toe
oŏ book		book, pull, look, cookie
ōō who	Pretend to scare S. ("Boo!") Pretend to cry. ("Boo-hoo") Play train. ("Choo-choo" or "Toot-toot")	oops, soup, spoon, cool, fruit, chew, shoe, tooth

Chart *(continued)*

OTHER VOWELS/DIPHTHONGS	EVENTS-GAMES	VOCABULARY
ûr b<u>ur</u>st	Make car or motor sounds. ("Ur-ur-ur")	work, hurt, shirt, bird
ẽr feath<u>er</u>	Same as above.	(only in unstressed syllables) butter, father, mother
ī b<u>uy</u>	Wave at S. ("Hi" or "Bye") Press your nose against S's. ("Look into my *eyes*.")	eye, bye-bye, pie, fly, why, tie, hi
ou c<u>ow</u>	Pretend to be hurt. ("Ow!" or "Ouch!") Make a loud sound. ("Pow!")	out, loud, clown, round, house
oi <u>oy</u>ster	Make pig sounds. ("Oink-oink") Bounce S. ("Boing, boing!")	boy, toy, coin

EARLY CONSONANTS	EVENTS-GAMES	VOCABULARY
b tu*b*	Wave to S. ("Bye-bye!") Scare S. ("Boo!")	ball, baby, box, book, balloon, belt, brush, bell, boy, bib, bunny, big
p *p*at	Pretend to shoot at S. ("Pow!") Pull a cork out of a bottle. ("Pop") Pop your lips. Blow a feather or blow out a match. Hold a thin strip of paper at S's nose, hanging it down to his mouth, and have him be a motor boat. ("Putt-putt")	pillow, paper, push, pencil, pan, pot, pants
m ca*m*era	Hum and let S feel your throat or nostril. Pretend to eat. ("Mm—good")	mirror, milk, mat, mama, move, mop
t an*t*	Say "Toot-toot" for a train whistle. Make fanfare sounds. ("Ta-ta")	table, top, turn, take, toy, truck, teeth, train
d *d*oll	Make bell sounds. ("Ding-dong") Sing a tune. ("Dee-dee-dee")	dog, doll, daddy, dish, do, dump, desk, dry, drop
n i*n*side	Make a motor sound. ("Na-na-na")	nut, nose, nurse, new, no
k pi*ck*le	Pretend to sneeze. ("K-K-choo!")	cry, clock, cat, can, cup, cake, cough, key, kiss, catch, keep, cold
g di*g*	Play Indian. ("Ugh") Pretend to race. ("On your mark, get set, *go*") Bounce S on your knee. ("Giddy-up")	go, good, give, gum, gun, glove, green, gate
ng ri*ng*	Ring a bell. ("Ding-dong" or "Bong") Bounce a ball. ("Bong")	ring, sing, tongue, bang

LATER CONSONANTS	EVENTS-GAMES	VOCABULARY
h *h*ot	Make laughing sounds. ("Ha-ha") Wave to S. ("Hi") Blow on a mirror (your breath condenses on it).	hello, hand, hot, hat, hair, hammer, happy, head, hear
w pa*w*	Make excited sounds. ("Wow!") Cry like a baby. ("Wah!") Play train. ("Woo-woo!") Whistle.	window, work, wagon, water, walk, wash, watch

Chart (continued)

LATER CONSONANTS	EVENTS-GAMES	VOCABULARY
f effort	Play a giant and chase S. ("Fe-fi-fo-fum") Wet S's finger, and dry it by blowing, pressing your upper teeth to your lower lip. Sing a tune. ("Fa-la-la")	fish, fork, face, food, fan, fat, flower, friend, fruit
v vine	Make a car sound. ("Va-room")	vase, vegetable, vest
l alley	Sing a tune. ("La-la-la") Wobble your tongue.	lip, lemon, like, light, lamp, lock, lost
r car	Growl at S ("R-r-r") or pretend to be a siren. Play with a toy phone. ("Ring")	run, read, rabbit, radio, reach, rock, rub, rain, rag
s sip	Deflate a balloon. ("S-S-S") Pretend to be a snake. Say "Psst" or whisper, saying "secrets."	sit, soup, see, sack, sandwich, sad, sink, smell, sneeze, snap, snow, spoon, stand
z fizz	Play with toy cars. ("Zoom!") Make buzzing sounds like a bee.	zipper, zoo, buzzer
sh ashen	Whisper to S. ("Sh!") Have S be teacher, telling you "Sh!" when there is too much noise.	shop, shoe, shake, show, ship, shirt

DIFFICULT COMBINATIONS	EVENTS-GAMES	VOCABULARY
th thick	Drop something. ("Thunk" as it hits bottom) Pretend to eat hot soup; put your tongue "out," and cool it by blowing.	thick, thin, threads, thirsty, throw
th this	Rock S. ("This way, that way")	mother, father, brother, this, that
hw why	Be excited. ("Whoo-pee!") Make sounds like the North Wind. ("Whh")	why, where, when, what, wheel
y yes	Clap your hands. ("Yipee" or "Yea") Jump back surprised. ("Yipes" or "Yow")	yellow, yes, you
ch archery	Make train sounds. ("Choo-choo") Dance with S. ("Cha-cha-cha") Sneeze. ("Achoo" or "K-choo")	chair, child, cheek, church, chalk, chicken, cheese, chain
j edge	Play with bells. ("Jingle")	juice, jar, jelly, jump
zh measure		

Stimulus Chart

Uses:
1. To select stimulus events that increase the child's responsiveness to the environment: vocalizing, babbling, smiling, laughing, interacting with others, gesturing; looking, listening, attending; moving, feeling, exploring. (Select those activities or materials that are likely to elicit the desired response.)
2. To select motivational materials within the guidelines of any program.
3. To outline informal activities for volunteers, aides, and parents.

SIGHT

By another person

Make faces at S. Move closer and farther away.
Play simple games like Peek-a-boo.
Wave your hand as in a greeting.
Act out simple songs or nursery rhymes.
Perform funny or unusual actions to surprise S.
Wink.
Move your hand slowly in front of S's eyes, then in different directions for S to watch (focus on and visually track).

Materials:

By toys

Play with the toy, or otherwise activate it.
Slowly move the object back and forth in S's range of vision.
Shake the object. Move it quickly to attract attention.
Make noise with the object by moving it.
Hide the object as S watches; then "find" it, or have S find it.

Materials:

wind-up toys, jack-in-the-box, music box, busy box, pull toys, toys on wheels (cars, trains), puppet, top, clear ball containing movable parts, mobiles

By self

Place a mirror directly in S's line of sight (e.g., in front while S is sitting, or above him while S is on his back), and allow S to "discover" its presence.
Help S move different parts of his body to make a reflection in a mirror. Move S closer, even touching the mirror.
Bring S's hands, arms, legs, feet into his range of vision, and shake them to attract his attention.
Sit behind S, and guide S to perform activities with his hands (clap, reach) in his range of vision.
Set up multiple mirrors around S so that he can see himself from many angles.

Materials:

mirror

By light

Move the light path slowly in different directions for S to focus on and track.
Turn the light off and on slowly, then more quickly, alternating patterns.
Shine the light on different parts of S's body and on other people.
Set up two lights, one to the left, one to the right of S. Alternate lighting first one, then the other. Use only one at a time.

Materials:

flashlight, blinking lights (tree ornaments)

By pictures

Slowly move the picture back and forth in S's range of vision.
Keep pictures at different distances from S.
Point to different items in the picture, and talk about them.
Help S trace lines in the picture with his finger.
Show different slides as S sits and looks.
Use large, bright, boldly colored graphics with horizontal, vertical, or diagonal lines.

Materials:

paper dolls, story books, magazines, picture cards, language activity cards, slides

SOUND

By voice

Greet S (Hi, How are you?, Bye) or say other common phrases.
Hum or sing songs.
Laugh.
Make funny sounds or nonsense syllables.
Talk in a rhythmic pattern or say nursery rhymes (See the Phonemes Chart to stimulate S to produce specific sounds).

Materials:

By bodily actions

Clap your hands.
Snap your fingers.
Stamp your feet.
Whistle.

Materials:

By musical instruments

Make sounds of varying degrees of loudness.
Beat the rhythms for different sounds, rhymes, or rhythm patterns.
Accompany a record or tape.
Strike or shake objects that have different tonal qualities.
Attach bells to S's wrists or ankles.

Materials:

bells, triangle, xylophone, drum, horn, sand blocks, cymbals, tambourine, toy organ or piano, shakers (maracas), filled containers (jars, cans, boxes filled with beads, beans, rice, water, coins), rattle

By toys

Use the object, or otherwise activate it.
Turn the object off and on briefly.
Hold the object close to S's ear, then move it (or S) farther away. Vary the distance and volume dramatically.
Alternate sounds between objects or using the same object (high—low pitch, loud—soft).
Hold the toy behind S (or otherwise out of his range of vision), and sound it.
Help S use the object.
Place a squeeze toy beside S, and roll him over the toy.
Play back S's own sounds (on a tape recorder).

Materials:

alarm clocks, jack-in-the-box, music box, radio, television, record player, tape recorder, talking doll, parts of a busy box, rubber balls and other squeeze toys, bicycle horn, toy telephone

MOTION

By your motions

Press against S firmly, then release him suddenly.
Bounce S on your knee (play Horsey).
Rock S back and forth or sideways (play Row-your-boat).
Swing S by his arms in a circle around you.
Toss S up in the air, and catch him.
Carry S piggy-back, bouncing him.
Pull S around in water (pool or large tub).
Wiggle S's arm, leg, or torso.
Swing S between two people by his arms and legs or in a blanket.
Roughhouse and tumble with S.

Materials:

By equipment

Help S use the equipment.
Leave S on a scooterboard for short periods so that he may move about freely.

Materials:

swing, large beach ball, rocking horse,

Chart *(continued)*

MOTION

Allow S to move about freely on a waterbed.
Place S over a large ball or cushion roll, and roll him back and forth or bounce him.

cushion roll, trampoline, tricycle, wagon, slide, scooterboard, waterbed, hammock

---

TOUCH

By movement (vibrations)

Place S's hand on the appliance, and turn it on so that he feels the vibrations.
Have S feel the strings or body of a musical instrument as you play.
Place S's hand on your neck as you hum or make other sounds that vibrate your vocal cords.
Stroke S with a vibrator.
Have S help you vacuum, and let him feel the suction and vibration.

Materials:

vacuum cleaner, vibrator, stringed instrument (guitar, piano), motor, speaker on a record player

By pressure

Guide S to push his fingers into the object or substance and to squeeze it, letting it move between fingers.
Guide S to manipulate the object or substance in a variety of ways: patting, rolling it between his palms, rubbing, poking.
Put different liquid substances in a container, and swish S's hand in it, allowing it to sift between his fingers. Or, pour the substance over S's hand or arm and smooth it over his skin.
Roll doughy substance (clay), and wrap it around S's hand at the wrist or fingers so that S pulls it to remove it.
Bury a bead or other object in the substance, and have S "find it."
Place objects of varying weights in bags. Assist S to pull each.
Attach weights (e.g., various weighted bean bags) to S's arms or ankles.

Materials:

sponge, nerf ball, bean bag, ball of loosely wound yarn, partially inflated beach ball, pillow; clay, play-dough, silly putty, flour paste; water, finger paints, whipped cream, shaving cream, body lotion; sand

By texture

Stroke S gently on the back of his hand with the materials.
Guide S to squeeze or rub the materials (back and forth or in a circular motion).
With tape, pat up and down gently on S's skin. (Do not press very hard.)
Blow several bubbles in a row to get S's attention, then help S poke or "catch" the bubbles.
Slowly pull a scarf or other material across S's torso, limbs, or face.

Materials:

felt, suede, fur, silk, cotton, leather, burlap, sandpaper, bumpy surface, stuffed animals, puppet, rubber, feathers, styrofoam bits, sand, dry leaves, crushed gravel, coins, popcorn, marshmallows, bubbles, scotch tape, string, hairbrush, paintbrush, touch-and-feel boks

By temperature

Blow S's hand with air of different temperatures.
Rub S's arm or leg with hot or cold cloths.
Move S's hand in a container of snow, ice, or varied water temperature.
Note: Be sure that the temperature is not so extreme that it will cause S to have seizures or other extreme neuro-muscular reactions.

Materials:

hairdryer, ice, snow, warm/hot/cold/cool water

TASTE/SMELL

By foods

Have S sniff the food before he eats or tastes it.
Cook food (e.g., cookies) so that it is hot when S smells, then eats it.

Materials:

vinegar, freshly baked items (cookies), pizza,

TASTE/SMELL

spaghetti, onion, sausage, salami, pepper, fresh fruit or vegetables. Refer to Foods Chart for sweet, sour, salty, bitter, and bland tastes

By nonedible substances

Rub the scent on S's body, dabbing some under his nose. Have S sniff different plants.

Materials:

perfume, powder, scratch and smell books, shaving lotion, body lotion, flowers, grasses

Directions for Using the Curriculum

Module 1: Program Selection, 472

Module 2: The Programs, 477

Module 3: General Instructional Procedures, 482

Module 4: Types of Programs, 491

MODULE 1:

Program Selection

INTRODUCTION

The Programmed Environments curriculum contains a wide range of programs. The first task that a teacher confronts is to select programs appropriate for each child. This task involves assessing the child's current skills, considering realistic long- and short-range objectives, and identifying programs that match the child's skill assessment and objectives.

The purpose of this module is to describe the four tools that facilitate program selection. These four tools are the:

1. Profile;
2. Curriculum Overview;
3. Class Observation Record; and
4. Program Overview for each individual program.

Based on the information presented in this module, you will be able to:

- Make appropriate observations on skills covered in this curriculum; and
- select appropriate programs to pretest.

PRELIMINARY INFORMATION

Profile

Before you observe in the classroom, you should analyze the Profile to determine the categories of behavior and their general sequence. The Profile, found on page 7, contains the titles of programs in the areas of Language, Cognitive, Motor, and Self-Help Skills. Within each section, programs are arranged in the order in which they are typically acquired, from simpler (bottom of the Profile) to more complex (top). The organization of the Profile summarizes the scope of the curriculum. This provides a rough picture of the approximate order of skills within each area and across areas. Lower level programs are not necessarily prerequisite to higher level skills.

The Curriculum Overview should be read next for an in-depth description of the skills, their interrelationships, and their acquisition over time. The Profile and Curriculum Overview contribute to a general understanding of the behaviors that may be taught with this curriculum.

Class Observation Record

With this broad picture, look at the Class Observation Record, pages 421-46, an ordered list of programs. It contains a general objective and an observation strategy for each program, as well as room for taking notes during observation. This information is abstracted from the individual programs. When you have completed the Class Observation Record, your observations will provide a reference for pretesting children on specific programs. This preliminary screening will assist you to identify the programs most likely to be taught.

INITIAL SCREENING PROCEDURES

What to Observe

We recommend that you observe and record data on each skill in the Class Observation Record, since skills are interrelated between and within curriculum areas. However, this procedure may be streamlined since one situation may provide information on a variety of different skills. For example, a child who imitates you performs many other behaviors at the same time. He responds to social interaction and responds to and repeats the model. He may also hold, reach for, and manipulate an object. Thus, each skill may not need to be observed in an isolated situation. Careful study of the Class Observation Record suggests ways to streamline observations.

When to Observe

Observation is a procedure that can be performed throughout the day during ongoing activities. Some skills will occur within your classroom routine, whereas other skills occur only in specific situations. You can determine from the Class Observation Record whether a skill is likely to occur in a natural setting, or if you must structure the situation to evaluate it.

Where possible, observation should occur during informal activities since these situations may best reflect the child's skills. Seemingly unstructured free-play with the child may be the setting where you systematically observe the specific skills listed on the Class Observation Record:

Does the child . . . respond to me? Make sounds? Name objects? Follow commands? Imitate?

What to Record

During initial observation, the child is given opportunities to perform the skill in several different situations with different materials. The basic information to be noted on the record form is whether the child performed the target skill. In addition, notes should clarify when and/or how well the child performed. This information can be represented as:

"Child is unable to perform the skill"; or
"Child can perform but only in certain situations" (with specifics cited); or
"Child can perform the skill whenever appropriate."

In addition to the target skill and its observation strategy, each program on the Class Observation Record indicates whether that program may be used to teach each of several closely related skills or concepts. Such programs are noted as "Cycle" programs because they may be reused or recycled to teach each of a set of related skills or concepts. For example, the same set of strategies with a change in materials may be used to teach the child either to match concrete objects or to match pictures. Each use of this program (matching objects or matching pictures) with the child is considered a "cycle." Thus, a cycle program is repeated several times to teach different but closely related skills or concepts through the same instructional sequence.

Because they are different though related, each skill or concept of a cycle program should be observed. For example, in the program Counting Rationally, each cycle represents a number concept: Count to one? two? three? four? five? These number concepts are related but different. Each should be evaluated. Or in Naming Objects, a child who can name a cup may not be able to name a shoe or a book. As indicated on the record form, data should be recorded on each skill or concept of a cycle program.

The following examples illustrate how to fill out the Class Observation Record:

RECEPTIVE SKILL

Skill	Objective	Observation	Cycle	Record
3. Following Cued Commands	Given a cued command (a verbal command given with accompanying gestures and context cues), S performs the requested action without assistance.	Point or gesture while you ask S to sit, stand up, hold your hand, give you what he's holding out, and the like, and record if he responds correctly.	Record each different command that S can perform. Each command is a cycle.	John *can perform: sit down stand up but not others*
OR				
4. Attending to Own Name	S turns his face toward the person who calls his name.	Position yourself anywhere in a quiet room with S (vary your direction relative to him). Call his name during activities, and record if he looks up at you.		Bill *with physical assistance only*

SELECTING PROGRAMS TO PRETEST

What to Consider

Your initial screening observations provide general information on the child's current skills and indicate those she may need to acquire. However, there may be a wide selection of potential programs (i.e., skills that the child cannot now perform). The next task then is to narrow this list of skills until you have identified a manageable number of appropriate programs to pretest. There are three main considerations in narrowing your choices:

- Priority goals for the child;
- the intent of each potential program; and
- the specified entry behaviors for each potential program.

474

All school districts require the writing of individual educational plans for each child based on input from parents, the classroom teacher, and other related professionals (discussed in module 7, Individual Educational Programs). This planning identifies the priority goals for the year. Given these broad goals, selection of programs for pretesting should focus on skills in the same curricular area(s) as these priority goals. For example, if the primary goal for a child is mobility, you would obviously look to the gross motor area as a priority to select programs to pretest.

Because each program contains information on the relationship of that skill to skills in other areas, you may also identify potential programs in other curricular areas. Although your priority for one youngster may be dressing skills, this may involve gross and fine motor skills as well. This information is presented in each Program Overview.

PROGRAM INTENT

The Program Overview

Each Program Overview, the first one to two pages of a program, contains the sections "Skill," "Entry Behaviors," "Objective," "Cycle," and "Follow-Up." An overview is specifically designed to aid you to identify appropriate programs to pretest. In general, this information covers the functional use of the skill ("Skill"); when it is typically taught ("Entry Behaviors"); the behavioral objective of the program with criterion statements ("Objective"); use of the program to teach related skills and concepts, if appropriate ("Cycle"); and generalization activities and follow-up programs ("Follow-Up").

To narrow choices within your priority area(s), you should read the Program Overview for each skill the child was unable to perform during screening observations. Although this is the general procedure, it does not require reading all program overviews in that area. Rather, we recommend that you read at least three overviews for programs that appear appropriate in the priority area. To select those three overviews, refer to your notes on the Class Observation Record for skills that the child was unable to perform. Select the program that has the lowest skill number; then select those that have the next higher numbers. The reason for reading at least three overviews is that the skills are not necessarily prerequisite to each other. Only by reading a selection of overviews will you be able to determine the most appropriate program(s) to pretest and teach at this time.

What Information to Look For

When reading the Program Overview, search for a match between your observations, the child's educational plan, and the intent of the program. Specific sections in the Overview clarify the intent of the program: "Skill," "Objective," and "Follow-Up." Read these sections, keeping your observations and goals in mind. For example, you observe that the child did not put on her sock when you requested; instead she put on her shoe. A review of Putting on a Shoe indicates the intent of that program is to teach a chain of motor responses. The observation suggests a language program to teach the child to discriminate between the words *shoe* and *sock*.

The second type of information you are looking for in the Overview is entry behaviors. Does the child now have those behaviors that will facilitate successful acquisition of the skill?

ENTRY BEHAVIORS

Some programs may be appropriate for your goal but may not be appropriate at this time because the child does not have the skills that facilitate successful acquisition, specified in "Entry Behaviors." These entry behaviors have been identified based on the existing skills exhibited by most children who have successfully used the program. Many of the entry behaviors have a program title listed after them: "S can lift his head and maintain an erect head position for 1 minute (e.g., Controlling Head Movements)." However, this reference does not mean that the child must have passed that particular program. Rather, it means that if the child does not exhibit the behavior, you may refer to that program to teach the skill.

Adaptations

The Entry Behaviors section also includes any skill that the child needs to sense the cues used (e.g., "S can hear") or to perform the response defined in the program (e.g., "S can pick up the object"). However, usually such "input-output" components of the task may be adapted for children with sensory or motor impairments. Therefore, these entry behaviors are immediately followed by suggested ways to adapt the specified program cues or responses (e.g., "S can hear the command. Or, adapt by using signing and/or gestures to convey the intent of the command").

Finally, the fact that the child does not exhibit a behavior does not necessarily mean that she cannot learn the skill at this time. Rather, it is unlikely that she will learn the skill through this program. If the skill is critical and the child does not exhibit the entry behavior, refer to another source or develop your own program based on the model provided in module 6, Developing Instructional Programs.

SUMMARY

Follow this procedure to select appropriate program(s) to pretest:

1. Study the information that summarizes the content of the curriculum
   a. The Profile (page 7);
   b. The Curriculum Overview (pages 1-10); and
   c. The Classroom Observation Record (pages 421-46).
2. Observe the child, writing your notes on the Class Observation Record for all curricular areas.
3. In the curricular area(s) where S's priority goals are listed, select for review at least the three lowest-numbered skills that the child was unable to perform.
4. Read the Overview of each of those programs. Check for the intent of the program and the entry behaviors that facilitate successful acquisition of the skill.

When you have completed these steps, select the program(s) that you consider most appropriate to pretest and teach at this time. This basic procedure is used any time you select a program during the year. You must, of course, update the information on the Class Observation Record.

MODULE 2:
The Programs

In this curriculum, a program is a set of specific strategies that evaluate and provide gradual, sequential learning. Each program contains the following components:

1. OVERVIEW

    SKILL INFORMATION: The information necessary to decide whether the program is appropriate to pretest (discussed in module 1, Program Selection).

2. PROGRAM

    PRETEST: An evaluation procedure used before instruction to verify that the child is unable to perform the skill.

    TEACHING STRATEGIES: Specified teaching procedures for systematic instruction and feedback as the child acquires the skill.

    POSTTESTS: An evaluation procedure used after instruction to verify that the child can perform the skill in at least three different situations.

    DATA COLLECTION: A system for recording and evaluating child performance before, during, and after instruction.

    The purpose of this module is to present general information on the contents of each program and to suggest how the programs may be adapted for use with children who manifest sensory and motor impairments. The general instructional procedures and their applications are critical to the successful use of the programs. For this reason, we highly recommend that you read and follow all procedures outlined in these modules, as well as the specific directions in each program. Based on the information in this module, you will be able to:

- Locate critical information on the Program; and
- make adaptations for specific sensory or motor impairments.

THE PROGRAM

Each Program contains this critical information:

1. Program type identification
2. Specifications of materials and chart(s)
3. General Strategy
4. Specifications for Conditions—Behavior—Criteria
5. Modifications/Suggestions

Program Type Identification

The program type identification is found directly under the program title on both the Overview and the Program. This indicates the data collection procedures to be followed on the program—4/5 data, rate data, skill analysis data, or chain data. These procedures are covered in module 4, Types of Programs. These procedures are program specific.

Specification of Materials and Chart(s)

Directly under the title before the main body of the Program are the titles *Materials* and *Chart*. The *Materials* section provides guidelines for the types of objects to use. Within these guidelines, you may use any that are appropriate to the child. The *Chart* section refers to any accompanying lists of options that you may use with this program. For example, Following Cued Commands is a cycle program through which you may teach a variety of commands. Its chart section refers to the chart titled *Cued Commands*, which is a list of suggested commands. From it you may select commands to teach through this program. All chart(s) referred to in the Programs are located on pages 451-70, directly after the programs, and are arranged in alphabetical order.

General Strategy and Conditions-Behavior-Criteria

The main body of the program is contained in the sections *General Strategy* and *Conditions-Behavior-Criteria*. The General Strategy defines the typical order of events for each *trial* or opportunity to respond in the program. Typical entries are:

ATTENTION: Suggestions to focus the child's attention to instruction.

CUES: Definitions of strategies specific to the program.

COMMAND: The request for the response.

LATENCY: How long to wait for a response to begin.

CORRECTION: Methods to correct errors that occur during instruction.

OTHER TRIALS: When to present new trials.

MODIFICATION: When to modify the program if the child is not meeting criterion.

Although the General Strategy describes a typical trial in the program, the actual events and their order may vary between tests and steps. The Conditions-Behavior-Criteria give this specification for the pretest (PRE), all learning steps in order, and all posttests (POST). *Conditions* specify which general strategy events are appropriate and their order; *Behavior* defines the response that is considered correct; and *Criteria* specify the number of times the response must be emitted in order to pass the test or step.

Immediately following the main body of the program are ways to modify it and strategies to use. Since this information is specific to the type of program, it will be discussed in module 4, Types of Programs.

ADAPTATION PROCEDURES

Since children may exhibit a range of sensory and motor impairments, the programs have been written assuming normal hearing, sight, and physical condition. However, any program may be adapted to compensate for a child with sensory or motor impairments. This adaptation may involve a change in either:

TASK CONDITIONS: Materials, commands, cues, or any specified condition under which the response is made.

RESPONSE REQUIREMENT: Specifications for the timing or type of response to be made.

Once an adaptation is selected, the standard program is used as written with this change in task conditions or response requirement for all tests and steps.

How to Identify Need for Adaptation

Because adaptations are compensations for specific physical disabilities, you can usually identify their need as you read the Program. Can the child use the standard task cues? (Can she see the specified visual cues, hear the auditory cues and commands?) Can the child physically perform the specified behavior? Occasionally, you may be unaware that a child will have difficulty until you actually begin instruction. Therefore, you may make adaptations any time the child is unable to perform the task due to a specific sensory or motor impairment.

Before you adapt a program, however, note that many programs may be individualized without an adaptation. For example, the objective on the Overview might say that the child "indicates" the named object, with the word *indicate* defined as "touch, pick up, or otherwise show the choice." In this case, the flexibility is already there, and there is no need to adapt the standard program.

Where to Find Suggestions for Adaptations

Although each Program Overview contains suggested adaptations specific to certain entry behaviors, these are only some of the possible strategies that you may use. They should not be considered necessary or exclusive. Often much more information can be obtained through discussions with physical, occupational or speech therapists, or other specialists working with the child. In addition, your own experiences with the child will be invaluable in making appropriate adaptations. Although the program may include some suggestions for using specific techniques such as sign language, you will need to consult other sources if you choose a method that requires specific training.

TASK CONDITIONS

How to Adapt Task Conditions

When you adapt task conditions, consider the type of cues that are used in the standard program to provide a stimulus for the response. Then, if the cue is inappropriate to the child, substitute another cue that will provide a more appropriate stimulus. For example, the following are some standard cues and possible substitutions:

Cue	Standard Adaptation Suggestions
verbal commands	*For Hearing Impaired:* Insure that the child looks at you at all times; use gestures with the command to point out materials or clarify your meaning; use sign language with the verbal command.
gestures (pointing, demonstrating)	*For Visually Impaired*: Make sounds instead of or in addition to your gesture to locate the object for the child; touch the child or have her feel the object or demonstration.
guidance	*For Visually Impaired*: Have the child explore with her hands to clarify the action.
position of objects	*For Visually Impaired*: Make sounds with the objects to locate them; have the child feel to locate them.

Note that in all situations you should insure the child's attention, select appropriate materials, and give all cues within her visual range.

RESPONSE REQUIREMENTS

How to Adapt Latency Requirements

When a child is able to perform the action but requires a long time to respond, usually the simplest adaptation is to extend the *latency* or time limit within which the child must begin to respond. In most programs the specified latency is 5 seconds after the command, and this time limit can be adapted to 10, 15, or 20 seconds. However, latency only involves the time between the last cue and the beginning of a response. On any program the child may take as long as she needs to perform the action as long as she starts within the latency and continues to respond. Thus, latency need only be adapted if the child takes longer than 5 seconds (or other specified latency) to start, not complete, a response.

How to Adapt Response Definitions

When the child is able to perform only an approximation of the defined response, adaptation requires redefinition of the response so that it is an action the child can perform. For example, if the program requires the child to "grasp an object, using her thumb and index finger" and the child's hand is paralyzed, you could adapt the program by redefining the response to "use two hands to hold the object." Adaptations in the response definition are used most with motorically impaired children. Note that you may use adaptive equipment with the child whenever appropriate.

How to Adapt Responses Requiring a Sequence of Actions

Some programs (specifically those in the Self-Help area) teach a response that involves the performance of a sequence of actions. For example, to put on a sock, the child has to bend her leg, bring the sock to her toes, and insert her foot. If the child is physically unable to perform one of the actions in the sequence (e.g., bend her leg unassisted), you may adapt the specified sequence by substituting another action(s) that enables her to complete the task without that part(s) she cannot perform. For example, in place of bending her leg, you might have the child use her hands to bring her leg up. The adapted sequence would be that the child holds her leg, brings it up to a bent position, brings the sock to her toes, and inserts her foot. Again, adaptive equipment may be used whenever appropriate.

1. Each program in the curriculum contains:

   a. An Overview with information necessary to decide whether the program is appropriate to pretest, and

   b. A Program with directions for teaching the concept or skill from pretesting through posttesting.

2. Although each program gives directions for administration, these directions should be used in conjunction with:

   a. Presentation procedures discussed in module 3, General Instructional Procedures; and

   b. Data collection procedures discussed in module 4, Types of Programs.

3. Any program may be adapted for children with sensory or motor impairments by adapting either:

   a. Task conditions; or

   b. Response requirements.

MODULE 3:
General Instructional Procedures

INTRODUCTION

Once a program has been selected as appropriate to pretest, the next task is to administer the pretest, then if failed, to present the program daily to teach the skill. When all learning steps are completed successfully, the skill is posttested to verify that the child has learned the skill. The purpose of this module is to describe those procedures for pretesting, teaching, and posttesting that are appropriate to all programs in the curriculum. These procedures and their applications to specific program types, discussed in module 4, Types of Programs, are critical to the successful use of this curriculum. Based on the information presented in this module, you will be able to:

- Present test trials appropriately;
- present instructional trials appropriately;
- present posttests in correct sequence; and
- structure appropriate sessions for administering programs.

PRETEST PROCEDURES

Pretest Model

Pretesting is used to verify whether a child can perform a particular skill. The general pretesting procedure is to present the child with various opportunities to perform the task (without trying to influence her performance), then record her behavior. Basically, each opportunity or *trial* in a test follows this model:

TEACHER INSURES READINESS	→	TEACHER PRESENTS TASK STIMULUS	→	CHILD RESPONDS	→	TEACHER RECORDS RESPONSE
Attention		Materials Cues Command				

From this model, you can see that the three components of pretest procedures are insuring the child's readiness to respond, presenting the task stimulus, and recording the response. These three components occur in every pretest trial.

Behavior problems of all types from passive (e.g., refusal to look up) to active (e.g., tantruming, off-task actions) indicate that the child is not ready to respond and will adversely effect child performance. Before any trial, it is imperative that the child is attending to you and the learning situation.

One strategy to get attention is to provide an attention cue. You might say the child's name or use other strategies to draw her attention to you and the instructional materials. Usually the best way to insure attention is to require the child to make eye contact with you. However, this may vary, depending on the specific child and task. In any case, the child should make some observable response that indicates readiness to respond. Module 5, Reinforcement and Instructional Control, gives further information to insure on-task behavior.

How to Present the Task Stimulus

Each program pretest states the conditions under which the child is expected to perform. These conditions consist of the materials, arrangement, your cues or actions, and the command. Your presentation should adhere to those guidelines since they insure a standard situation in which the response can occur. Although there is some individual flexibility in materials selection and actual presentation, this flexibility remains within the program guidelines.

Two types of problems may arise in the task presentation: the omission or the addition of task cues. The omission of a specified condition may make the task more difficult than need be, while the addition of some extra assistance may make the task simpler than outlined. Many times these teacher errors can be prevented by careful program study and self-monitoring during trials. Typical points to notice are:

- Arrangement of materials;
- specified cues to be given; and
- addition of unwanted cues while you wait for a response
- (leaning, smiling, frowning, nodding).

How to Record the Response

Once the child has had an opportunity to respond, her behavior is recorded on a *data sheet* (a sheet for writing responses for one child on one program). Although the four types of programs have different data systems, they all use common recording symbols:

+ ... The child responded correctly and met the description of the behavior specified in the program (i.e., a "correct response").

− ... The child responded but did not meet the description of behavior specified (i.e., "an error").

θ ... The child made no response within the *latency* or time limit for beginning a response as specified in the program (counted as "error").

How to Provide Nondifferential Feedback during the Pretest

The objective of the pretest is to determine that the child does or does not demonstrate a behavior. It is important that you do not provide feedback to the child until you receive her response. Do not state that a response is correct or incorrect. Do not provide cues that might indicate the correct response. Instead, interact with the child in a friendly but neutral manner. Then clear away the materials, if appropriate, and go on to the next activity or trial. This is called *nondifferential feedback* because it is the same whether the response is correct or incorrect. Specific *differential* feedback is appropriate when you teach, not when you test.

Summary of Pretest Procedures

Give the pretest to verify that the child cannot perform the skill.

1. Get the child's attention.
2. Present task cue(s):
   a. Give all the cues described in the program; or
   b. give only those cues described in the program.
3. Wait for a response, up to the specified latency.
4. Record the child's response on the data sheet:
   a. Use one data sheet for one program for one child; and
   b. use "+", "−", and "θ" symbols.
5. Continue to give trials until the test is completed

After the pretest is completed, decide whether to teach the program.

1. Begin instruction on this program if the child fails the pretest.
2. Discontinue instruction on this program if the child passes the pretest:
   a. File the completed data sheet; and
   b. select another program for potential instruction.

TEACHING PROCEDURES

Model

Trials given during teaching steps or phases also assess a child's response under standard conditions. However, they go beyond the testing procedures and provide specific feedback on performance in order to improve the child's *next* response.

The general teaching procedure is to present the child with various opportunities to perform a task. Then based on her response, specific feedback is given to either increase the probability of a correct response or remediate an error. Finally the child's response to the original task is recorded. Each learning trial follows this basic model:

TEACHER INSURES READINESS Attention → TEACHER PRESENTS TASK STIMULUS Materials Cues Command → CHILD RESPONDS → TEACHER GIVES SPECIFIC FEEDBACK → TEACHER RECORDS RESPONSE

From this model, you can see that the four components of teaching procedures are: to insure the child's readiness to respond, to present the task stimulus, to provide specific feedback, and to record the response. Three of these components (insuring readiness, presenting the stimulus, and recording the response) are essentially the same as the components in pretesting procedures. For these components, the same information applies except that the specific instructions for the task cues and the description of the required responses are different, as specified on the Program. The feedback component of teaching procedures is the basic difference between testing and teaching.

How to Increase the Likelihood of a Correct Response

The purpose of specific feedback after a correct response is to increase the likelihood that the child will emit that response on the next trial. This procedure is called *posi-*

tive reinforcement. In other words, when a child makes a correct response, you reinforce that behavior to make it more likely to occur again. Any item or event that is used to strenghten a response is called a *positive reinforcer*. Since only positive reinforcement is referred to in this curriculum, the terms *reinforcer* and *reinforcement* are used.

Reinforcement should follow the response *immediately* so that the child associates the response with the reinforcer. Any item or event may be a potential reinforcer for a child: food, activities, tokens, praise. The effectiveness of any reinforcer varies from child to child and from day to day. Any reinforcer should be presented immediately after the response and should include praise that states why the response is correct: "Good. You picked up the shoe!" More specific information on reinforcement and its general use is contained in module 5, Reinforcement and Instructional Control.

How to Correct Errors

When the child makes an *error*, either the wrong response or no response within the specified latency, specific feedback is given immediately to enable the child to respond correctly at the next opportunity. This procedure is called *correction*. During correction the child has a chance to practice the response with extra assistance which is *in addition to* the task cues specified for the trial. Once the child has successfully practiced the response with extra assistance, correction is over. Then a new trial is presented under the original task conditions.

Each program indicates what type of correction to use. Some programs give specific directions in the General Strategy section to correct errors. However, many programs simply direct you to use "general correction procedures." In this case, you may select one of the three following procedures, depending on the type of error, the nature of the task, and existing program cues:

- Extra directions to refocus the child's efforts on the task;
- a demonstration of the task; or
- physical guidance to perform the task.

Correction Procedure: Refocus

Refocus requires you to *intercept* (physically interrupt) the mistake if possible, then redirect the child's attention to the task. This indicates that a correction is needed but not how it should be accomplished. This procedure is usually successful with children if they have previously performed the task correctly; it simply calls their attention to the fact that an error has occurred. This example illustrates how to refocus to correct an error: The teacher gives Sara a command: "Sara, pick up the shoe," and points to a selection of objects. Sara starts to pick up a bowl.

1. intercept immediately	Stop Sara from picking up the bowl. (error)
2. refocus attention with extra directions	"Sara, look carefully at *all* the objects."
3. repeat command (with all specified cues)	"Pick up the *shoe*."
4. observe latency for practice response	Wait for Sara to respond.
5. record	Write either " − " for the original error, or write " −(R+)" to indicate not only the error but also what correction was used and how the child responded with refocusing.
	We recommend that you record the correction in addition to the original error.

Correction Procedure: Demonstration

In *demonstration*, the child receives necessary information through extra directions and a demonstration of the task itself. You *intercept*, give a demonstration with extra directions, and then repeat the task request. Demonstration is usually effective with children who imitate fairly consistently and with tasks that are easily demonstrated. The following is an example of demonstrating to correct an error:

1. intercept immediately	Stop Sara from picking up the bowl. (error)
2. demonstrate with extra directions	"Sara, look, I'm picking up the shoe."
3. repeat command (with all specified cues)	"Pick up the *shoe*."
4. observe latency for the practice response	Wait for Sara to respond.
5. record	Write either " − " for the original error, or write " − (D +)."

Correction Procedure: Guidance

In *guidance*, you *intercept*, then give the child extra directions while you physically assist her to practice the response. It is most effective with tasks that teach a motor response or with children who do not respond successfully to refocus or demonstration. The following is an example of guiding to correct an error:

1. intercept immediately	Stop Sara from picking up the bowl. (error)
2. repeat the command (with all specified cues)	"Pick up the *shoe*."
3. guide a practice response with extra directions	"This is the *shoe*."
4. record	Write either " − " for the original error, or write " −(G +)."

Note

If the procedure you used is not effective (e.g., the child makes an error on the practice response), try another procedure until the child practices once successfully with extra assistance. After the child makes one successful response with extra assistance, return to the original task conditions. Give trials without the extra assistance. If for any reason none of the correction procedures (or variations on them) work, stop for the day, ending on a positive note. Note that an error at any time reflects a problem. Each time an error occurs, correct it but pause to reassess the situation to determine why the error occurs. Both task confusion *and* behavior problems can result in an error. After you correct the child, stop and evaluate the situation. If an error appears to be caused by a behavior problem, handle that first before you continue instruction.

Summary of Teaching Procedures

After failing the pretest, give the child learning trials as specified in the program.

1. Get the child's attention.
2. Present task cue(s):
    a. Give all the cues described in the program; or
    b. give only those cues described in the program.
3. Wait for a response, up to the specified latency.

4. When a response occurs (or latency is up), immediately give specific feedback:
  a. Reinforce a correct response; or
  b. correct an error by one or more of the following methods:
   (1) Give extra directions
   (2) Demonstrate the task
   (3) Physically guide the child to complete the task
   (4) Use specific program corrections
5. After you provide feedback, record the original response on the data sheet:
  a. Continue to use the same data sheet as the one on which the pretest for that child on that program was recorded; and
  b. use "+", "−", and "θ" symbols.
6. Start a new trial.

Continue to give trials as specified in the program until the child has gone through all learning steps or phases.

POSTTEST PROCEDURES

Model

The purpose of posttesting is to verify that the child can perform the skill in at least three different situations. Hence, every program contains three separate posttests, each with slightly different task conditions. In any one posttest, trials are given according to the procedures described in pretesting:

TEACHER INSURES READINESS	→	TEACHER PRESENTS TASK STIMULUS	→	CHILD RESPONDS	→	TEACHER RECORDS RESPONSE
Attention		Materials Cues Command				

Note that like pretesting, no specific feedback is provided. In other words, responses are neither reinforced nor corrected during a posttest.

When to Posttest

After the child has successfully completed all learning steps or phases, she is given the first posttest on the skill. This first posttest is identical to the pretest. It has the same task conditions as the last learning step or phase of the program except for the procedural difference between testing and teaching. Whereas specific feedback (i.e., reinforcement, correction) is given during learning trials through the last learning step or phase, no specific feedback is given during the first posttest (or any other test).

After the child successfully completes the first posttest, she is given in sequence the second and third posttests, each containing new task conditions. When the child has successfully completed all three posttests in order, she has completed the program. At that time, refer to "Follow-Up" in the Program for generalization activities and new programs.

Summary of Posttest Procedures

Give the first posttest after the child successfully completes all learning steps or phases.

1. Give the child an attention cue(s).
2. Present task cue(s):
  a. Give all the cues described in the program; or
  b. give only those cues described in the program.

3. Wait for a response, up to the specified latency.
4. Record the child's response on the data sheet:
   a. Continue to use the same data sheet as the one on which the pretest and teaching steps or phases for that child and that program was recorded; and
   b. continue to give trials until the test is completed.

After the first posttest is successfully completed, give the second posttest with its new task conditions.

After the second posttest is successfully completed, give the third posttest with its new task conditions.

After the third posttest is successfully completed, the program is complete.

1. File the completed data sheet.
2. Plan other generalization activities on this skill.
3. Select another program(s) for potential instruction.

SESSION PROCEDURES

Components

A *session* is each time period in which program trials are presented to the child. Procedures for structuring a session insure the child's optimal performance on the task at hand, whether it is a test situation or part of the learning steps or phases. The three specific session components effecting child performance are the preliminary warm-up, the pace, and the length of the session.

How to Present a Warm-Up

Like an attention cue before a trial, a short *warm-up* activity at the beginning of each session insures that the child is ready to respond. A warm-up may consist of a review demonstration of the previous day's task, an opportunity for the child to explore novel materials, or any brief activity that helps the child focus on instruction. The purpose of a warm-up is not to provide direct instruction but rather to relax and prepare the child for work through various preliminary activities.

How to Pace the Session

Another variable that affects performance is the *pace* of the session (i.e., the speed at which trials are presented). An overly slow pace can cause boredom while a rapid-fire pace may create tension. Either extreme may produce a behavior problem, such as resistance, refusal to work, responding to distractions, and so on. Ways to prevent such problems are to pace the trials by allowing time in between to talk, rest, or play. This pacing will vary, depending upon the child, the time of day, and other conditions, such as the child's attention span, health conditions, and so forth. By observing how the child responds, you may speed up or slow down trials to keep her attention.

Whenever behavior problems occur during a session, discontinue trials and data collection momentarily since you are not getting the child's optimal performance. Before you continue the session, get the child's attention and re-establish instructional control. Eliminate the source of distraction, draw the child's attention back to the task, or use other behavior management strategies. These are discussed in module 5, Reinforcement and Instructional Control. After the child is ready to attend, resume the session or begin again later.

Whatever your pace, you should always encourage the child's attention to the task. Pause before a trial to praise and reinforce her readiness to work. This reinforcement should not follow immediately after a correct response. That feedback is specific to the test or teaching procedure. Instead, reinforcement for readiness or attention is given *before* a trial, when the child is exhibiting appropriate behavior. This reinforcement may be included as part of the attention procedures for any trial. When reinforcement is given for appropriate behavior, it should include specific praise for the behavior (e.g., "You pay such good attention!" or "You're really ready to work!").

How to Determine Length of a Session

Although an eventual goal is for 15-minute sessions, the actual length of the session will depend upon the individual child. Sessions that are too short hinder progress since the child has only a few opportunities to work on the skill. On the other hand, sessions that run too long usually cause behavior problems such as fidgeting and distraction. A general guideline is to work for 10 to 15 minutes unless there is a behavior problem. In that case, the problem should be handled before you present additional trials since the child is no longer responding to the task.

Regardless of the actual length of the session, it should always end on a positive note so that the child learns to enjoy instruction. After the last task trial is completed, have the child perform some other task that she enjoys and can do well. This may be helping put away materials, getting a toy for free play, or any other reinforcing activity that denotes the end of the session.

How to Handle Procedural Errors

All of the procedures described for pretesting, teaching, posttesting, and structuring the session provide optimal conditions for the child's performance. Whenever the child must respond to a task and these conditions are not fulfilled, a *procedural error* has occurred. In this case, simply circle the child's recorded response on your data sheet, and indicate the circumstances:

$\ominus^{PE}$ . . . Forgot to get her attention.

$\oplus^{PE}$ . . . Gave an extra cue on the task.

$\ominus^{PE}$ . . . Started the session without a warm-up.

$\ominus^{PE}$ . . . Pace resulted in tantrum.

$\oplus^{PE}$ . . . Reinforced the response on this test.

$\ominus^{PE}$ . . . Forgot to correct this response during instruction.

$\oslash^{PE}$ . . . Session too long (behavior deteriorated).

The PE marking indicates that the circled response will not be counted toward criterion and that another trial will be presented to replace this trial. You may decide to circle several responses on a step or even an entire session, and mark it PE. There are a variety of situations that would make this necessary, for example, when another student continues to interfere with instruction.

SUMMARY

1. Present each program in the following order:
   a. Pretest;
   b. teaching steps or phases; and
   c. posttests in consecutive order.
2. Present test trials in the following order:
   a. Get attention;
   b. present task cues as specified;
   c. observe latency; and
   d. record response without giving feedback.

3. Present teaching trials in the following order:
   a. Get attention;
   b. present task cues as specified;
   c. observe latency;
   d. give feedback as appropriate:
      (1) reinforcement
      (2) correction; and
   e. record response.
4. Instructional sessions should contain the following components to insure optimal child performance:
   a. Warm-up;
   b. appropriate pace of trials;
   c. appropriate length of instruction; and
   d. reinforcing activity at the end.
5. When errors in any of the above procedures (Items 1–4) prevent optimal child performance, the problem should be remediated and the trial(s) or session repeated.

MODULE 4:
Types of Programs

A variety of skills are covered in this curriculum. Some skills require the child to increase her general responding to stimuli in the environment; some, to develop her muscle tone, strength, coordination and balance; others, to perform a sequence of actions to complete a task; and still others to discriminate and respond appropriately to increasingly more complex stimulus cues. Because of this range of behaviors, no single data collection system is sufficient to record progress on each instructional program. On the other hand, it is not necessary to have a unique data collection system for every program. For these reasons, we have developed four basic data systems. The data system appropriate to each program is identified immediately under the title on each Overview and Program. The four basic program types in this curriculum are:

1. *Rate Data:* Early stimulation programs that elicit responses to environmental stimuli when responses initially occur at a low rate. Learning is documented as the frequency of responding during a 10-minute session increases. Strategies focus on finding and using stimuli that effectively increase responding.

2. *4/5 Data:* Higher language and cognitive programs that focus on skills that initially occur only with assistance or extra cue(s). Learning is documented as the child performs the skill with increasingly less teacher assistance. The focus of the intervention strategy is to add then systematically remove (fade) these cues.

3. *Skill Analysis:* Basic motor programs that develop muscle tone, strength, coordination, and balance. Each skill is broken into discrete components. Learning is defined as an increase in the number of components completed without assistance. Strategies focus on exercises to develop specific strength and balance skills.

4. *Chain (Task Analysis):* Self-help programs that request the child to complete a behavioral chain in sequential order. Each skill is analyzed into sequential parts. Learning is defined as an increase in parts completed without assistance. The child is taught to complete parts of the chain and to complete the chain in correct order.

The purpose of this module is to describe these four types of programs and their applications to the general procedures presented in module 3. Each of the sections has been written to stand alone, so you need to read only the section(s) that is relevant to the program(s) you have selected to use. However, because you may be using all four types at some point, we highly recommend that you read the four sections. Based on the information presented in this module, you will be able to:

- Present, record, and evaluate child performance on pretests;
- present, record, and evaluate child performance on instructional sequences;
- modify instructional sequences as needed, based on child performance; and
- present, record, and evaluate child performance on posttests, with remediation if needed.

SECTION 1:
Rate Data Programs

Some programs take an existing but random action or sound and increase its frequency to a rate sufficient for its use in more complex learning. In such programs, various stimuli are presented, and over successive program steps, the child learns to respond more and more frequently. The criterion or frequency required on each step or test is a specified *rate* of response, or the number of responses that occur within a specified time interval. These have been identified as *rate data* programs.

Stimuli in rate data programs may include any of a variety of visual, auditory, or tactile cues by an object or person. Each program specifies guidelines for the stimuli you present to elicit the defined response. However, within those guidelines, you may use any stimulus that is effective with your child. Note that the stimulus elicits an unassisted response and, thus, comes before that response. Since complete guidance for a response occurs at the same time as the response, it is never used as a stimulus in the rate data programs. It may, however, be used as a correction procedure.

How to Determine a Correct Response

Each rate data program is structured to increase the frequency of a specific class of responses, such as vocal responses. Within the response guidelines, a variety of different responses may be counted as correct. For example, if the desired response is *vocal,* any phoneme is correct as long as it meets the program guidelines. In other words, in all steps and tests, a correct response is one that is elicited by specified stimuli and that meets the program specifications without guidance.

How to Measure Progress

In rate data programs, the child is required to make correct responses more frequently over successive 10-minute sessions. In other words, successive steps have basically the same task conditions (stimuli) and behaviors but different criteria. Each test and step specifies the minimum number of responses that must be emitted without guidance during this 10-minute session for the child to meet criterion.

The criteria in rate data programs require the child to increase the rate and variety of her responses. This dual criteria insures that the child learns more than one stereotypic response. If, for example, the program is used to increase vocal responses, any phoneme may be a correct response. However, more than one phoneme must be emitted to meet criterion.

As long as the child meets criterion on each successive step, she is demonstrating progress. If, however, the child fails to meet this criterion on any step, the standard steps need to be *modified* or expanded. This modification involves breaking a step into smaller steps to allow for more gradual progress. Thus, progress is documented as the child meets successive criteria on the standard steps with these modifications.

How to Present a Rate Data Session

During the session, the child is presented with stimuli and given as many trials or opportunities to respond as possible. Because the criterion standard is a ratio of correct responses to time, it is important that each session last 10 minutes. The response ratio is effected if you should increase or decrease the length of the session.

Another variable that can affect response rate is the frequency of trials. If a child begins to respond, trials usually occur at a rapid rate so that criterion is met. However, if a child does not respond (typically in rate data programs, an error is *no* response rather than an overt action), it is necessary to slow the pace to the specified latency. The criterion for each step has been set to allow the slowest appropriate pace (e.g., the number of trials that can be given in 10 minutes if the entire latency has to elapse for each trial). If the pace is slowed even further, the child will receive insufficient trials to meet criterion.

How to Record Rate Data

The standard data sheet for rate data programs is found on page 447. It contains space to write information and lines to record responses. It can be used to record responses made by one child on one program, from pretest through posttest. Hence, all documentation of progress during skill acquisition (i.e., responses on each step and any modifications) is accumulated on the same sheet. (Extra sheets may be attached, of course, to provide more space.)

PRETEST PROCEDURES

How to Present a Pretest Trial

The general test procedures for all programs specify that an attention cue is given before each trial, all task cues are presented as specified, and each response is recorded without any specific feedback. On rate data tests, there is a slightly different application to these rules. For example, attention is still important, but rate data programs are for the nonresponding child. To require eye contact before every trial is often impractical in terms of the intent of the program, the current behaviors of the child, and the pace at which trials may occur. In addition, the stimuli presented include by definition almost all activities that may be used as attention cues. Therefore, in a rate data test, you may begin the trial (i.e., begin to present stimuli) before the child is actually attending. However, the child should always be in a position in which she is ready to respond.

In rate data pretests, there is one exception to the rule that no specific feedback is given after a response. Some rate data programs specifically state that you should imitate a correct response since this is part of a natural interaction. However, the child is not praised for a correct response nor does she receive any correction for an error. The only feedback specifically used on some rate data tests is the imitation of a correct response.

How to Record a Pretest

From the general trial model, each stimulus or trial in a rate data test results in either a correct response or an error (overt action or no response within the specified latency). However, as has been noted before, rate data criterion is based only on the number of correct responses in relation to time, not in relation to errors or to the total number of responses. At times, it may be difficult to record data and present stimuli at a rapid pace. Since errors are not calculated in the criterion measure, you may write down only +'s or use a wrist counter to keep a tally of the total number of correct responses. In addition, you should record the different responses made to insure that a variety is included in the total number of correct responses.

For example, full recording might look like this:

PRE   +000+0+ +000+0+000+0+ +   different sounds: ä, ŭ, ĕ, m, d

You may simply write the total number of correct responses if you used a wrist counter:

PRE Total = 9 + 's   different sounds: ä, ŭ, ĕ, m, d

The total number of correct responses determines whether the child met criterion:

PRE + + + + + + + +   different sounds: ä, ŭ, ĕ, m, d

How to Score a Pretest

By looking at the total number of correct responses, a decision can be made as to whether the child passed the test or needs work on the skill. If the total is the same or more than the criterion specified (including the number of different responses), the child has passed the pretest. Any total less than criterion indicates failure. A child cannot fail a test until the full 10 minutes have elapsed.

TEACHING PROCEDURES

How to Present a Teaching Trial

The teaching trials in rate data programs follow the general teaching procedures, with specific applications. Before a stimulus is presented, the child's readiness to respond is insured either by an attention cue or by the child's position, as discussed in the pretest section. Each trial is presented according to the General Strategy guidelines. After latency, the child's response is immediately reinforced or corrected as appropriate, and then recorded. As in rate data pretesting, you may shortcut recording by writing only the correct responses.

How to Reinforce a Correct Response

When the child makes a correct response during a teaching step, immediately reinforce her and state why the response is correct: "GOOD, YOU SAID "AH!" Some rate data programs specify that the correct response be imitated as another kind of feedback. This imitation is in addition to any other type of reinforcement.

How to Correct an Error

Each rate data program gives specific directions to correct errors. If a motor response is required, correction is usually physical guidance to perform an action within the program guidelines. However, it is impractical if not impossible to physically guide a vocal response. (Note that cues such as stroking the face or even patting the throat are tactile stimuli and do not actually guide the child to push air through her vocal cords.) Because it is unrealistic to attempt to physically guide a vocal response, the vocal rate data programs typically have no correction other than to go on to another trial.

How to Score a Step

Rate data steps are recorded in a manner similar to test recording. Although each stimulus could result in a correct response or an error that may be corrected, only the total number of correct responses is essential to document criteria. Therefore, only the total number of correct responses, either written individually or from a tally on a wrist counter, need be recorded on the data sheet. By comparing this tally to the criterion, it can be determined if the child is responding at an appropriate rate, with the appropriate number of different responses.

On rate data programs, the child is allowed a minimum number of sessions that do not meet criterion before the step is modified or expanded. If the child has not responded at the criterion rate after the fourth attempt (i.e., fourth 10-minute session), write *M* to indicate modification should occur. That step is then broken down into smaller successive steps. This type of modification allows the child to increase her rate of responding more gradually than the children did on whom the program was standardized.

The following example illustrates how rate data steps are scored:

Date	Min.	Step	Response	Comments
			S/1 Criterion	= any 5 responses
10/16	10	S/1	+++	first session: criterion not met
10/17	10	S/1	++	second session: criterion not met
10/18	10	S/1	+++++	pass: go on to S/2
			S/2 Criterion	= 10 responses, 2 different actions
10/19	10	S/2	actions: turn, poke, shake ++++++	first session: criterion not met
10/20	10	S/2	actions: pull, turn ++++	second session: criterion not met
10/23	10	S/2	actions: poke, pull +++++	third session: criterion not met
10/24	10	S/2	actions: shake, turn ++++++++	Ⓜ fourth session: criterion not met

Whenever four sessions have been presented and step criterion has not yet been met, that change should be modified according to the following procedures.

MODIFICATION PROCEDURES

Types of Modification

Because rate data programs allow you to select any stimuli within the stated guidelines, you may change those task conditions at any time without modification. In these programs, modification involves adding extra steps that change the criterion more gradually. The two basic choices are:

- Add extra practice on the previous step; and
- increase the rate more gradually.

These two alternatives may be used in addition to the suggestions listed for specific programs.

In some cases, the child may pass the last step only after two or three attempts. Or, the child may perform inconsistently from day to day. If this occurs, allow the child to repeat the last step that she performed successfully. She might repeat the step several times before she progresses to the step where failure occurred. The modification would appear on the data sheet like this:

Date	Min.	Step	Response	Comments
			S/1 Criterion	= any 5 sounds
10/15	10	S/1	++ ä ŭ	first session
10/16	10	S/1	+ ŭ	second session
10/17	10	S/1	ŭ ä m +++++++++	pass: go on to S/2
			S/2 Criterion = 10	sounds, 2 different
10/18	10	S/2	+++++ m ŭ	first session
10/19	10	S/2	++++ ă k ŭ	second session
10/22	10	S/2	++++++ ŭ	third session
10/23	10	S/2	+++++ ŭ Ⓜ	fourth session
			modification: on each of	meet S/1 criterion 4 days
10/24	10	S/2A	+++++ d ŭ	day 1: pass
10/25	10	S/2B	+++++++++ m ä	day 2: pass
10/26	10	S/2C	+++++++ k ŭ m	day 3: pass
10/29	10	S/2D	++++++++ ŭ m ĕ	day 4: pass
			Modification to original	complete: return S/2
10/30	10	S/2	ä ŭ g +++++++++	pass: go on to S/3

Note that the modification steps were coded *A, B, C* and so on, to the number of the step which the child failed. As soon as the child passes the modification step(s), repeat the original step.

Increasing the Rate More Gradually

A program may be modified by adding steps that increase the performance criterion gradually. The modification would look like this on the data sheet:

Date	Min.	Step	Response	Comments
			S/1 Criterion	= any 5 actions
10/15	10	S/1	++	first session
10/16	10	S/1	+++	second session
10/17	10	S/1	++	third session
10/18	10	S/1	+++ Ⓜ	fourth session
			modification more	= increase rate gradually
10/19	10	S/1A	++++	S/1A = any 2 actions: pass
10/22	10	S/1B	+++	S/1B = any 3 actions: pass
10/23	10	S/1C	+++++	S/1C = any 4 actions: pass
			modification return	complete: to original S/1
10/24	10	S/1	++++++	pass: go on to S/2

The child progresses through the program until failure occurs, progresses through a series of modification steps, then on through the final steps.

POSTTEST PROCEDURES

How to Present a Posttest Trial

After the child passes the last program step, she is ready to be posttested, using the general testing strategies that apply to rate data tests. Response readiness is insured; task cues are presented; and after latency, the response is recorded. As noted in pretesting, the imitation of a correct response is allowed as specific feedback. As in all programs, rate data posttesting insures the presence of the skill in at least three different situations: POST 1 is in the same situation as the teaching steps, while POST 2 and 3 contain slight variations in task conditions. These posttests are presented in order.

How to Remediate a POST 1 Failure

Since POST 1 is identical to the last program step except for the general procedural difference between testing and teaching (i.e., specific feedback), a failure in POST 1 suggests a problem with reinforcement. Usually this problem can be remedied by reviewing the last step (with reinforcement) to build the child's "confidence" in her own response, then by repeating POST 1 (without reinforcement). For example:

Date	Min.	Step	Response	Comments
			Criterion = 25	responses, 5 different acts
10/22	10	POST 1	total = 14 +'s actions: pull, push, turn, poke, bang	fail: review last step
10/23	10	S/5	total = 29 +'s actions: bang, turn, push, pull	pass: repeat POST 1
10/24	10	POST 1	total = 26 +'s actions: turn, poke, shake, push, pull	pass

How to Remediate a POST 2 or 3 Failure

When the child can respond at the criterion rate without extra feedback, she is ready to try varied situations on POST 2, then POST 3. Here, failure may indicate a need to review the skill in the *new* situation: Teach the program steps again but with the specified changes. However, since the child has already performed at the criterion rate under the old conditions, the rate may increase more rapidly this time.

To review, present the first step. (Remember that in a rate data program, successive steps are the same except for the criterion). At the end of this session, you can identify the child's initial rate of response in the new situation. Based on this initial rate, write and circle the step code for the step on which the child has just met criterion (i.e., the highest step at which the child met criterion during the session). Continue to review all steps in order. You may skip steps if the child's high level of performance warrants it. Then repeat the posttest that was failed. For example:

Date	Min.	Step	Response	Comments
			criterion :	Post 2 = 25 responses, 5 different
10/25	10	POST 2	Total = 9 +'s, 3 different	fail = review all steps in the new situation
			criterion :	S/1 = 5 responses S/2 = 10 responses, 2 diff.
10/26	10	S/1 (S/2)	Total = 11 +'s, 3 different	pass: count as S/2, since child met criterion for that step, as well as S/1
			criterion :	S/3 = 15 responses, 3 different

499

Date	Min.	Step	Response	Comments
10/28	10	5/3	total = 15 +'s, 3 different	pass
			criterion: 4 different	5/4 = 20 responses, 5/5 = 25 responses, 5 different
10/29	10	5/4 (5/5)	total = 26 +'s, 5 different	pass: count as 5/5, since child met criterion for that step as well as 5/4: go on to POST 2
			Criterion:	POST 2 = 25 responses, 5 different
10/30		POST 2	total = 28 +'s, 6 different	pass
10/31		POST 3	total = 26 +'s, 7 different	pass

This shortcut procedure may be used anytime a child is meeting higher than specified criterion during instruction.

Follow-Up

After the program is complete (i.e., the child has passed POST 3), you will need to insure that the child continues to generalize the skill to new situations and maintains her level of performance. To write such a program, refer to module 6, Developing Instructional Programs. In addition, the "Follow-Up" section of the Program Overview indicates ways to use the skill in other situations and other programs in the curriculum that may be appropriate to teach at this time. Thus, to conduct follow-up:

- Write a program to insure use and generalization; and
- continue to other suggested programs as appropriate.

SUMMARY

1. Each rate data program is recorded on a separate data sheet.
2. A pretest is given to verify that the child cannot perform the skill:
   a. Trials are given by general pretest procedures with the specification that:
      (1) The child must be in a position to attend, even if she does not make eye contact; and
      (2) a correct response is imitated on some programs.
   b. Only correct responses are recorded.
   c. The child must respond correctly the specified number of times during the 10-minute session.
   d. A testing session lasts 10 minutes.
3. Steps are taught in order:
   a. Trials are given by general teaching procedures.
   b. All correct responses are reinforced; some are also imitated.
   c. All errors are corrected as specified in the program.
   d. Only correct responses need to be recorded.
   e. A session lasts 10 minutes.
   f. A passed step is one in which the child meets criterion during the 10-minute session.

g. When four sessions elapse and the child has not met criterion on a single step, write an Ⓜ to indicate that modification will occur.

4. Modification consists of writing extra step(s) to:
   a. Add extra practice on the previous step; or
   b. increase the rate more gradually; or
   c. use specific strategies as suggested in the program.

5. Three posttests are given to verify that the child can perform the skill in three different situations:
   a. Trials are given by general posttesting procedures, as applied to rate data.
   b. A test is passed when the child meets criterion during the 10-minute session.
   c. POSTS 1, 2, and 3 are given in order.
   d. Failure on POST 1 is remediated by reviewing the last step, then repeating POST 1.
   e. Failure on Post 2 or 3 is remediated by reviewing all steps with the new task cues, then repeating the failed test.
   f. When reviewing steps, if the child meets a higher criterion than that specified for the step you are teaching, count the higher step as passed.

SECTION 2:
4/5 Data Programs

OVERVIEW

Characteristics

Some programs require the child to respond appropriately to increasingly more complex stimulus cues. Behaviors are shaped through successive steps or approximations. Cue properties are added to the stimuli, then faded out gradually so that the child eventually responds with no cues and without other assistance. (This procedure is referred to as *stimulus shaping, cueing-fading,* and *prompting-fading* in different curricula.) The programs in this curriculum have a criterion standard that requires the child to respond correctly 4 out of 5 trials on each step before she progresses to the next step. To emphasize this characteristic, they have been called *4/5 data* programs.

How to Determine a Correct Response

In the Program, each test and step has specifications for each task cue. These indicate the conditions for a correct response. The 4/5 data programs require careful study since cues change from step to step. Since conditions change from step to step, the standards for a correct response also change.
Some of the cues that often occur in 4/5 data programs are:

VERBAL CUES: Gestures or extra directions separate from and in addition to the command.
DEMONSTRATION: Partial or complete modeling of the task.
GUIDANCE: Partial or complete physical assistance in performing the task.
MATERIALS: Use of color, size, shape, position, or other properties to indicate a particular response.
RESPONSE PRACTICE: Practice of the response (by demonstration or guidance) before the command.
DELAYED CUE: Presentation of a cue 3 seconds after latency begins if the child is not initiating a correct response.

Note that although standard cues are often used, cues are always fully described in the General Strategy section of the Program.

How to Measure Progress

In the 4/5 data programs, a high percentage of correct responses is required to demonstrate the skill on each step and test. This percent is reflected in the ratio "4 correct out of 5 trials." The child demonstrates progress by meeting this criterion on each step. If, however, the child fails to meet this criterion on any step (i.e., she makes too many errors), the standard steps need to be *modified* or expanded so that progress can be adequately measured. In 4/5 data programs, such modification involves breaking that step into smaller steps to allow for more gradual progress. Thus, progress in skill acquisition is documented as the child meets successive criterion on the standard steps, with modifications (extra steps).

The standard data sheet for recording child performance on 4/5 data programs is found on page 447. It contains space to write identifying information and horizontal lines to record responses. It can be used to record responses made by one child on one program, from pretest through posttest. Hence, all documentation of progress during skill acquisition (i.e., responses on each step and any modifications) is accumulated on the same sheet. (Extra sheets may be attached, of course, to provide more space.)

PRETEST PROCEDURES

How to Present a Pretest Trial

All trials on 4/5 pretests, are given according to the general pretest procedures. Prior to each trial, an attention cue is given to insure that the child is ready to respond. All task cues for each trial are presented as specified. After each response, record $+$, $-$, or θ (no response, counted as an error) without giving specific feedback.

How to Score a Pretest

A defined number of correct responses are required to meet criterion on 4/5 program pretests. If the child makes two errors, testing stops. If the child makes incorrect responses, additional trials are presented. If the child makes four correct responses, she has passed the program. The following examples illustrate how pretests are scored:

PASS: 4 correct	FAIL (needs instruction): 2 errors	
+ + + +	− −	+ + − −
+ − + + +	+ − −	− + + + −
+ + − + +	− + −	+ − + + −
+ + + − +	+ − + −	+ + − + −
− + + + +	− + + −	+ + + − −

TEACHING PROCEDURES

How to Present a Teaching Trial

The presentation of teaching trials in 4/5 programs follows general teaching procedures. Each trial is preceded by an attention cue to insure response readiness, all task cues are presented as specified for the step, and all responses receive feedback, either reinforcement for correct responses (as defined by the conditions and behavior for the step) or immediate correction for errors. Responses are recorded as $+$, $-$, or θ (counted as an error).

How to Correct an Error

The 4/5 data programs typically direct you to use general correction procedures. Thus, you may elect to refocus (R), demonstrate (D), or use guidance (G) to cover errors. Because errors are critical to determine when modifications are needed, we highly recommend that after each error, you record in parentheses which correction procedure you used and whether the child performed with this correction as suggested in module 3, General Instructional Procedures. In other words, rather than marking just " − " for the original error, we recommend that you record " − (R +)" with the information on correction noted in parentheses.

How to Score a Step

Although two errors indicate failure on a 4/5 test, teaching steps allow a minimal amount of error to occur so that the child has an opportunity to learn through the correction feedback. On 4/5 data steps, more than five trials may be given to allow the child a chance to learn through correction. The first few errors (up to three) are not counted in the learning criterion. That is, only the *last* five trials of a step count toward criterion. As long as the child has not made four errors, continue to present trials until she either passes the step by responding correctly 4 out of the last 5 trials or makes a fourth error.

Instead of *failure*, excessive error (defined as four errors) indicates that the child's learning is progressing more slowly than did the learning of students on whom the program was standardized. In other words, excessive error reflects that the change in stimulus conditions or response requirements between steps is too great for this particular child. When excessive error occurs, the program is individualized by expanding or modifying the step to provide for more gradual changes in task conditions. When a fourth error occurs before the child passes the step, mark an *M* on the data sheet, and indicate that modification is needed.

Notice that whenever an error occurs, it is corrected, and the corrected response is recorded in parentheses. However, only the responses outside of parentheses (i.e., responses NOT receiving correction assistance) are counted. If a session ends in the middle of a step, all responses are cumulative, meaning that you do not need to start the step over at the next session. Count all responses on the step, regardless of when the trials occurred.

The following examples illustrate how to record and score step data:

PASS: 4 correct out of the last 5 trials	MODIFY: any 4 errors on a step (before criterion is met)
+ + − (R +) + + + − (D +) + + +	+ − (R +) + − (R +) − (D +) − (D +) Ⓜ
− (R +) − (D +) + + − (R +) + + + − (G +) + + − (G +) + +	− (R +) − (D +) − (D +) − (G +) Ⓜ
− (R − D +) + − (D +) + + + − (G +) − (G +) − (G +) + + + +	+ + − (G +) + − (D +) + + − (D − G +) − (G +) Ⓜ

Whenever four errors have been made before step criterion is met, that step is modified according to the following procedure.

MODIFICATION PROCEDURES

Types of Modification

There are several ways to expand a 4/5 program to allow for more gradual learning. Each method involves adding an extra step(s) to bridge the gap between the previous step (that the child has passed) and the current step causing difficulty (where the child made four errors). The main choices are:

- Add extra practice on the previous step;
- fade out the existing cue(s) more gradually;
- add a new kind of cue, then fade it out gradually; and
- add delayed cues.

You may also use specific modification suggestions in the program. By adding a step(s) to provide for one of these modifications, the program is expanded at the point where the individual child needs more work. Note that these modifications follow typical strategies also found in some standard programs. In addition, general information on writing cueing-fading strategies is included in module 6, Developing Instructional Programs.

Adding Extra Practice

In some cases, the child may simply require some extra practice on the previous step before she can succeed on the current step. This often occurs when the child made errors on the previous step before she passed it. In addition, it may occur with a child who performs inconsistently from day to day. Remember that standard programs contain only the number of trials typically needed. Any one child may require more repetition than this.

In this situation, a modification step(s) is added between the previous step and the current step. The new step(s) is identical to the previous one but has more trials, still in the 4 correct out of 5 criterion ratio. Depending on how much extra practice is needed, the modification step(s) might require: 8 correct out of 10 trials, 12 correct out of 15 trials, or 4 correct out of 5 trials on each of 4 different days. This last modification would look like this on the data sheet:

Date	Min.	Step	Response	Comments
10/15	15	5/1	+-(R+)-(O+)+++ -(O+)+	pass
10/16	9	5/2	-(R+)-(R+)-(O+)-(O+)Ⓜ	fail: 4 "errors"
			modification: 4/5 criterion	repeat 5/1 with for 4 different days.
10/17	8	5/2A	+-(R+)+-(R+)+++	Day 1: pass
10/18	7	5/2B	-(O+)-(R+)++++	Day 2: pass
10/19	9	5/2C	++++	Day 3: pass
10/22	6	5/2D	++++	Day 4: pass;
			modification complete: return to	original 5/2
10/23	9	5/2	-(R+)++++	pass: continue to 5/3

Note that the modification steps are coded *A, B, C,* and so on, to the number of the step originally failed. Then, as soon as the child passes the modification, repeat the original step.

Fading an Existing Cue More Gradually

As noted before, the steps in 4/5 data programs typically describe a *fading* procedure in that the cue or extra assistance is gradually faded out or removed in the successive steps. When a child makes four errors on one step, this may indicate that the extra assistance has been removed too quickly. In this case, a new step(s) is added between the previous step, which the child passed, and the current one, where she has made four errors. This new modification step has the same type of cue as in the previous step, but in a less obvious form. In each modification step, the cue is presented in a less obvious way until it is in the level specified.

For example, if the child is to pick the correct choice, Step 1 may specify that you hold out the object to the child, and Step 2 may have you only tap the object as a cue. The modification steps might fade this cue more gradually and would appear like this on the data sheet:

Date	Min.	Step	Response	Comments
10/16	8	S/1	++++	pass (object held out)
10/17	10	S/2	-(R+)-(0+)+-(R+)-(R+) ⓜ	fail: 4 errors (object tapped)
			modification:	child picks up object when:
10/18	7	S/2A	++++	S/2A: object is held half way out to child (4/5): pass
10/19	9	S/2B	++++	S/2B: object is held one-third way to child (4/5): pass
10/20	8	S/2C	++++	S/2C: object is picked up then replaced and tapped (4/5): pass
			modification complete:	return to original S/2 (object is tapped)
10/23	7	S/2	+-(R+) +++	pass: continue to S/3

Adding a New Cue, Then Fading It Out

However, in some cases, it may be difficult to objectively describe or present an intermediate cue between two steps in the standard program. Or, the child may begin to respond consistently to some irrelevant cue. In these situations, you may modify by adding steps with a new cue to insure that the child focuses on the critical part of the task.

The first modification step is the same as the current step (where the child made four errors) with the addition of a new cue. The rest of the modification steps fade out this cue until it is completely removed, leaving the original step. For example, the standard step may include a cue to point to an object. Since it would be confusing to "partially point," extra cues or directions might be used to modify the step. The data sheet would look like this:

Date	Min.	Step	Response	Comments
10/16	7	S/4	++++	pass (with pointing cue)

Date	Min.	Step	Response	Comments
10/17	10	S/5	-(R+)-(R+)-(R+)-(0+) Ⓜ	fail: 4 errors (no cues)
			modification	S finds the object:
10/18	6	S/5A	++++	S/5A: with cues "Look under the cup" (4/5) - pass
10/19	9	S/5B	+-(R+)+++	S/5B: with cue "Look all around" (4/5) - pass
			modification	complete: return to original S/5 (no cues)
10/21	8	S/5	++++	pass: last step, go on to POST 1

Adding Delayed Cues

Sometimes a modification may involve the use of a delayed cue. A *delayed cue* is presented after latency has already begun, such as after 3 seconds. A delayed cue is based on initial child response. It is presented only if the child begins to make the wrong response, or makes no response, during those 3 seconds. At this point, the delayed cue is given. (Note that until the delayed cue is given, no error should be recorded, since this cue is part of the task conditions for the response.) If the child is already making a correct response, the delayed cue is omitted. This strategy is often used to fade demonstrations or verbal cues, either those in the standard program or those added during modification.

For example, one step in the program may require the child to respond after a demonstration, and the next step might include no cue. To modify the program, you might add a step that incorporates a delayed demonstration (e.g., demonstrate after 3 seconds if the child is not responding correctly). More trials might be added in the 4/5 ratio (e.g., 8/10, 16/20). The modification might look like this on the data sheet:

Date	Min.	Step	Response	Comments
10/16	8	S/5	++++	pass (with demonstration)
10/17	10	S/6	-(0+)-(0+)-(0+) Ⓜ	fail: 4 errors no cues
			modification:	use delayed demonstration for 8 correct out of 10 trials
10/18	9	S/6A	+++++	(continue tomorrow)
10/19	5	S/6A cont'd	+++	pass: modification complete- return to original s/6
10/20	7	S/6	++-(0+)++	pass: last step, go on to POST1

507

Thus, the child continues through the program and meets criterion on each step, including modification steps.

POSTTEST PROCEDURES

How to Present a Posttest

All trials on 4/5 posttests are given according to the general posttest procedures. An attention cue is given to insure readiness, the task cues are presented as reinforcement or correction. In addition to these general trial procedures, the three posttests on a 4/5 program are presented in order:

POST 1	After the child passes the last teaching step
POST 2	After the child passes POST 1
POST 3	After the child passes POST 2

Each 4/5 posttest is scored the same way as a pretest. A maximum of five trials are given with 4 correct out of the possible 5 trials being "pass." Two errors indicate failure.

How to Remediate a POST 1 Failure

POST 1 is identical to the last program step except for the general procedural difference between teaching and testing: reinforcement and correction of responses. If the child can pass the last step but not POST 1, the change in the procedure (i.e., no reinforcement or correction) may have "confused" the child. Usually this problem can be remedied by reviewing the last step (with specific feedback). After this review, repeat POST 1 again but reinforce the child for attending and being ready to work. For example,

POST 1	+ − + −	"Seemed unsure when I gave no feedback."
S/5	+ + + +	"Performed well with reinforcement."
POST 1	+ − + + −	"Still unsure; I'll repeat S/5 with feedback on every other response."
S/5	+ + + +	"Did well with this reduced feedback."
POST 1	+ + − + +	"Pass: go on to POST 2."

How to Remediate a POST 2 or 3 Failure

Since POST 2 and 3 conditions are slightly different, failure here may indicate a need to review the skill in the new situation. Teach the program steps again but with the *new* change. When a child fails either POST 2 or POST 3, all steps should be reviewed with the new cues. However, since the child has been through these steps before, learning may progress more quickly this time. Anytime the child responds correctly on the first two trials of a review step, you may shortcut the rest of the trials for that step and go on to the next step. If she makes an error on either of the first two trials of a step, correct that error and give trials on that step until the child responds correctly 4 out of the last 5 trials. Then go on to the next step until all steps have been reviewed. For example,

POST 2	− −	"Fail: teach steps with new conditions."
S/1	+ − (R +) + + +	"Error in second trial: teach step to criterion."
S/2	+ +	"First 2 responses correct: go on to next step."
S/3	+ +	

S/4	− (R+) + + + +	"Error in first trial: teach step to criterion."
S/5	+ +	"Pass: repeat POST 2."
POST 2	+ + − + +	"Pass."
POST 3	+ + + +	"Pass: program complete."

Follow-Up

After the program is complete (i.e., the child has passed POST 3), you will need to insure that the child continues to generalize the skill to new situations and maintains her level of performance. To write a program, refer to module 6, Developing Instructional Programs. In addition, the "Follow-Up" section of the Program Overview indicates ways to use the skill in other situations and other programs in the curriculum that may be appropriate to teach at this time. Thus, to follow-up:

- Write a program to insure use and generalization; and
- continue to other suggested programs as appropriate.

DISCRIMINATION PROGRAMS

How to Identify a Discrimination Program

Several programs in the language and cognitive areas require the child to *discriminate* (respond differently) between two different concepts. For example, to teach the word *shoe*, it is necessary to teach the child to pick a shoe when the word *shoe* is spoken, and conversely, not pick a shoe when the word *cup* is spoken (i.e., pick the cup). OR, in a program that teaches matching, the child must learn to pick up the bowl when a sample bowl is displayed but pick the spoon when it is the sample.

All programs of this type state in the Objective and the Conditions-Behavior-Criteria sections that the child must respond correctly to both concepts ("4 correct out of 5 for each target"). As specified in the General Strategy on these programs, trials for the two concepts are randomly alternated. The child cannot pass a step or test if she meets criterion on only one of the two concepts.

How to Record a Discrimination Program

To facilitate scoring, responses to each concept are kept on separate lines and labeled. For example, if the child is to discriminate cup and spoon, all pretest trials for cup are recorded on one line, and all pretest trials for spoon are recorded on the line immediately underneath. This separation of data for the two concepts is used on all steps and tests throughout the program.

How to Score a Discrimination Program

On any test or step, the child must respond correctly 4 out of 5 trials on each concept in order to pass. On tests, this means that she cannot make two errors on any one concept, although she can make one error on each and still pass (i.e., meet 4 out of 5 on each). For example:

Test Pass:	cup	+ + − + +	PASS: 4 correct out of 5 on
	spoon	+ − + + +	each concept, with trials randomly alternated

OR

Test Fail:	cup	+ − + −	FAIL: 2 errors on *cup*, with trials
	spoon	+ − +	randomly alternated

On steps, the errors are cumulative, meaning that a total of four errors (regardless of which concept) indicates a need for modification. For example:

| Step Pass: | cup | $+\ +\ -(R+)\ +\ +$ | PASS: 4 correct out of the last 5 trials on each concept, with trials randomly alternated |
| | spoon | $-(R+)\ -(D+)\ +\ +\ +\ +$ | |

| Step Fail: | cup | $+\ +\ -(D+)$ | |
| | spoon | $-(D+)\ -(R+)\ -(R+)\ Ⓜ$ | FAIL: 4 errors total, with trials randomly alternated |

SUMMARY

1. Each 4/5 data program is recorded on a separate data sheet.

2. A pretest is given to verify that the child cannot perform the skill:
   a. Trials are presented with general pretest procedures.
   b. The child must respond correctly 4 out of 5 trials to pass.
   c. Testing stops when two errors have been made.

3. Steps are taught in order:
   a. Trials are presented with general teaching procedures.
   b. All correct responses are reinforced.
   c. All errors are corrected by Refocus, Demonstration, or Guidance.
   d. Correction is recorded in parentheses but does not count toward criterion.
   e. Trials are given until the child responds correctly 4 out of 5 trials, OR until four errors are made on the step.
   f. When four errors are made on a step, write Ⓜ to indicate modification will occur.

4. Modification consists of writing an extra step(s):
   a. Add extra practice on the previous step.
   b. Fade out program cues more gradually.
   c. Add a new cue, and fade it out gradually.
   d. Add a delayed cue, then remove it.
   e. Use additional strategies suggested in specific programs.

5. Three posttests are given to verify that the child can perform the skill in three different situations:
   a. Trials are presented with general posttesting procedures, which include no correction.
   b. A test is passed when the child responds correctly 4 out of 5 trials.
   c. POST 1, 2, and 3 are given in order.
   d. Failure on POST 1 is remediated by reviewing the last step, then repeating POST 1.
   e. Failure on POST 2 and 3 is remediated by reviewing all steps with the new task cues, then repeating the failed test.
   f. When reviewing steps, if the child responds correctly on the first two trials of a step, skip the rest of the trials on that step, and go on to the next step.

SECTION 3:
Skill Analysis Programs

Some skills require the child to develop muscle tone, strength, coordination, and/or balance to perform the target. In these programs, the motor components of the skill have been analyzed into discrete subskills the child must be able to perform to master the target behavior. Skill acquisition is documented as the child learns to perform increasingly more of the subskills, until she can combine all of them as she performs the target unassisted. Since the target skill has been broken down into motor components, these programs have been called *skill analysis* programs in this curriculum.

The skill analysis curriculum includes most programs in the Fine and Gross Motor areas, as well as those that involve mouth control in Eating Skills (i.e., Chewing) and Expressive Language Skills (i.e., Shaping Words). Because all of these programs involve muscle development, we highly recommend that you use them only after consultation with a physical, occupational, or speech therapist. In particular, if the child exhibits delayed development, as well as specific handicaps (e.g., cerebral palsy, cleft palate), these programs should be used only under supervision by the specialist. With this caution in mind, these programs offer a structured procedure to teach skills that involve motor control. Any additions or deletions recommended by the specialist should be integrated into the standard program.

Each skill analysis program specifies the conditions for and the definition of the target skill and each subskill. In the Conditions-Behavior-Criteria section, each subskill is numbered for identification. These subskills need not be taught sequentially, but they have been presented in the typical order in which they are required. The last numbered "component" is a restatement of the target skill, emphasized with an asterisk. Throughout the standard program, only the unassisted performance of these components (under the specified conditions) is considered correct.

In the skill analysis programs, the child gradually acquires more of the subskills until she can perform the target, unassisted. Daily instruction is presented on one or more subskills, and probe data is taken each week to determine the subskills she can perform unassisted. The child demonstrates progress when new subskills are evidenced on successive probes. If, however, the child fails to perform new subskills, the standard subskills need to be *modified* or broken into smaller components so that her progress can be more adequately measured. Thus, progress on skill acquisition is documented as the child performs more subskills on successive probes, with modifications if needed.

Children require much time and practice during skill acquisition because these programs focus on muscle development. Depending on the individual child, you can expect to modify these programs frequently. Although this is true, the standard program and the specified modification procedures will enable you to systematically teach and document progress.

Where to Record the Data

The standard data sheet for recording skill analysis programs is found on page 449. It contains space to write identifying information. Boxed sections are located below, for each test and probe. Extra sheets may be used. Numbered blanks and five corresponding columns of numbers are located within each box. Fill in the blanks with the word or phrase that corresponds to the parts of the program. The number columns are provided to record performance on each subskill. Cross out those numbers you do not need. This data sheet is used to record all performance on the program, from pretest through posttest. Additional sheets may be needed.

PRETEST PROCEDURES

How to Present a Pretest Trial

Skill analysis pretests follow the typical sequence: provide an attention cue before every trial, present the task cues for the target skill, observe latency, and record the child's response without differential feedback.

Skill analysis programs often make use of a natural consequence for a reinforcer. If the child sits and attends, she may play with a toy. However, if she loses her balance, she won't be able to reach the toy. As indicated in the General Strategy, present the "natural consequence" if the child performs the target. However, do not praise or otherwise reinforce the response. If an error occurs, intervene only if the child is about to seriously hurt herself (e.g., fall backward).

How to Record a Pretest

The child's pretest performance is recorded next to the number designated for the target behavior. The standard symbols " + ", " − ", and "θ" (no response, counted as an error) are used. Each boxed section has room for five trials. During the pretest, record only the appropriate number for the target behavior:

*6. Target   6+ 6− 6+ 6+ 6+

Record the *pre* for pretest, the date, and the time required to complete the task. If trials are given at different times during the day, add the total number of minutes:

SUMMARY: PROBE # _PRE_

Date: _10/27_   Min. _15_

How to Score a Pretest

The child must meet the specified criterion of 4 correct responses out of 5 trials to pass the pretest. Continue to present trials until she has either performed the target unassisted four times or has made two errors. Testing stops after two errors since the child can no longer meet test criterion. For example:

*6. Target	6+	6−	6+	6+	6+	PASS: 4 correct out of 5 trials

OR

*6. Target	6−	6+	6−	6	6	FAIL: 2 errors

If a child fails the pretest, present a probe at the next session. Give the first probe to obtain diagnostic information. This procedure is described in the next session.

TEACHING PROCEDURES

Two basic procedures are used during the instructional phase of skill analysis programs:

- Daily practice on the subskills(s); and
- weekly probes to document acquisition of new subskills.

Since the instructional phase begins with a probe for baseline information, weekly probes will be discussed first.

PROBES

When to Take Probes

Although it is possible to record every skill opportunity on skill analysis programs, data collection has practical difficulties. First, data recording is often awkward when you must physically assist the child to complete a motor response chain. Second, progress may be slow. The increase in parts completed from one day to the next is usually negligible. For these reasons, probes are taken only once every fifth instructional day (i.e., 4 days of practice, then a probe day).

How to Present a Probe Trial

Probe trials are presented with general teaching procedures: Insure attention before every trial, present task cues as specified, observe latency, and give immediate feedback on each response, either reinforcement for correct responses or correction on errors. In the skill analysis probes, however, there is a specific application of the term *trial*.

One or more component skills may occur when the target skill is performed. For example, in sitting (target), the child must keep her head up, balance her trunk and keep it erect, and use her limbs as needed for support or balance. The conditions for each program part are specified to enable you to obtain information on a single component behavior. Therefore, one trial gives the opportunity to perform only one subskill.

How to Reinforce a Correct Response

Feedback is given immediately after performance on every subskill trial. Many programs specify a natural consequence, which should occur after the child performs the subskill or target. During instruction, this consequence should be presented as soon as the part is completed, whether performed with or without assistance. In addition, praise and/or other reinforcement is presented for a correct (unassisted) response.

How to Correct an Error

Each skill analysis program directs you to correct an error on a part by using any of the Suggestions listed after the Conditions-Behavior-Criteria section. These suggestions describe specific guidance and exercise strategies. Typically, it is easiest to use just the guidance strategies on probe trials, although any strategy is appropriate during daily practice.

In general, record the response for the subskill or target next to the appropriate number in the boxed section, using the symbols " + ", " − ", or "θ" (counted as an error). Trials on the subskills may be presented in any order. However, you do not need to give trials for each subskill on every probe.

In the early part of the instructional phase, it is inappropriate to probe the more difficult behaviors if the child's response deficits are severe. For example, in sitting (target), if the child can sit erect only with support at the shoulders (earlier subskill), she obviously cannot sit erect and use only her hands for balance (more difficult subskill). On the other hand, in the later part of the instructional phase, the child has already performed less difficult subskills to criterion and is now performing more difficult subskills that rely on the child's existing abilities. You do not need to probe those less complex skills. In addition, since it is time-consuming to probe each subskill, probe only those that are appropriate for the child.

Where the subskill or target is obviously too difficult for the child, you may omit trials on those parts. But you should indicate that the trial was omitted for this reason. In this case, write NA for "not appropriate to probe" next to the appropriate number(s) in the trial columns for that probe.

When the child has already performed a subskill at least the number of times recommended in the Criterion for that part during a previous probe(s), you may omit trials on that part(s). But you should indicate that the trial was omitted for this reason. In this case, write " ✓ " next to the appropriate number(s) to indicate that the child has previously performed that subskill to criterion. This marking should only be used when the child performs a more difficult subskill correctly during the probe. If she makes errors on the more difficult subskill, you should not assume that the child can still perform the easier subskill, even though she may have performed it to criterion. Note that the subskill criterion is only a suggestion for the minimum number of times a child should perform the subskill before you consider using the " ✓ " marking.

One column on the data sheet might appear like this:

1 ✓	The child previously met criterion on Parts 1 and 2, so you assume she still has those subskills, as demonstrated by her performance on Part 3. She was unable to perform Parts 4 and 5 unassisted on the probe; so Parts 6, 7, and 8 (target) were not probed at this time.
2 ✓	
3 +	
4 −	
5 −	
6 NA	
7 NA	
*8 NA	

Thus, the child was presented with trials for only Parts 3, 4, and 5. Note that these trials may be presented in any order and at different times during the day.

On a probe, up to five columns may be used, meaning up to five trials on each subskill. Based on the task and the child's endurance, we highly recommend giving five trials per appropriate subskill so that you have better information on the child. If you give fewer than five trials per subskill, give the same number of trials on each one. In any case, completely fill in those columns you use (e.g., mark "NA" or " ✓ " as appropriate). The data sheet for a probe might look like this:

1. ___	1 ✓	1 ✓	1 ✓	1 ✓	1
2. ___	2 ✓	2 ✓	2 ✓	2 ✓	2
3. ___	3 +	3 +	3 +	3 +	3
4. ___	4 −	4 +	4 −	4 −	4
5. ___	5 −	5 −	5 −	5 −	5
6. ___	6 NA	6 NA	6 NA	6 NA	6

| 7. _____ | 7 *NA* | 7 *NA* | 7 *NA* | 7 *NA* | 7 |
| *8. *target* | *8 *NA* | *8 *NA* | *8 *NA* | *8 *NA* | *8 |

How to Score a Probe

Progress on skill analysis programs is determined by an increase in the number of parts performed without assistance from one probe to the next. Count each " ✓ " as an assumed correct response and each "NA" as an assumed error. To determine the average number of parts completed, add the number of parts correct on all columns used. From the previous data sheet example, the child performed a total of 13 correct responses (counting " ✓ "'s and " + "'s) and 4 columns were used. Thus she performed an average of 3.25 parts correctly per column (13 ÷ 4).

Fill in this information in the space provided for that probe:

SUMMARY: PROBE # __3__
Date: _10/15_   Min. _30_ (total)
Average +'s per column _3.25_

Then fill in the average parts completed from the previous probe. (On Probe 1, this number is automatically 0.) The average parts gained between these probes is the difference between these two numbers. To continue this example, the data sheet would appear like this:

Ave. +'s per column on last probe _2.75_
Average parts gained _.5_

As long as the average parts gained is greater than 0, the child is progressing on successive probes. For example:

SUMMARY: PROBE # __3__
Date: _10/15_ Min. _30_
Average +'s per column _3.25_
Ave. +'s per column last probe _2.75_
Average parts gained _.5_

SUMMARY: PROBE # __4__
Date: _10/22_ Min. _25_
Average +'s per column _3.5_
Ave. +'s per column on last probe _3.25_
Average parts gained _.25_

When to Modify

If the child has not gained new skills (parts) after two successive probes, her progress is not occurring rapidly enough to be measured. Write Ⓜ after the second successive probe after the "Average parts gained 0." Modification procedures will be discussed after Daily Practice.

When to End the Individual Phase

When the child has performed the target skill 4 out of 5 trials on a probe, the instructional phase of the program is over. Until the child meets this criterion on a probe, instruction continues through two basic procedures: daily practice and weekly probes. Note that the child may learn to perform the target without necessarily meeting the suggested criterion on certain subskills. In this case, the only required criterion is to perform the target 4 out of 5 trials.

DAILY PRACTICE

How to Present Daily Practice

During daily practice, you may work on one or more subskills the child was unable to perform on the last probe. Specific strategies are described for each part under

Suggestions. Although you do not need to record response-by-response data, you should record on the data sheet that daily practice was given, as well as the time that was spent.

Spaces for you to record the dates and times of these practice sessions are on the data sheet under the summary probe information. There is space to record four sessions. After you complete the fourth daily session, present the next probe session to evaluate whether the child has made progress. Thus, although there is flexibility in the daily practice sessions, performance is always documented at regular intervals through probe sessions.

How to Use the Suggestions

Some *suggestions* describe how to apply a standard shaping procedure to teach the subskill. These suggestions usually involve gradual increases of time or distance. For example, to maintain an erect head position, the child is placed in position and reinforced for any brief interval of keeping her head up. Gradually, her head is kept erect for longer intervals before she is reinforced. Or, the child is first reinforced for any upward movement when her head is down. Gradually she is required to lift her head farther before she is reinforced.

Other *suggestions* describe how to apply a standard fading procedure to the subskill. At first, the child is physically guided to perform the task. Gradually she is required to perform more on her own before she is reinforced. For example, to maintain an erect head position, the child's head is held in position. Gradually less pressure is exerted on her head so that she must use her own muscles to help hold it up. The pressure is gradually decreased as her muscles strengthen, until she can maintain the position on her own.

A third type of *suggestion* involves the use of specific materials or equipment, such as wedges, beach balls, and standing tables. Each item is pictured with the child in position. These strategies usually involve a shaping or fading procedure as described above, while using the specified materials. After the child can perform the subskill with the materials, these materials are removed.

Caution

As noted before, consult a specialist before you use any of the skill analysis programs. Some suggestions that are appropriate for one child may be ineffective with or detrimental to another. After you have determined that a particular strategy is appropriate for your child, you may find that the child is resistant (e.g., refuses to perform; exhibits inappropriate behaviors, such as crying). Many children with severely delayed motor development resist learning new positions and skills. When this occurs and you are certain that the strategy is appropriate to the child, you should insist on some performance. This does not mean, however, that sessions on motor skills should involve a daily fight. Sessions should always be presented with as much reinforcement as possible. When the child resists a new position, movement, or activity, take time for her to get used to the new situation. If necessary, reinforce whenever she allows you just to touch her or place her in position. Gradually raise your criterion until she is reinforced only for performing.

Many children require relaxation exercises each day before they are ready to work on new skills. When this is appropriate, get instructions specific to your child from a physical therapist or other specialist. Use these relaxation exercises prior to every test, probe or daily session, and include the time required to complete them in the total time recorded for that session.

MODIFICATION PROCEDURES

How to Modify the Subskills

After you have worked on the selected strategy(ies) for a week, probe to determine whether the child can perform more subskills without assistance. Anytime she makes no gain in new parts on two successive probes, the program should be modified. This will enable you to document more gradual learning. Breaking a subskill into smaller components enables you to document increments of these smaller components during probes.

Each part may be further task analyzed by following the information included in the Suggestions. Although you may use a strategy informally during daily practice, in modification you actually revise the list of parts to obtain finer probe data. For example, where the strategy suggests increasing time, you could modify by specifying the time increments:

ORIGINAL	MODIFICATION
When the child's head is placed erect, she will maintain this position for 1 minute.......................................	A for 2 seconds
	B for 5 seconds
	C for 10 seconds
	D for 15 seconds
	E for 30 seconds
	F for 1 minute

Note that the modification is coded *A, B, C,* and so on, to the number of the subskill that is modified.

If the strategy suggests increasing distance, you can specify increments for distance:

ORIGINAL	MODIFICATION
When a toy is placed 5 feet away, the child will crawl forward to reach it	A 1 foot away
	B 2 feet away
	C 3 feet away
	D 4 feet away
	E 5 feet away

Or, if the strategy suggests fading assistance, you can specify the levels of assistance:

ORIGINAL	MODIFICATION
When the child is placed on her stomach with her head up and trunk at a 45° angle supported by her forearms, she will maintain this position for 1 minute	A when resting on a wedge
	B when held at the shoulders
	C when held at the elbows
	D unassisted

Further information on writing shaping or cueing-fading strategies is contained in module 6, Developing Instructional Programs.

With this expanded list of subskills, your probe data will reflect more gradual increments in the skill. Instruction then continues as before: Daily practice and weekly probes, using this expanded list of parts.

POSTTEST PROCEDURES

How to Present a Postest

After the child has passed instruction (i.e., performed the target correctly four out of five trials on a probe), she is ready to be posttested. Posttesting is essentially the same as pretesting. On each trial, response readiness is insured, task cues are presented, latency is observed, and the response on the target skill is recorded next to the appropriate number on the data sheet. Criterion is 4 correct responses out of 5 trials. Two errors indicate failure. As in all programs, posttesting insures the presence of the skill in at least three different situations. POST 1 is conducted with the same conditions as instruction (except, of course, for reinforcement or correction). POSTS 2 and 3 contain slight variations in these task conditions.

How to Remediate a Posttest Failure

When failure occurs on a posttest (two errors), review the instructional phase. Begin daily practice and weekly probing until the child performs the target skill to criterion on a probe. Then repeat the failed posttest. Note that if the failure occurs in POST 2 or 3, the instructional program should be reviewed with the *new* conditions.

Follow-Up

After the program is complete (i.e., the child has passed POST 3), you will need to insure that the child continues to generalize the skill to new situations and maintains her level of performance. To write a program, refer to module 6, Developing Instructional Programs. In addition, the "Follow-Up" section of the Program Overview indicates ways to use the skill in other situations and other programs in the curriculum that may be appropriate to teach at this time. Thus, to conduct follow-up:

- Write a program to insure use and generalization; and
- continue to other suggested programs as appropriate.

SUMMARY

1. Use the skill analysis programs only after consultation with a physical, occupational, or speech therapist as appropriate.
2. Record each skill analysis program on a separate data sheet (or set of sheets).
3. A pretest is given to verify that the child cannot perform the skill:
   a. Trials are presented with general pretesting procedures, with the addition of any specified natural consequences.
   b. Each response is recorded in one trial column next to the number specified for the target (last number in the list of parts).
   c. Each response is recorded as $+$, $-$, or θ.
   d. The child must respond correctly 4 out of 5 trials to pass.
   e. Testing stops after two errors.
4. The instructional phase consists of two procedures:
   a. Daily practice is given, using the Suggestions section of the program; and
   b. weekly probes are presented to document acquisition of new parts.
5. A probe is given immediately after a failed pretest, then every fifth instructional day thereafter (e.g., 4 days of practice between each):
   a. All probe trials are given with general teaching strategies.
   b. One trial is the opportunity to perform one subskill or the target.
   c. Give trials for each subskill, except:
      (1) When the child met the suggested criterion on that subskill on a previous probe(s); and
      (2) when the child is obviously unable to perform the subskill.
   d. Up to five trials are recorded for each appropriate subskill.
      (1) Completely fill in all columns used.
      (2) Record $+$, $-$, or θ for those subskills probed.
      (3) Record ✓ for subskills previously demonstrated.

(4) Record NA for parts not probed due to obvious inability to perform.

   e. Learning is defined as an increase in the parts (or average number of parts) completed between probes.

   f. If the child has competed an average of no new parts after two successive probes, write Ⓜ to indicate that modification will occur.

   g. Instruction continues until the child can perform the target 4 out of 5 trials on a probe.

6. Modification is the expansion of one or more subskills into smaller components:

   a. A subskill may be broken down into increments of time, distance, or decreasing levels of assistance.

   b. Daily instruction remains the same with the expanded list of subskills.

   c. Weekly probes continue with use of the expanded list of subskills.

7. Three posttests are presented to verify that the child can perform the skill in three different situations:

   a. Tests trials are presented with general testing procedures.

   b. Each response is recorded in one trial column next to the number specified for the target.

   c. The child must respond correctly 4 out of 5 trials on each test to pass.

   d. POST 1, 2, and 3 are presented in order.

   e. Failure on any posttest is remediated by reviewing the instructional phase until the child performs the target 4 out of 5 trials. Then the failed posttest is repeated.

Chain Programs

OVERVIEW

Characteristics

Some skills require the child to perform a sequence of actions to complete a task. In these programs, the task has been analyzed into sequential parts. Skill acquisition is documented as the child gradually learns to perform an increasing number of parts, until she can chain them all in order. These programs are called *chain* programs in this curriculum.

How to Determine a Correct Response

Each chain program contains the definition and the sequential components of the target behavior. Under Behavior in the Program, each component is listed and numbered sequentially for identification. The last numbered "component" on each task sequence is a restatement of the target skill, emphasized with an asterisk. Throughout the program, only the unassisted performance of this part is considered correct.

How to Measure Progress

In the chain programs, the child gradually acquires more parts until she can perform the entire task unassisted. Daily instruction is given on the parts, and probe data is taken each week to determine how many parts she can complete unassisted. When she performs new parts without assistance on successive probes, the child demonstrates progress. If, however, the child fails to perform new parts unassisted, the standard parts need to be *modified* or expanded so that her progress can be adequately measured. This modification involves breaking a part into smaller components to permit more gradual progress. Thus, progress on skill acquisition is documented as the child performs more parts unassisted on successive probes, with modifications.

Where to Record the Data

The standard data sheet for chain programs is found on page 449. It contains space to write identifying information. Below this heading are boxed sections for each test and probe. You may need extra sheets. There are numbered blanks and five corresponding columns of numbers in each section. Fill in each blank with a word or phrase so that each part is identified by its corresponding number. Each program part is identified by a number. Cross out those numbers you do not need. This data sheet is used to record all performance on the program, from pretest through posttest.

PRETEST PROCEDURES

How to Present a Pretest Trial

Chain program pretest trials require you to present an attention cue before every trial, present the task cues for the target skill as specified, observe latency, and record the child's response without giving any specific feedback. However, there is a particular application to these procedures.

These programs often include a natural consequence. For example, if the child puts on her coat (target), she is ready to go outside; until she puts it on, she cannot go outside. As indicated in the General Strategy, present the "natural consequence" if the child performs the target.

However, do not praise or otherwise reinforce the response. If an error occurs, intervene only if the child is about to seriously hurt herself (e.g., fall down backward) or if she is becoming very frustrated with the task (e.g., cannot get her head out of the shirt because her arm is stuck).

How to Record a Pretest

On a pretest, the child's performance is recorded next to the number specified for the target in the program. The standard symbols "+", "−", and "θ" (no response, counted as an error) are used. Each boxed section has room for five trials. Use only the appropriate number for the target from each of the columns during the pretest:

*6. Target   6 + 6 + 6 + 6 − 6 +

In addition, next to the boxed section, record that this was a pretest required to complete the probe. If trials are given at different times during the day, add the total number of minutes:

SUMMARY: PROBE # PRE
Date: 10/27   Min. 11

How to Score a Pretest

To pass the pretest, the child must meet the specified criterion of 4 correct responses out of 5 trials. Continue to present trials as specified until she has either performed the target unassisted four times or has made two errors. Testing stops after two errors since the child can no longer meet test criterion. For example:

*6. Target   6 + 6 − 6 + 6 + 6 +   PASS: 4 correct out of 5 trials

OR

*6. Target   6 − 6 + 6 − 6   6   FAIL: 2 errors

TEACHING PROCEDURES

During the instructional phase of chain programs, there are two main procedures:

- Daily practice on the part(s); and
- weekly probes to document acquisition of new parts.

Because the instructional phase begins with a probe for baseline information, weekly probes will be discussed first.

PROBES

When to Take Probes

Although it is possible to record every skill opportunity on chain programs, data collection has practical difficulties. First, because progress on these skills is often slow, the increase in parts completed from one day to the next is often negligible. Second, during instruction (discussed later) you may wish to focus on one or two parts rather than have the child go through the entire task sequence every time. Third, data recording is often awkward when you need to assist the child, particularly when you are conducting instruction in a natural setting (e.g., in the bathroom). For these reasons, probes are taken only once every fifth instructional day (i.e., 4 days of practice, then a probe day).

How to Present a Probe Trial

Probe trials are presented with general teaching procedures: Insure attention before every trial, present task cues as specified, observe latency, and give immediate feedback on each response, either reinforcement for correct responses or correction of errors. Each probe trial presents the opportunity to perform all parts of the task in order once. The task cues for the target are presented, and the child is allowed to perform each part on her own. If she does not begin to perform the first part correctly within latency, she is corrected to complete that part. The completion of this part, with or without assistance, is the condition for the next successive part. If the child does not begin the second part within latency, she is corrected. This procedure continues until she has an opportunity to perform each part in order without assistance.

How to Reinforce a Correct Response

Feedback is given on each part of the task, not just after the entire task has been completed. The child receives reinforcement if she completes each behavior correctly, or correction if she makes an error, either an overt action or no response within the latency. Although some parts may occur very rapidly, immediate feedback should be given whenever possible.

On programs that specify a natural consequence, this should be presented as soon as the task is completed, whether performed with or without assistance. For example, if the natural consequence of putting on a coat (target) is to go outside, the child may go outside as soon as she puts her coat on, with or without assistance. In addition, praise and/or other reinforcement is presented for the correct (unassisted) response.

How to Correct an Error on a Part

Each chain program specifies that you may use any of the general correction procedures (refocus, demonstration, guidance) or any of the Suggestions listed for the part after the Conditions-Behavior-Criteria section. Regardless of the strategy you use, any assistance that includes extra directions is considered correction for an error. Therefore, be sure to allow latency to elapse for that part (unless an overt error occurs).

How to Record Probe Trials

Record the responses for each part of the task next to the appropriate number in the boxed section. For each trial, use one column. However, because each number in a column represents an opportunity to perform, only + 's need to be recorded. An unmarked number indicates error. A + by the last number (the one identifying the target) automatically means a + on all parts, whether or not they are marked. For example:

The child performed Parts 1 and 5 unassisted	The child only needed assistance on Part 4	The child performed all parts unassisted	
1 +	1 +	1 +	1
2	2 +	2 +	2
3	3 +	3 + or 3
4	4	4 +	4
5 +	5 +	5 +	5
*6	*6	*6 +	*6 +

On a probe, up to five trials are presented. However, they may be offered at different times during the day rather than in one session. It would be unreasonable to ask the child, for example, to put on her coat five times in a row. We highly recommend that you give five trials so that you have better information on the child. However, you may give fewer trials, depending on the task and the child's endurance.

How to Score a Probe

Progress on chain programs is defined as an increase in the number of parts completed without assistance from one probe to the next. To determine the average number of parts completed per trial on the probe, add up the number of parts correct on all trials, and divide by the number of trials given. Note that if the child performs the target, she automatically receives credit for all parts. For example, on five trials, if the child completes 2, 3, 2, 2, then 3 parts correctly, she has performed an average of 2.4 parts per trial (12 ÷ 5).

Fill in this information in the space provided for that probe:

SUMMARY: PROBE # __1__
Date: _9/27_ Min. _15_
Average +'s per column _2.4_

Then fill in the average parts completed from the previous probe. (On Probe 1, this number is automatically 0.) The average parts gained between these probes is the difference between these two numbers. To continue this example, the data sheet would appear like this:

Ave. +'s per column on last probe __0__
Average parts gained _2.4_

As long as the average parts gained is greater than 0, the child is progressing on successive probes. For example:

SUMMARY: PROBE # __1__
Date: _9/27_ Min. _15_
Average +'s per column _2.4_
Ave. +'s per column on last probe __0__
Average parts gained _2.4_

SUMMARY: PROBE # __2__
Date: _10/3_ Min. _20_
Average +'s per column _3.8_
Ave. +'s per column on last probe _2.4_
Average parts gained _1.4_

When to Modify

If the child has not gained any new parts after two successive probes, her progress is not occurring rapidly enough to be measured by this program. Write Ⓜ after the second successive probe after the "Average parts gained 0." Modification procedures will be discussed after Daily Practice.

When to End the Instructional Phase

When the child has performed the target skill 4 out of 5 trials on a probe, the instructional phase of the program is over. Until the child meets this criterion on a probe, instruction continues, using the two basic procedures: daily practice and weekly probes. Note that if for any reason the child can perform the target skill but cannot perform all the parts, she should receive credit on the target. Criterion is based only on performance of the target, not the parts.

DAILY PRACTICE

How to Present Daily Practice

During daily practice, you may conduct sessions in either of two ways. First you may present trials on the task exactly as you would during a probe, with the exceptions that you need not take response-by-response data and that you need not limit the session to five trials. Or, you may work on specific strategies described in each program under Suggestions. In either case, you may structure the session as you wish without recording data on every response. However, you should note on the data sheet that daily practice was presented and record the total time you worked on the task.

Spaces for you to record the dates and times of these practice sessions are on the data sheet under summary probe information. There is space to record four sessions. The fourth daily session is followed by a probe session to determine if the child has acquired additional skills. Thus, although there is flexibility in the daily practice sessions, performance is always documented at regular intervals through probe sessions.

How to Use the Suggestions

Each program contains suggestions to remediate errors. Some suggestions involve the addition of cues or physical assistance. For example, if the child is having difficulty grasping a shirt at a particular place, you might add a cue such as a colored tab to remind her where to grasp. Such a suggestion is a specific application of a standard cueing-fading strategy. During daily practice, you might give the child repeated practice grasping the tab, grasping where you point, and then grasping the appropriate place without any cues. After working on this specific part (and others) for a week, you can determine on the probe whether the child can now perform the parts without assistance.

Other suggestions include ways to chain together two or more parts that are typically learned as a unit. These suggestions give specific information to apply a standard forward or backward chaining procedure to this skill. For example, if you are teaching the child to perform three parts (A, B, and C) in order, using a chaining strategy, you would first guide her to perform all three parts in sequence. For forward chaining, teach her to perform the first part (A). For backward chaining, you would start by teaching her to perform the last part (C). The practice steps would be:

Forward Chain	*Backward Chain*
(1) You guide or assist S to perform *A, B,* and *C* in sequence.......	
(2) S completes A alone (first part); you assist to perform B and C.	(2) You assist to complete *A* and *B;* and S completes *C* alone (last part).
(3) S completes *A* and *B* (first two parts); you assist to perform *C*.	(3) You assist to complete *A;* S completes *B* and *C* alone (last two parts).
(4) S completes *A, B,* and *C* in sequence..............	

The suggestions indicate where these strategies are particularly appropriate. But you may use them any time during daily practice. After you have worked on a strategy for a week, probe to determine whether the child can perform more parts without assistance.

MODIFICATION PROCEDURES

How to Modify the Parts

A program should be modified to document more gradual acquisition if the child does not demonstrate a gain in parts completed on two successive probes. Essentially, this modification in a chain program is an expansion of the number of parts. By breaking one part into smaller components, you can document acquisition of these smaller components during probes.

The Suggestions describe how to analyze behaviors into smaller component parts. Although you may have used a strategy informally during daily practice, in modification, you actually revise the list of parts to obtain finer probe data. For example, in putting on a T-shirt, a child is having difficulty pushing her head through the neck opening. You could modify that part to specify a series of smaller actions that are performed in sequence to complete that part (e.g., a shaping strategy):

ORIGINAL	MODIFICATION
4. pushes head through opening	4. A pushes head in at least 2 inches
	B pushes head in to her eyes
	C pushes head in past her nose
	D pushes head in to her chin
	E pushes head through opening

Note that the added parts are coded *A, B, C,* and so on, to the number of the expanded part.

Another way to modify this same part would be to specify decreasing amounts of assistance (e.g., a cueing-fading or a chaining strategy):

ORIGINAL	MODIFICATION
4. pushes head through opening	4. A pushes head through opening with complete guidance
	B pushes head in to eyes unassisted, with guidance to push the rest of the way
	C pushes head in to mouth unassisted, with guidance for final pull
	D pushes head through opening (unassisted)

Further information on writing shaping, cueing-fading, and chaining strategies is contained in module 6, Developing Instructional Programs. With this expanded list of parts, your probe data will reflect more gradual increments in the skill. Instruction then continues as before: Daily practice and weekly probes, using this expanded list of parts.

POSTTEST PROCEDURES

How to Present a Posttest

After the child has passed instruction (i.e., performed the target correctly 4 out of 5 trials on a probe), she is ready to be posttested. Posttesting is essentially the same as pretesting. On each trial, response readiness is insured, task cues are presented, latency is observed, and the response on the target skill is recorded next to the appropriate number on the data sheet. Criterion is 4 correct responses out of 5 trials. Two errors indicate failure. As in all programs, posttesting documents skill acquisition in at least three different situations. POST 1 is conducted with the same conditions as instruction (except, of course, for reinforcement or correction). POSTS 2 and 3 contain slight variations in these task conditions.

How to Remediate a Posttest Failure

When failure occurs on a posttest (two errors), review the instructional phase. Begin daily practice and weekly probing until the child performs the target skill to criterion on a probe. Then repeat the posttest. Note that if the failure occurs in POST 2 or 3, the instructional program should be reviewed with the *new* conditions.

Follow-Up

After the program is complete (i.e., the child has passed POST 3), you will need to insure that the child continues to generalize the skill to new situations and maintains her level of performance. To write a program, refer to module 6, Developing Instructional Programs. In addition, the "Follow-Up" section of the Program Overview indicates ways to use the skill in other situations and suggests other programs that may be appropriate to teach at this time. Thus, to conduct follow-up:

- Write a program to insure use and generalization; and
- continue to other suggested programs as appropriate.

SUMMARY

1. Record each chain program on a separate data sheet (or set of sheets).
2. A pretest is given to verify that the child cannot perform the skill:
   a. Trials are presented with general pretesting procedures and specific natural consequences.
   b. Each response is recorded in one trial column next to the number specified for the target (last number in the list of parts).
   c. Each response is recorded as $+$, $-$, or θ.
   d. The child must respond correctly 4 out of 5 trials to pass.
   e. Testing stops after two errors.
3. The instructional phase consists of two procedures:
   a. Daily practice, using the Suggestions section of the program; and
   b. weekly probes to document acquisition of new parts.
4. Probes are given immediately after a pretest is failed, then every fifth instructional day thereafter (i.e., 4 days of practice between each):
   a. All probe trials are presented with general teaching procedures.
   b. Up to five trials are recorded during a probe session.
      (1) One opportunity to perform each part is recorded in each trial column.
      (2) Only $+$'s are recorded; an unmarked number in a trial column indicates error.
      (3) A $+$ by the last number (target) means that the entire skill was performed correctly.
   c. Learning is documented by an increase in the parts (or average number of parts) completed between probes.
   d. If the child has completed no new parts after two successive probes, write Ⓜ to indicate that modification will occur.
   e. Instruction continues until the child performs the target 4 out of 5 trials on a probe.

5. Modification is the expansion of the number of parts listed in the task sequence:
   a. A part may be broken down into smaller sequential actions or into decreasing levels of assistance.
   b. Daily instruction remains the same with the expanded task sequence.
   c. Weekly probes continue with use of the expanded task sequence.

6. Three posttests are presented to verify that the child can perform the skill in three different situations:
   a. Test trials are presented with the general testing procedures.
   b. Each response is recorded in one trial column next to the number specified for the target.
   c. The child must respond correctly 4 out of 5 trials on each test to pass.
   d. POST 1, 2, and 3 are presented in order.
   e. Failure on any posttest is remediated by reviewing the instructional phase until the child performs the target 4 out of 5 trials. Then the failed posttest is repeated.

Supplementary
Information

Module 5: Reinforcement and Instructional Control, 529

Module 6: Developing Instructional Programs, 535

Module 7: Individual Educational Programs (IEP), 548

MODULE 5:

Reinforcement and Instructional Control

INTRODUCTION

A behavioral approach to instruction focuses on these events:

$$\text{ANTECEDENT EVENTS} \longrightarrow \text{CHILD RESPONSE} \longrightarrow \text{CONSEQUENT EVENTS}$$

To increase appropriate child behavior, you can structure these antecedent and consequent events to:

- Arrange antecedent events to facilitate appropriate behavior *before* a response occurs; and
- arrange consequent events *after* a response occurs to increase the frequency of a desired response or decrease the frequency of an interfering behavior.

This module describes some basic techniques to arrange antecedent and consequent events, which affect child behavior during instruction. However, it is not possible to cover all behavioral techniques in a few short pages, so we have included further references in the Bibliography. Based on the information presented here, you will generally be able to:

- Select and use reinforcers (consequent events) appropriately;
- select and teach on-task behaviors; and
- manage antecedent events in the classroom.

SELECTING AND USING REINFORCERS

How to Select Reinforcers

Although the sequence described in the introduction is "antecedent-response-consequence," it is important to identify appropriate consequences before you attempt to modify child behavior. A *positive reinforcer* is any item or event that can be used to increase behavior. In practice, this means anything that the child has shown a preference for and will work to obtain:

Consumables (ice cream, candy, cereal, milk)

Sensory events (tickling, water play, rocking, music)

Preferred activities (favorite toys, going outside)

Social events (attention, praise, smiles, hugs)

Tokens (chips, play money, to trade in for other reinforcers)

Marks (stars, checkmarks, grades)

Because all children are different, reinforcers are usually different for each child. By definition, only those items that increase a child's behavior are reinforcers for that child. You can never assume that something is a reinforcer for one child just because other children respond to it.

You first need to identify reinforcers for each child. One way is to ask parents, or the child herself if possible, what she likes. However, it is often difficult to determine reinforcers for a child. To do this, select a variety of objects or activities to which you think the child will respond. For suggestions, refer to the Stimulus Chart on page 467. Then systematically present the different items that you have selected. Note those to which the child responds by smiling, reaching toward, laughing, or otherwise indicating some positive response. Those that increase these behaviors can be considered reinforcers for that child.

How to Use Reinforcers

Once reinforcers have been identified, they can be used as consequences for appropriate behavior. Whenever the child performs a desired behavior, present a reinforcer immediately. This should be done every time you observe the child performing the desired behavior, until she consistently performs that target response. The close temporal pairing of the response and reinforcer is very important. Delay allows other behaviors to occur so that there is a less obvious association between the response and consequence, and possibly, even an undesired association with another response. Note that the instructional programs in this curriculum allow the child to receive reinforcement for every correct response during the instructional steps or phases. Reinforcement for appropriate behavior is presented in addition to the reinforcement for correct responses on the program task.

The effectiveness of any one reinforcer depends on how often it is used. As with anything, a reinforcer that is used again and again eventually loses its effectiveness. An obvious example is the use of food as a reinforcer. Even if milk is very reinforcing for a child, it will lose its effectiveness or "appeal" after a meal. To insure that a particular reinforcer maintains its effectiveness, you should use it only occasionally and vary it with other reinforcers. One strategy is to offer the child several reinforcers from which she may choose. Thus, although a reinforcer should be presented immediately after each appropriate response, the reinforcer itself should vary. In this way, you can use reinforcers to increase behaviors.

TEACHING ON-TASK BEHAVIORS

How to Identify "Appropriate" Behaviors

The first step in managing child behavior is to identify exactly what you wish the child to do. Each behavior you select as a target should be defined so that you or any other observer can determine whether or not the child is responding in that manner. In addition, the child should be able to produce that behavior or some approximation of it. These targets should be behaviors that are of immediate practical value or that are considered "on-task" behaviors because they facilitate instruction. Some examples of on-task behaviors are:

Sits in chair facing the teacher (neither moves the chair nor moves around in the chair).

Positions hands so that they are on her lap (not in her mouth, playing with her hair, hitting, or throwing materials).

Looks toward the teacher or materials when requested to do so.

Remains quiet during a task, and attends to the teacher.

When to Work on On-Task Behaviors

Many children may exhibit few on-task behaviors; however, they should not be eliminated from instruction just because they are distractible or do not attend to the task. Rather, on-task behaviors should be taught as an integral part of the programs. During instruction, you will shape on-task and program target behaviors. In addition, you may need to work on on-task behaviors intermittently during the day. If a child emits few on-task behaviors, you may need to shape *sitting* or *hands down* behavior during five or six short sessions interspersed throughout the day. In addition, you may need to assist her to demonstrate these behaviors before you present each program trial during an individual instructional session. Gradually, as the child's on-task behavior increases, instructional skill will be acquired more rapidly.

The programs of the curriculum Profile have been developed with children who exhibited few on-task behaviors. When these programs are appropriate for your child, they provide excellent opportunities to work on program tasks and on-task behaviors simultaneously. However, certain other programs are more difficult to use when extreme behavior problems occur. You may need to work on on-task behavior in isolation before you use those typically found in the upper two-thirds of the Profile, particularly in Language and Cognitive Skills. This decision, of course, will be based on the extent of the problem. Wherever possible, though, integrate on-task behavior drills into your regular instructional session.

How to Teach On-Task Behaviors

When you want the child to exhibit a specific behavior (e.g., put hands down, look at you), first tell the child to do it. This command should be spoken in a firm, clear voice with as few words as possible and should be used consistently every time you want that particular behavior to occur. It should not contain the word *good* since that could be misunderstood as praise rather than as a command. Some typical commands are "Look," "Listen," "Hands down," "Sit straight," or the child's name (to look at you). After you give the command, pause and wait for the child to comply. (Always look directly at the child throughout the command and pause.) Then, if the child performs the behavior, immediately reinforce it with praise and any other effective reinforcer. If the child does not perform the behavior, repeat the command as before. Physically assist her to do so, but make no other comments. Reinforce as soon as she performs the behavior with this assistance.

As you present the command at different times, gradually give less assistance and reinforce each closer approximation of the behavior. When the child complies on command without assistance, gradually increase the length of time she maintains the behavior before you present the reinforcer. For example, to teach the child to remain in her seat, you may first need to position the child and hold her in place for 5 seconds. When she sits on command, you can gradually increase the time from 5 to 10, 15, 20, 30 seconds or longer.

This procedure—present a command and reinforce appropriate behavior (or its approximation)—is used before every instructional trial and at intermittent times during the day until the child performs the behavior consistently on command. When the child performs consistently, you may fade out the reinforcer.

How to Fade the Use of Continuous Reinforcement for Appropriate Behavior

At first many children respond only to reinforcers like food or sensory events and do not respond to praise alone. As described earlier, to shape on-task behavior, praise is always presented with a reinforcer that is effective with that child. The first step in fading continuous reinforcement is to fade the original reinforcer (e.g., food, toy). Though praise is still given for every occurrence of appropriate behavior, the reinforcer is presented only after every other response. If the behavior is still produced consistently, you may continue to fade the reinforcer; if not, reintroduce the reinforcer after every appropriate response. Gradually offer the reinforcer less frequently (e.g., every second, third, fourth, then fifth time the behavior occurs), but continue to praise the child each time. At this point, praise is acting as a reinforcer since it is increasing or maintaining appropriate behavior. The original reinforcer should be presented randomly as a back-up to maintain the effectiveness of the praise.

This step is extremely important for instructional sessions because praise is usually presented more quickly and easily than many other reinforcers. By using praise for each appropriate behavior (correct responses and on-task behaviors) and fading other reinforcers systematically, you can gradually maintain appropriate behavior by praise and eventually present the back-up reinforcer only at the end of the session. Keep in mind that this is a very gradual process.

The second step in fading continuous reinforcement is to fade the use of praise gradually. (Note that this step is appropriate to maintain on-task behaviors. However, praise with or without a back-up reinforcer is required for every correct response on the program task during instruction, according to general instructional procedures.) The praise for on-task behavior is gradually decreased in frequency until it is presented occasionally rather than continuously. This process follows the same basic procedure as fading the original reinforcer. As long as the child consistently performs on-task behaviors, praise is given less frequently, until you make only occasional comments on the child's behavior. Again, the back-up reinforcer can still be used to maintain the effectiveness of praise.

How to Decrease Inappropriate Behavior

Often undesired or inappropriate behavior occurs and interferes with the production of the desired behavior. When an inappropriate behavior occurs, it should be ignored (e.g., not reinforced by your attention). Look down or away from the child, and discontinue any ongoing activity. In addition, give other children who are behaving appropriately reinforcers for their behavior, thus providing models for the misbehaving child. As soon as the child exhibits any appropriate behavior, even an apprixibation, immediately reinforce it, and continue the activity.

However, if the inappropriate behavior is dangerous or disrupts other children, direct intervention may be necessary. The purpose of intervention is to interrupt the behavior as quickly as possible. Interruption should be conducted in a neutral manner with little excitement, attention, or comment. For example, give a command and/or physically stop the behavior. As soon as the misbehavior is interrupted, the child should be ignored briefly until she produces any appropriate behavior, which should then be immediately reinforced. If the behavior is dangerous or persistent, you may want to consider using punishment or presenting aversive stimuli. Refer to the Bibliography for other sources of information.

By strategically presenting different consequences (reinforcement for all appropriate behaviors and withholding reinforcement for undesirable behaviors), you can increase the child's on-task behaviors. The strategies described here may be used informally throughout the day. However, if you find that you need a formal program, refer to module 6, Developing Instructional Programs. The procedures described there for "cueing-fading" can be used with the information here to teach the child to perform on command. Once she can perform unassisted, the procedures for increasing the frequency of her performance can be used to maintain the on-task behavior.

Sometimes it is possible to set up situations to avoid behavior problems in the classroom before they occur. The next section covers this topic.

MANAGING ANTECEDENT EVENTS IN THE CLASSROOM

Many things in the classroom environment may provide a stimulus for inappropriate behaviors. For example, wide open areas may be a stimulus for running around the room. It is possible to teach appropriate behaviors under these conditions, however, it is often easier to rearrange the environment. The management of antecedents requires that you arrange the environment to facilitate appropriate child behavior and, if possible, preclude inappropriate behavior.

As behavior problems or "off-task" behaviors occur (those that intefere with instruction), an assessment of the stimulus conditions can lead to changes, insuring that the problem does not reoccur. "What elements of the situation appear to create distraction, frustration, or boredom? How can these conditions be changed?" The conditions you may need to change depend on the type of inappropriate behavior. For example, if the child sits unoccupied or rocks, you may wish to place toys in an easily accessible place for her. But if she throws toys frequently, you may wish to keep particular toys out of reach, but make sure the child is occupied in play with an individual who can prevent this behavior. Thus, you will need to assess each situation involving recurrent inappropriate behavior before deciding upon changes.

Ways to Prevent Off-Task Behavior

Certain off-task behaviors are common with different children, and teachers often use some standard strategies to prevent their occurrence. Common strategies that you may use are:

If the child frequently gets up during instruction	Place her chair back to the wall with a table in front of her. Sit opposite so that she cannot push away from the table.
If the child frequently grabs at materials	Keep materials behind you until time for use. Position materials only after she has her hands in her lap, with or without assistance.
If the child frequently plays with materials and does not respond	Change materials, or allow her to explore new materials before using them with a program.
If the child frequently touches the child next to her	Separate the two by space, or a barrier, or by sitting between them.
If the child is frequently distracted by other activities in the classroom	Conduct the session in another room, or in a partitioned section of the room, or change the time of the session.
If the child refuses to respond or responds inappropriately after a few minutes	Limit the session to 2 or 3 minutes. When she maintains on-task behavior for this length of time, gradually increase the session length, and/or alternate activities during the session.
If the child usually does not perform at a particular time (e.g., before lunch)	Change her schedule to provide an easier activity at that time.

These strategies can prevent the reoccurrence of some problems. You can devise your own strategies, specific to the situation. Keep in mind that the management of antecedents is used to facilitate appropriate behavior before it (or any other response) occurs. Once a behavior occurs, consequences (reinforcement for appropriate behavior and withholding reinforcement for inappropriate behavior) are used to manage that behavior after it occurs.

SUMMARY

1. Positive reinforcers are items or events that increase behavior and may be identified by observing the child's behavior:
   a. Once identified, reinforcers should be presented immediately after the child performs an appropriate behavior.
   b. To keep their effectiveness, reinforcers should be varied.
2. On-task behaviors are those that facilitate instruction:
   a. Wherever possible, they should be taught as an integral part of instructional programs.
   b. They are taught by presenting a command and reinforcing approximations of the behavior.
   c. Continuous reinforcement for on-task behavior is faded by first pairing praise with the original reinforcer, fading the original reinforcer, then fading praise.
3. Inappropriate behaviors are decreased by strategically presenting different consequences—reinforcement for appropriate behaviors and withholding reinforcement for inappropriate behaviors.
4. On-task behaviors may be facilitated by managing antecedent (stimulus) events.

MODULE 6:

Developing Instructional Programs

The general process in teaching a new skill is to select an existing skill and change it over gradual steps into the desired skill. To develop an instructional program to teach the skill, focus on three critical questions:

1. What is the desired skill?
2. What skill does the child have now that would facilitate learning the desired skill?
3. What does she need to learn to shape the current skill into the desired skill?

This module presents information to answer these questions. After reading this module, you will be able to:

- Define a target skill;
- write appropriate steps to teach the skill with a data system to measure progress; and
- apply the information to the standard programs in the curriculum.

PRELIMINARY CONSIDERATIONS

How to Select a Target Skill

Target skills are selected for the child based on educational goals in relation to her present functioning. For example, if the goal for the child is to feed herself independently and the child can now pick up pieces of food and eat them, a target skill for immediate instruction might be to use a spoon or a cup.

To select a realistic target skill, you need to be familiar with the order in which skills are typically acquired. For the programs in this curriculum, each program "Objective" is a target skill, and module 1, Program Selection, discusses procedures to identify appropriate target skills for your students. In addition, module 7, Individual Programs, describes procedures to identify long- and short-range objectives (targets) in general. Whatever procedure you use, the selection of the target skill is the preliminary step to develop an instructional program.

How to Specify a Target Skill

Once you have selected a target, define it in behavioral terms. Not only do you need to specify the behavior itself in observable (measurable) terms, but you also need to state the conditions under which the child must perform, and how often she must perform (criterion). Points to consider are:

Is the response or behavior defined so that it can be observed reliably? (Can different observers agree whether or not the behavior occurred?)

Can the response be observed easily without requiring extensive observation periods? (Can the response be defined for a short time interval? as a small unit?)

Should the child perform on command or initiate the action on her own?

What type of materials or equipment will she use?

Will she be allowed any type of cues or assistance, or must she perform independently?

Is there a time limit for beginning and/or completing the response?

Does she need to perform the skill at all times, or is a less stringent criterion acceptable?

The answers to these questions will help you define the target skill for each individual child. For example, in eating with a spoon, the following definitions are only a few of the possibilities, depending upon how you want the child to perform at the end of the program:

Using an adapted spoon, the child will feed herself at least five bites of pudding at lunchtime on 3 consecutive days (no cues or assistance).

The child will pick up the (standard) spoon and feed herself one bite of pudding within 10 seconds of a command at least five times in a row during one lunch period (no assistance).

The child will use a (standard) spoon to feed herself at least half a cup of pudding within 10 minutes of presentation of food 4 out of 5 days (no cues or assistance).

Obviously, the conditions, behavior, and criterion that you specify depend upon the level of performance desired in the child's immediate environment. Often a child does not need to perform with complete independence or function independently at all times. To set a high standard may be unrealistic and unnecessary at one point but appropriate at another. Your specification of the target is critical to set a realistic goal. It is also critical to determine the starting point for instruction.

How to Identify an Initial Skill for Instruction

Once you have defined the target, you can compare the child's current performance to these target standards. In particular, you are looking for current skills that are related to or resemble the target, although they do not meet your specifications for the target in terms of conditions, behavior, and/or criteria. Points to consider are:

Does she perform the target but not up to your frequency or time limit standards?

Does she perform the target but at the wrong time (to another stimulus)?

Does she perform the target but only with assistance?

Does she make any response that physically resembles the target?

When you can answer these questions, you can identify the point at which to begin instruction. Based on the initial skill the child exhibits, you can then determine how to structure a program so that she will produce the target.

The difference between the initial skill and the target skill usually falls into one of two categories:

1. The child cannot perform the target under the specified conditions but does perform some approximation with or without assistance; or
2. the child can perform the target under the specified conditions but does not meet your standards for either frequency (how often she performs) or duration (how long she performs).

Based on the desired target and the initial starting point that you have identified, select the category (either develop response production or increase performance standards, respectively) that is most appropriate. Note that for the first category, you may also need to increase the child's performance standards *after* she learns to produce the target response under the specified conditions. The next section describes strategies to outline programs based on specific changes within each of these general categories.

PROGRAMS TO DEVELOP RESPONSE PRODUCTION

Types of Strategies

There are two strategies to shape the child's production of the target skill:

- Accept an approximation of the response, then gradually require closer approximations (response shaping); and
- add stimulus cues that facilitate or assist the child's performance, then decrease the amount of these cues gradually (cueing-fading).

The first strategy is known as *response shaping* or *reinforcing successive approximations*; the second has been called *cueing-fading, prompting-fading*, or *stimulus-response shaping*. A third strategy, *chaining*, has elements of both, since it involves the use of stimulus cues (assistance), as well as approximations of the response when the behavior is a skill comprised of a sequence of actions:

- Add stimulus cues to facilitate performance of each action in a sequence; then
- gradually remove those cues in order, starting from either the first action in the sequence (forward chaining) or the last action (backward chaining).

When to Use Response Shaping

Shaping is a strategy that gradually changes the topography or physical appearance of a response into a more desired form. It is used primarily when the target skill is a particular motor action that the child does not currently perform, perhaps through lack of coordination or muscle tone. Although it is often used to teach basic motor skills or speech production, it is usually combined with cueing-fading so that stimulus cues are used to facilitate each approximation of the response.

When to Use Chaining

Chaining also focuses on the motor production of the action itself. However, it is used only when the action is comprised of an ordered sequence or chain of independent actions. It is often used to teach self-help tasks, such as dressing skills, or vocational tasks, such as putting together a product. However, this strategy focuses on the production of the chain, not any one particular action. It is often used after each action has been taught by shaping. In addition, it has a built-in cueing-fading strategy to teach the sequence of actions.

When to Use Cueing-Fading

Cueing-fading assumes that the child can already perform or can quickly learn the action itself. The strategy focuses on the stimulus conditions that exist before a response occurs. It is typically used to teach concept or language skills, where the response serves only to indicate understanding or use of a concept. The visual, tactile, or auditory cues focus attention on the critical elements of the task. Cueing-fading is a very effective method to teach the child when to make a particular response or to indicate what type of response is required.

How to Outline the Steps

Based on the above information, you can select the strategy that appears most appropriate to teach the child to produce the target response, either shaping, chaining, or cueing-fading. After you select the strategy, outline the steps between the initial skill that the child can perform and the target skill. The first task is to identify the intermediate behaviors that should be shaped. Although you identify intermediate behaviors, the way these behaviors are determined is different for each strategy.

Intermediate Behaviors Required to Shape a Response

In shaping, the child learns to produce finer and finer motor approximations of the skill. The intermediate behaviors are the gradual changes in the topography or physical appearance of the response between the initial and target skill. These intermediate behaviors comprise the outline of the steps. For example, the steps in shaping the target "pushing a button" might be:

Step 1:   Child moves her arm in any way.

Step 2:   Child moves her arm in the direction of the button.

Step 3:   Child moves her arm so that her hand is within 6 inches of the button.

Step 4:   Child touches the button with her hand.

Step 5:   Child touches the button with tips of her finger(s).

Step 6:   Child pushes the button.

As the child progresses through the steps, she gradually produces a closer approximation of the skill until on the last step, she produces the target itself.

Intermediate Behaviors Required to Chain a Response

In chaining, the target is a sequence of actions, and the child learns to complete more actions in the sequence. To identify the intermediate behaviors, you first identify the actions that comprise the target. For example, the sequence for putting on a sock might be:

Part 1:   Grasp sock at cuff.

Part 2:   Bend leg.

Part 3:   Insert toes into cuff of sock.

Part 4:   Pull sock over ball of the foot.

Part 5:   Pull sock over heel.

Part 6:   Straighten cuff on leg.

From this sequence or task analysis, you can specify the order in which the child learns to complete the task. This order is then the list of intermediate behaviors. You may either specify that the child learns the first part first (forward chaining) or the last part first (backward chaining). For this sequence, the intermediate behaviors would be:

Forward Chain		Backward Chain	
Step 1:	Teacher assists Student to perform all parts		
Step 2:	S performs Part 1 alone; T assists Parts 2–6.	**Step 2:**	T assists Part 1–5; S performs Part 6 alone.
Step 3:	S performs Parts 1–2 alone; T assists Parts 3–6.	**Step 3:**	T assists Parts 1–4; S performs Parts 5–6 alone.
Step 4:	S performs Parts 1–3 alone; T assists Parts 4–6.	**Step 4:**	T assists Parts 1–3; S performs Parts 4–6 alone.
Step 5:	S performs Parts 1–4 alone, T assists Parts 5–6.	**Step 5:**	T assists Parts 1–2; S performs Parts 3–6 alone.
Step 6:	S performs Parts 1–5 alone; T assists Part 6.	**Step 6:**	T assists Part 1; S performs 2–6 alone.
Step 7:	S performs Parts 1–6 alone		

As the child progresses through the steps, she is gradually performing more parts of the sequence on her own, until she can produce the entire sequence without assistance.

Intermediate Behaviors for Cueing-Fading

In cueing-fading, the child first performs the response with extra assistance, which is then gradually faded or removed. Define the form of assistance, and specify how it will be faded out. For example, if the target requires the child to push a particular button, the cues might be:

	Extra Cues/Assistance	Fading Strategy
Materials:	*size*—the correct button is larger than others.	Present smaller and smaller buttons until all choices are the same size.
	color—the correct button is painted red to attract attention, while all the other choices are white.	Paint more and more of the red button white until all choices are the same color.
	position—the correct button is closer than others.	Gradually move the button (or child) farther until all choices are equidistant.
Teacher:	*gestures*—point toward, nod to, or tap the correct button.	Make the gesture less obvious.
	extra directions or tone of voice—tell the child which button is correct.	Reduce the amount of extra directions, reduce volume.
	facial expression—smile, nod when the child aims for the correct button.	Make your expression less obvious.
	physical guidance—assist the child to push the correct button.	Reduce the force of your grasp, until you barely touch the child.
	demonstration—touch the correct button as a model.	Wait 1 second for the child to start, then demonstrate. Wait before you demonstrate so

combined cues—gesture to the correct button, demonstrate pushing it, then physically guide the child to perform.

that the child responds without a model.

Gradually remove each cue in order—stop guiding, then modeling, then gesturing, until no extra cues are given.

Once you identify a cue(s) and ways to remove it, the intermediate behaviors are the decreasing levels of assistance under which the child performs. If you use combined cues, for example, the steps might be:

Step 1: After extra directions and demonstration, child performs the target with physical guidance.

Step 2: After extra directions and demonstration, child performs the target (without guidance).

Step 3: After extra directions, child performs the target (without demonstration or guidance).

Step 4: Child performs the target (without assistance).

As the child progresses through the steps, she performs the response with less assistance until she can perform the target on her own.

How to Write Intra-Program Steps

Once you have broken the target into steps or intermediate behaviors, you then need to specify the criterion or standard of performance for each step. This criterion is used to determine when the child has passed a step and is ready to progress to the next one. Usually a standard criterion is used, such as 4 correct out of 5 trials, or correct performance on 80% of the trials. Thus, the child must perform each intermediate behavior to criterion before she progresses to the next step.

Your program must also include a decision point for a program modification. You may identify this point as a certain number of errors (e.g., the child was unable to perform the intermediate behavior after five trials on the step) or as a certain time interval (e.g., the child was unable to perform the intermediate behavior after 5 days of instruction on the step). Whatever this point, it is critical to provide a system for evaluating the success of the steps you have written. If the child meets criterion on successive steps, the steps are appropriate for teaching the skill. If she fails to meet step criterion after a certain specified point, the steps need to be modified or changed.

How to Modify a Step

If the step needs to be modified, break it into smaller intermediate behaviors. For shaping, this means identifying smaller topographical changes in the physical appearance of the response. In cueing-fading, you should identify ways to remove the cue or assistance more gradually. With the chaining strategy, you need to break the sequence of actions into smaller independent actions to teach in order. Thus, when you modify, you are adding extra steps to provide more instruction when the child encounters difficulty.

Other Components of the Program

Once you have outlined the steps with criterion standards and a modification point, you are ready to prepare the full program. The program should contain the following components with specified materials, stimulus cues, and criterion standards:

- A *pretest* of the target skill to verify that the child cannot perform the skill; the *steps* of sequenced intermediate behaviors; and
- a *posttest* (identical to the pretest) to verify that the child can perform the target after instruction.

In addition, consequences for the child's responses should be specified for these components. During the pretest or posttest, specific feedback on performance should not be given, neither reinforcement for correct responses nor correction for errors. For the steps, however, you should specify how you will reinforce each correct performance of the intermediate behavior and how you will correct each error.

Finally, the program should specify a data system for recording each child response during tests and steps. Usually, the symbols are " + " for a correct response and " − " for errors. Performance is recorded after each opportunity and is kept on a data sheet by test and step. For example:

PRETEST	− −	FAIL (cannot meet criterion of 4 correct out of 5 possible)
Step 1	+ + + +	PASS: 4 correct (out of 5 possible)
Step 2	+ − + + +	PASS: 4 correct (out of 5 possible)

By systematically recording each response made during the program, you have a written record of child performance on each step or test, program modifications, and child performance on the modification steps. This data system is an integral part of the program.

Summary

The program that you write to teach the child to produce the target skill should contain:

- A statement of the *target objective* in behaviorial terms;
- a *pretest, teaching steps, and a posttest,* containing:
    specified *conditions* (materials, task cues),
    definition of a *correct response,* and
    statements of *criterion* performance;
- specified *reinforcers* for correct responses during the steps;
- stated strategies for interrupting or *correcting errors* during the steps;
- response-by-response *recording* of child performance; and
- a *criterion system* for evaluating progress during instruction and revising the program as needed.

By preparing a shaping, chaining, or cueing-fading strategy with the above elements, you have written a systematic instructional program to teach the child to perform a skill that was not in her initial repertoire of behaviors.

PROGRAMS TO INCREASE PERFORMANCE STANDARDS

Types of Strategies

The second general category of programs contains those that increase performance standards (how often or long the child responds correctly). These are targets the child has demonstrated that she can perform but does not do so as often as you desire. In other words, these programs increase the consistency of the child's performance. There are three basic ways to measure consistent performance:

- Percent of correct responses to the total responses;
- frequently of correct responses in a given time interval (i.e., response rate); or
- percent of time intervals when the correct response occurs.

When to Use Percent of Correct Responses

Percent of correct responses is easiest to use when the target can be defined in terms of a discrete stimulus (task cues, materials, command) and one child response. Many cognitive, motor, and self-help skills fall into this group. The child is given a command and is expected to respond to that command. Because each trial or opportunity to respond is discrete, it is relatively easy to keep track of each response as either correct " + " or error " − ". The percent of correct responses is then a ratio of correct responses to the total responses made:

$$\frac{\text{total } +\text{'s}}{\text{total } +\text{'s and } -\text{'s}} \times 100$$

For example, if the child made 8 correct responses out of 10 opportunities, she performed correctly on 80% of the trials.

When to Use Rate of Correct Responses

At other times, the target might be performed in a situation where it is difficult to identify one discrete opportunity to perform. The child might be constantly presented with different stimuli to increase her responding behaviors. Often this strategy is used with a nonresponsive child (e.g., the profoundly retarded). Because the relationship between one discrete stimulus and one response is hard to define and because discrete responses may occur very rapidly, it is often easier to compare correct responses to time rather than to total opportunities. The rate of correct responses is then the frequency of responses in a given time interval:

$$\frac{\text{total } +\text{'s}}{\text{specified time}}$$

For example, the child produced 20 vocal sounds (20 +'s) in 10 minutes (the specified time). The number of times S did not respond is not noted. However, you have a baseline for evaluating later performance (e.g., 25 +'s in 10 minutes, 10 +'s in 10 minutes).

When to Use Percent of Time

A third situation is when the target is a behavior that you wish the child to perform continuously. For example, you might want the child to hold her head up continuously during a 10-minute session or some other time period. Many social skills and on-task behaviors fall into this category. In this situation it is difficult to identify one discrete response since the behavior is to be performed continuously. However, you can observe the child at short intervals (e.g., every 10 or 15 seconds) during the time period and observe whether or not she is exhibiting the behavior at that time. By recording her performance as " + " (exhibits the behavior) or " − " (does not exhibit the behavior) at specified intervals, you can approximate the percent of the time she exhibited the behavior. The percent of the time is then a ratio of the time intervals when the behavior occurred to the total intervals observed:

$$\frac{\text{total intervals with } + \text{ recorded}}{\text{total intervals in the time period}} \times 100$$

For example, if you observe the child at 15-second intervals during 10 minutes and she exhibits the behavior on 35 out of the possible 40 intervals (4 per minute x 10 minutes), the child is performing the target approximately 90% of the time.

How to Evaluate Initial Performance

From the above information, you can select the appropriate method to measure the frequency of the child's performance—percent of correct responses, rate of correct responses, or percent of the time when the correct response is occurring. After you have selected the method of measurement, take baseline to determine the child's initial frequency of performance. Although you observed that the child could perform the target occasionally during your preliminary work, your baseline data will reflect the precise frequency with which the child performs the target. Only with this initial measurement can you adequately measure increases in performance.

How to Take Baseline Data

According to the conditions you specified for the target behavior, present the child with opportunities to perform. During baseline, do not give the child specific feedback on her performance (neither reinforcement for correct responses nor correction for errors). Simply record her performance under the target conditions. This recording will be easiest if you prepare an appropriately structured data sheet. For percent correct data, it is best to present a standard number of trials that is a multiple of 100. Ten trials are often given since this converts to percentage easily. Your raw data sheet can be divided into 10 boxes to aid in data collection:

Date 9/24	1	2	3	4	5	6	7	8	9	10	% correct
Baseline:	+	−	−	+	−	−	−	−	+	−	30 % correct

For percent of the time data, a similar sheet can be used, although the number of boxes will depend on the number of time intervals you plan to observe and the total time period for your observations. Several standard methods are every 15 seconds for 5 minutes (20 observations), every 30 seconds for 5 minutes (10 observations), and every minute for 10 minutes (10 observations). Your data sheet can be set up to record this easily:

Date 9/15	1 min	2 min	3 min	4 min	5 min	6 min	7 min	8 min	9 min	10 min	% time in 10 minutes
Baseline:	−	+	−	−	+	+	+	−	−	−	40% of the time

For rate data, it is often easiest to use a wrist counter to keep tally of the correct responses made during the specified time interval:

Date 10/10   Number of responses in 10 minutes

Baseline: *Tally*: 10 responses

It is usually best to take baseline data on more than 1 day. If the behavior is performed erratically, record baseline for several days. These data provide the child's initial frequency of performance on the target.

How to Increase Performance

Once you have established the child's initial performance, use feedback to increase her performance during intervention. This feedback is usually reinforcement for correct responses, and either correction or withholding of reinforcement for errors. This contingent feedback should be specified before you begin intervention and presented systematically for each response. In addition, you should take data as you did during baseline but under these new contingencies for the intervention phase.

How to Graph Progress During Intervention

Progress is documented as the child increases her percent or rate of performance, until she performs at criterion. Although progress can be determined by looking at the raw data sheet, it is often easier to observe if you graph the raw data. On the bottom of the graph (going across), write the days on which you recorded the data. On the vertical, record the percent or rate of the target behavior. The graph for percent correct or percent of time would then look like the one shown below. The graph for rate data would be similar, but instead of percent, record the number of responses within the specified standard time period (e.g., during a 10-minute session).

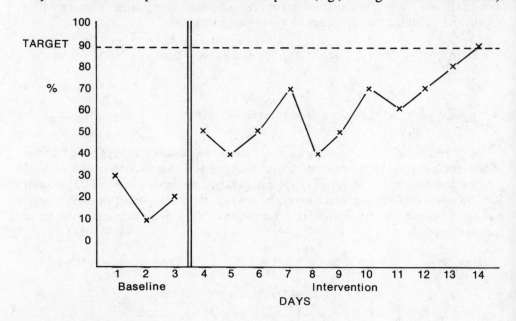

When to Modify Your Intervention Strategy

All programs should include a decision point to determine when a modification must be made. This point is usually specified as the number of days you allow the child to meet each increase in rate or percent. For example, one point might be that the child has 5 days to increase from 20% to 40% correct responding. If the child increases to 40% within this time period, your strategy is successful to that point. If she does not, you will need to change to another reinforcement or correction strategy. These modification points are critical to evaluate the success of your intervention.

When to Take Post-Intervention Data

Once the child performs the target behavior to your specified criterion standards, take post-intervention data. At this time, record data under the same conditions as baseline—no reinforcement or correction. If the child performs to criterion, you can say that intervention was successful. If not, reinstitute the intervention phase as needed until the child can perform to criterion under the baseline or post-intervention conditions.

Summary

The program that you write to increase the child's performance standards should contain:

- A statement of the *target objective* in behavioral terms;
- a *baseline period* to establish initial performance frequency;
- an *intervention phase* with specified contingent feedback for correct responses and errors;
- a *criterion system* to evaluate progress during intervention and revise the intervention strategy as needed; and
- a *post-intervention period* to document criterion performance after intervention.

By writing a program to increase the frequency of target performance with these elements, you have specified a systematic procedure based on either percent correct responding, rate of correct responding, or percent of time where that correct responding is occurring.

APPLICATIONS TO THE CURRICULUM

Ways to Apply Programming Techniques

Although you may use any of the descriptions to develop programs on your own, particularly for on-task behaviors, these procedures also have direct applications to this curriculum. The better you understand these procedures, the more you will be able to individualize and use the standard programs with your students. The programming procedures described here have two main applications in the use of this curriculum:

- Modifications in the standard programs; and
- generalization after completion of any program.

MODIFICATIONS IN THE STANDARD PROGRAMS

4/5 Data and Rate Data Programs

Two of the four types of programs in this curriculum have been described here: The *4/5 data* programs are based on the cueing-fading procedure, and the *rate data* programs are based on the measurement procedure of rate of correct responding. Modification procedures for these programs are covered in their respective modules but in more specific detail. The other two types of standard programs, *chain* and *skill analysis*, are organized somewhat differently than the procedures described here, but their modifications include these procedures to shape the response (cueing, fading, shaping, chaining).

Chain Programs

The *chain* programs all contain a task analysis of the sequence of actions that comprise the target skill. The data collection system in the standard programs is based on regular probes on performance of those parts in order: Daily instruction organized as you wish, and weekly probes on all parts. If the child does not complete more parts after two successive probes, the program is then modified. The modification procedures for those programs are essentially the techniques discussed in chaining procedures. Thus, you may use these chaining procedures to modify the standard program if you wish to take response-by-response data each day.

You may reorder the steps in a standard program into a forward or a backward chain. We leave this option for several reasons. First, the appropriateness of forward or backward chaining is usually based on the individual child, so this is flexible in the standard program. Second, data collection on a trial-by-trial basis is often awkward with self-help skills, so regular probes can be substituted unless the child is not progressing (i.e., requires modification). Thus, the chaining procedures described here are directly applicable to the use of the *chain* programs.

Skill Analysis Programs

The *skill analysis* programs contain a list of motor subskills, which the child combines to perform the target skill. The data collection system in the standard programs is based on regular performance probes of each of these parts: Daily instruction organized as you determine on specific subskills, and weekly probes on each part. If the child cannot perform more subskills after two successive probes, the program is then modified. The modification procedures for those programs are the techniques discussed in shaping and cueing-fading. Thus, you may use these techniques to modify the standard program if you wish to take response-by-response data daily.

For example, you can take one subskill listed in the standard program and write a shaping or cueing-fading sequence of steps as described here. Although we note that skill analysis programs often require individualization or modification, use of the Suggestions in the programs is flexible for several reasons. First, the number of intermediate steps needed for shaping or cueing-fading is based on the individual child's motor development and is difficult to standardize. Second, data collection on a trial-by-trial basis is often awkward and may reflect little change in performance from trial to trial. Hence, regular probes are substituted unless the child is not progressing (i.e., requires modification). Thus, the shaping and cueing-fading procedures described here are directly applicable to the use of *skill analysis* programs.

GENERALIZATION

All of the standard programs require the child to perform the target to a certain criterion before she completes the program, either 4 correct out of 5 trials (4/5 data, chain, skill analysis) or a specified number of responses in 10 minutes (rate data). However, the child usually needs to maintain these standards after she has completed the program and in other situations as well. The procedures described here to maintain or increase performance standards are directly applicable after the completion of any standard program.

4/5 Data, Chain, and Skill Analysis Programs

Most of the programs, particularly the 4/5 data, the chain, and the skill analysis programs involving movement (e.g., Walking), can be easily followed up by taking intermittent data with the percent of correct responding procedures described here. All of these programs require a discrete response to be formed after a command or require a discrete stimulus. After you complete these programs, initiate a measurement system to collect percent correct responding data at regular intervals (e.g., each week) in different situations.

The skill analysis programs involving the maintenance of a position (i.e., Controlling Head Movements, Sitting, and Standing) are all easily converted to a percent of time measurement system, since the child is expected to maintain her position throughout a time period. Once the child passes these programs, initiate a percent of time data system at regular intervals (e.g., each day or week) in different situations to insure maintenance of the skill.

The *rate data* programs use a data collection system to measure frequency of responding in relation to time, since stimuli are present continuously. However, the eventual goal is for the child to respond to one discrete stimulus. Although the programs in the curriculum that are specified as follow-up skills for each *rate data* program move the child toward that goal, you may also use generalization to further this end. To do this, initiate a percent of correct responding measurement system after the child completes the standard *rate data* program. In this generalization program, present one stimulus, and record whether the child responds to it. At first her percent of correct responding to a single stimulus will probably be quite low, since she previously responded only to a variety of stimuli. However, in time, her percent correct will increase to a realistic target, perhaps 50% of the stimuli presented. This follow-up is critical for children who initially respond only at a very low frequency.

SUMMARY

1. Target skills should be written in objective terms with specifications for the behavior, the conditions under which it will be performed, and criterion standards for performance.
2. Program strategies fall into two basic categories
   a. Response production programs teach the child to perform the target when she cannot do so initially; and
   b. performance standards programs teach the child to emit the behavior more frequently or for longer periods if she performs the target inconsistently.
3. Response production programs have steps that specify intermediate behaviors:
   a. Cueing-fading, shaping, and chaining are the three basic procedures.
   b. The program should contain specifications (conditions, behavior, criteria, consequences) for a pretest, all teaching steps, and a posttest.
   c. Data should be collected on responses given on each test or step.
4. Performance standards programs measure increasing frequency of correct responding:
   a. Correct responding may be evaluated in relation to total responses or time.
      (1) Percent of correct responses in the total number of responses emitted.
      (2) Rate of correct responses in a specified time period.
      (3) Percent of time a correct response occurs.
   b. The program should contain specifications (conditions, behavior, criteria, consequences) for a baseline period, an intervention phase, and a post-intervention period.
   c. Data should be collected on responses during each phase.
5. These (Items 1–4) strategies may be used to write independent programs or to expand existing programs in this curriculum:
   a. Modification procedures described for the standard programs in this curriculum use the response production strategies—shaping, chaining, and cueing-fading.
   b. Generalization for the standard programs involves the use of performance standards programs—percent correct, rate, and percent of time.

MODULE 7:
Individualized Education Programs

INTRODUCTION

According to Public Law 94–142, an *individualized education program* (IEP) is a written statement for each handicapped child and includes:

- A statement of the child's present level of educational performance;
- a statement of annual goals with short-term objectives;
- a statement of the educational services to be provided and the extent to which the child will participate in regular educational programs;
- the projected date for initiation of such services and their anticipated duration; and
- appropriate objective criteria and evaluation procedures and schedules, on at least an annual basis, for determining whether the instructional objectives are being achieved.

The IEP is to be developed by a committee composed of at least one school administrator, the teacher, one or both of the parents, and the child where appropriate. This committee must meet prior to the onset of any services and at least once a year thereafter to evaluate and revise the IEP if necessary.

As a teacher, you are directly involved in most phases of the IEP. This module provides information to assist you to fulfill your role in the development of the IEP, using this curriculum. Based on this information, you will be able to use this curriculum with other sources to:

- Assess the child's present educational performance;
- determine annual goals with short-term objectives; and
- evaluate and document efforts to achieve those objectives.

ASSESSMENT
Types of Assessment

There are several factors to consider when assessing the child's present level of educational performance. Not only is her performance on specified tasks evaluated but also her medical status and physical condition as they relate to performance. With many severely and profoundly retarded individuals, medical and physical evaluations have direct impact on the development of the IEP. Although these evaluations are usually conducted by a specialist, you may be asked to participate under their supervision, and in any case, you will need to apply the information to your programming decisions in the classroom.

The medical evaluation will describe health conditions that may effect educational programming decisions. Factors such as diet, seizures, allergies, and physical stamina are evaluated. The physical evaluation is usually conducted by a physical or occupational therapist to determine specific therapy needs, reflexes, positioning, adaptive equipment, physical limitations, and the like. In addition, sensory deficits in sight and hearing may be evaluated by an opthamologist or audiologist respectively to determine need for adaptive media. A speech therapist may also be involved. Although you may be asked to participate in such evaluations, your role is usually to provide the specialist with any related information you have about the child, so that she may make a more adequate evaluation.

Educational Assessments

You have a much greater role in the evaluation of the child's performance on educational tasks. Although some local agencies have diagnosticians who conduct preliminary educational assessments, you will probably be participating in this assessment in the classroom, either on your own or in conjunction with the diagnostician.

Criteria for Assessment Tools

Some local agencies use one or more specific assessment tools, frequently the TARC (Sailor and Mix), the LAP (Sanford), or the BCP (VORT Corporation), which are referenced in the Bibliography with other assessment tools. Other times you may have your option of which test or checklist to use. There are several criteria for selecting an appropriate assessment tool. First, the one that you select or ones you use in combination should cover a wide range of skills in language, motor, social, self-help, and cognitive tasks appropriate to the child's current level. You should be able to use the tool to identify both skills the child can perform, as well as those she cannot. For example, a preschool assessment test may give little diagnostic information about a profoundly retarded individual, since she may be unable to perform any of the tasks.

Second, the tool you select should describe what skills to teach next if the child is unable to perform certain tasks. This prescriptive information is usually a sequence of tasks. An assessment test that presents tasks without such a sequence provides current information on the child but little prescriptive information for later planning. If at all possible, the tool should direct you to specific programs to teach those skills, either by suggesting curricular sources or by including such programs as a complementary component of the materials.

Application to This Curriculum

In module 1, Program Selection, procedures are described for using the Class Observation Record to make initial observations on tasks covered in this curriculum. This initial assessment should be used in conjunction with other assessment tools and should not be used exclusively, since it cannot possibly cover all skills that you need to assess. With this in mind, the assessment procedures for this curriculum provide a basis for conducting an educational assessment to identify appropriate instructional objectives and implement them.

GOALS AND SHORT-TERM OBJECTIVES

Annual Goals

After the child's current medical status, physical condition, and educational performance have been assessed, the committee meets to determine annual goals with short-term objectives and the services needed to meet those goals. Although you will have considerable input at this meeting, decisions are made as a group, with input from the administrator, specialists, and particularly, the parents. Your role is to present the diagnostic assessment information you have accumulated on the child and to assist in setting priorities and reasonable goals for the year.

Long-Range Goals

Usually the long-range goals for the severely or profoundly retarded during their school years are so basic that they are almost self-evident. To:

> Communicate needs;
> follow simple commands;
> walk or negotiate herself independently;
> use common objects;
> feed herself;
> toilet herself;
> dress herself;
> perform simple self-care tasks;
> initiate positive interactions with others; and
> interact positively with peers and adults.

Realistic Annual Goals

With these functional goals in mind, identify approximations of these skills that the child can realistically achieve in a year. Your assessment information, along with the other evaluations, provides the basis for this estimate.

In addition, you will need to consider priorities and the educational services available. Realistic goals depend upon factors such as:

> The child's current skills;
> the order in which skills are typically acquired;
> the child's age;
> physical care needs (feeding, toileting, rest);
> attendant medical or physical problems;
> teacher-child ratio in the classroom;
> therapy needs and available personnel; and
> school attendance expectations (half-day, recurrent illnesses).

With these factors in mind, the committee sets realistic annual goals with the services needed to meet those goals (e.g., class placement, physical therapy).

SHORT-TERM OBJECTIVES

Once the annual goals have been determined, each is broken down into a set of short-term objectives, providing instruction toward the goal and for evaluating the child's performance during the year. Your input will be critical for the development of the IEP.

How to Identify Short-Term Objectives

Short-term objectives are sequenced skills that are the targets for direct instruction during the year. Typically, information on such skill sequences can be found in developmental scales of early child behaviors and behavioral checklists. As noted in assessment, a device that provides such a sequence simplifies your planning in that you assess current skills and identify targets for instruction at the same time. To apply information provided by other specialists, add objectives specific to the individual child based on their recommendations.

Because each short-term objective is evaluated according to PL 94–142 guidelines, these targets must be stated in behavioral terms. That way, you can document whether or not the child achieved the objective during the year. Thus, you should specify the target behavior, the conditions under which it will be performed, and the criterion standards for performance. Although the program to teach the skill is not included in the IEP, this statement of the target objective with measurable criteria is required. In addition, each short-term objective is usually assigned to a specific person who will be responsible for implementation and evaluation.

Applications to This Curriculum

By using the program selection techniques discussed in module 1 and pretesting to verify appropriate programs, you have identified short-term objectives that are available through this curriculum. Where appropriate, you may simply take the "Objective" from the program selected, and write this on the IEP. In addition, if you are developing your own targets and programs, you may use the procedures discussed in module 6 to identify, write, and implement instruction on other target objectives.

EVALUATION AND DOCUMENTATION

Accountability

Although you are required to specify and evaluate performance on the short-term objectives that you are responsible for, you are also responsible for making "good faith efforts" to assist the child to meet the objectives and goals on the IEP. In addition, parents may complain, ask for revisions in the IEP, or invoke due process procedures if they feel that these efforts are not being made. Thus, you or the agency may be held accountable for demonstrating or documenting "good faith efforts" in teaching the short-term objectives. Many agencies, therefore, require you to document your efforts during the year, not only to improve classroom instruction but also to verify that "good faith efforts" have been made. This is particularly true with persons who manifest severe developmental retardation, whose progress may be very slow. Your documentation comes primarily from two sources:

- The written program, containing specifications for everything you do to teach the target objective; and
- child performance data on the program, including pretest or baseline data, indicating the need for instruction; data on all learning steps or phases; and posttest or post-intervention data, documenting acquisition of the target objective.

Applications to This Curriculum

If you use the programs and procedures in this curriculum, you have documented good faith efforts in teaching these target objectives. In addition, the modification procedures give specific guidelines for individualizing programs when progress is not occurring as rapidly as targeted. These modification procedures are critical in demonstrating good faith efforts when the target objective is not being achieved within your projected time frames on the IEP.

In addition, the procedures for developing your own programs, discussed in module 6, will also enable you to document good faith efforts on other target objectives. These procedures may be applied to any target objective you have identified from developmental scales, behavioral checklists, or recommendations from particular specialists. Thus, this curriculum, along with the modules, provides a basic structure to develop, implement, and document child performance on target objectives listed in the child's IEP.

How to Organize Documentation

After the IEP has been written, the committee is required to meet at least once a year to evaluate the child's progress on target objectives. Your local agency, however, may have guidelines requiring more frequent review by the committee. In any case, you will need to keep your documentation sources organized for easy use during the day and for easy reference when compiling information for the committee meeting. We suggest keeping child folders with accumulated information. But whatever system you use should involve as little of your time as possible for the maximum benefits.

Ongoing Documentation

Lesson plans (i.e., written programs) are used in the classroom daily. However, after you have become skilled in using them, they may not be used in the instructional session but rather as a reference both before and after the school day or the instructional session. In addition, any one lesson plan or program may be repeated or used with several students. Because of these factors, it is helpful to keep all programs in a central place in the classroom for quick referral. For example, you may set up a planning table or area for keeping bound curricula (e.g., this curriculum) or folders containing programs you have written. In addition, you may want to post activities for volunteers on a wall chart.

Data sheets, on the other hand, have to be readily available for use whenever they are needed. One way to organize them is to hang clipboards, one for each child, holding the data sheets for each program on which the child is receiving instruction. Then you can simply pick up the clipboard each time you work with the child. Another method is to post data sheets or wall charts wherever instruction occurs, such as in the bathroom (with data transferred later onto a data sheet). Once a program is complete, the data sheet should be placed in the child's folder so that only current data sheets are kept out in the classroom.

Although the programs and data sheets are the primary sources of documentation, there are two particular situations where secondary or summary information may be kept:

- When the class size requires a daily schedule to organize "who does what when"; and
- when your local guidelines require you to document overall instructional time throughout the day.

Whatever method you use to prepare a schedule (by child, by time, by instructional agent, by activity), this summary should account for each child's total day. This daily summary should include information on instructional programming, therapy, group activities, and class routines or care-taking time (feeding, toileting, rest). Such a summary can demonstrate how the child's IEP is being met on a daily basis.

How to Keep a Child's Folder

All information that is not used daily should be accumulated in a central place, such as the child's folder. During the course of the year, the child's folder will contain more and more information on her progress:

- A copy of the IEP;
- a copy of each program used or a listing of where to locate them in the curricular materials you are using;
- data sheets on all completed programs; and
- daily summaries or schedules, if appropriate.

It will be helpful if you make notes on the copy of the IEP once a month indicating the program(s) used to teach each objective and a statement of child performance to date. By preparing this information at regular intervals, it will be much easier to compile all information for the end-of-the year evaluation.

The End-of-the Year Evaluation

At the end of the school year, the committee meets to evaluate the effectiveness of the child's IEP in terms of the achievement of the listed instructional objectives. After determining what progress has been made, based on your input from the child's folder and input from other members of the committee, the committee then draws up a new IEP for the upcoming year. To some extent, new assessments may be made. But the evaluation of the child's performance at the end of the year is basically an assessment of her current skills for starting the new year. Thus, the cycle continues—assessment, planning, implementation, evaluation.

SUMMARY

1. The child's IEP is written annually by a committee and must contain:
   Assessment of current performance;
   annual goals with short-term objectives;
   educational services to be provided; and
   evaluation procedures and schedules.

2. You will play a major role in writing and implementing the IEP. You will:
   a. Conduct or participate in assessment, particularly the educational assessment.
   b. Assist in setting priorities and realistic annual goals.
   c. Assist in listing target objectives for each annual goal.
   d. Implement instruction on specific objectives during the year.
   e. Document child performance on those objectives during the year.

3. You will be expected to document good faith efforts to assist the child to achieve those objectives stated in the IEP:
   a. The written programs specify your implementation strategies.
   b. The child data sheets document performance during implementation.

4. This curriculum, with the procedures described in the modules, can assist you to fulfill your role in writing and implementing the IEP:
   a. Observation and program selection procedures assist you to assess current performance to determine instructional objectives for the year.
   b. The programs and the specified procedures, particularly for modifications, enable you to implement instruction on specific objectives and to document all efforts to meet the objective.

Bibliography

ASSESSMENT

Balthazaar, E.E. *Balthazaar scales of adaptive behavior for the profoundly and severely mentally retarded.* Champaign, Ill.: Research Press, 1971.

BCP—The Santa Cruz special education management system. Palo Alto, Calif.: VORT Corporation, 1973.

Cohen, M., & Gross, P. *The developmental resource* (Vol. I and II). New York: Grune & Stratton, 1979.

Haring, N.G. (Ed.). *Developing effective individualized education programs for severely handicapped children and youth.* Washington, D.C.: Department of Health, Education and Welfare, Office of Education, Bureau of Education for the Handicapped, August 1977.

Nihara, K., Foster, R., Shellhaus, M., & Leland, H. *AAMD adaptive behavior scales.* Washington, D.C.: American Association on Mental Deficiency, 1974.

Sailor, W., & Mix, B.J. *The TARC assessment inventory for retarded children.* Lawrence, Kan.: H & H Enterprises, 1975.

Sanford, A.R. *Learning accomplishments profile.* Chapel Hill, N.C., Winston-Salem, N.C.: Kaplan School Supply Corporation, 1970.

Uzgiris, I., & Hunt, J. McV. *Assessment in infancy: Ordinal scales of psychological development.* Urbana: University of Illinois Press, February 1975.

BEHAVIOR MANAGEMENT

Axelrod, S. *Behavior modification for the classroom teacher.* New York: McGraw-Hill, 1977.

Becker, W.C. *Parents are teachers.* Champaign, Ill.: Research Press, 1971.

Becker, W.C., Engelmann, S., & Thomas, D.R. *Teaching: A course in applied psychology.* Chicago: Science Research Associates, 1971.

Bijou, S.W. *Child development: The basic stages of early childhood.* Englewood Cliffs, N. J.: Prentice-Hall, 1976.

Bijou, S.W., & Baer, D.M. *Child development I.* Englewood Cliffs, N. J.: Prentice-Hall, 1961.

Bijou, S.W., & Baer, D.M. *Child development II.* Englewood Cliffs, N. J.: Prentice-Hall, 1965.

Buckley, N.K., & Walker, H.M. *Modifying classroom behavior: A manual of procedures for classroom teachers.* Champaign, Ill.: Research Press, 1972.

Hall, R.V. *Managing behavior: Behavior modification series.* Lawrence, Kan.: H & H Enterprises, 1971.

Haring, N.G. Measurement and evaluation procedures for programming with the severely / profoundly handicapped. In E. Sontag (Ed.), *Educational programming for the severely and profoundly handicapped.* Reston, Va.: Division on Mental Retardation, The Council for Exceptional Children, 1977.

Kaufmann, J.M., & Snell, M.E. Managing the behavior of severely handicapped persons. In E. Sontag (Ed.), *Educational programming for the severely and profoundly handicapped.* Reston, Va.: Division on Mental Retardation, The Council for Exceptional Children, 1977.

Kiernan, C.C., & Woodford, F.P. *Behavior modification with the severely retarded.* Amsterdam: Associated Scientific Publishers, 1975.

Mash, E.J., Handy, L.C., & Hamerlynck, L.A. *Behavior modification approaches to parenting.* New York: Brunner / Mazel Publishers, 1976.

Patterson, C.R., & Gullion, M.F. *Living with children.* Champaign, Ill.: Research Press, 1968.

Smith, R.M., & Neisworth, J.T. *Modifying retarded behavior.* Boston: Houghton Mifflin, 1973.

Sulzer-Azaroff, B., & Mayer, G.R. *Applying behavior analysis procedures with children and youth.* New York: Holt, Rinehart & Winston, 1977.

Tompson, T., & Grabowski, J. *Behavior modification of the mentally retarded.* New York: Oxford University Press, 1977.

GENERAL

Anderson, D.R., Hodson, G.D., & Jones, W.G. *Instructional programming for the handicapped student.* Springfield, Ill.: Charles C Thomas, 1975.

Brown, L., Crowner, T., Williams, W., & York, R. *Madison's alternative for zero exclusion: A book of readings* (Vol. 5). Madison, Wis.: Madison Public Schools, 1975.

Fredricks, H.D.B., & Baldwin, V. L. et al. *A data based classroom for the moderately and severely handicapped* (2nd ed.). Monmouth, Or.: Instructional Development Corporation, 1977.

Fredricks, H.D.B. et al. *The teaching research curriculum for moderately and severely handicapped.* Springfield, Ill.: Charles C Thomas, 1976.

Guide to early developmental training. Wabash Center for the Mentally Retarded. Boston: Allyn & Bacon, 1977.

Hanson, M. *Teaching your Down's syndrome infant: A guide for parents.* Baltimore: University Park Press, 1977.

Haring, N.G. Measurement and evaluation procedures for programming with the severely and profoundly handicapped. In E. Sontag (Ed.) *Educational programming for the severely and profoundly handicapped.* Reston, Va.: Division on Mental Retardation, The Council for Exceptional Children, 1977.

McLean, J.E., Yoder, D.E., & Schiefelbusch, R.L. *Language intervention with the retarded.* Baltimore: University Park Press, 1972.

Shearer, D., Billingsley, J., Frohman, A., Hilliard, J., Johnson, F., & Shearer, M. *The Portage project* (Experimental edition). Portage, Wis.: Portage Project, Cooperative Educational Service Agency No. 12, 1976.

Williams, W. Procedures that enhance the maintenance and generalization of induced behavioral change. *American Association for the Education of the Severely / Profoundly Handicapped.* Seattle: University of Washington, April 1, 1975.

LANGUAGE

Bricker, D., Dennison, L., & Bricker, W. A language intervention program for developmentally young children. Miami, Fla.: *Mailman Center for Child Development Monograph Series No. 1,* 1976.

DuBose, R.F. Development of communication in non-verbal children. *Education and Training of the Mentally Retarded,* February 1978, *13* (1).

Engelmann, S., & Osborn, J. *Distar language.* Chicago: SRA, 1970, 1976.

Guess, D., Sailor, W., & Baer, D.M. *A speech and language training program for severely handicapped persons.* (Revised, field tested manual). Kansas Neurological Institute and The University of Kansas, 1975.

Hanson, M. *Teaching your Down's syndrome infant: A guide for parents.* Baltimore: University Park Press, 1977.

Kent, L. *Language acquisition program for the severely retarded.* Champaign, Ill.: Research Press, 1974.

Tawney, J.W., & Hipsher, L.W. *Systematic language instruction: The Illinois program.* Washington, D.C.: USOE, Bureau of Education for the Handicapped, Grant No. 7–1025, 1970.

York, R., Williams, W., & Brown, P. Teacher modeling and student imitation: An instructional procedure and teacher competency. *AAESPH Review,* November 1976, *1* (8).

COGNITIVE PROGRAMMING

Bove, M. (College of St. Joseph, Rutland, Vermont). Language for non-imitative SMR. Chicago CEC Convention, 1976.

Bricker, D., Dennison, L., & Bricker, W. A language intervention program for developmentally young children. Miami, Fla.: *Mailman Center for Child Development Monograph Series No. 1,* 1976.

Engelmann, S., & Carnine, D. *Distar arithmetic: An instructional system.* Chicago: SRA, 1969.

Feingold, A. *Teaching arithmetic to young children.* New York: John Day, 1965.

Gladstone, D., & Gladstone, J. *Mathematics involvement program.* Chicago: SRA, 1971.

Karnes, M. *Early childhood enrichment series.* Springfield, Mass.: Milton Bradley, 1970.

Resnick, L.B., Wang, M.C., & Kaplan, J. Behavior analysis in curriculum design: Sequenced introductory mathematics curriculum. *Monograph No. 2 University of Pittsburgh, Learning Research and Development Center,* December 1970.

Young, B. *Nuffield mathematics project.* New York: John Wiley & Sons, 1967.

MOTOR

Brazelton, T.B. *Infants and mothers: Differences in development.* New York: Dell, 1969.

Bricker, D., Davis, J., Wahlin, L., & Evans, J. A motor training program for the developmentally young. Miami, Fla.: *Mailman Center for Child Development Monograph Series No. 2,* 1976.

Buttram, B., & Brown, G. *Developmental physical management for the multi-disabled child.* University, Ala.: University of Alabama, 1976.

Finnie, N. *Handling the young cerebral palsied child at home.* New York: E.P. Dutton, 1975.

Guide to early developmental training. Wabash Center for the Mentally Retarded. Boston: Allyn & Bacon, 1977.

Hanson, M. *Teaching your Down's syndrome infant: A guide for parents.* Baltimore: University Park Press, 1977.

Levy, J. *The baby exercise book.* New York: Pantheon Books, 1973.

SELF-HELP

Campbell, P. Daily living skills. In N.G. Haring (Ed.), *Developing effective individualized education programs for severely handicapped children and youth.* Washington, D.C.: Department of Health, Education and Welfare, Bureau of Education for the Handicapped, August 1977.

DeVore, M.S. *Individualized learning program for the profoundly retarded.* Springfield, Ill.: Charles C Thomas, 1977.

Finnie, N. *Handling the young cerebral palsied child at home.* New York: E.P. Dutton, 1975.

Fredricks, H.D.B. et al. *The teaching research curriculum for moderately and severely handicapped.* Springfield, Ill.: Charles C Thomas, 1976.

Foxx, R., & Arzin, N. *Toilet training the retarded.* Champaign, Ill.: Research Press, 1975.

Lent, J. *Project MORE.* Parsons: The University of Kansas Bureau of Child Research, 1975.

Linford, M.D., Hipsher, L.W., & Silikovitz, R.G. Self-help instruction. *Systematic instruction for retarded children: The Illinois program.* Washington, D.C.: USOE, Bureau of Education for the Handicapped, Grant No. 7–1025, 1970.

McCormack, J.E. *Manual of alternative procedures: Activities of daily living.* Medford: Massachusetts Center for Program Development and Evaluation, 1976.

Schmidt, P. Feeding assessment and therapy for the neurologically impaired. *AAESPH Review,* November 1976, *1* (8).

Somerton, E., & Turner, K. *Pennsylvania training model: Individual assessment guide.* Harrisburg: Pennsylvania Department of Education, 1975.

Utley, B., Holvoet, J., & Barnes, K. Handling, positioning and feeding the physically handicapped. In E. Sontag (Ed.), *Educational programming for the severely and profoundly handicapped.* Reston, Va.: Division on Mental Retardation, The Council for Exceptional Children, 1977.

Glossary

adaptation: a change in stimulus cue(s) or response standards in a program to compensate for sensory or motor impairments; suggested strategies;

attention: the child's readiness to respond to a task as demonstrated by eye contact or some other observable behavior; part of general trial procedures; how to teach.

chain programs: programs in this curriculum that teach the child to perform a sequence of actions that comprise the target skill; procedures;

chaining: general strategy for teaching the child to perform a sequence of actions by systematically removing assistance on each action in order; how to write a chaining strategy; applications to this curriculum;

class observation record: record form for making initial screening observations on skills covered in this curriculum; form; procedures for using;

command: verbal request for the child to perform a specific action;

correction: specific feedback presented immediately after an error occurs to enable the child to practice the task with extra assistance; *see also* general correction procedures; part of general trial procedures;

criterion: standard of performance required;

cueing-fading: general strategy for teaching the child to perform a task by presenting extra assistance, then gradually and systematically removing that assistance; how to write a cueing-fading strategy; applications to this curriculum;

cue: presentation by the teacher that provides a stimulus for a particular response;

curriculum overview: description of the order in which skills taught in this curriculum are typically acquired;

cycle: section on each Program Overview that specifies the repetition of that program, if appropriate, to teach related skills or concepts; procedures.

data sheet: sheet for recording all responses on a program; 4/5 Data and Rate Data Programs; Skill Analysis and Chain Programs;

delayed cue: cue that is presented after latency if the child has not initiated a correct response; description;

demonstration (D): presentation of a model of the correct or desired response; as a correction procedure;

discriminate: to respond differentially to different stimuli; discrimination programs.

entry behaviors: section of each Program Overview that lists behaviors that facilitate acquisition of the target skill; use;

error (− or θ): a response that does not meet program specifications for a correct response, either an overt action or no response within latency.

follow-up: section of each Program Overview that suggests generalization activities and future programs to consider;

4/5 data programs: programs in this curriculum that teach the child to perform a task by systematically removing assistance on successive steps; procedures.

general correction procedures: strategies to correct an error by refocusing, demonstration, or guidance; description;

generalize: to perform the same response to different stimuli or in different settings; generalization;

guidance (G): physical assistance to perform the correct or desired response; as a correction procedure.

latency: time limit in which the child must initiate a response; adaptations.

modify: to expand the number of program steps or parts to document more gradual increments in the skill; modifications for Rate Data; for 4/5 Data; for Skill Analysis; for Chain.

natural consequence: event that typically follows the performance of a particular action in the natural environment.

pace: speed at which trials are presented; description;

posttest (POST): evaluation procedure to verify that the child can perform the skill after instruction; general procedures;

pretest (PRE): evaluation procedure to verify whether the child can perform the skill to determine need for instruction; general procedures;

procedural error (PE): situation in which the child does not have optimal conditions for performance; how to remediate;

profile: chart of all programs in this curriculum; form;

program: set of strategies for teaching and evaluating instruction on a skill; components of programs in this curriculum; how to develop instructional programs; section of a program in this curriculum that contains information for using the program; description;

program overview: section of a program in this curriculum that contains information for selecting the program; description.

rate data programs: programs in this curriculum that increase the child's rate of responding; procedures;

refocusing (R): presentation of extra directions to focus the child's attention on a critical part of the task; as a correction procedure;

reinforce: to increase the occurrence of a behavior; how to select and use reinforcers; reinforcement as a part of general instructional procedures.

session: time period in which program trials are presented; length;

shaping: general strategy for teaching the child to perform a skill by reinforcing closer and closer approximations; how to write a shaping strategy applications to this curriculum;

skill analysis programs: programs in this curriculum that teach the child to perform subskills that are combined as part of the target skill; procedures;

stimulus: object or event that is presented to elicit a response.

task conditions: specified stimuli (command, cues) used to elicit a particular response; *see also* cue;

trial: opportunity to respond under specified task conditions.

warm-up: preliminary activities to relax a child prior to a session; description.